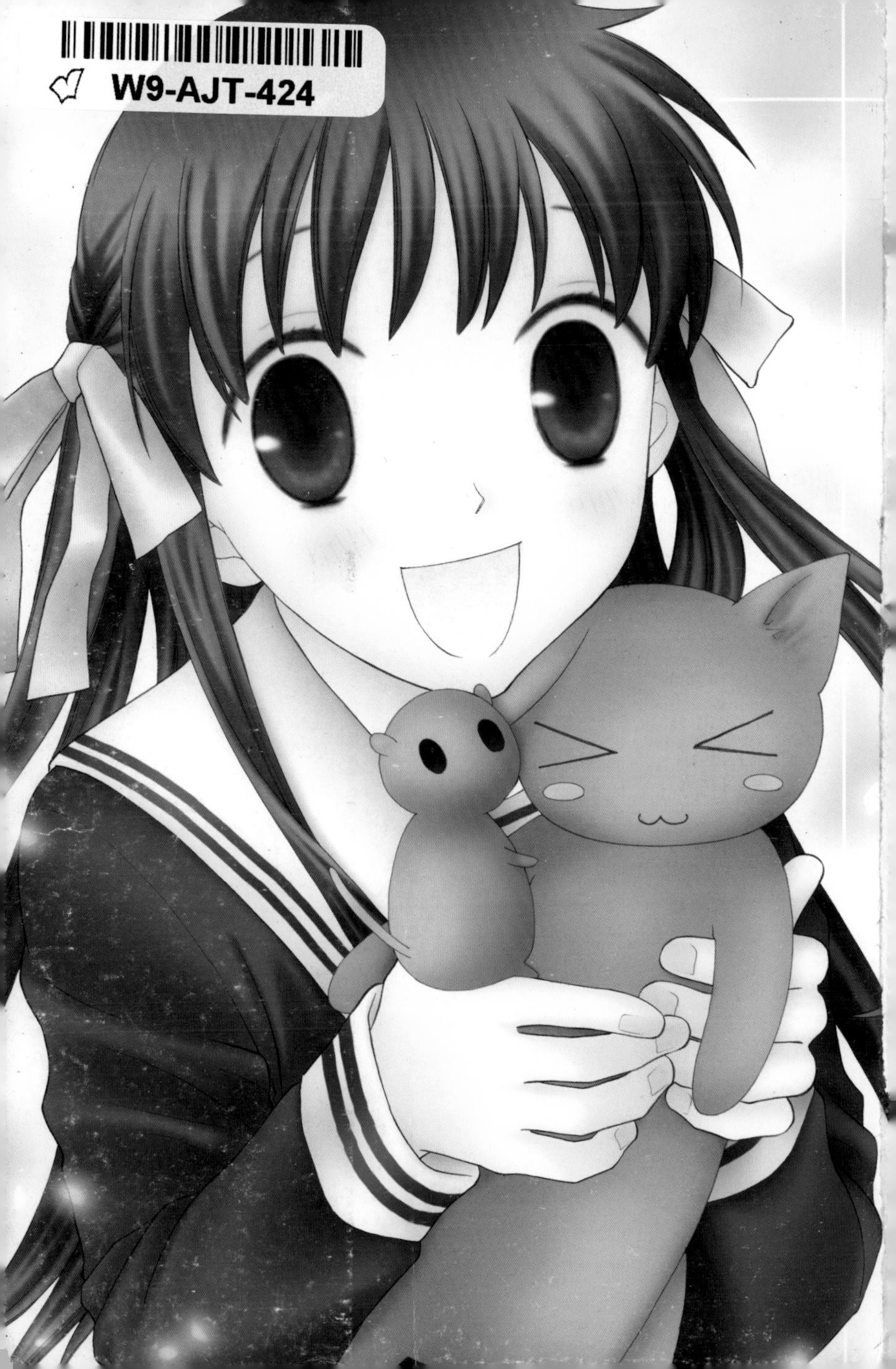

NICE TO MEET YOU AND HELLO! THIS IS TAKAYA. HOW ARE YOU? ONCE I STARTED TO WRAP UP FURUBA, IT REALLY FELT LIKE IT HAD BEEN A LONG TIME COMING. BUT EVEN NOW, WHENEVER I THINK OF YOU FINE PEOPLE WHO LOVE "FRUITS BASKET", I FEEL THAT TRULY, IN SOME WAYS, THE STORY WILL NEVER BE OVER. I THINK TO MYSELF, "YOU ALL CONTINUE TO LET IT LIVE ON IN YOUR HEARTS... MY WORK IS CHERISHED BY SO MANY..." AND I KEENLY REALIZE HOW FULL OF GRATITUDE I AM. THANK YOU. I THINK BACK TO WHEN I STARTED DRAWING FURUBA, HOW THERE WERE TIMES WHEN I THREW MYSELF INTO IT WHOLE-HEARTEDLY, WITH AN ALMOST DESPERATE DEVOTION, IN ORDER TO MAKE IT THROUGH. I CAME OUT OF THOSE TIMES REALIZING THAT FURUBA HAD BEGUN TO TRAVEL THE WORLD, AND WAS BEING READ BY FANS ALL OVER THE GLOBE. IT'S TIMES LIKE THESE THAT I THINK THAT THERE CAN'T BE ANY GREATER HAPPINESS THAN TO BE A MANGA CREATOR. TRULY, THANK YOU. THE EVER KIND AND SMILING TOHRU, BASHFUL KYO, AWKWARD YUKI, AND ALL THE OTHER CHARACTERS... THANK YOU FOR LOVING THEM SO MUCH. FOR THAT, I LOVE ALL OF YOU IN RETURN. TRULY, TRULY THANK YOU.

高屋奈月.

Natsuki Takaya

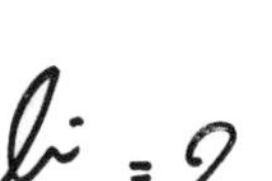

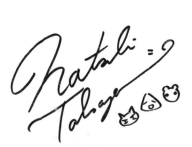

Fruits Basket™

Volume 23

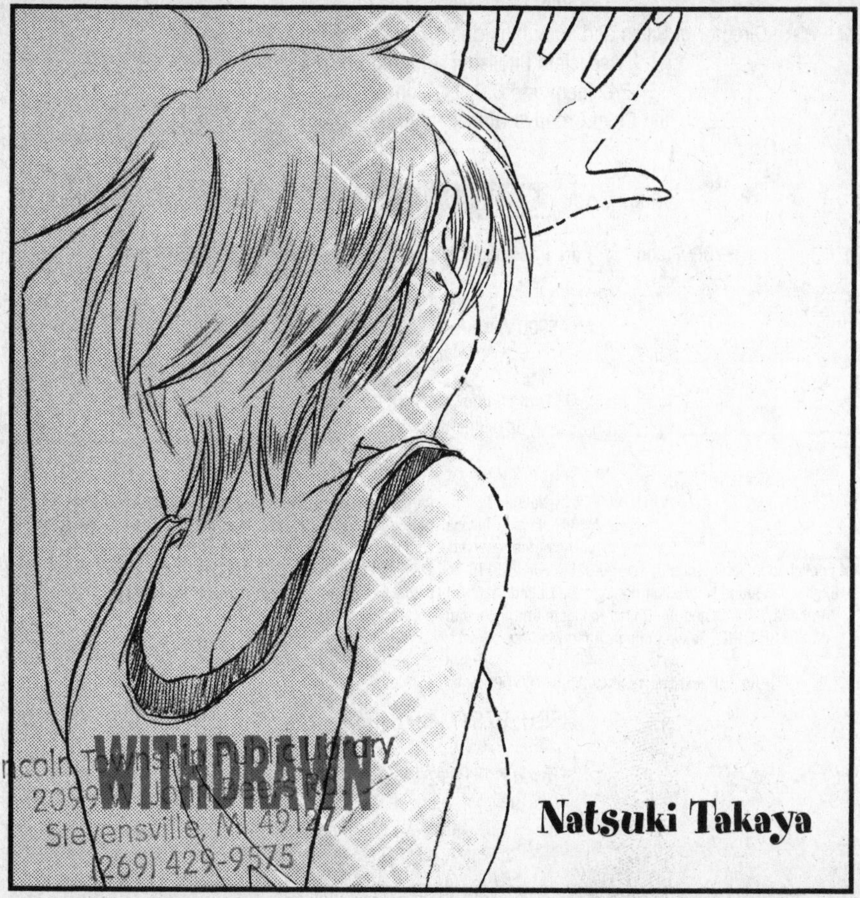

Natsuki Takaya

Fruits Basket Volume 23
Created by Natsuki Takaya

Translation - Alethea & Athena Nibley
English Adaptation - Lianne Sentar
Retouch and Lettering - Star Print Brokers
Production Artist - Rui Kyo
Graphic Designer - Louis Csontos

Editor - Alexis Kirsch
Print Production Manager - Lucas Rivera
Managing Editor - Vy Nguyen
Senior Designer - Louis Csontos
Director of Sales and Manufacturing - Allyson De Simone
Associate Publisher - Marco F. Pavia
President and C.O.O. - John Parker
C.E.O. and Chief Creative Officer - Stu Levy

A TOKYOPOP® Manga

TOKYOPOP and are trademarks or registered trademarks of TOKYOPOP Inc.

TOKYOPOP Inc.
5900 Wilshire Blvd. Suite 2000
Los Angeles, CA 90036

E-mail: info@TOKYOPOP.com
Come visit us online at www.TOKYOPOP.com

ISBN: 978-1-4278-0827-1

First TOKYOPOP printing: July 2009
10 9 8 7 6 5 4 3 2 1
Printed in the USA

Fruits Basket ™

Volume 23

By
Natsuki Takaya

HAMBURG // LONDON // LOS ANGELES // TOKYO

Fruits Basket ™

Table of Contents

STORY SO FAR...

Hello, I'm Tohru Honda, and I have come to know a terrible secret. After the death of my mother, I was living by myself in a tent, when the Sohma family took me in. I soon learned that the Sohma family lives with a curse! Each family member is possessed by the vengeful spirit of an animal from the Chinese Zodiac. Whenever one of them becomes weak or is hugged by a member of the opposite sex, that person changes into his or her Zodiac animal!

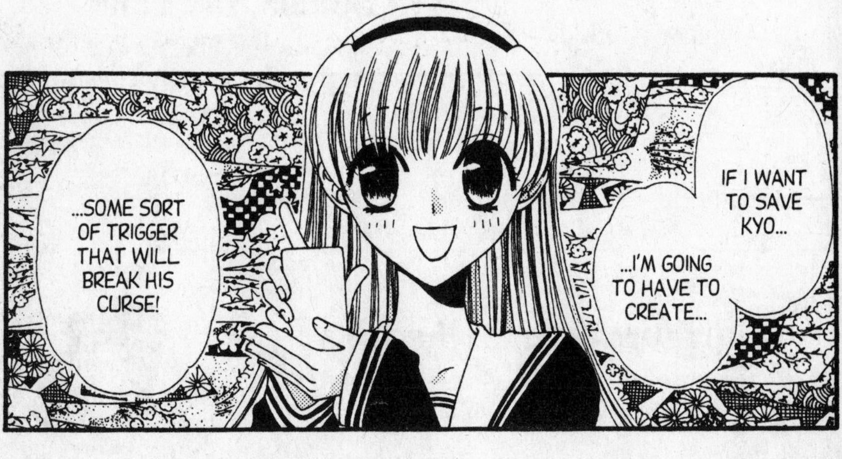
IF I WANT TO SAVE KYO...
...I'M GOING TO HAVE TO CREATE...
...SOME SORT OF TRIGGER THAT WILL BREAK HIS CURSE!

Tohru Honda

The ever-optimistic heroine of our story. An orphan, she now lives in Shigure's house, along with Yuki and Kyo, and is the only person outside of the family who knows the Sohma family's curse.

Yuki Sohma, the Rat

Soft-spoken. Self-esteem issues. At school, he's called "Prince Yuki."

Kyo Sohma, the Cat

The Cat who was left out of the Zodiac. Hates Yuki, leeks and miso. But mostly Yuki.

Kagura Sohma, the Boar

Bashful, yet headstrong. Determined to marry Kyo, even if it kills him.

Fruits Basket Characters

Mabudachi Trio

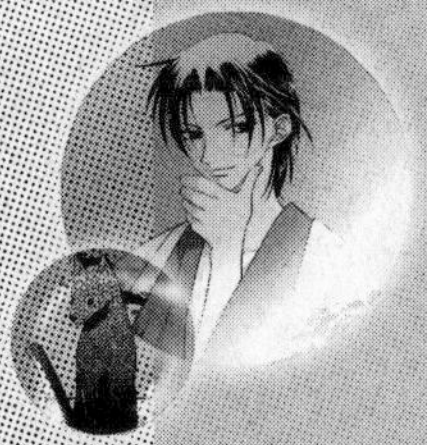

Shigure Sohma, the Dog

Enigmatic, mischievous and a little perverted. A popular novelist.

Hatori Sohma, the Dragon

Family doctor to the Sohmas. Only thing he can't cure is his broken heart.

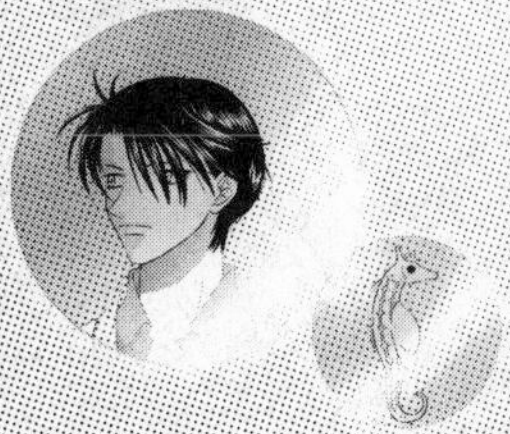

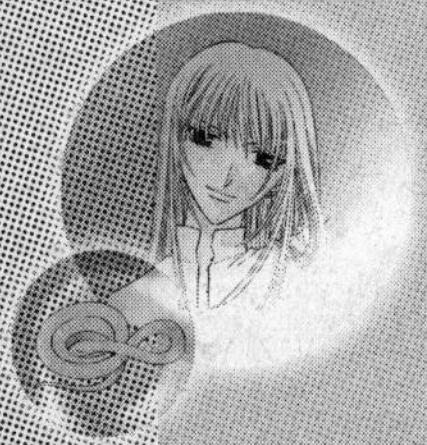

Ayame Sohma, the Snake

Yuki's older brother. A proud and playful drama queen…er, king. Runs a costume shop.

Saki Hanajima

"Hana-chan." Can sense people's "waves." Goth demeanor scares her classmates.

Arisa Uotani

"Uo-chan." A tough-talking "Yankee" who looks out for her friends.

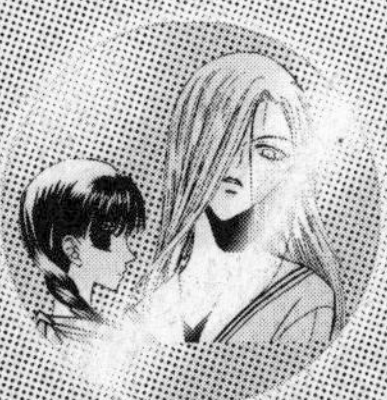

Tohru's Best Friends

Hiro Sohma, the Ram (or sheep)

This caustic tyke is skilled at throwing verbal barbs, but he has a soft spot for Kisa.

Momiji Sohma, the Rabbit

Half German. He's older than he looks. His mother rejected him because of the Sohma curse. His little sister, Momo, has been kept from him most of her life.

Hatsuharu Sohma, the Ox

The nicest of guys, except when he goes "Black." Then you'd better watch out. He was once in a relationship with Rin.

Kisa Sohma, the Tiger

Kisa became shy and self-conscious due to constant teasing by her classmates. Yuki, who has similar insecurities, feels particularly close to Kisa.

Fruits Basket Characters

Isuzu "Rin" Sohma, the Horse

She was once in a relationship with Hatsuharu (Haru)...and Tohru leaves her rather cold. Rin is full of pride, and she can't stand the amount of deference the other Sohma family members give Akito.

Ritsu Sohma, the Monkey

This shy, kimono-wearing member of the Sohma family is gorgeous. But this "she" is really a he!! Cross-dressing calms his nerves.

Kureno Sohma, the Rooster (or bird)

He is Akito's very favorite, and spends almost all of his time on the Sohma estate, tending to Akito's every desire. Kureno was born possessed by the spirit of the Bird, but his curse broke long ago...which means we've never seen him transformed. He pities Akito's loneliness, and can't bring himself to leave her.

"God"

Akito Sohma

The head of the Sohma clan. A dark figure of many secrets. Treated with fear and reverence. It has recently been revealed that Akito is actually a woman!

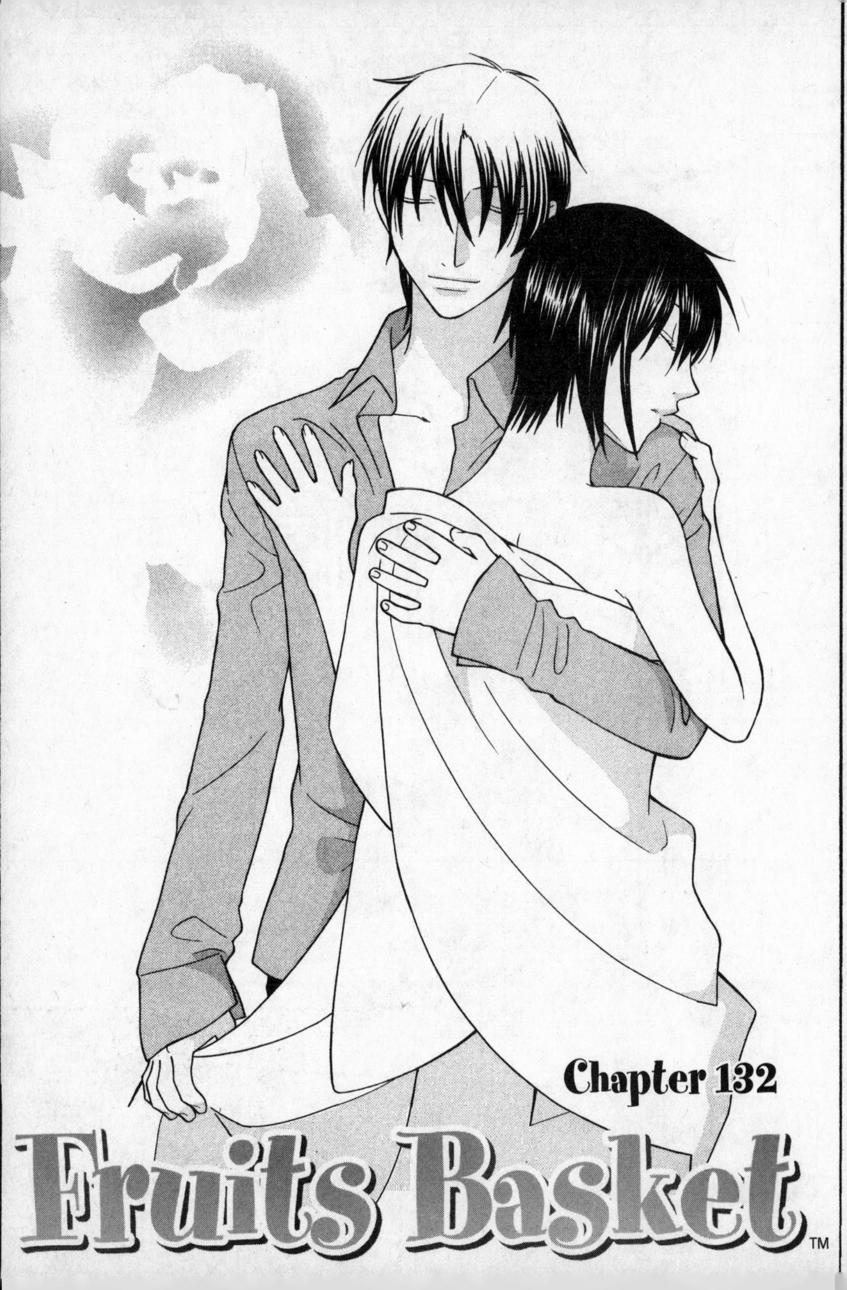
Chapter 132
Fruits Basket™

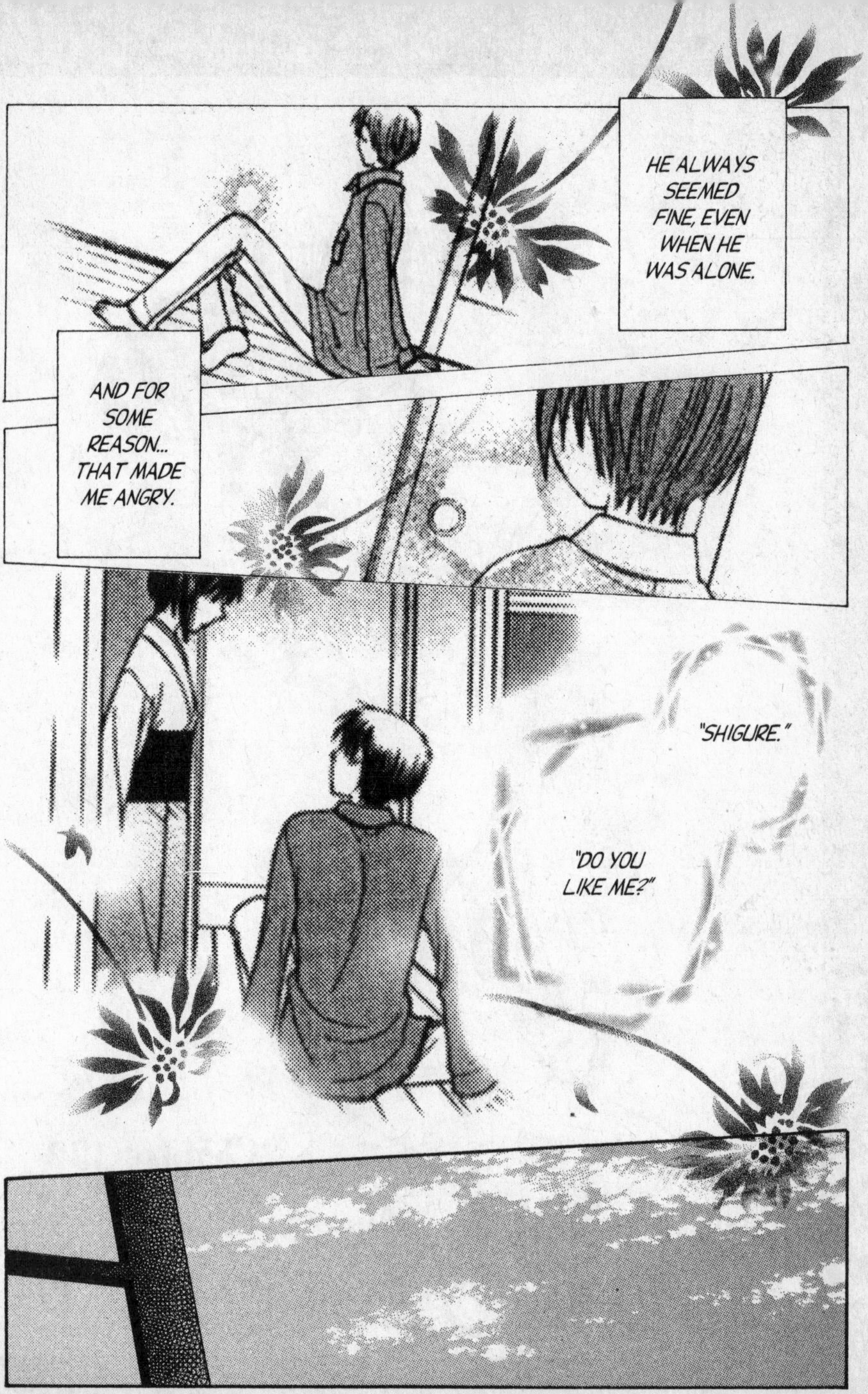
HE ALWAYS SEEMED FINE, EVEN WHEN HE WAS ALONE.
AND FOR SOME REASON... THAT MADE ME ANGRY.
"SHIGURE."
"DO YOU LIKE ME?"

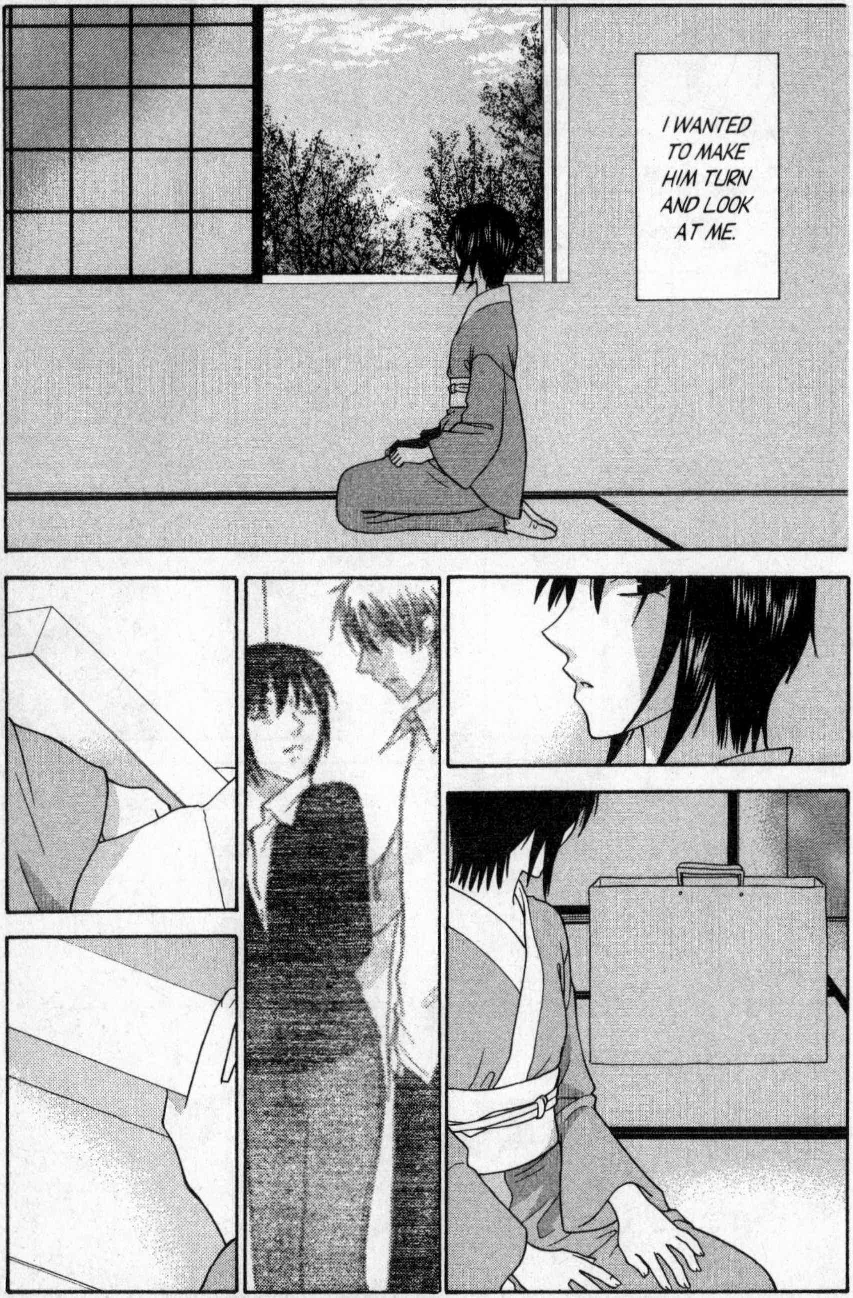
I WANTED TO MAKE HIM TURN AND LOOK AT ME.

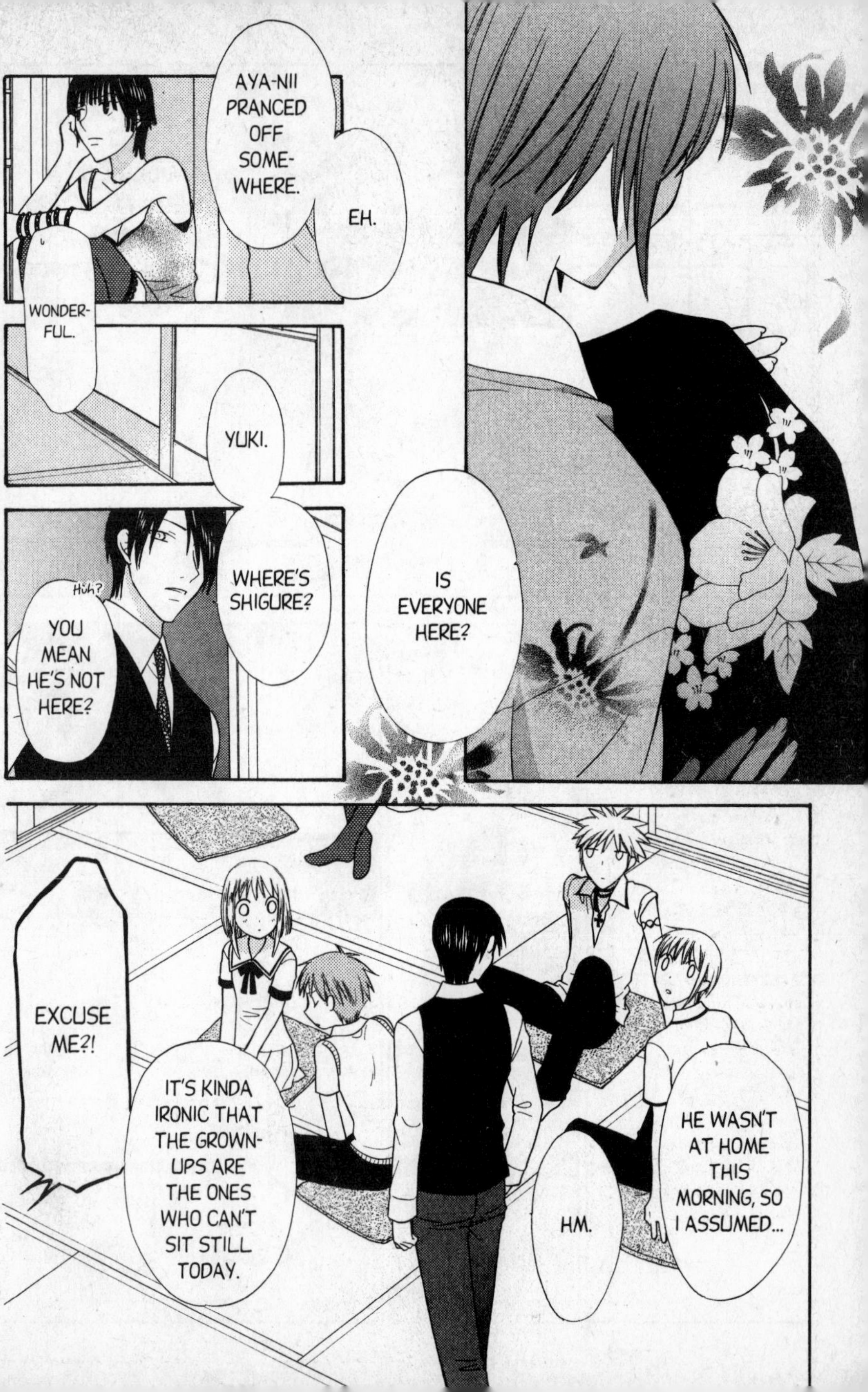
IS EVERYONE HERE?
AYA-NII PRANCED OFF SOME-WHERE.
EH.
WONDER-FUL.
YUKI.
WHERE'S SHIGURE?
Huh?
YOU MEAN HE'S NOT HERE?
HE WASN'T AT HOME THIS MORNING, SO I ASSUMED...
HM.
IT'S KINDA IRONIC THAT THE GROWN-UPS ARE THE ONES WHO CAN'T SIT STILL TODAY.
EXCUSE ME?!

Fruits Basket

Nice to meet you and hello. This is Takaya. Furuba has finally reached its final volume, and Kyoko-san adorns the last cover. It starts with Tohru and closes with Kyoko-san. I had decided that from the beginning. She has a bright, full-faced smile, fitting of Kyoko-san. ...All said and done, this has been a long series. It's thanks to all of you that it was able to go on. I think it must be hard to keep reading something for a long time. Thank you very much. ✤ ✤ I went on a sort of break after Furuba ended, but with little things here and there, I'm still doing lots of work. I was like, "Huh?" (laugh) But a vacation where I'm doing nothing would probably be hard on me in its own way, so maybe it's better this way...maybe.

Now then, laughing or crying, this is the end of Furuba. Please enjoy it!

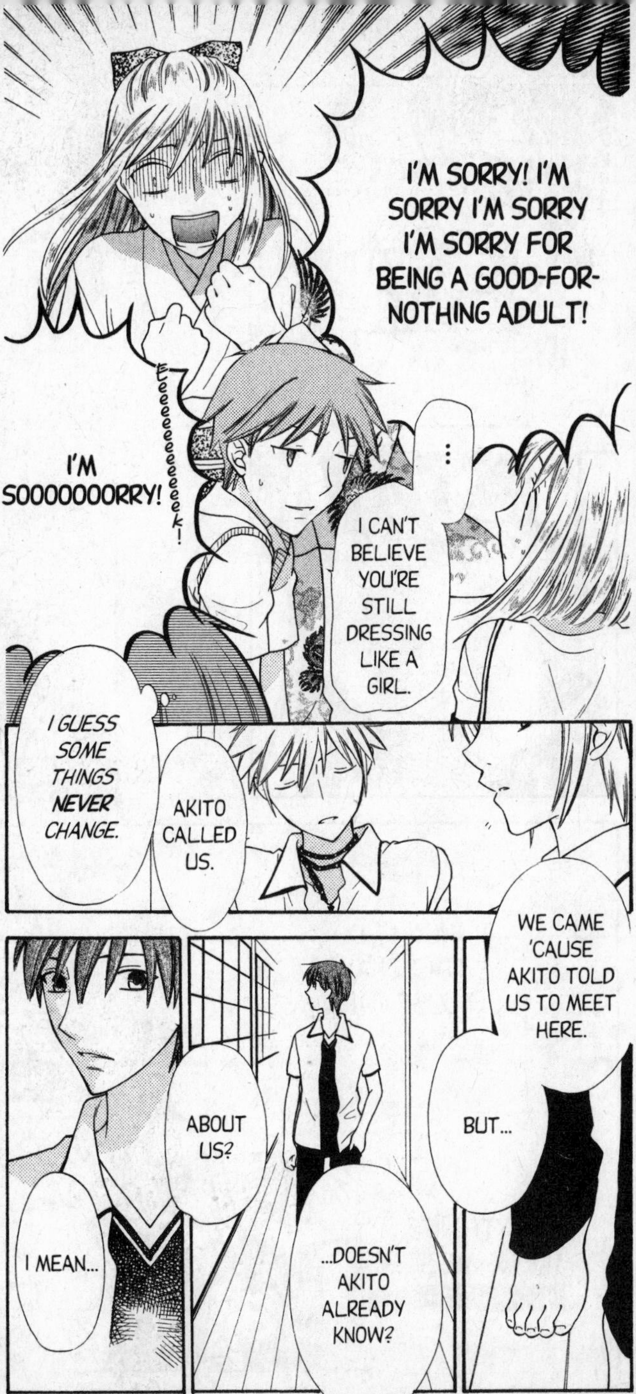
I'M SORRY! I'M SORRY I'M SORRY I'M SORRY FOR BEING A GOOD-FOR-NOTHING ADULT!
Eeeeeeeeeeeeek!
I'M SOOOOOOORRY!
...
I CAN'T BELIEVE YOU'RE STILL DRESSING LIKE A GIRL.
I GUESS SOME THINGS **NEVER** CHANGE.
AKITO CALLED US.
WE CAME 'CAUSE AKITO TOLD US TO MEET HERE.
BUT...
...DOESN'T AKITO ALREADY KNOW?
ABOUT US?
I MEAN...

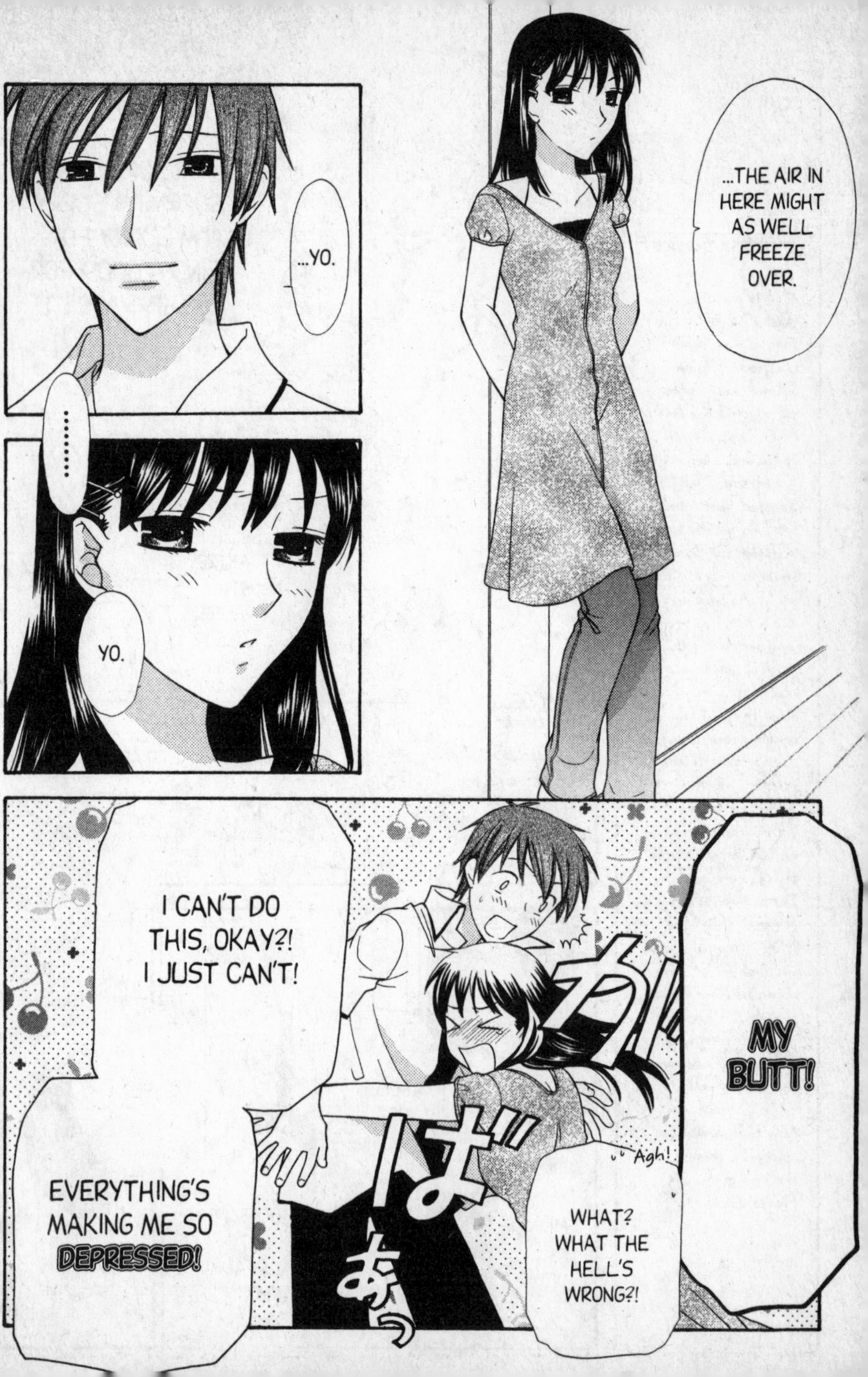
...THE AIR IN HERE MIGHT AS WELL FREEZE OVER.
...YO.
......
YO.
MY BUTT!
I CAN'T DO THIS, OKAY?! I JUST CAN'T!
Agh!
WHAT? WHAT THE HELL'S WRONG?!
EVERYTHING'S MAKING ME SO DEPRESSED!

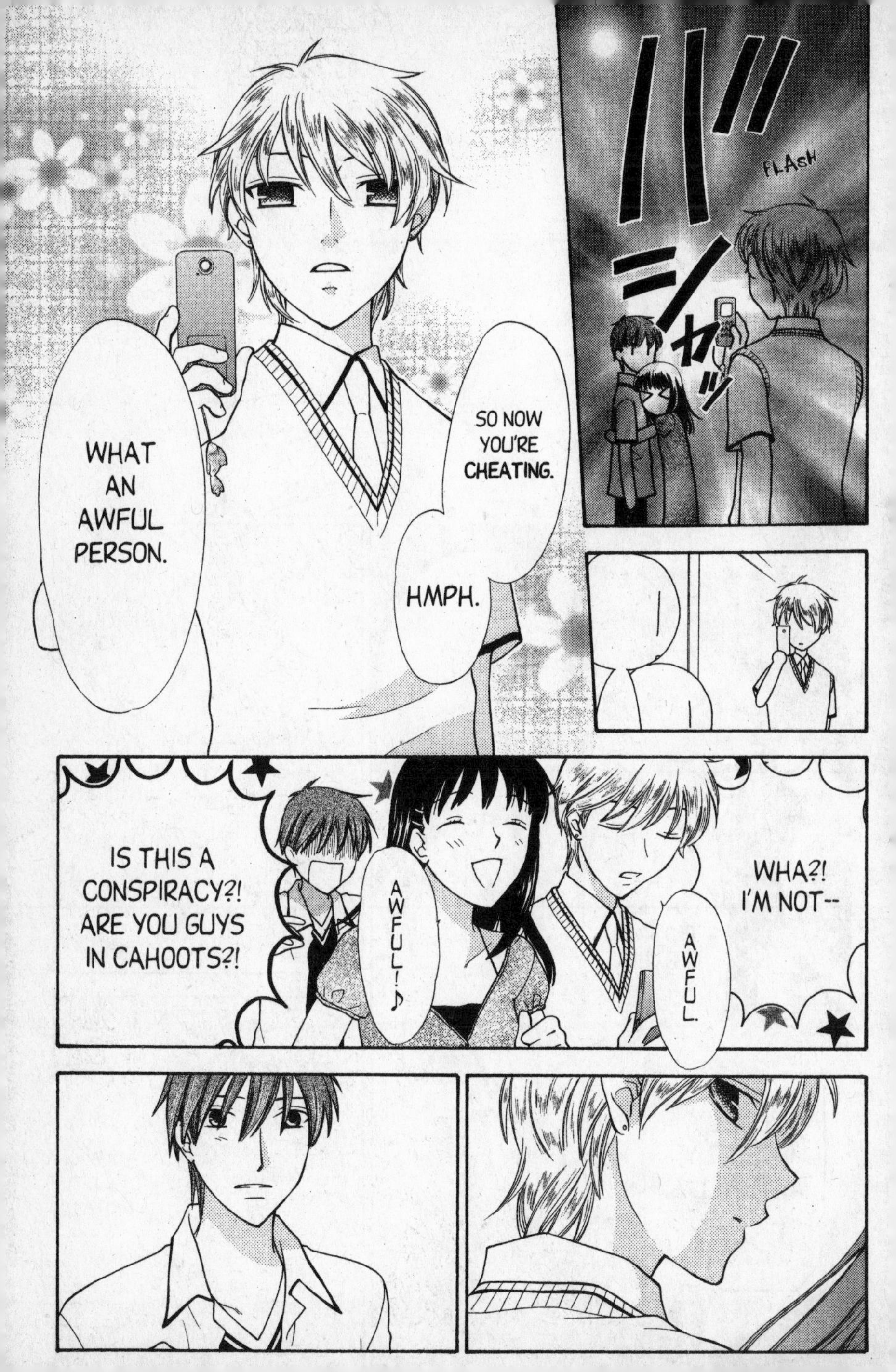
FLASH
SO NOW YOU'RE CHEATING.
HMPH.
WHAT AN AWFUL PERSON.
WHA?! I'M NOT--
AWFUL.
AWFUL!♪
IS THIS A CONSPIRACY?! ARE YOU GUYS IN CAHOOTS?!

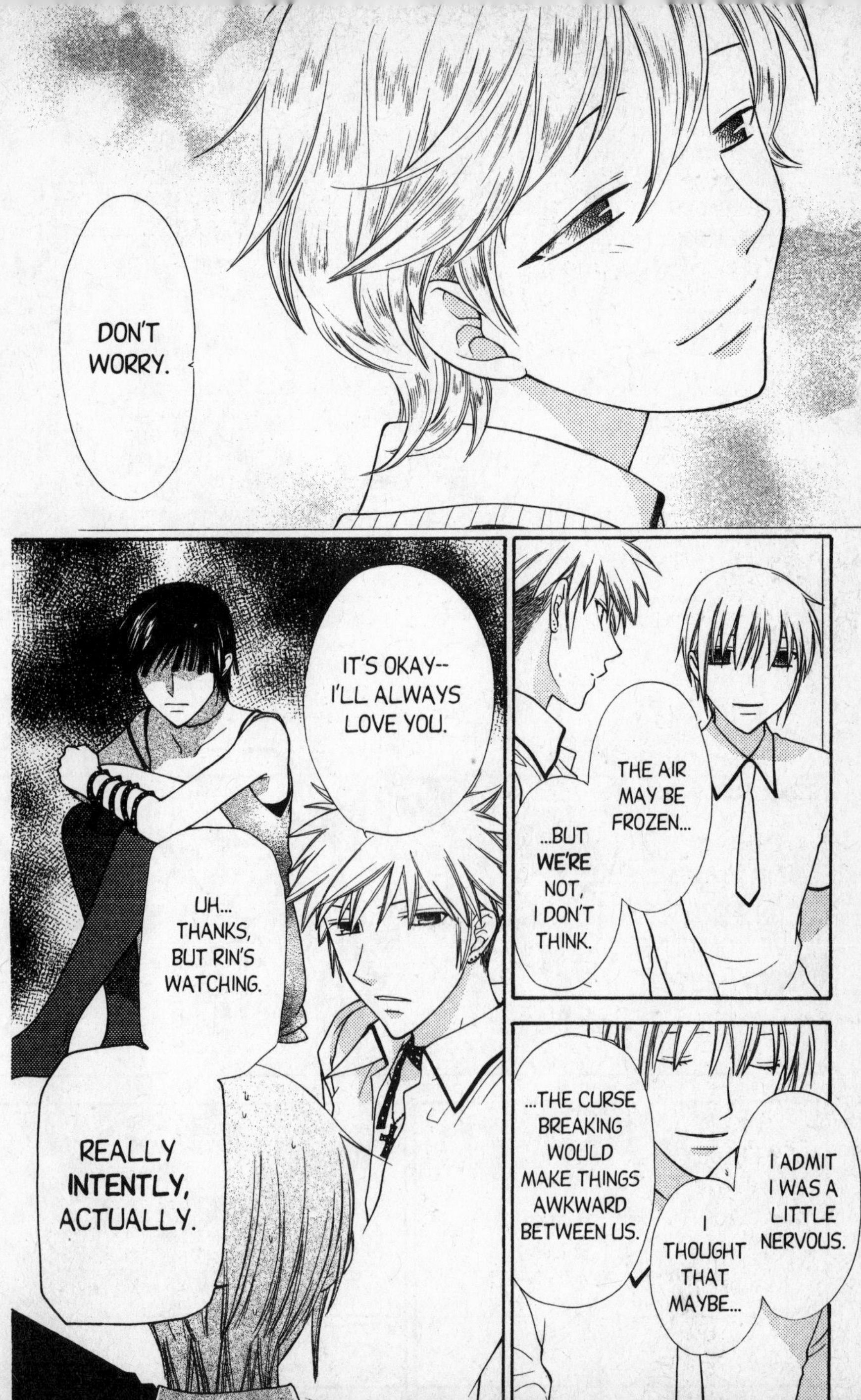
DON'T WORRY.
THE AIR MAY BE FROZEN...
...BUT WE'RE NOT, I DON'T THINK.
I ADMIT I WAS A LITTLE NERVOUS.
I THOUGHT THAT MAYBE...
...THE CURSE BREAKING WOULD MAKE THINGS AWKWARD BETWEEN US.
IT'S OKAY-- I'LL ALWAYS LOVE YOU.
UH... THANKS, BUT RIN'S WATCHING.
REALLY INTENTLY, ACTUALLY.

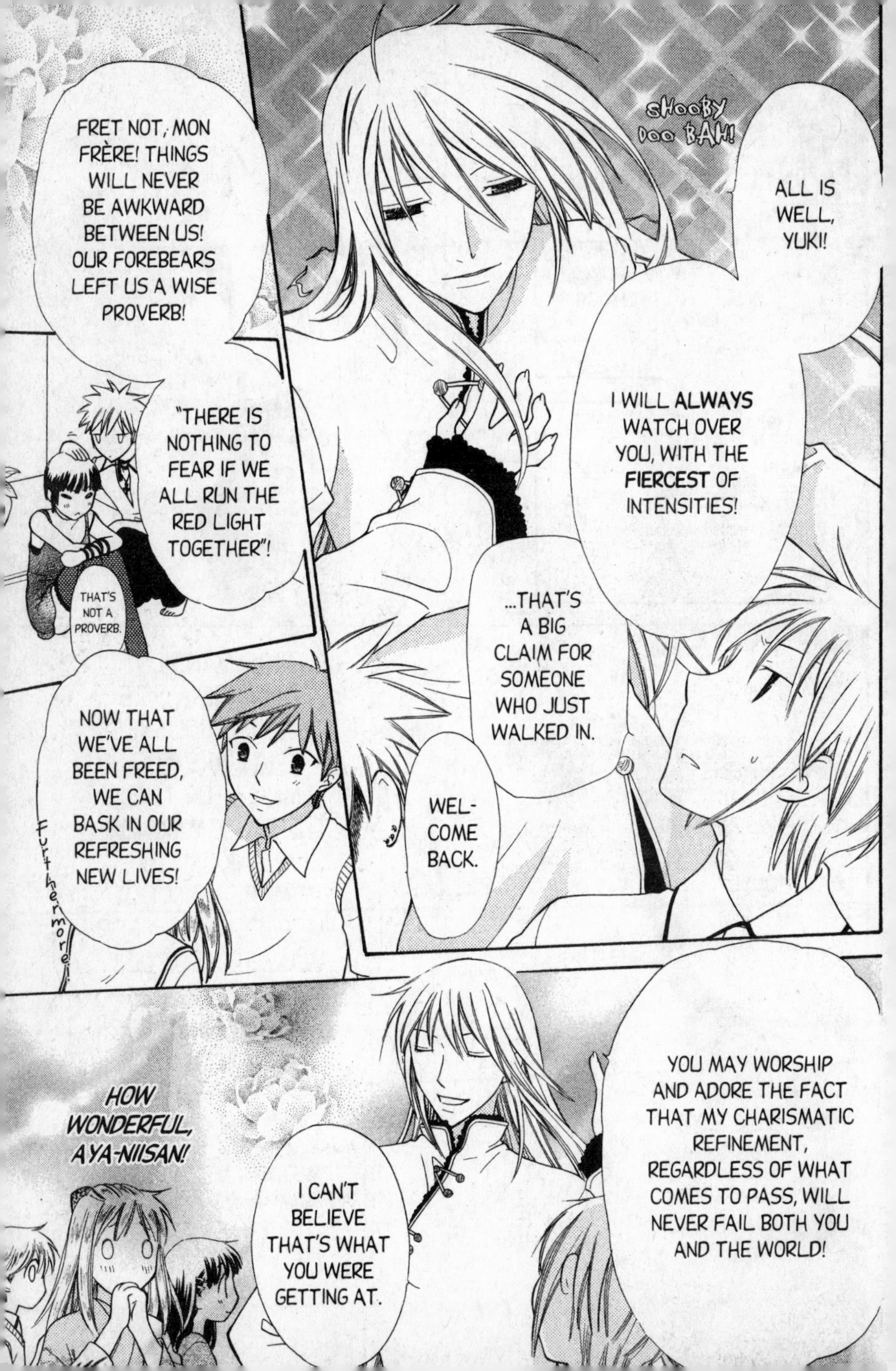

SHOOBY DOO BAH!
ALL IS WELL, YUKI!
I WILL ALWAYS WATCH OVER YOU, WITH THE FIERCEST OF INTENSITIES!
...THAT'S A BIG CLAIM FOR SOMEONE WHO JUST WALKED IN.
WEL-COME BACK.
FRET NOT, MON FRÈRE! THINGS WILL NEVER BE AWKWARD BETWEEN US! OUR FOREBEARS LEFT US A WISE PROVERB!
"THERE IS NOTHING TO FEAR IF WE ALL RUN THE RED LIGHT TOGETHER"!
THAT'S NOT A PROVERB.
NOW THAT WE'VE ALL BEEN FREED, WE CAN BASK IN OUR REFRESHING NEW LIVES!
Furthermore!
YOU MAY WORSHIP AND ADORE THE FACT THAT MY CHARISMATIC REFINEMENT, REGARDLESS OF WHAT COMES TO PASS, WILL NEVER FAIL BOTH YOU AND THE WORLD!
I CAN'T BELIEVE THAT'S WHAT YOU WERE GETTING AT.
HOW WONDERFUL, AYA-NIISAN!

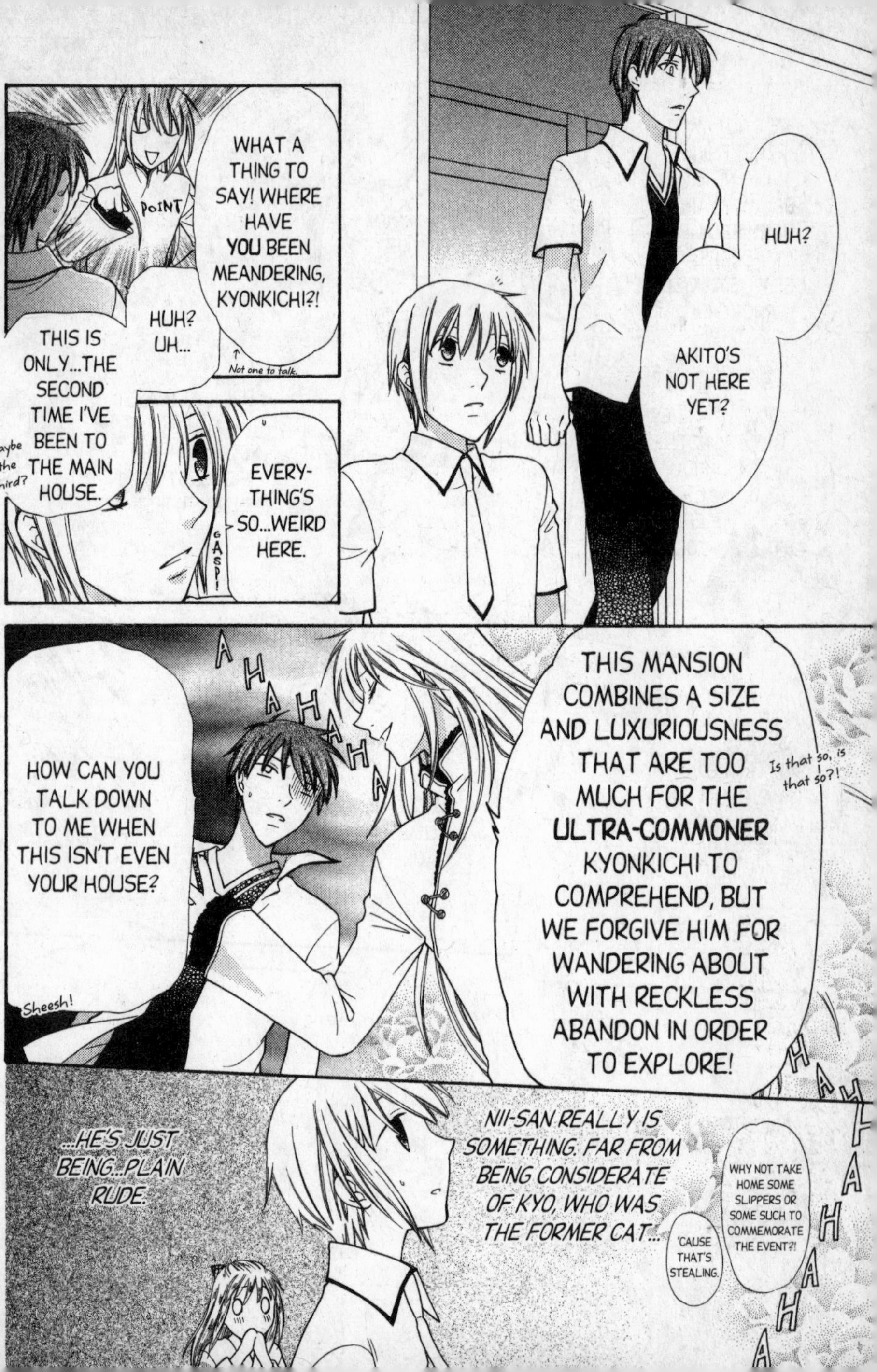
HUH?
AKITO'S NOT HERE YET?
WHAT A THING TO SAY! WHERE HAVE **YOU** BEEN MEANDERING, KYONKICHI?!
Not one to talk.
HUH? UH...
THIS IS ONLY...THE SECOND TIME I'VE BEEN TO THE MAIN HOUSE.
Maybe the third?
EVERYTHING'S SO...WEIRD HERE.
GASP!
THIS MANSION COMBINES A SIZE AND LUXURIOUSNESS THAT ARE TOO MUCH FOR THE **ULTRA-COMMONER** KYONKICHI TO COMPREHEND, BUT WE FORGIVE HIM FOR WANDERING ABOUT WITH RECKLESS ABANDON IN ORDER TO EXPLORE!
Is that so, is that so?!
AHAHAHAHA
HOW CAN YOU TALK DOWN TO ME WHEN THIS ISN'T EVEN YOUR HOUSE?
Sheesh!
NII-SAN REALLY IS SOMETHING. FAR FROM BEING CONSIDERATE OF KYO, WHO WAS THE FORMER CAT...
WHY NOT TAKE HOME SOME SLIPPERS OR SOME SUCH TO COMMEMORATE THE EVENT?!
'CAUSE THAT'S STEALING.
AHAHAHAHAHA
...HE'S JUST BEING...PLAIN RUDE.

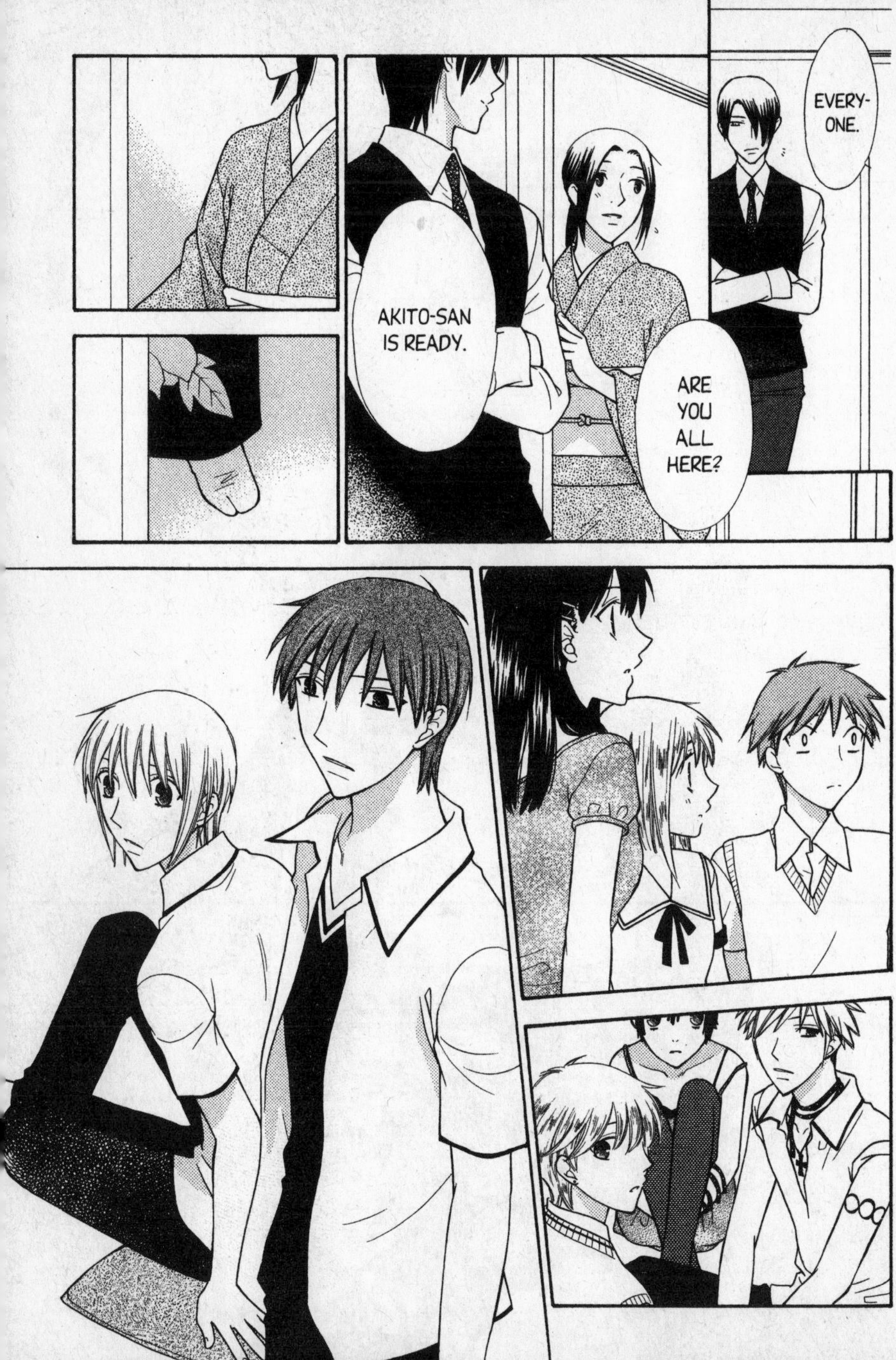
EVERY-ONE.
ARE YOU ALL HERE?
AKITO-SAN IS READY.

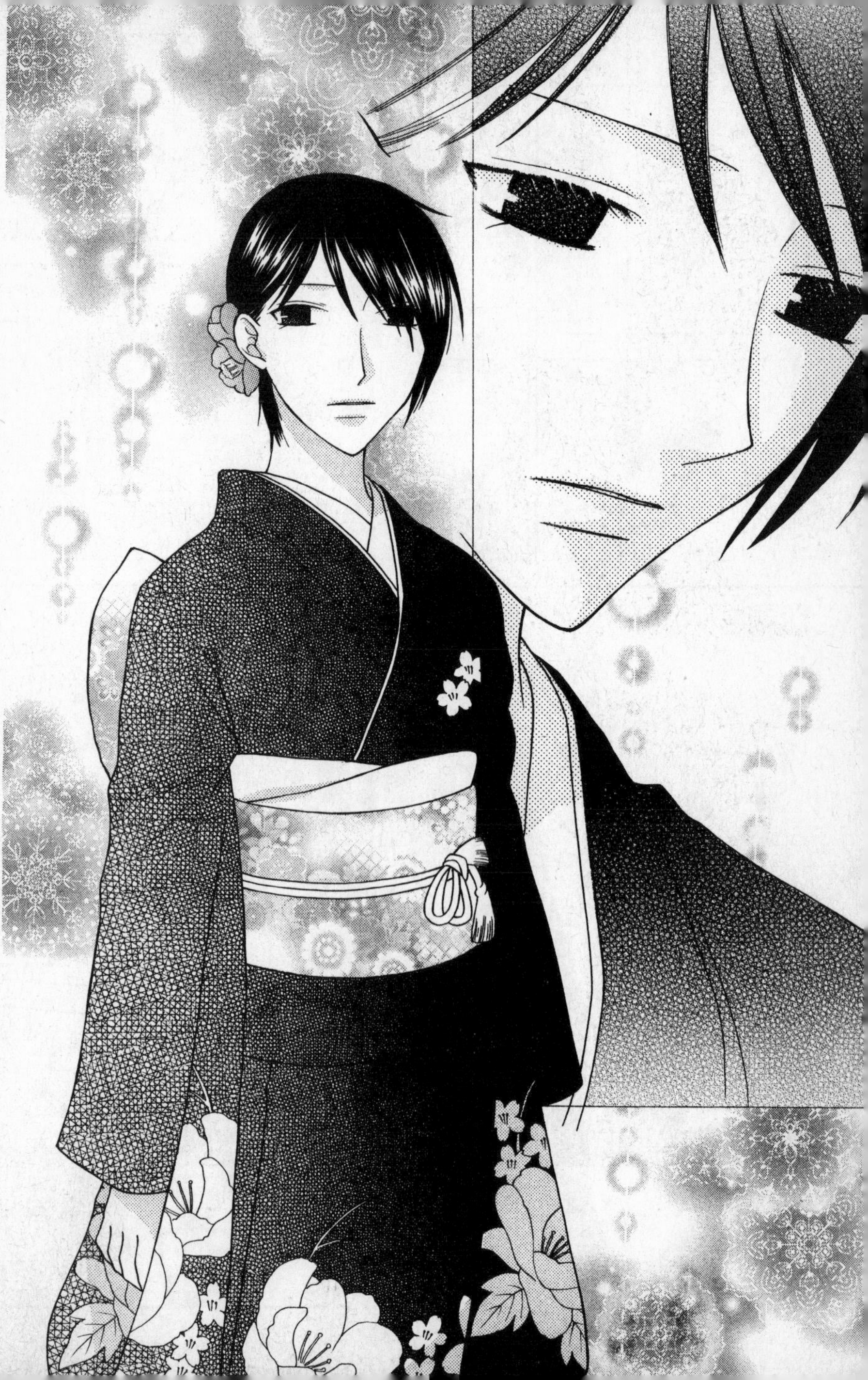

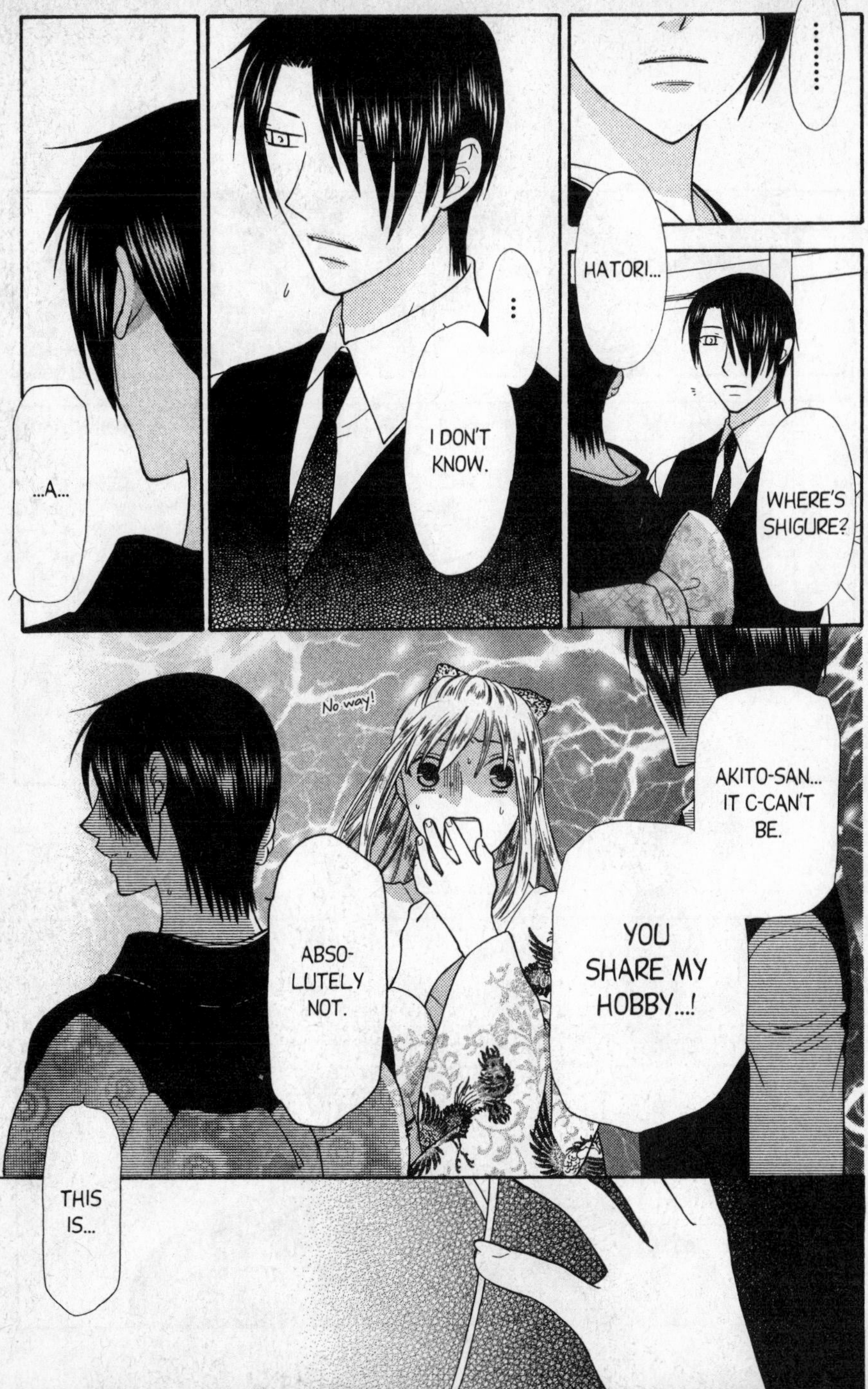
......
HATORI...
WHERE'S SHIGURE?
...
I DON'T KNOW.
...A...
AKITO-SAN... IT C-CAN'T BE.
YOU SHARE MY HOBBY...!
No way!
ABSO-LUTELY NOT.
THIS IS...

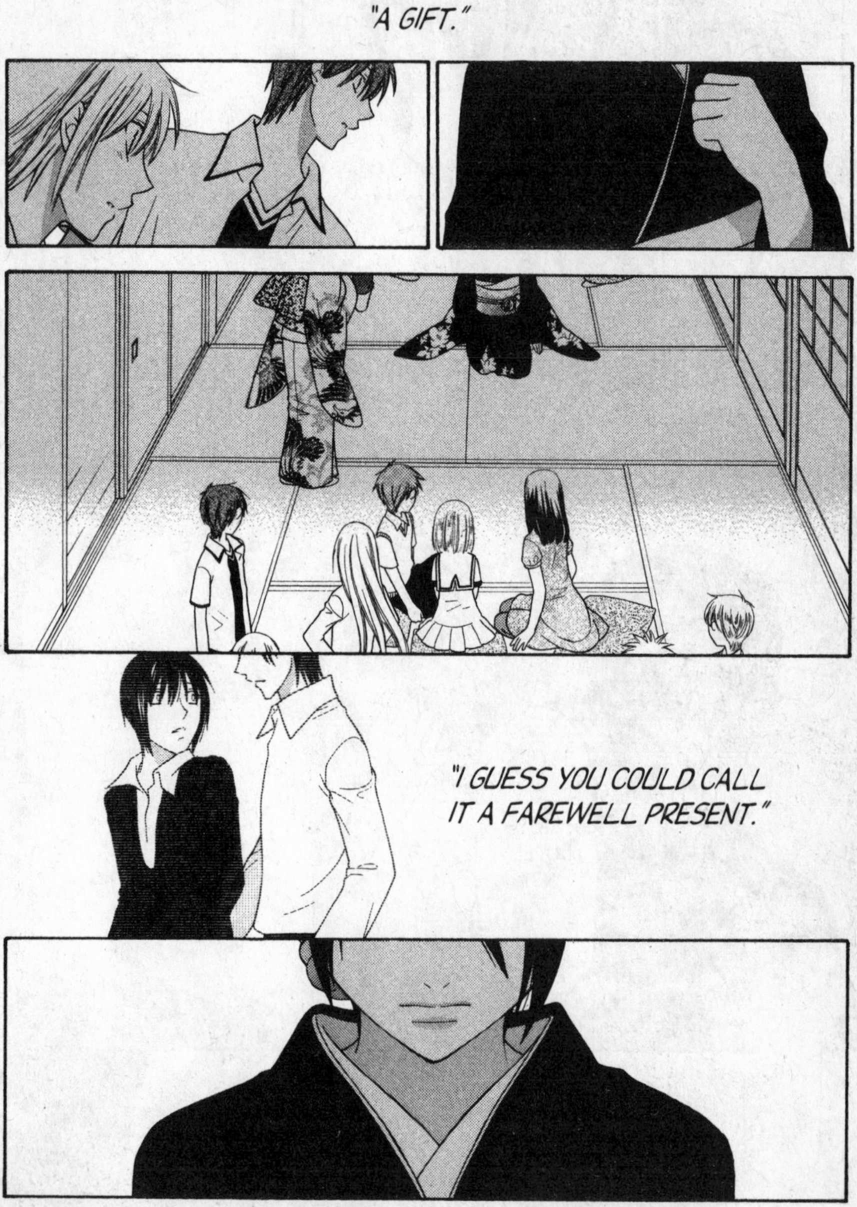
"A GIFT."
"I GUESS YOU COULD CALL IT A FAREWELL PRESENT."

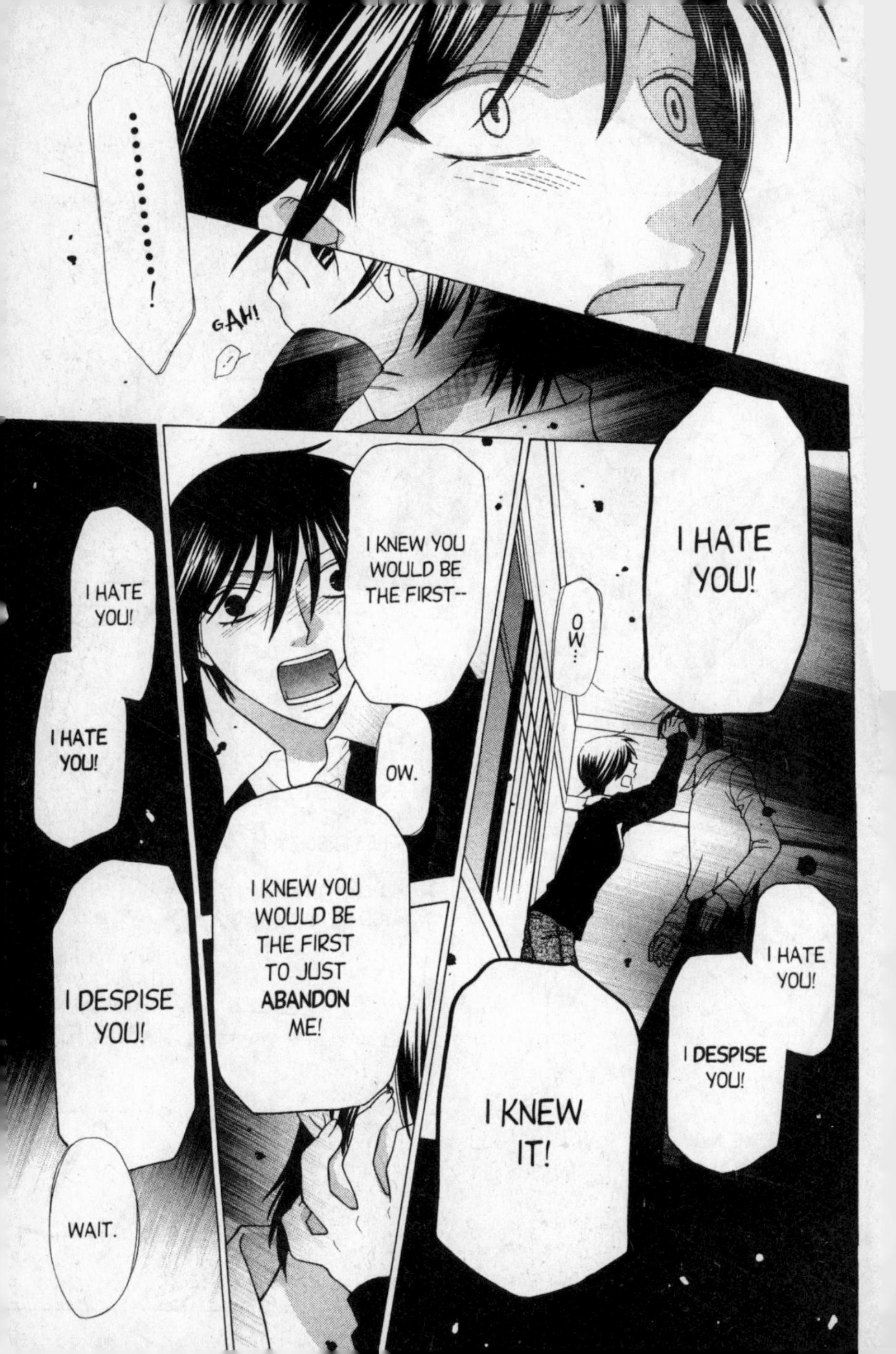
......!
GAH!
I HATE YOU!
OW...
I HATE YOU!
I DESPISE YOU!
I KNEW IT!
I KNEW YOU WOULD BE THE FIRST--
OW.
I KNEW YOU WOULD BE THE FIRST TO JUST ABANDON ME!
I HATE YOU!
I HATE YOU!
I DESPISE YOU!
WAIT.

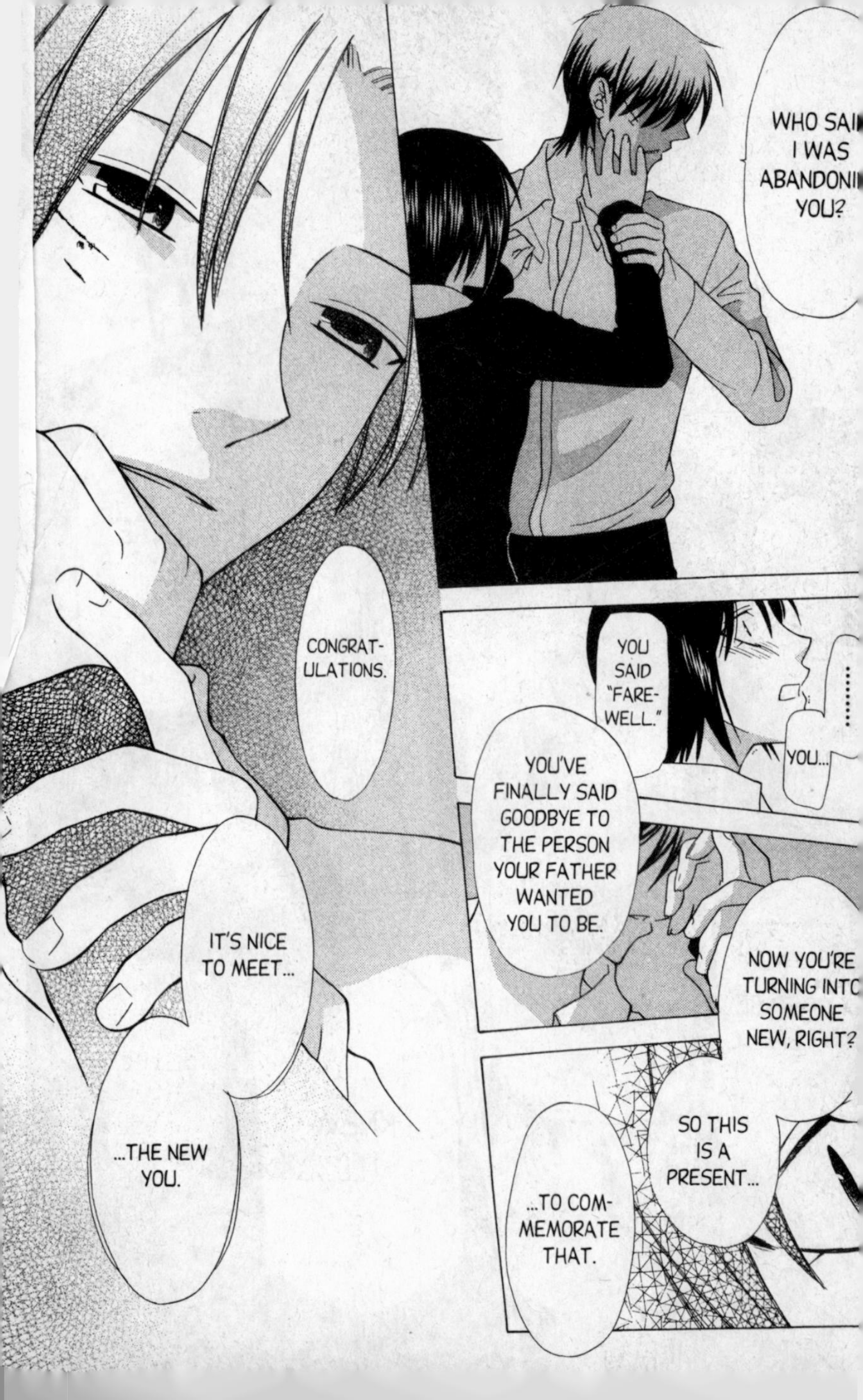
WHO SAI I WAS ABANDONI YOU?
....
YOU...
YOU SAID "FAREWELL."
YOU'VE FINALLY SAID GOODBYE TO THE PERSON YOUR FATHER WANTED YOU TO BE.
NOW YOU'RE TURNING INTC SOMEONE NEW, RIGHT?
SO THIS IS A PRESENT...
...TO COMMEMORATE THAT.
CONGRATULATIONS.
IT'S NICE TO MEET...
...THE NEW YOU.

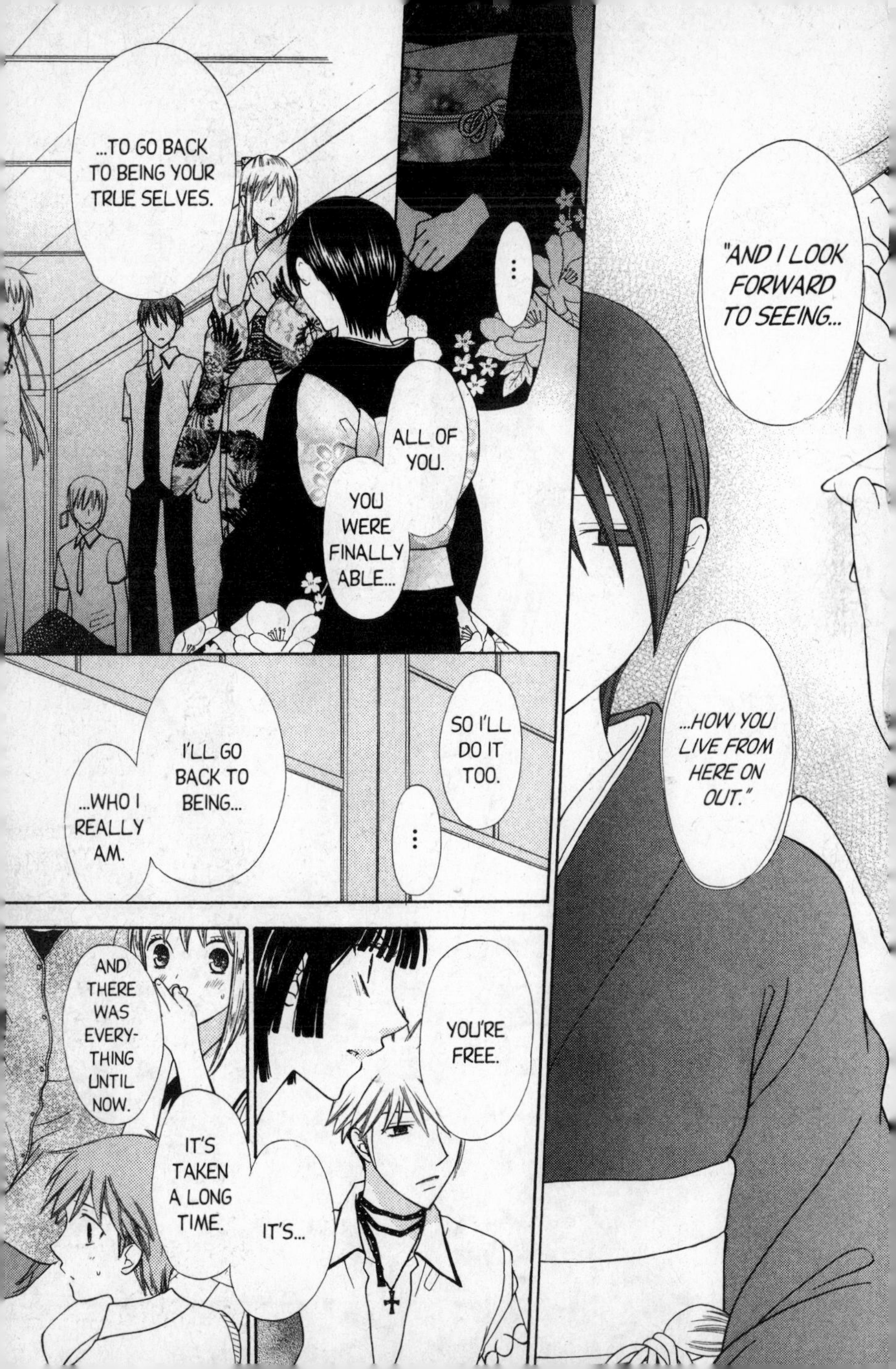
"AND I LOOK FORWARD TO SEEING...
...HOW YOU LIVE FROM HERE ON OUT."
...
ALL OF YOU.
YOU WERE FINALLY ABLE...
...TO GO BACK TO BEING YOUR TRUE SELVES.
SO I'LL DO IT TOO.
...
I'LL GO BACK TO BEING...
...WHO I REALLY AM.
YOU'RE FREE.
IT'S...
IT'S TAKEN A LONG TIME.
AND THERE WAS EVERY-THING UNTIL NOW.

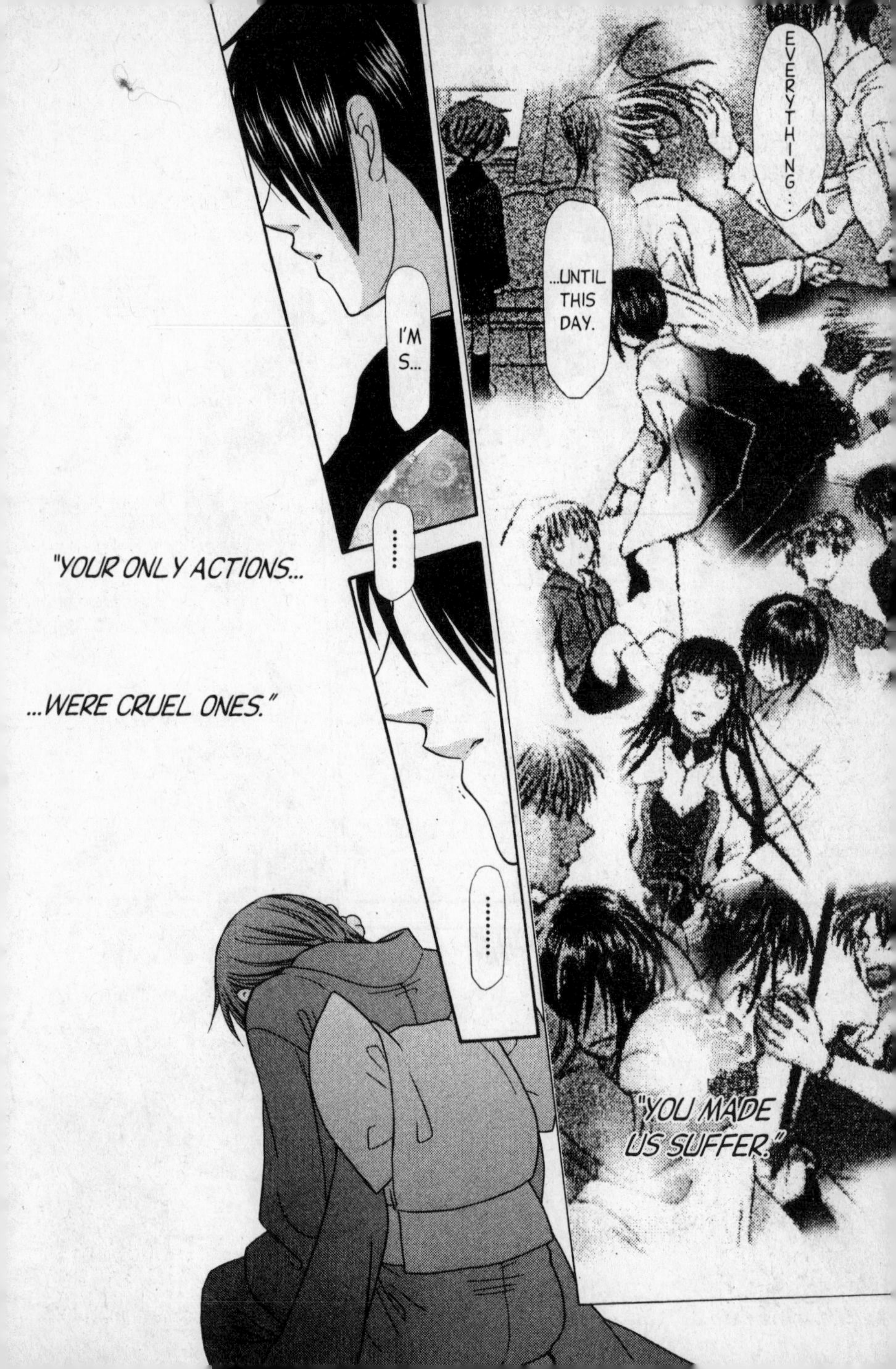
EVERYTHING...
...UNTIL THIS DAY.
"YOU MADE US SUFFER."
I'M S...
......
....
"YOUR ONLY ACTIONS...
...WERE CRUEL ONES."

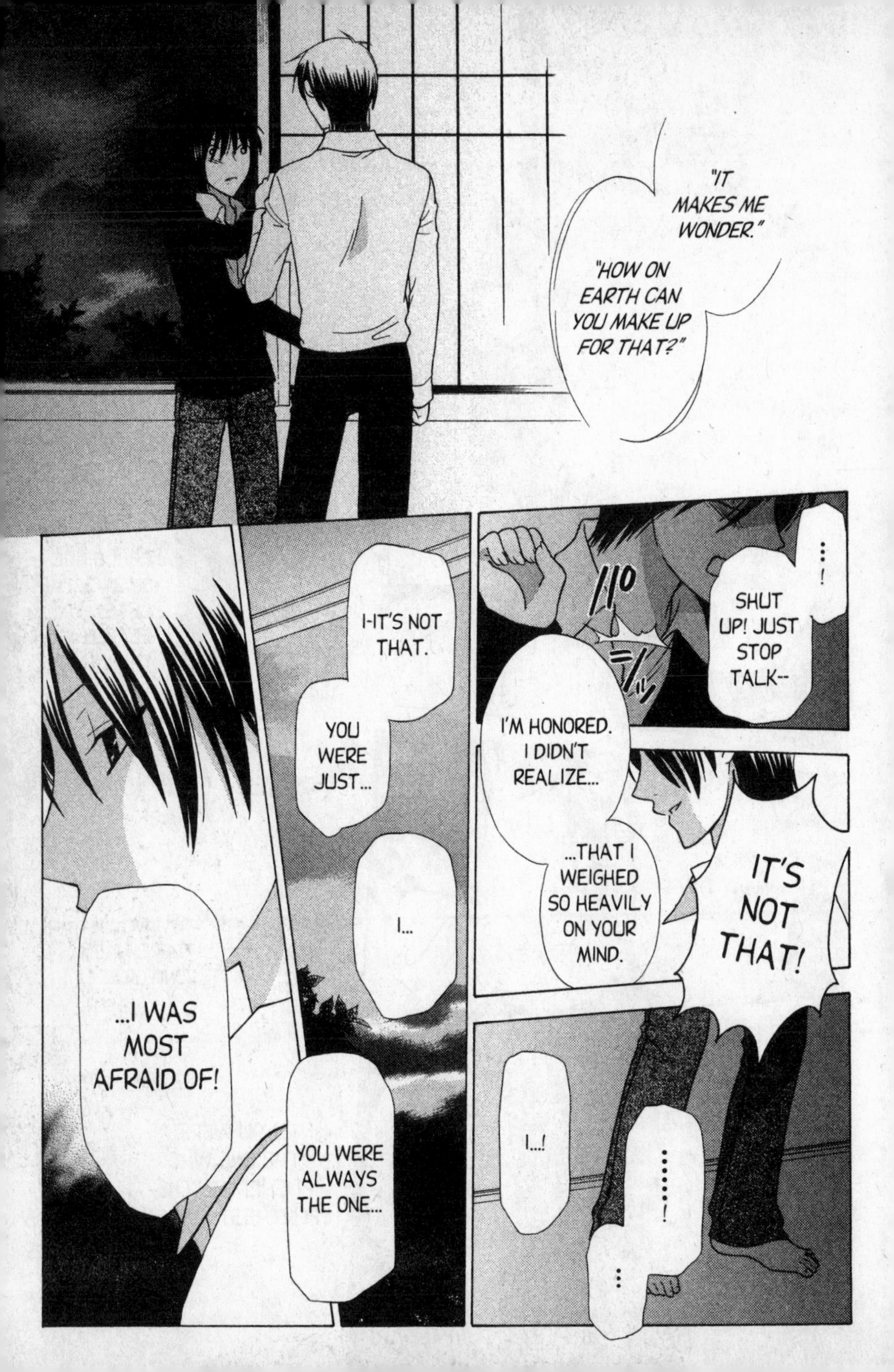
"IT MAKES ME WONDER."
"HOW ON EARTH CAN YOU MAKE UP FOR THAT?"
...!
SHUT UP! JUST STOP TALK--
I'M HONORED. I DIDN'T REALIZE...
...THAT I WEIGHED SO HEAVILY ON YOUR MIND.
IT'S NOT THAT!
......!
I...!
...
I-IT'S NOT THAT.
YOU WERE JUST...
I...
YOU WERE ALWAYS THE ONE...
...I WAS MOST AFRAID OF!

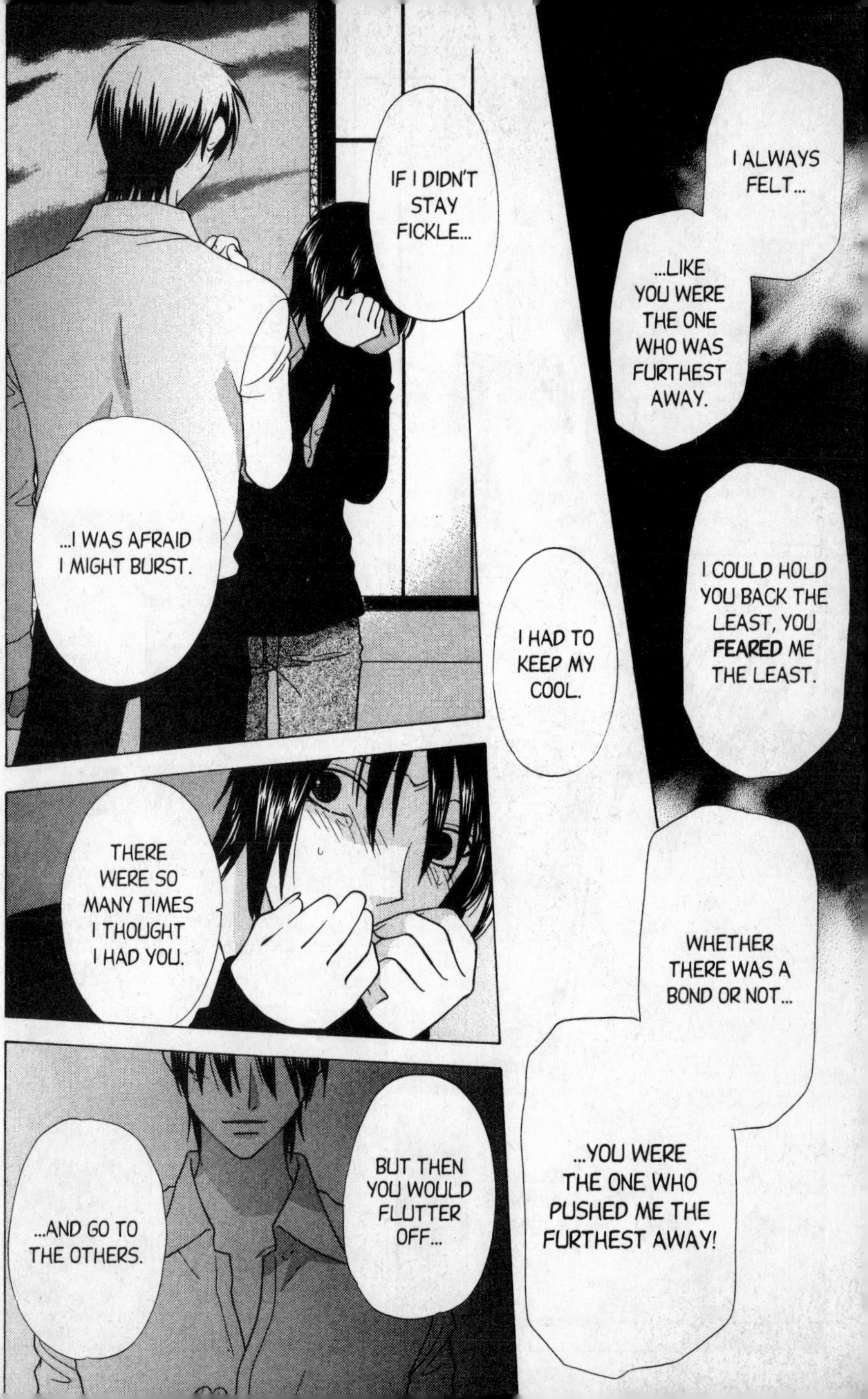
I ALWAYS FELT...
...LIKE YOU WERE THE ONE WHO WAS FURTHEST AWAY.
I COULD HOLD YOU BACK THE LEAST, YOU FEARED ME THE LEAST.
WHETHER THERE WAS A BOND OR NOT...
...YOU WERE THE ONE WHO PUSHED ME THE FURTHEST AWAY!
IF I DIDN'T STAY FICKLE...
...I WAS AFRAID I MIGHT BURST.
I HAD TO KEEP MY COOL.
THERE WERE SO MANY TIMES I THOUGHT I HAD YOU.
BUT THEN YOU WOULD FLUTTER OFF...
...AND GO TO THE OTHERS.

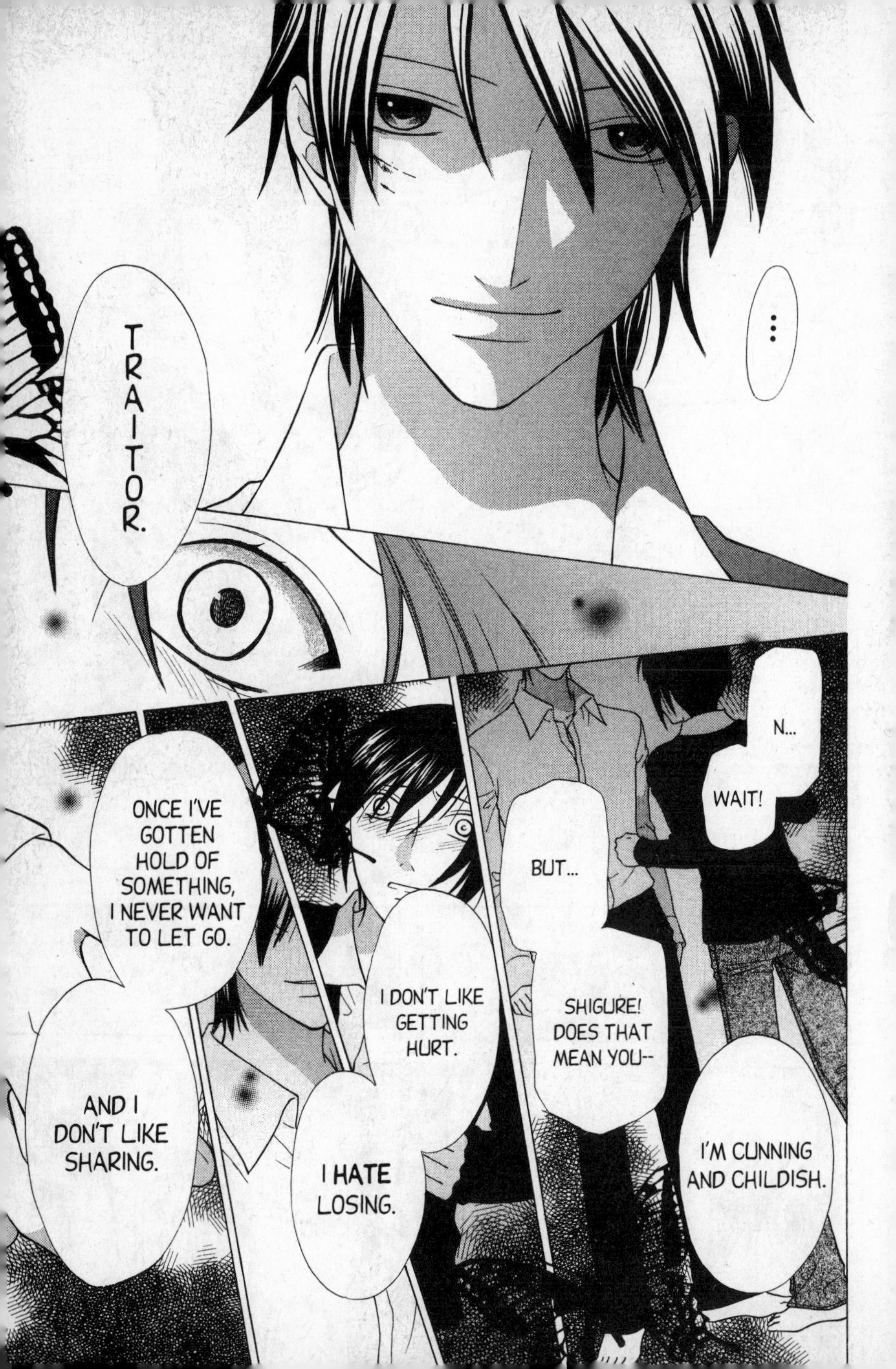
...
TRAITOR.
N... WAIT!
BUT...
SHIGURE! DOES THAT MEAN YOU--
I'M CUNNING AND CHILDISH.
I DON'T LIKE GETTING HURT.
I HATE LOSING.
ONCE I'VE GOTTEN HOLD OF SOMETHING, I NEVER WANT TO LET GO.
AND I DON'T LIKE SHARING.

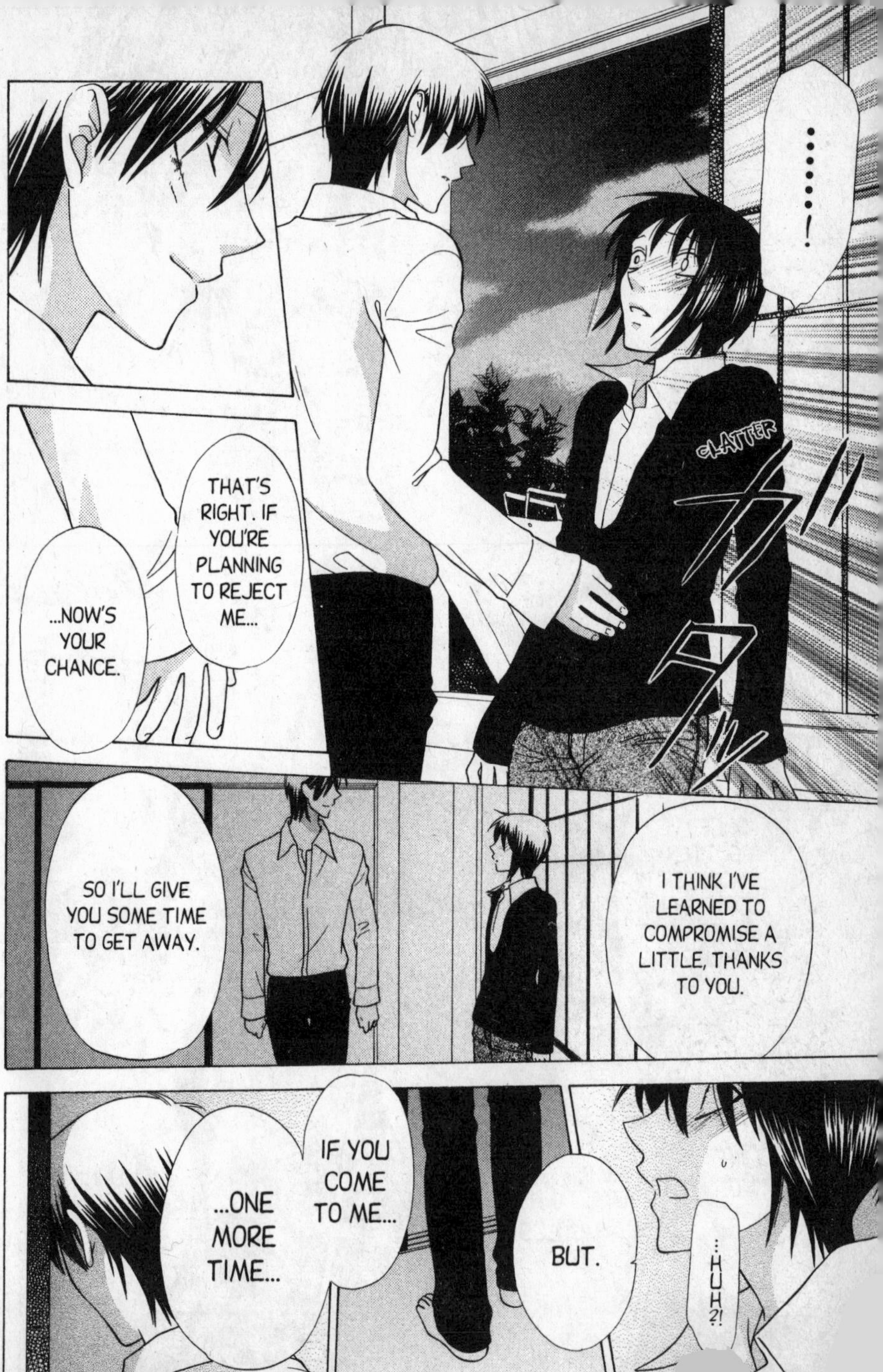
……!
CLATTER
THAT'S RIGHT. IF YOU'RE PLANNING TO REJECT ME...
...NOW'S YOUR CHANCE.
I THINK I'VE LEARNED TO COMPROMISE A LITTLE, THANKS TO YOU.
SO I'LL GIVE YOU SOME TIME TO GET AWAY.
...HUH?!
BUT.
IF YOU COME TO ME...
...ONE MORE TIME...

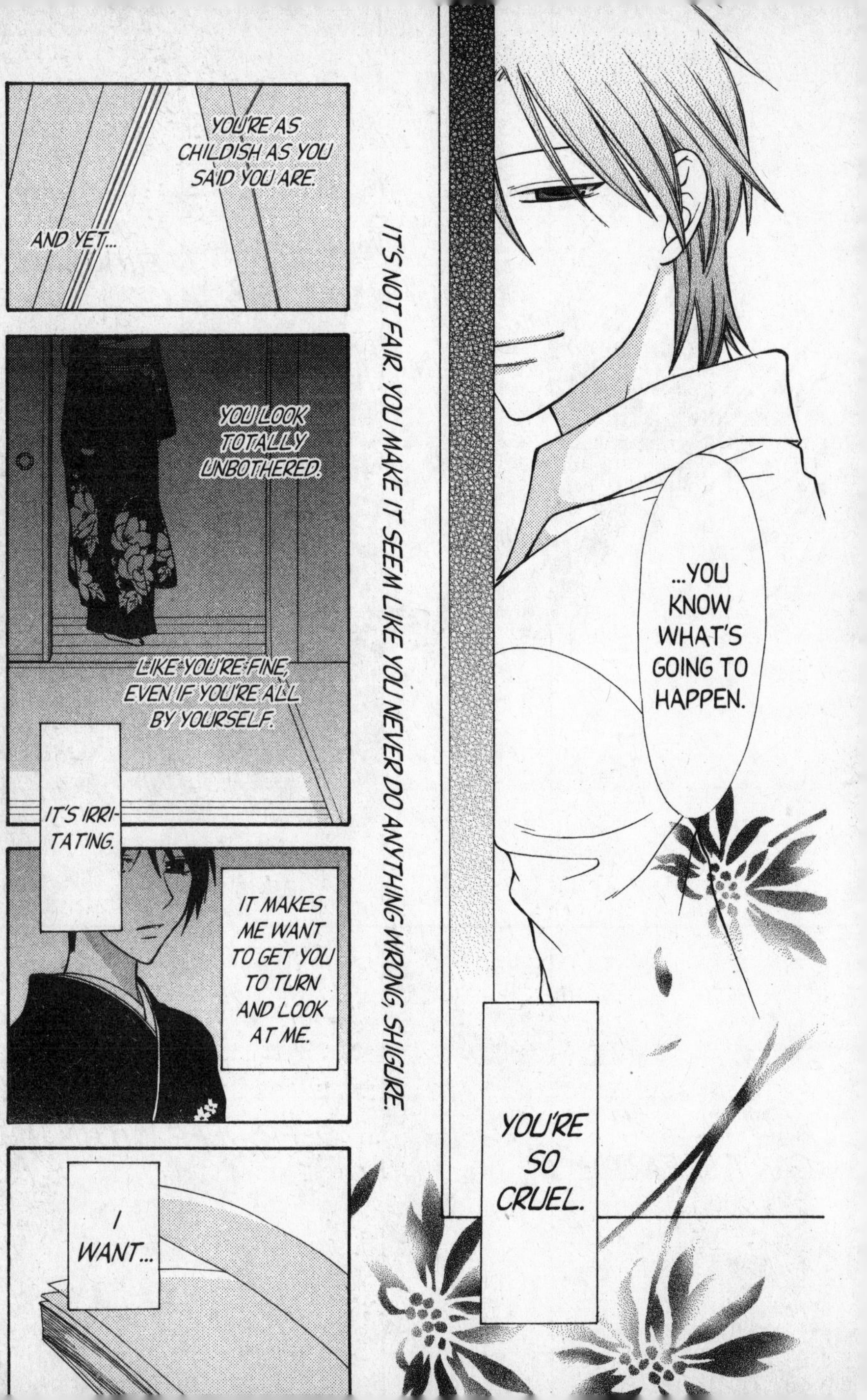
...YOU KNOW WHAT'S GOING TO HAPPEN.
YOU'RE SO CRUEL.
IT'S NOT FAIR. YOU MAKE IT SEEM LIKE YOU NEVER DO ANYTHING WRONG, SHIGURE.
YOU'RE AS CHILDISH AS YOU SAID YOU ARE.
AND YET...
YOU LOOK TOTALLY UNBOTHERED.
LIKE YOU'RE FINE, EVEN IF YOU'RE ALL BY YOURSELF.
IT'S IRRI-TATING.
IT MAKES ME WANT TO GET YOU TO TURN AND LOOK AT ME.
I WANT...

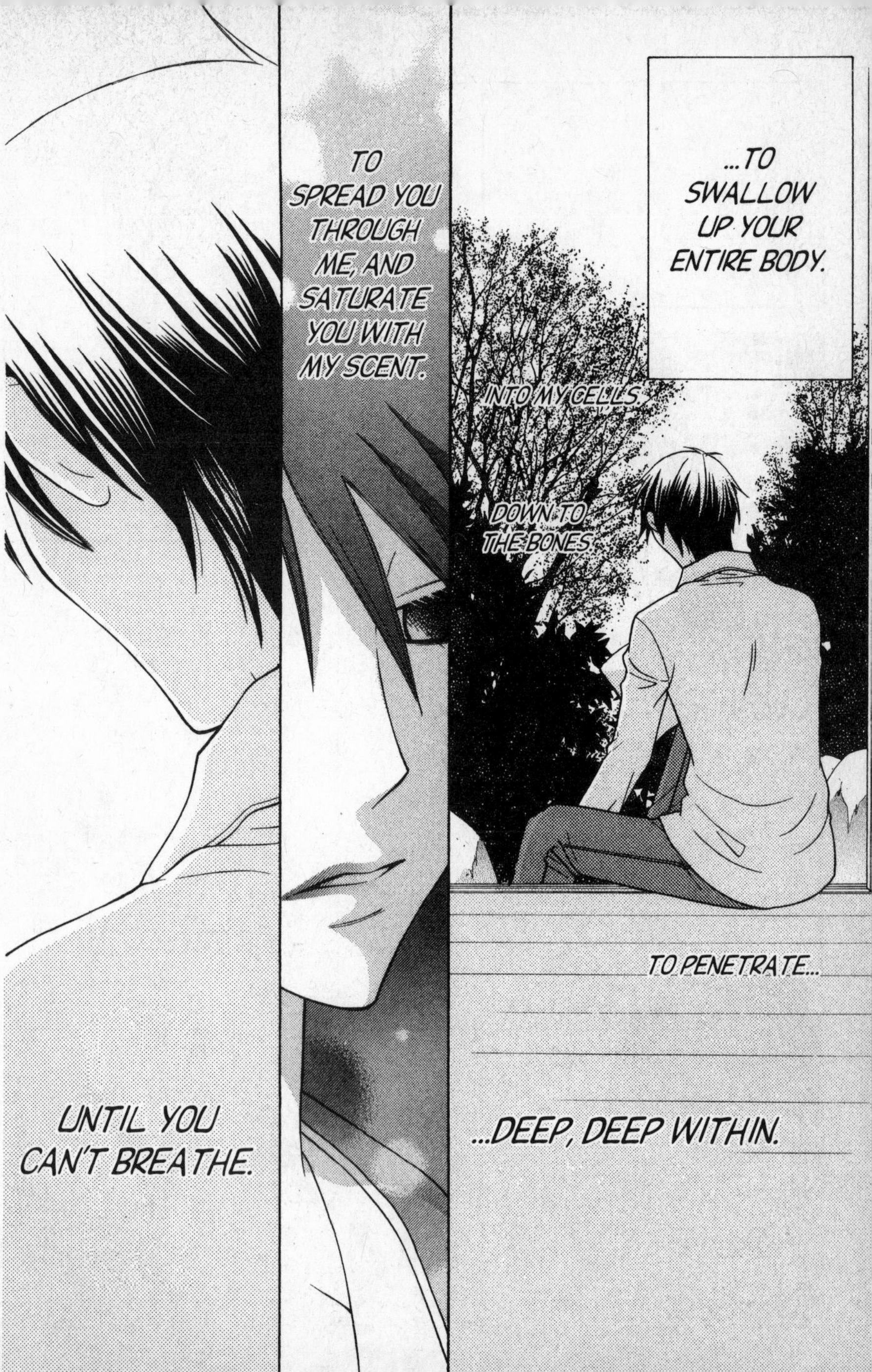
...TO SWALLOW UP YOUR ENTIRE BODY.
INTO MY CELLS.
DOWN TO THE BONES.
TO PENETRATE...
...DEEP, DEEP WITHIN.
TO SPREAD YOU THROUGH ME, AND SATURATE YOU WITH MY SCENT.
UNTIL YOU CAN'T BREATHE.

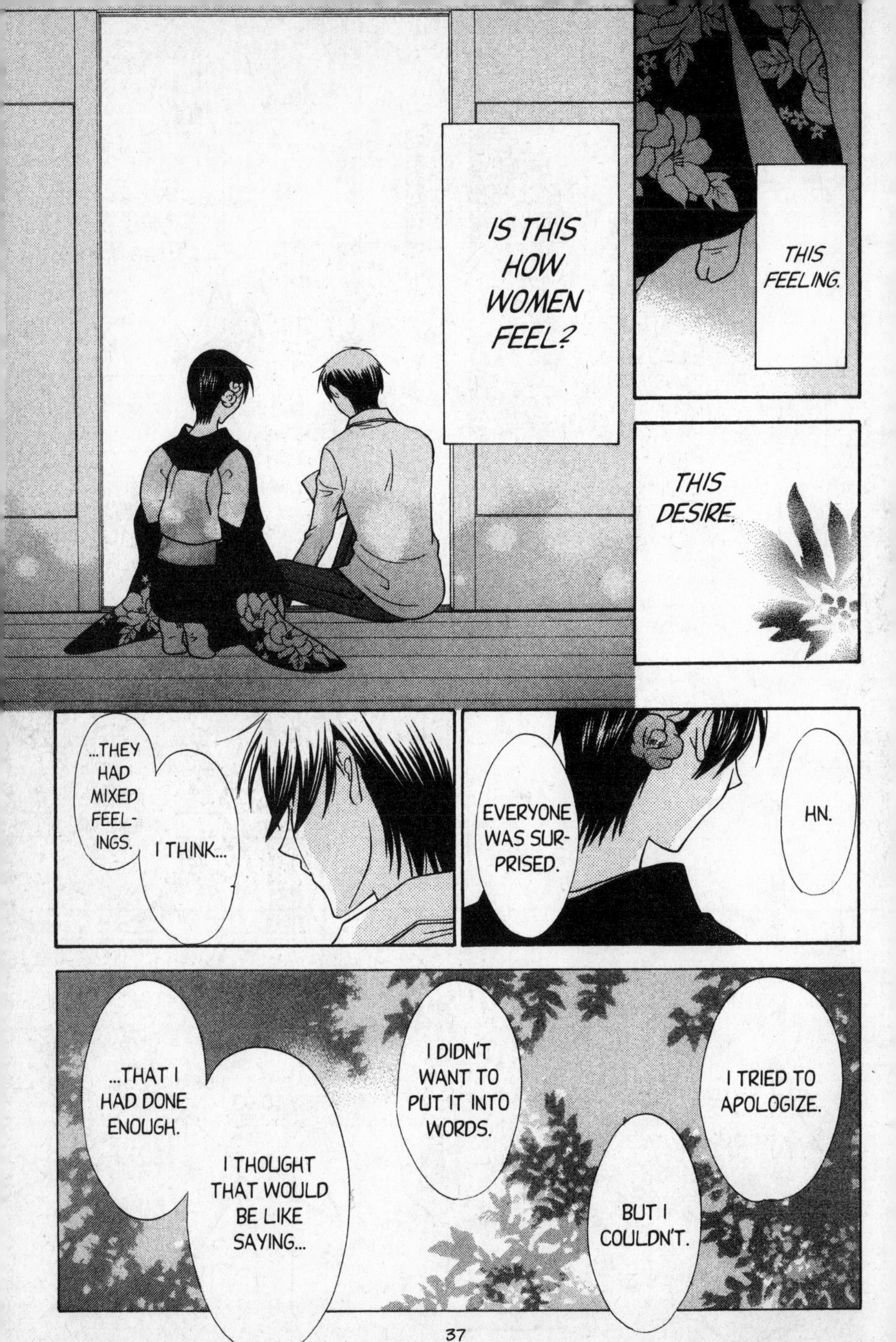
THIS FEELING.
THIS DESIRE.
IS THIS HOW WOMEN FEEL?
HN.
EVERYONE WAS SURPRISED.
I THINK...
...THEY HAD MIXED FEELINGS.
I TRIED TO APOLOGIZE.
BUT I COULDN'T.
I DIDN'T WANT TO PUT IT INTO WORDS.
I THOUGHT THAT WOULD BE LIKE SAYING...
...THAT I HAD DONE ENOUGH.

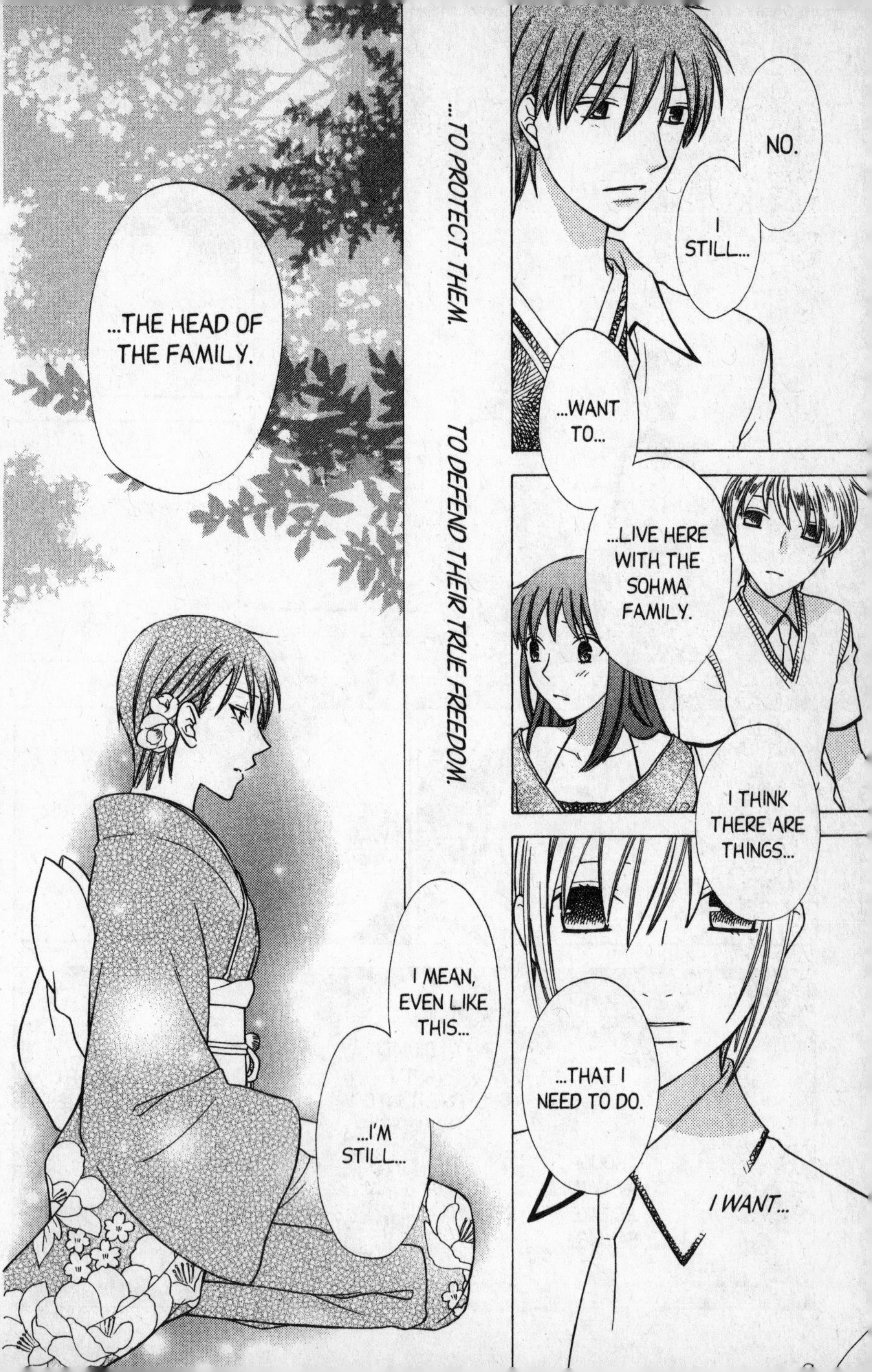
NO.
I STILL...
...WANT TO...
...LIVE HERE WITH THE SOHMA FAMILY.
I THINK THERE ARE THINGS...
...THAT I NEED TO DO.
I WANT...
...TO PROTECT THEM.
TO DEFEND THEIR TRUE FREEDOM.
I MEAN, EVEN LIKE THIS...
...I'M STILL...
...THE HEAD OF THE FAMILY.

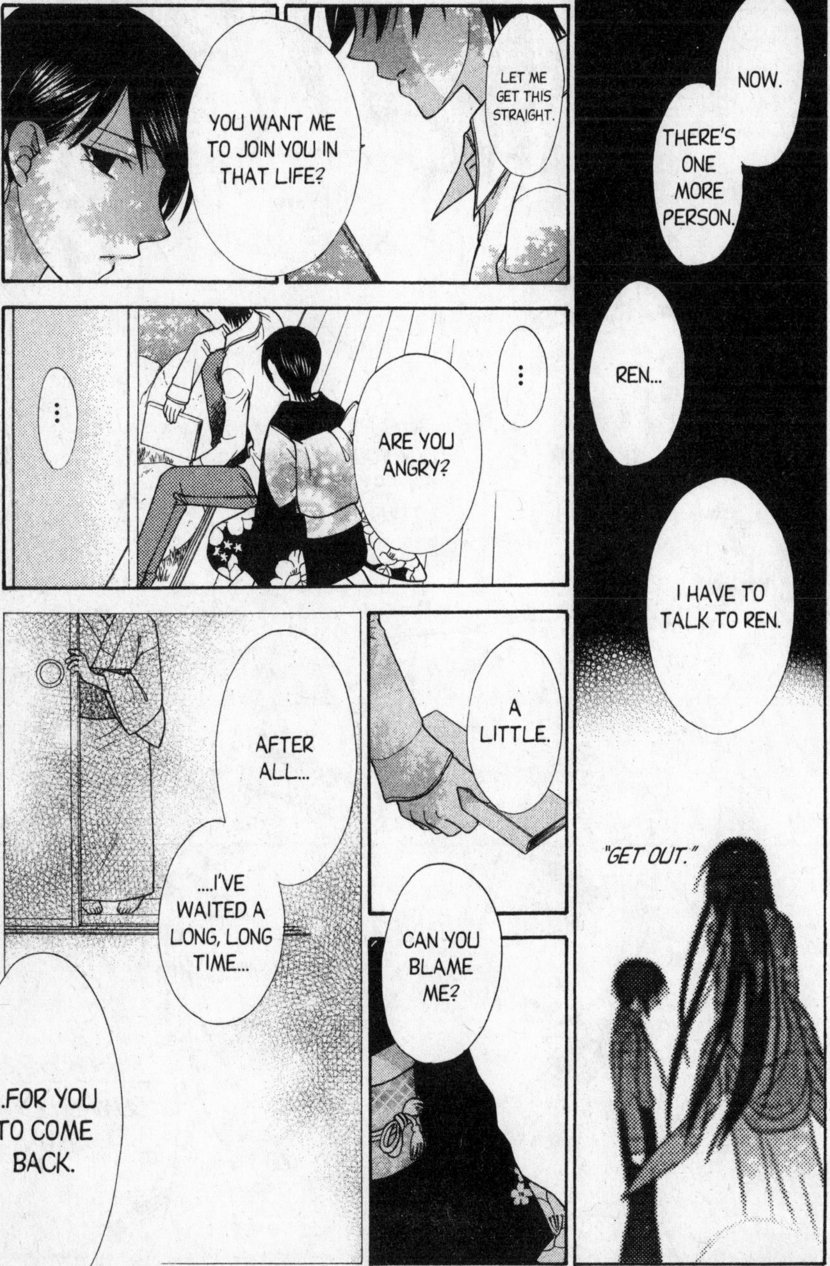
NOW.
THERE'S ONE MORE PERSON.
REN...
I HAVE TO TALK TO REN.
"GET OUT."
LET ME GET THIS STRAIGHT.
YOU WANT ME TO JOIN YOU IN THAT LIFE?
...
ARE YOU ANGRY?
...
A LITTLE.
CAN YOU BLAME ME?
AFTER ALL...
....I'VE WAITED A LONG, LONG TIME...
...FOR YOU TO COME BACK.

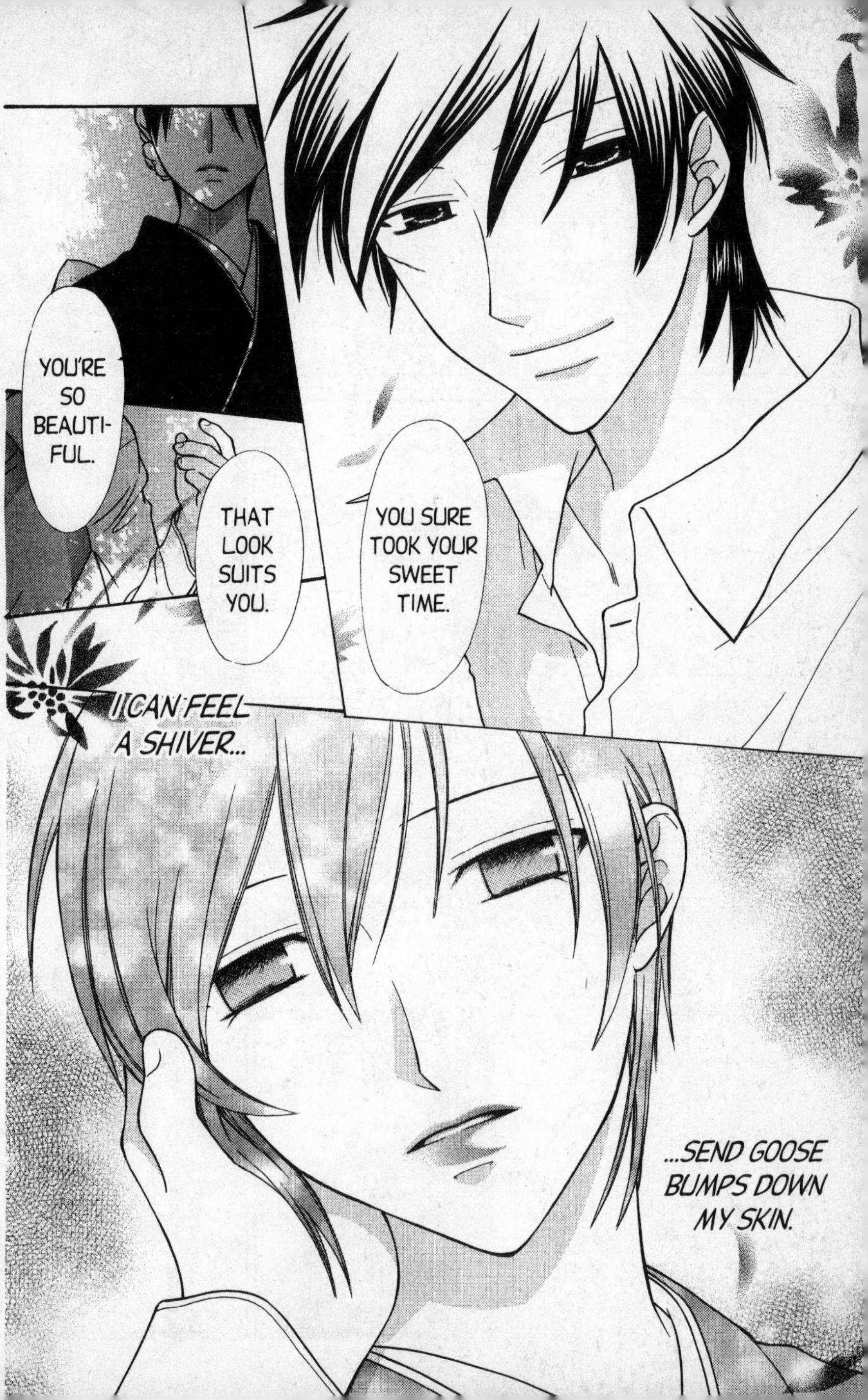
YOU SURE TOOK YOUR SWEET TIME.
YOU'RE SO BEAUTIFUL.
THAT LOOK SUITS YOU.
I CAN FEEL A SHIVER...
...SEND GOOSE BUMPS DOWN MY SKIN.

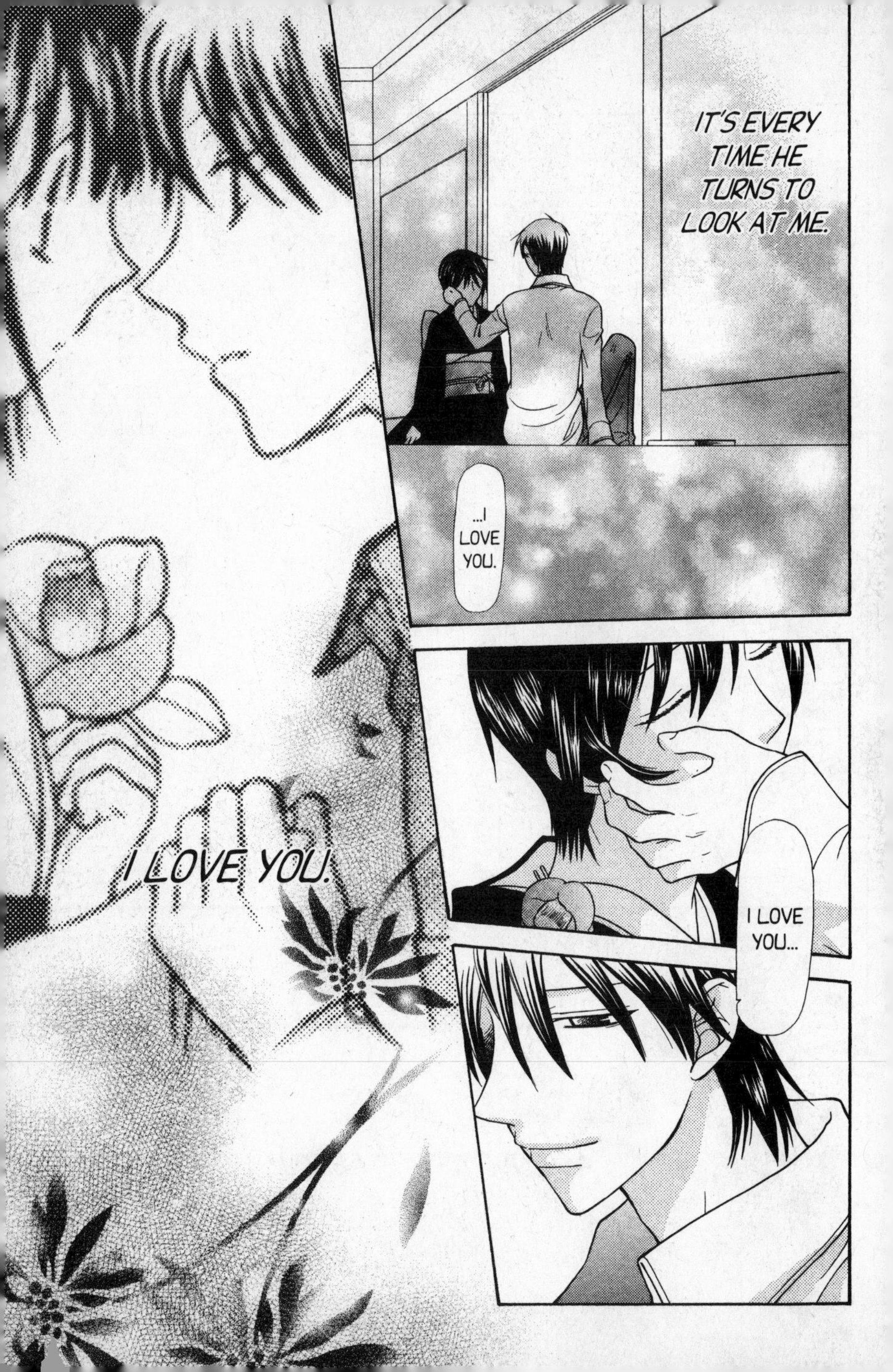
IT'S EVERY TIME HE TURNS TO LOOK AT ME.
...I LOVE YOU.
I LOVE YOU...
I LOVE YOU.

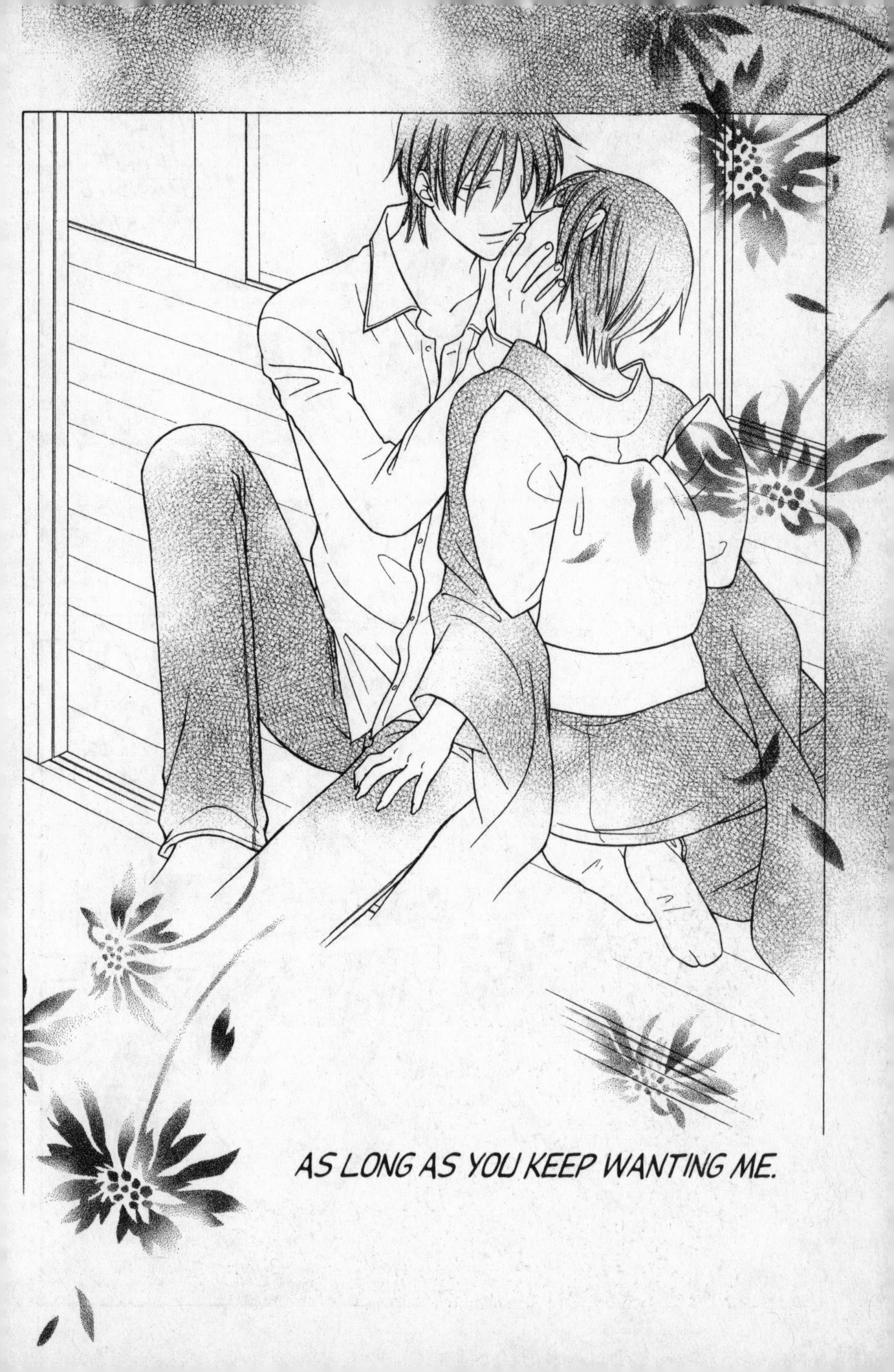
AS LONG AS YOU KEEP WANTING ME.

Chapter 133

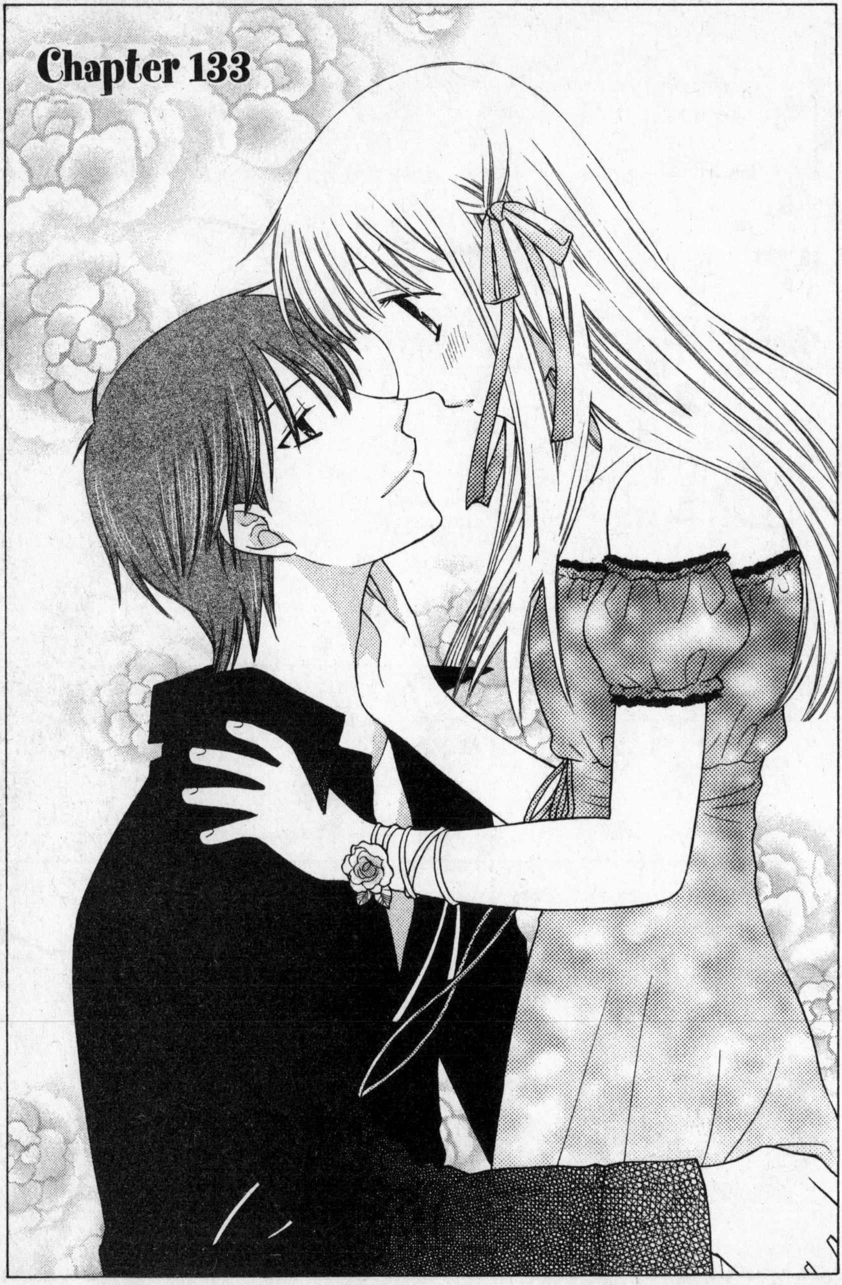

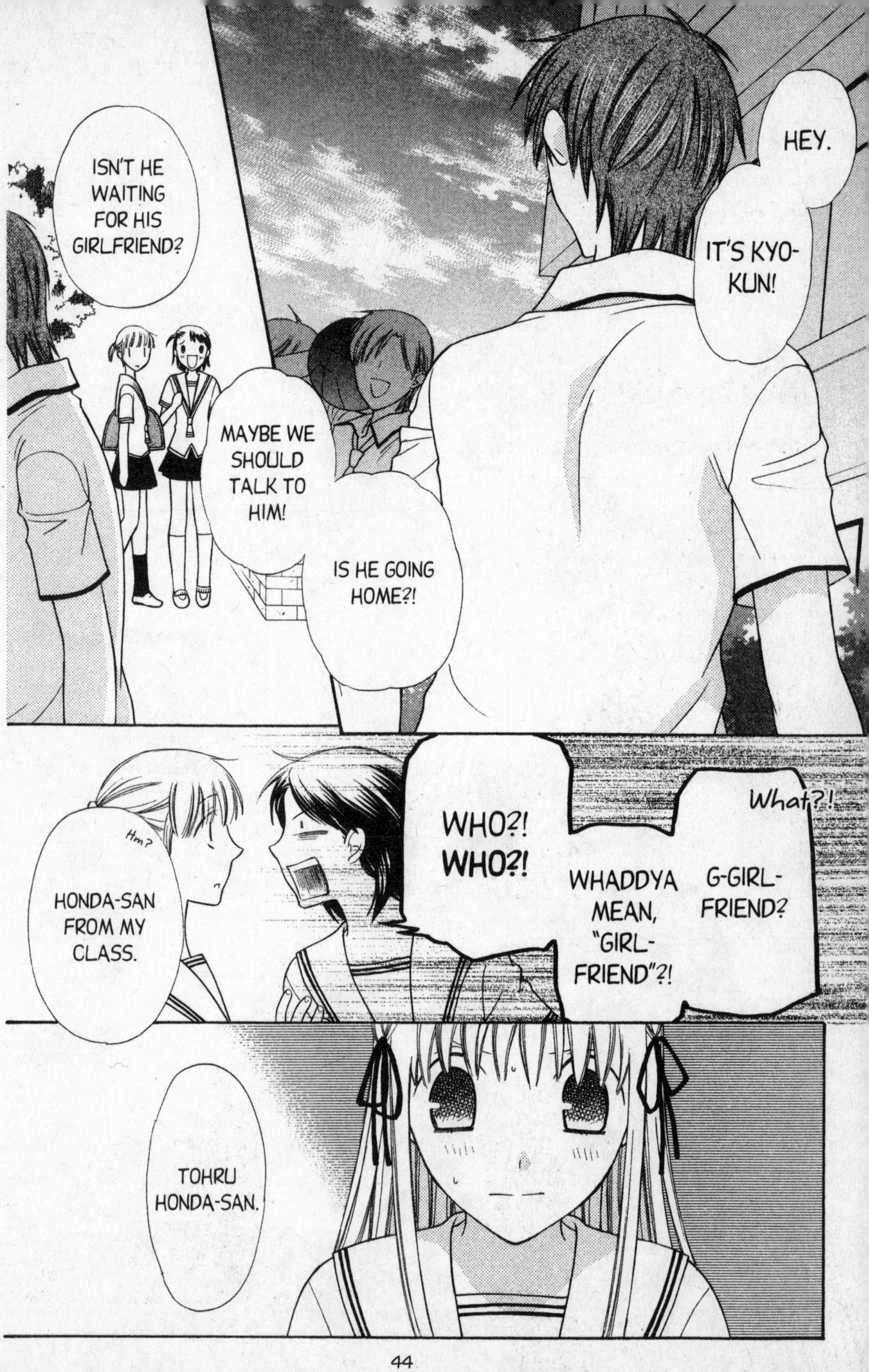
HEY.
IT'S KYO-KUN!
IS HE GOING HOME?!
MAYBE WE SHOULD TALK TO HIM!
ISN'T HE WAITING FOR HIS GIRLFRIEND?
What?!
G-GIRL-FRIEND?
WHADDYA MEAN, "GIRL-FRIEND"?!
WHO?! WHO?!
Hm?
HONDA-SAN FROM MY CLASS.
TOHRU HONDA-SAN.

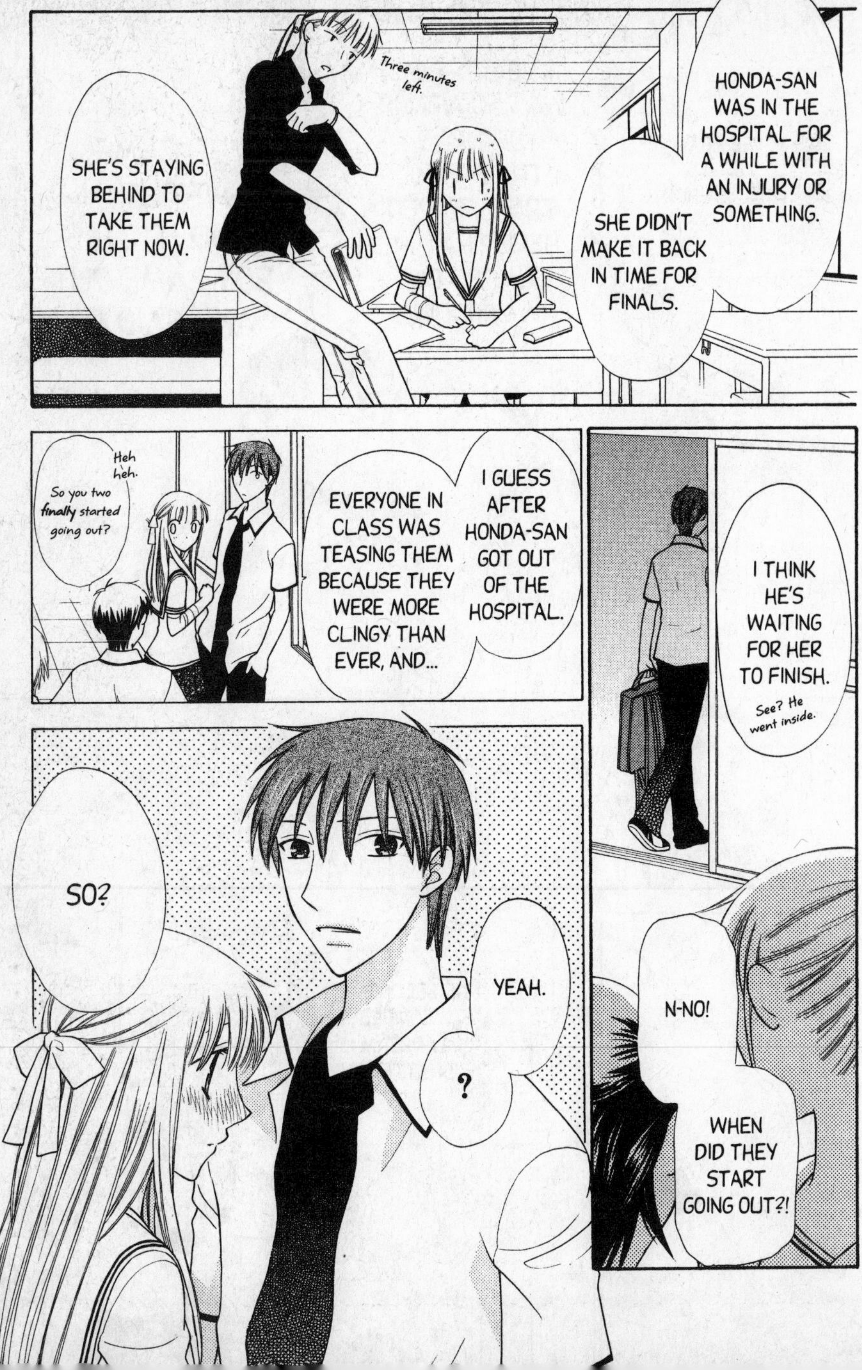

HONDA-SAN WAS IN THE HOSPITAL FOR A WHILE WITH AN INJURY OR SOMETHING.
SHE DIDN'T MAKE IT BACK IN TIME FOR FINALS.
Three minutes left.
SHE'S STAYING BEHIND TO TAKE THEM RIGHT NOW.
I THINK HE'S WAITING FOR HER TO FINISH.
See? He went inside.
I GUESS AFTER HONDA-SAN GOT OUT OF THE HOSPITAL.
EVERYONE IN CLASS WAS TEASING THEM BECAUSE THEY WERE MORE CLINGY THAN EVER, AND...
Heh heh.
So you two finally started going out?
N-NO!
WHEN DID THEY START GOING OUT?!
YEAH.
?
SO?

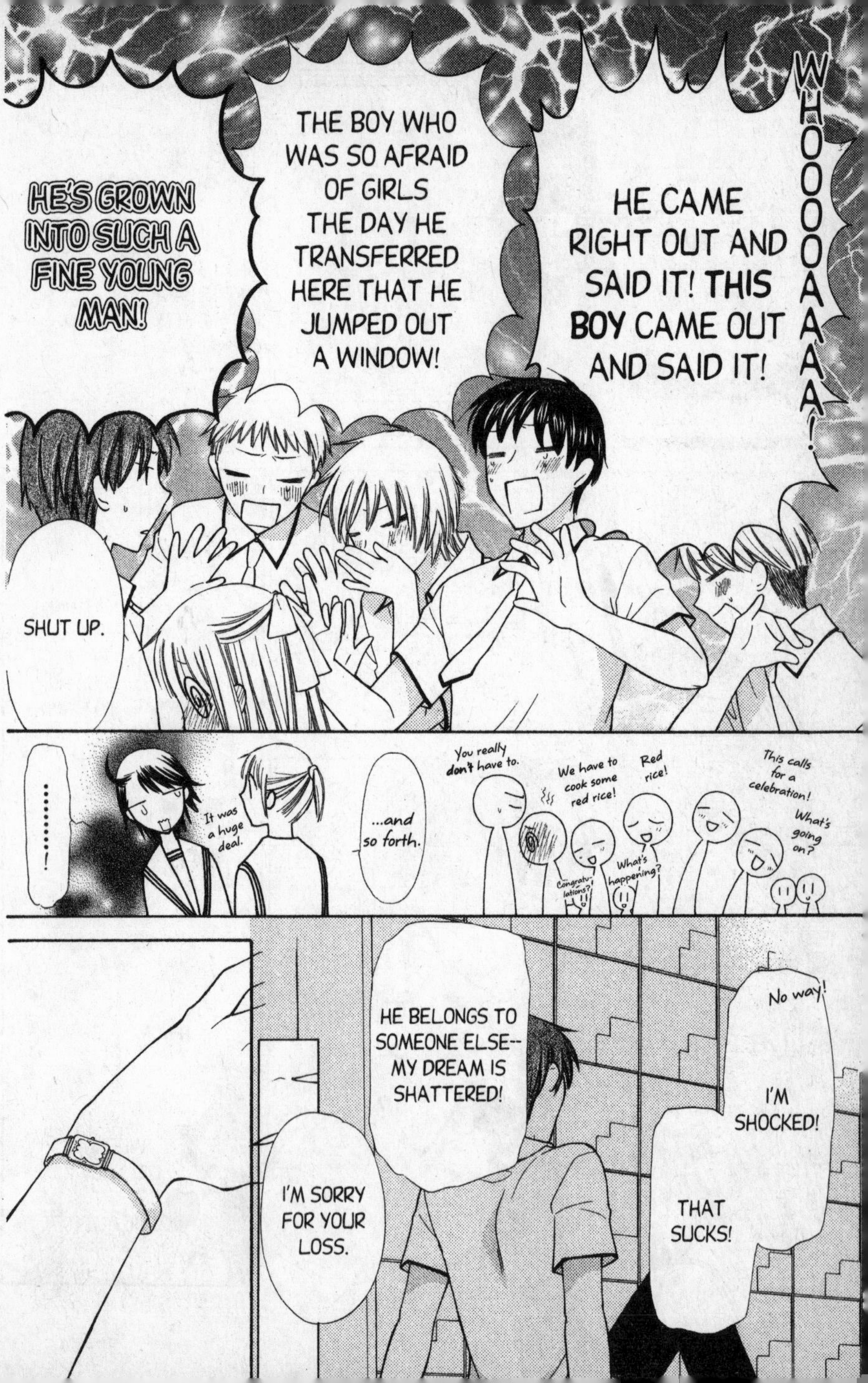
WHOOOOOAAAA!
HE CAME RIGHT OUT AND SAID IT! THIS BOY CAME OUT AND SAID IT!
THE BOY WHO WAS SO AFRAID OF GIRLS THE DAY HE TRANSFERRED HERE THAT HE JUMPED OUT A WINDOW!
HE'S GROWN INTO SUCH A FINE YOUNG MAN!
SHUT UP.
What's going on?
This calls for a celebration!
Red rice!
What's happening?
We have to cook some red rice!
Congratulations?
You really don't have to.
...and so forth.
It was a huge deal.
......!
No way!
I'M SHOCKED!
THAT SUCKS!
HE BELONGS TO SOMEONE ELSE-- MY DREAM IS SHATTERED!
I'M SORRY FOR YOUR LOSS.

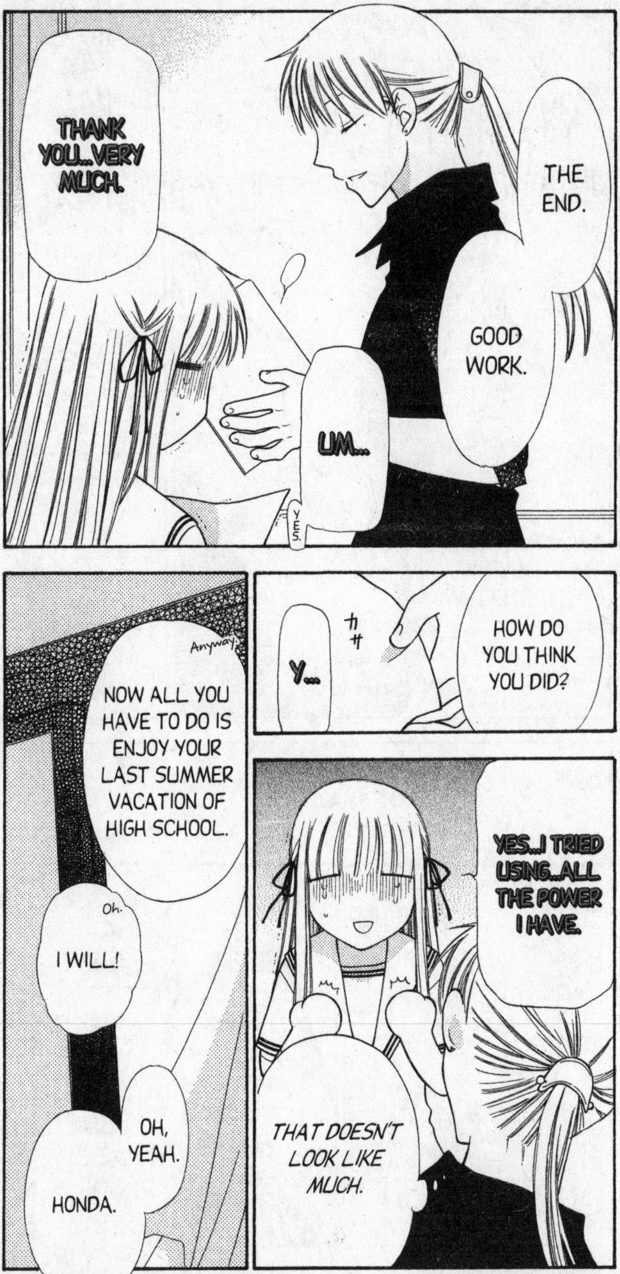
THE END.
GOOD WORK.
THANK YOU...VERY MUCH.
UM...
YES.
HOW DO YOU THINK YOU DID?
カサ
Y...
YES...I TRIED USING...ALL THE POWER I HAVE.
THAT DOESN'T LOOK LIKE MUCH.
Anyway,
NOW ALL YOU HAVE TO DO IS ENJOY YOUR LAST SUMMER VACATION OF HIGH SCHOOL.
Oh.
I WILL!
OH, YEAH.
HONDA.

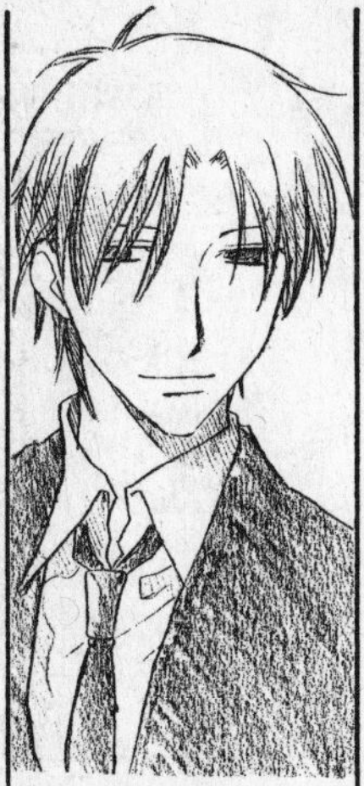

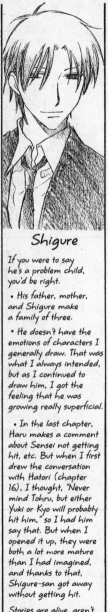

Shigure

If you were to say he's a problem child, you'd be right.

- *His father, mother, and Shigure make a family of three.*
- *He doesn't have the emotions of characters I generally draw. That was what I always intended, but as I continued to draw him, I got the feeling that he was growing really superficial.*
- *In the last chapter, Haru makes a comment about Sensei not getting hit, etc. But when I first drew the conversation with Hatori (chapter 16), I thought, "Never mind Tohru, but either Yuki or Kyo will probably hit him," so I had him say that. But when I opened it up, they were both a lot more mature than I had imagined, and thanks to that, Shigure-san got away without getting hit.*

Stories are alive, aren't they? (laugh)

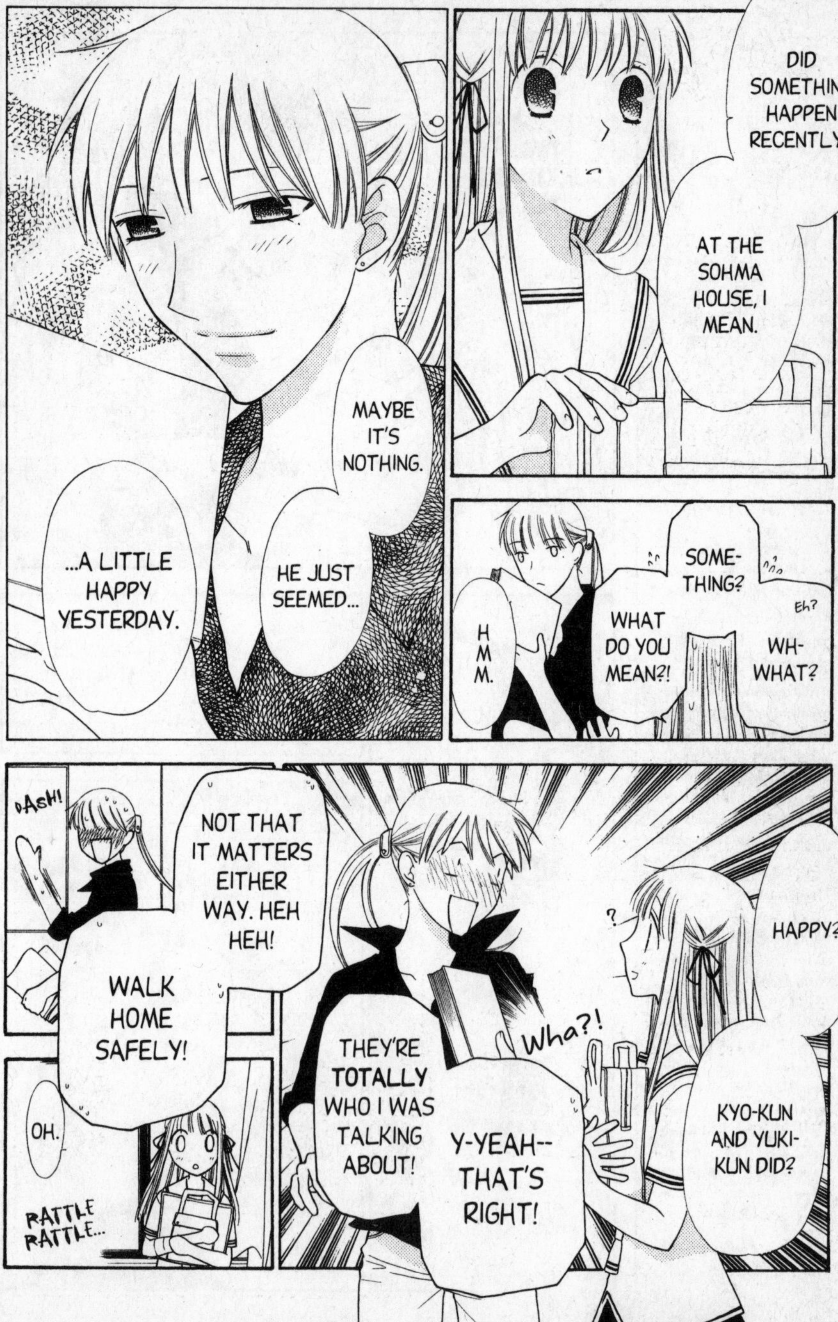
DID SOMETHING HAPPEN RECENTLY?
AT THE SOHMA HOUSE, I MEAN.
SOME-THING?
Eh?
WH-WHAT?
WHAT DO YOU MEAN?!
HMM.
MAYBE IT'S NOTHING.
HE JUST SEEMED...
...A LITTLE HAPPY YESTERDAY.
HAPPY?
KYO-KUN AND YUKI-KUN DID?
Wha?!
Y-YEAH--THAT'S RIGHT!
THEY'RE TOTALLY WHO I WAS TALKING ABOUT!
NOT THAT IT MATTERS EITHER WAY. HEH HEH!
DASH!
WALK HOME SAFELY!
OH.
RATTLE RATTLE...

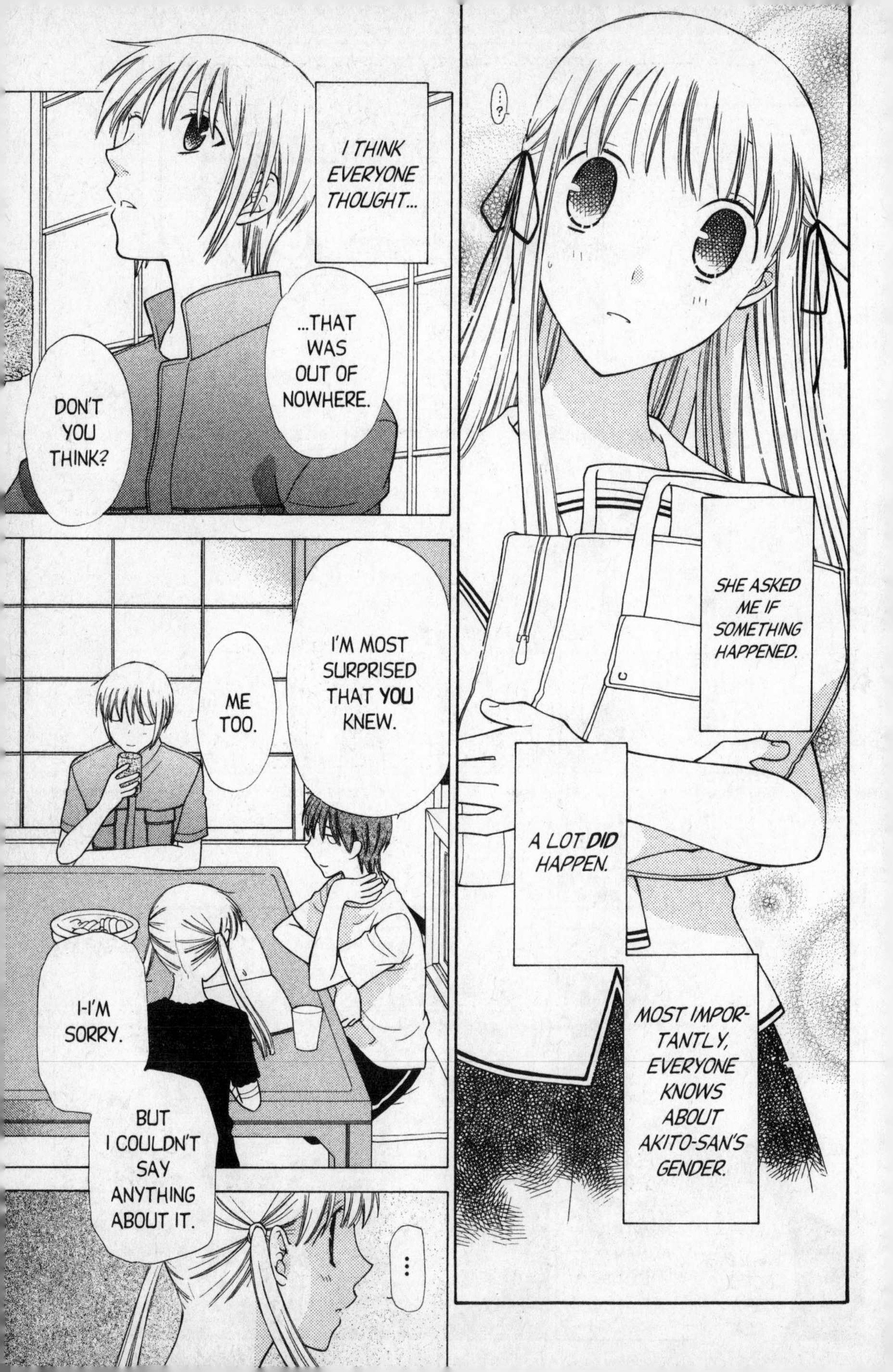
...?
SHE ASKED ME IF SOMETHING HAPPENED.
A LOT DID HAPPEN.
MOST IMPORTANTLY, EVERYONE KNOWS ABOUT AKITO-SAN'S GENDER.
I THINK EVERYONE THOUGHT...
...THAT WAS OUT OF NOWHERE.
DON'T YOU THINK?
I'M MOST SURPRISED THAT YOU KNEW.
ME TOO.
I-I'M SORRY.
BUT I COULDN'T SAY ANYTHING ABOUT IT.
...

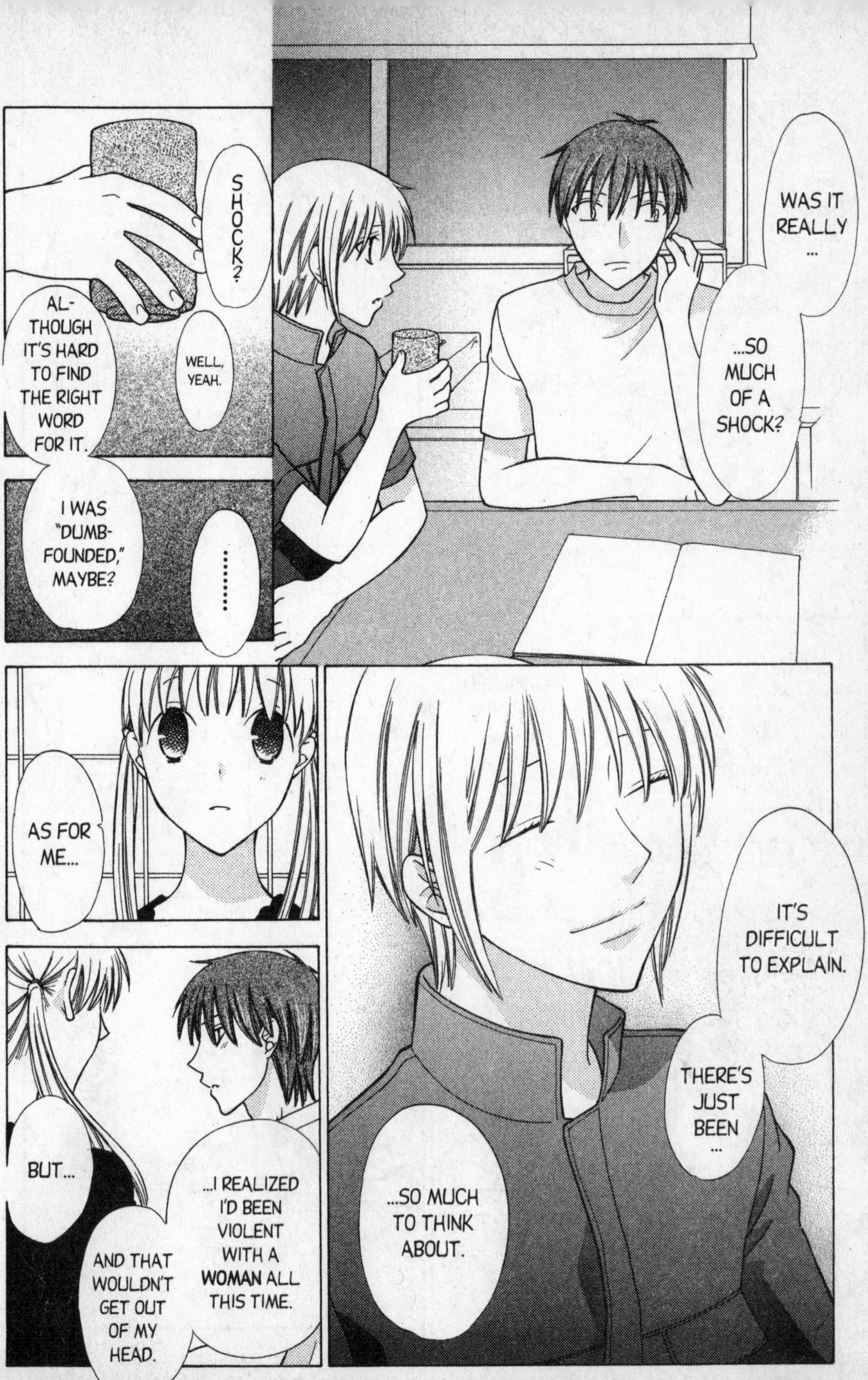
WAS IT REALLY ...
...SO MUCH OF A SHOCK?
SHOCK?
WELL, YEAH.
ALTHOUGH IT'S HARD TO FIND THE RIGHT WORD FOR IT.
......
I WAS "DUMBFOUNDED," MAYBE?
IT'S DIFFICULT TO EXPLAIN.
THERE'S JUST BEEN ...
...SO MUCH TO THINK ABOUT.
AS FOR ME...
BUT...
...I REALIZED I'D BEEN VIOLENT WITH A **WOMAN** ALL THIS TIME.
AND THAT WOULDN'T GET OUT OF MY HEAD.

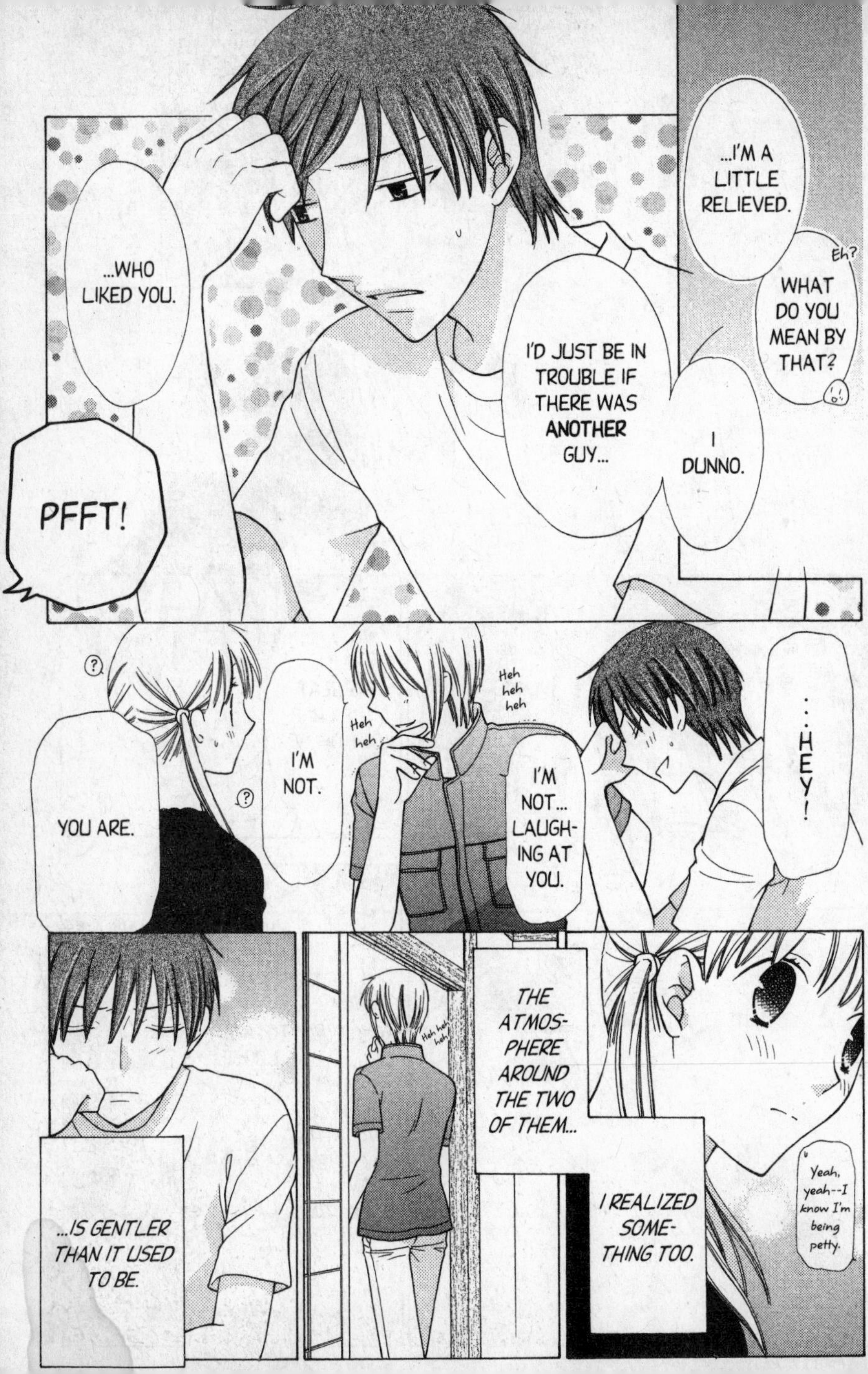
...I'M A LITTLE RELIEVED.
Eh?
WHAT DO YOU MEAN BY THAT?
I DUNNO.
I'D JUST BE IN TROUBLE IF THERE WAS **ANOTHER** GUY...
...WHO LIKED YOU.
PFFT!
...HEY!
Heh heh heh
I'M NOT... LAUGHING AT YOU.
Heh heh
I'M NOT.
YOU ARE.
Yeah, yeah--I know I'm being petty.
I REALIZED SOMETHING TOO.
THE ATMOSPHERE AROUND THE TWO OF THEM...
Heh heh heh
...IS GENTLER THAN IT USED TO BE.

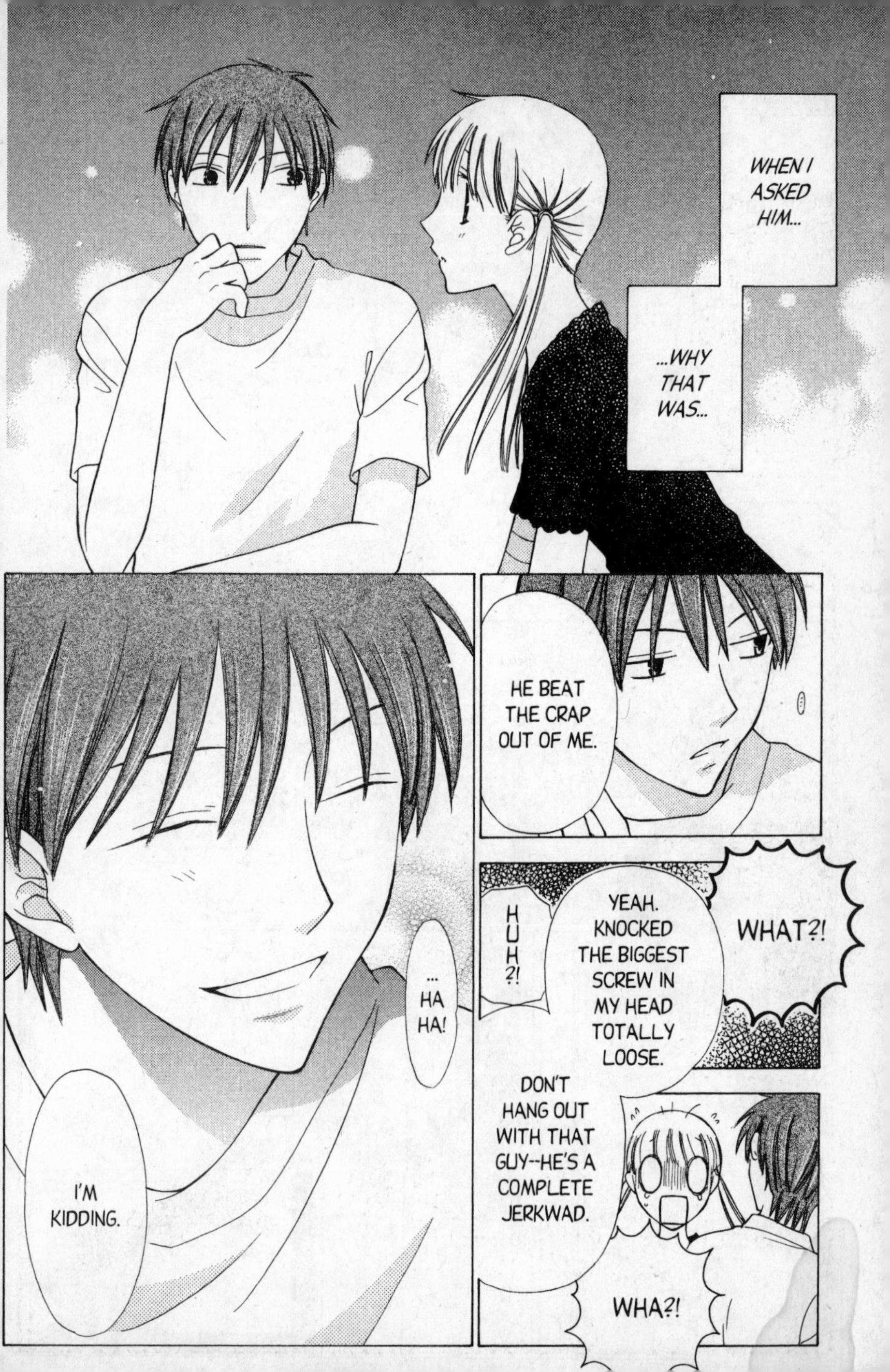
WHEN I ASKED HIM...
...WHY THAT WAS...
HE BEAT THE CRAP OUT OF ME.
WHAT?!
YEAH. KNOCKED THE BIGGEST SCREW IN MY HEAD TOTALLY LOOSE.
HUH?!
DON'T HANG OUT WITH THAT GUY--HE'S A COMPLETE JERKWAD.
WHA?!
...HA HA!
I'M KIDDING.

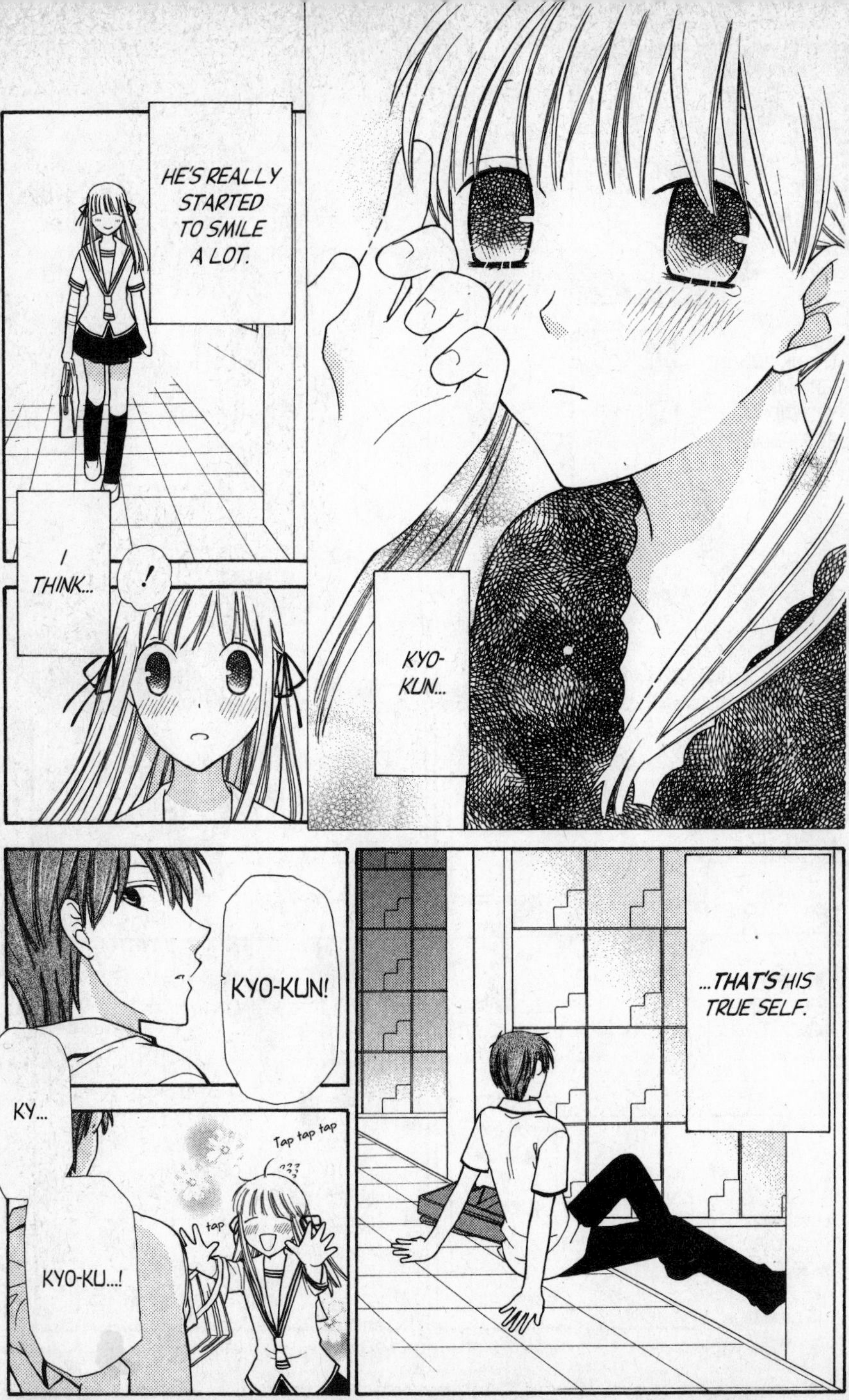
KYO-KUN...
HE'S REALLY STARTED TO SMILE A LOT.
I THINK...
!
...THAT'S HIS TRUE SELF.
KYO-KUN!
KY...
Tap tap tap
tap
KYO-KU...!

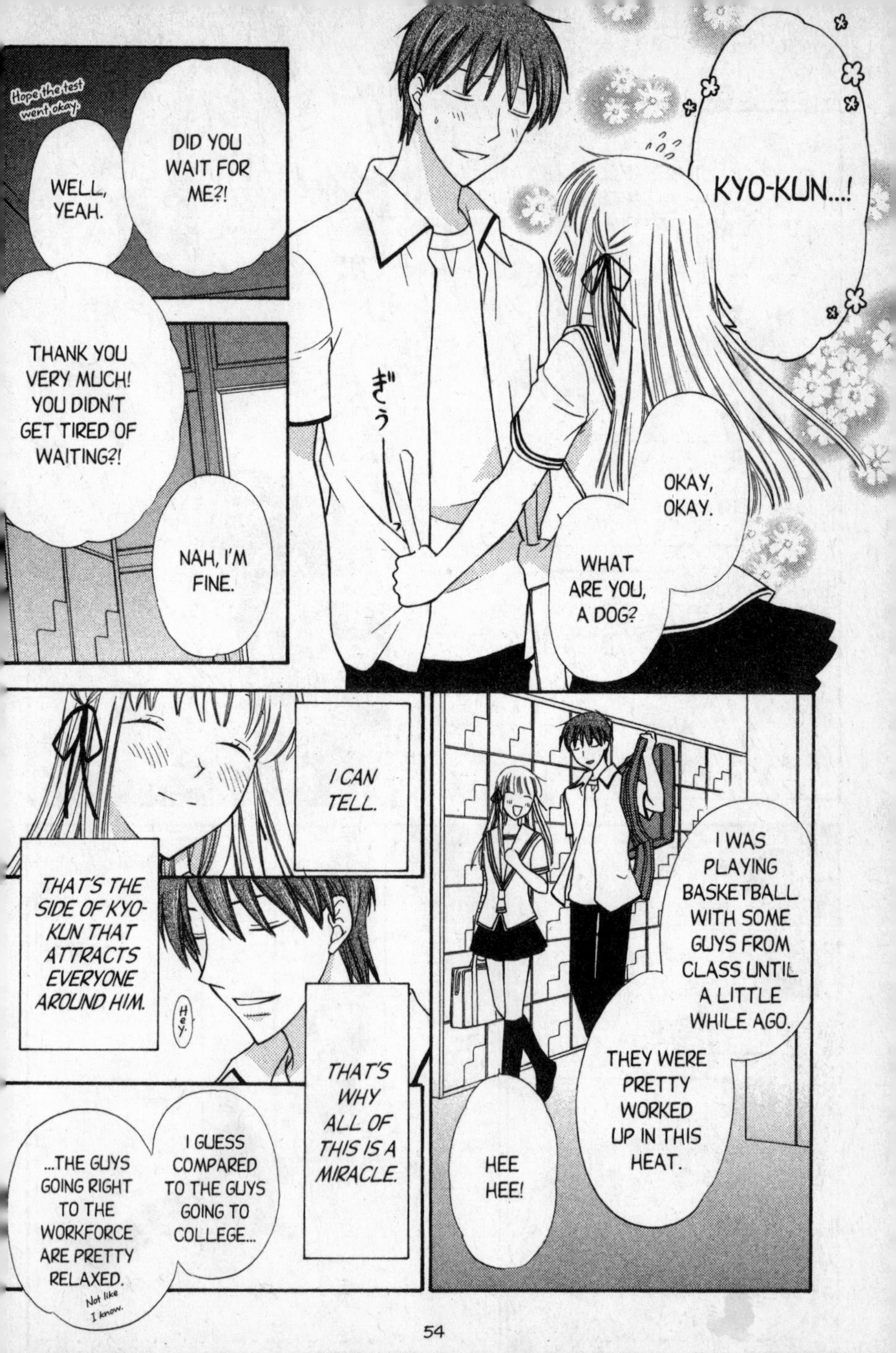
KYO-KUN...!
ぎう
OKAY, OKAY.
WHAT ARE YOU, A DOG?
DID YOU WAIT FOR ME?!
WELL, YEAH.
Hope the test went okay.
THANK YOU VERY MUCH! YOU DIDN'T GET TIRED OF WAITING?!
NAH, I'M FINE.
I WAS PLAYING BASKETBALL WITH SOME GUYS FROM CLASS UNTIL A LITTLE WHILE AGO.
THEY WERE PRETTY WORKED UP IN THIS HEAT.
HEE HEE!
I CAN TELL.
THAT'S THE SIDE OF KYO-KUN THAT ATTRACTS EVERYONE AROUND HIM.
Hey.
THAT'S WHY ALL OF THIS IS A MIRACLE.
I GUESS COMPARED TO THE GUYS GOING TO COLLEGE...
...THE GUYS GOING RIGHT TO THE WORKFORCE ARE PRETTY RELAXED.
Not like I know.

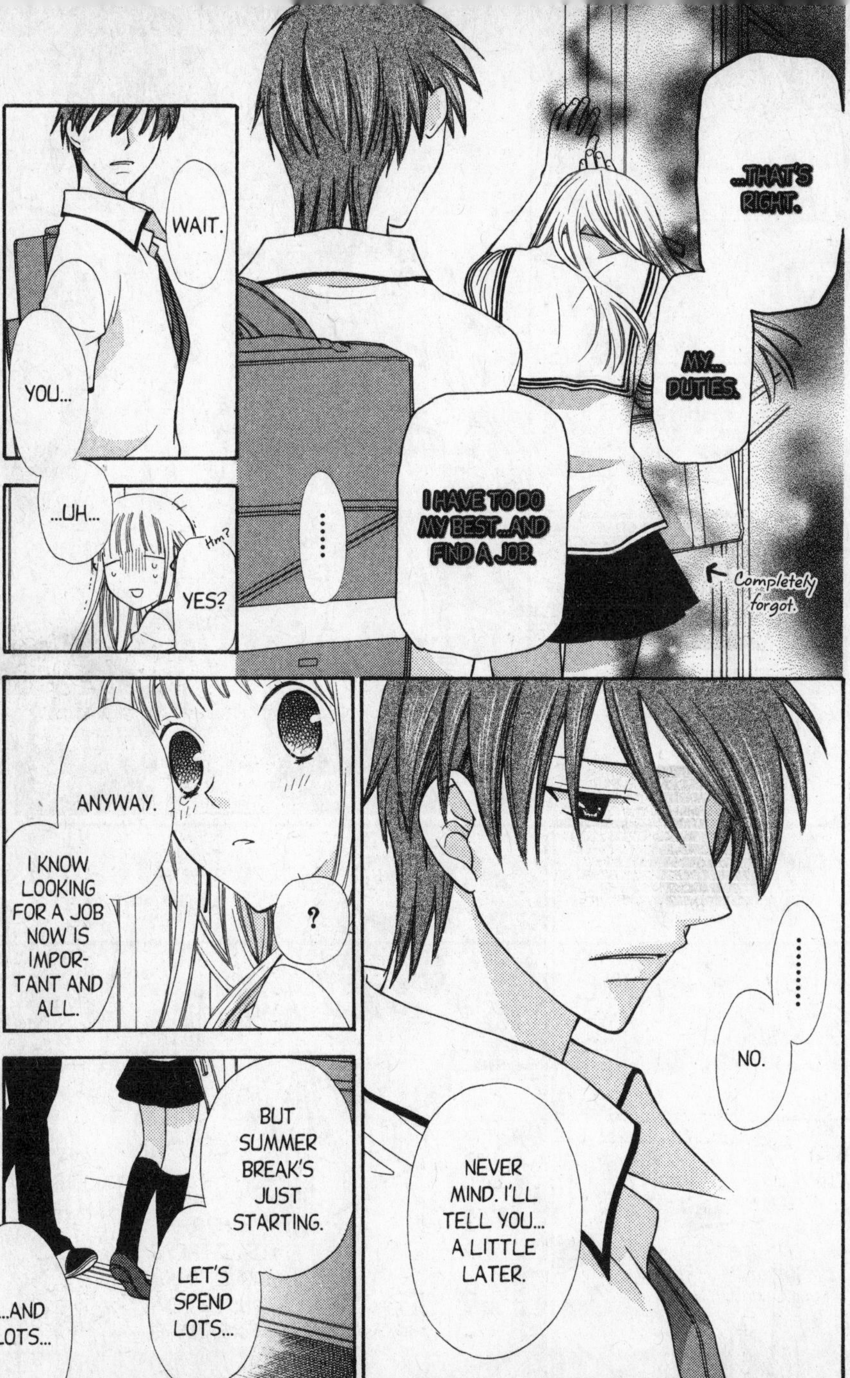
...THAT'S RIGHT.
MY... DUTIES.
I HAVE TO DO MY BEST...AND FIND A JOB.
Completely forgot.
......
WAIT.
YOU...
...UH...
Hm?
YES?
......
NO.
NEVER MIND. I'LL TELL YOU... A LITTLE LATER.
ANYWAY.
I KNOW LOOKING FOR A JOB NOW IS IMPOR-TANT AND ALL.
?
BUT SUMMER BREAK'S JUST STARTING.
LET'S SPEND LOTS...
...AND LOTS...

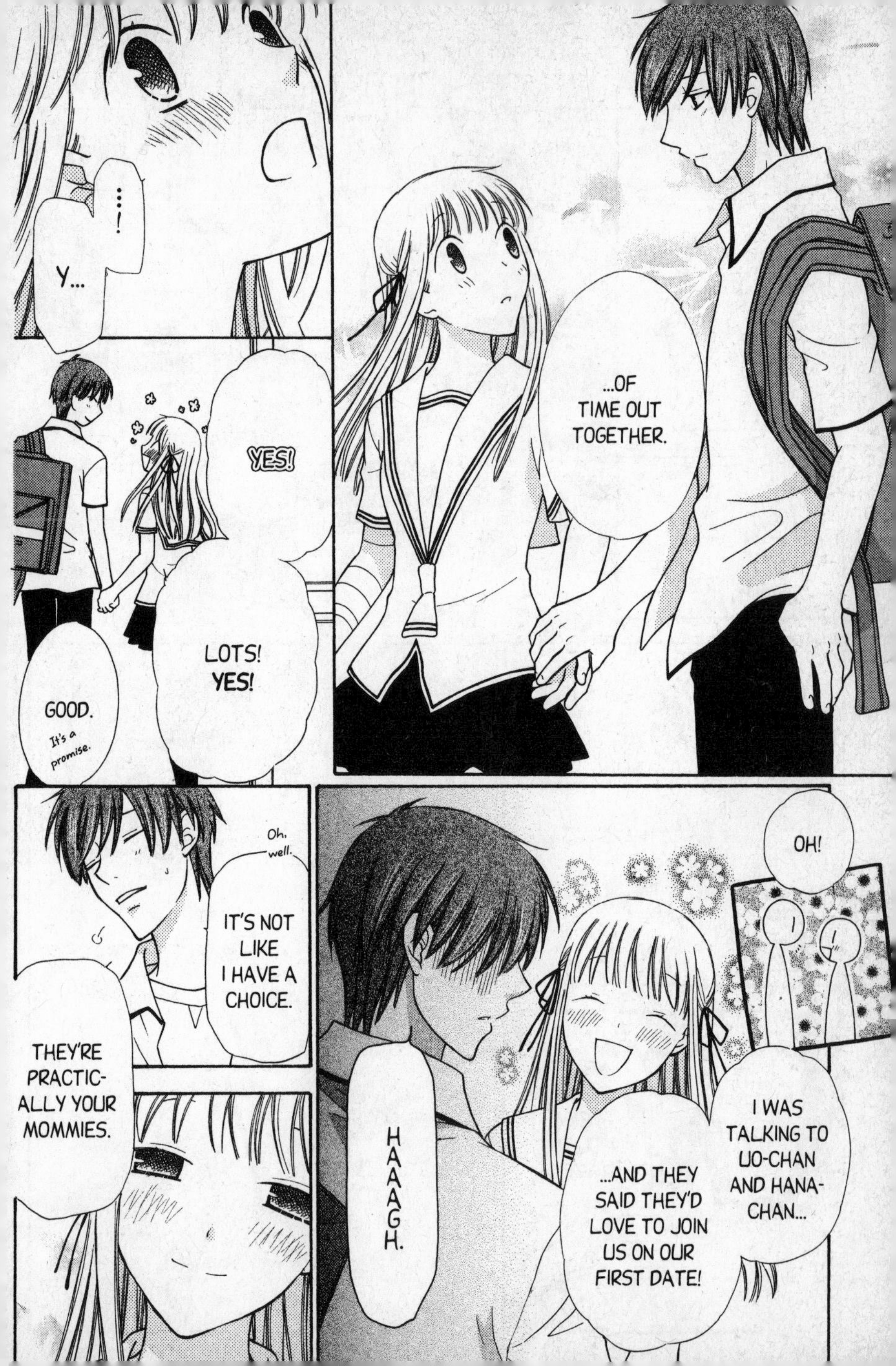
...OF TIME OUT TOGETHER.
...!
Y...
YES!
LOTS! YES!
GOOD.
It's a promise.
OH!
I WAS TALKING TO UO-CHAN AND HANA-CHAN...
...AND THEY SAID THEY'D LOVE TO JOIN US ON OUR FIRST DATE!
HAAAGH.
Oh, well.
IT'S NOT LIKE I HAVE A CHOICE.
THEY'RE PRACTIC-ALLY YOUR MOMMIES.

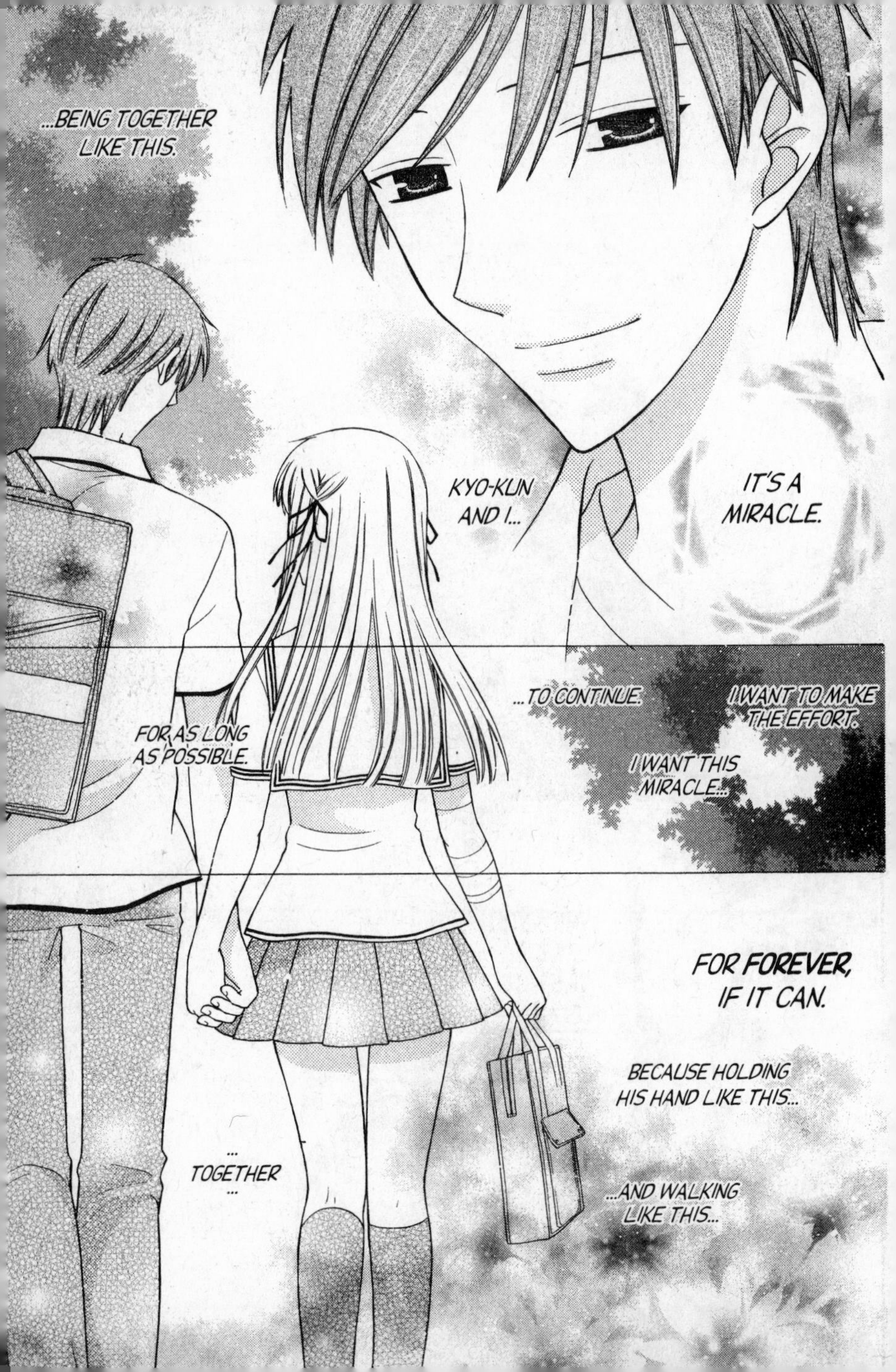
IT'S A MIRACLE.
KYO-KUN AND I...
...BEING TOGETHER LIKE THIS.
I WANT TO MAKE THE EFFORT.
...TO CONTINUE.
I WANT THIS MIRACLE...
FOR AS LONG AS POSSIBLE.
FOR **FOREVER**, IF IT CAN.
BECAUSE HOLDING HIS HAND LIKE THIS...
...AND WALKING LIKE THIS...
... TOGETHER ...

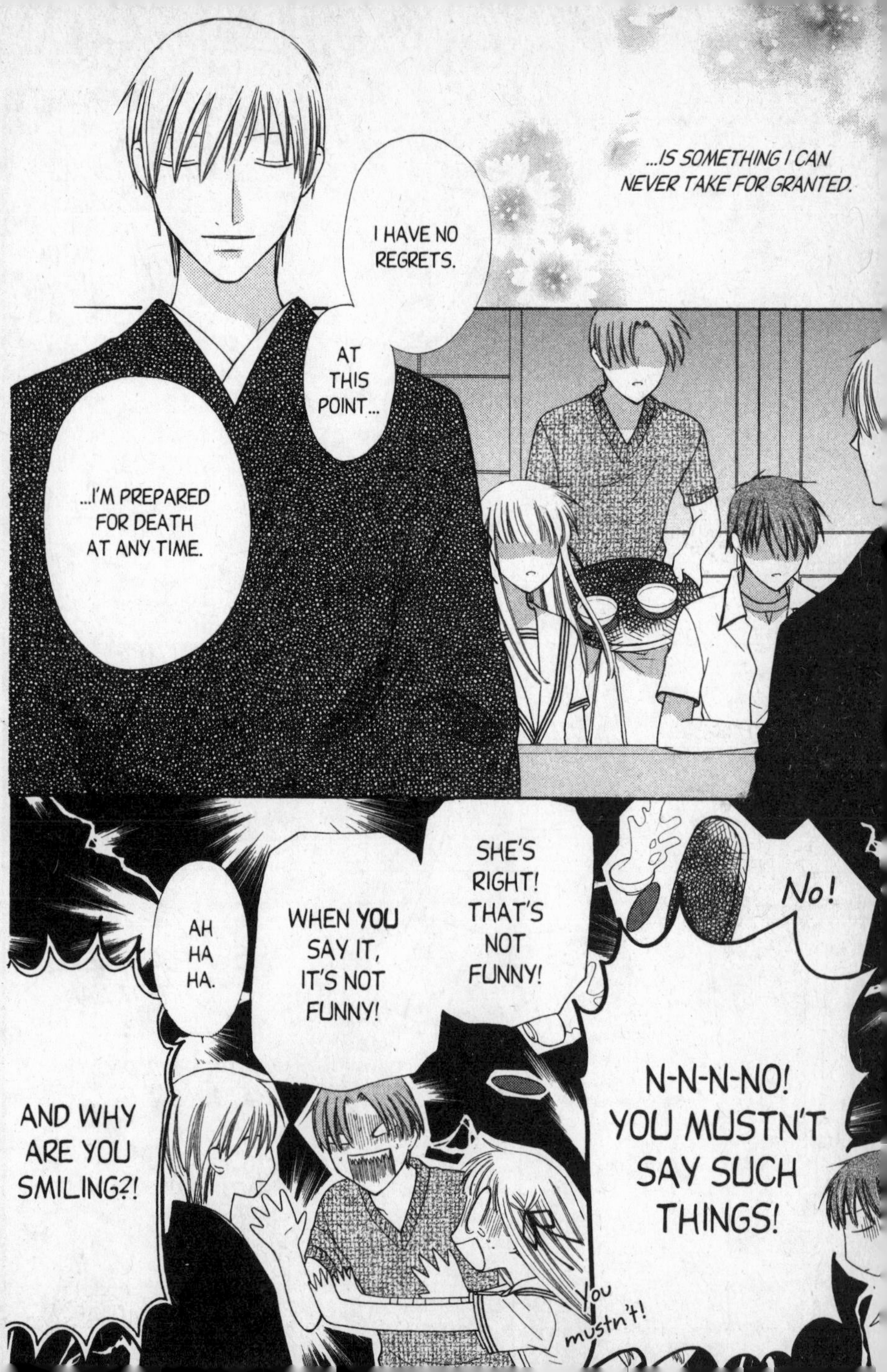
...IS SOMETHING I CAN NEVER TAKE FOR GRANTED.
I HAVE NO REGRETS.
AT THIS POINT...
...I'M PREPARED FOR DEATH AT ANY TIME.
No!
SHE'S RIGHT! THAT'S NOT FUNNY!
WHEN YOU SAY IT, IT'S NOT FUNNY!
AH HA HA.
N-N-N-NO! YOU MUSTN'T SAY SUCH THINGS!
You mustn't!
AND WHY ARE YOU SMILING?!

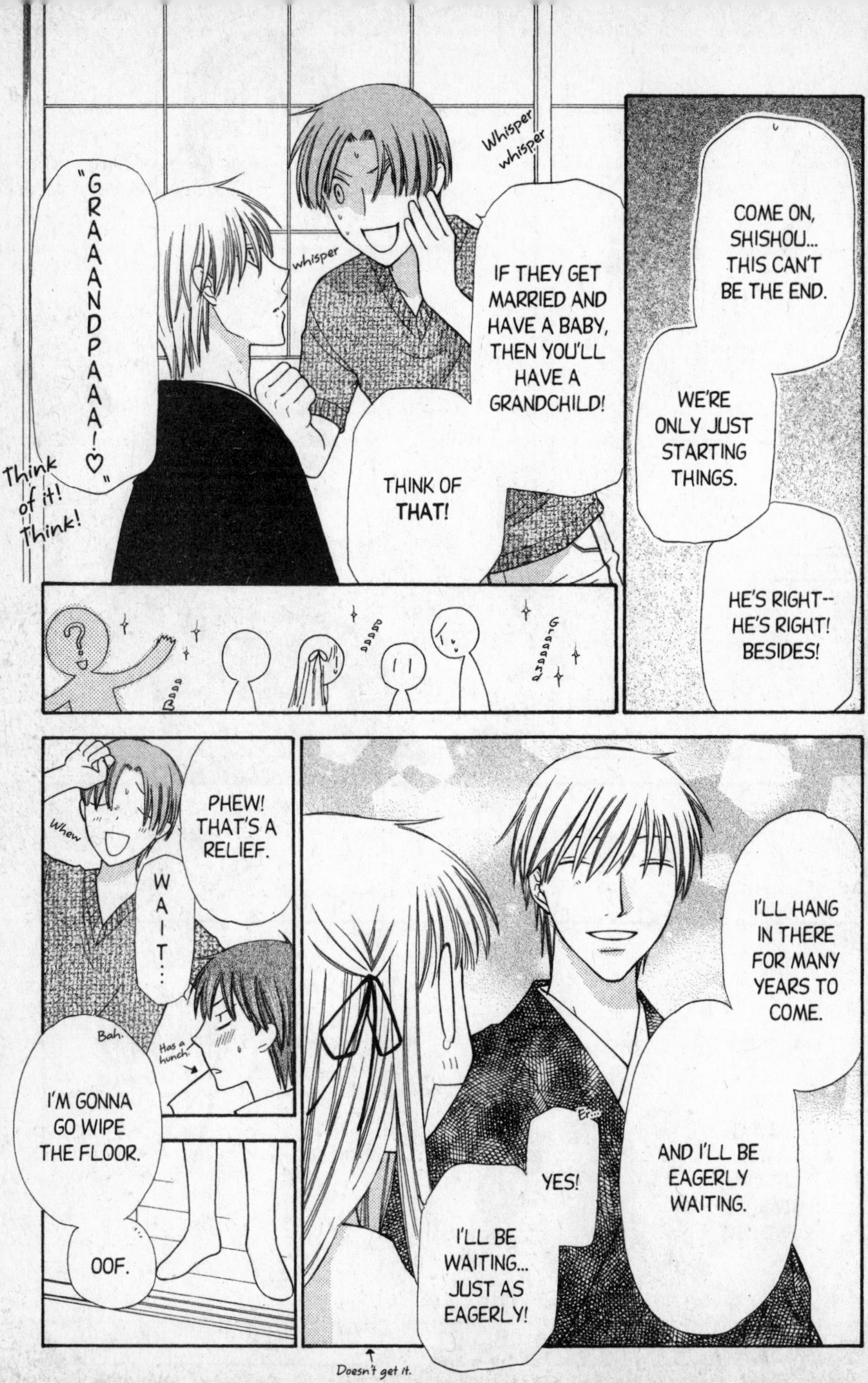
COME ON, SHISHOU... THIS CAN'T BE THE END.
WE'RE ONLY JUST STARTING THINGS.
HE'S RIGHT-- HE'S RIGHT! BESIDES!
Whisper whisper
IF THEY GET MARRIED AND HAVE A BABY, THEN YOU'LL HAVE A GRANDCHILD!
THINK OF THAT!
whisper
"GRAAAANDPAAAA!♡"
Think of it! Think!
I'LL HANG IN THERE FOR MANY YEARS TO COME.
AND I'LL BE EAGERLY WAITING.
Er...
YES!
I'LL BE WAITING... JUST AS EAGERLY!
Doesn't get it.
PHEW! THAT'S A RELIEF.
Whew
WAIT...
Bah.
Has a hunch.
I'M GONNA GO WIPE THE FLOOR.
OOF.

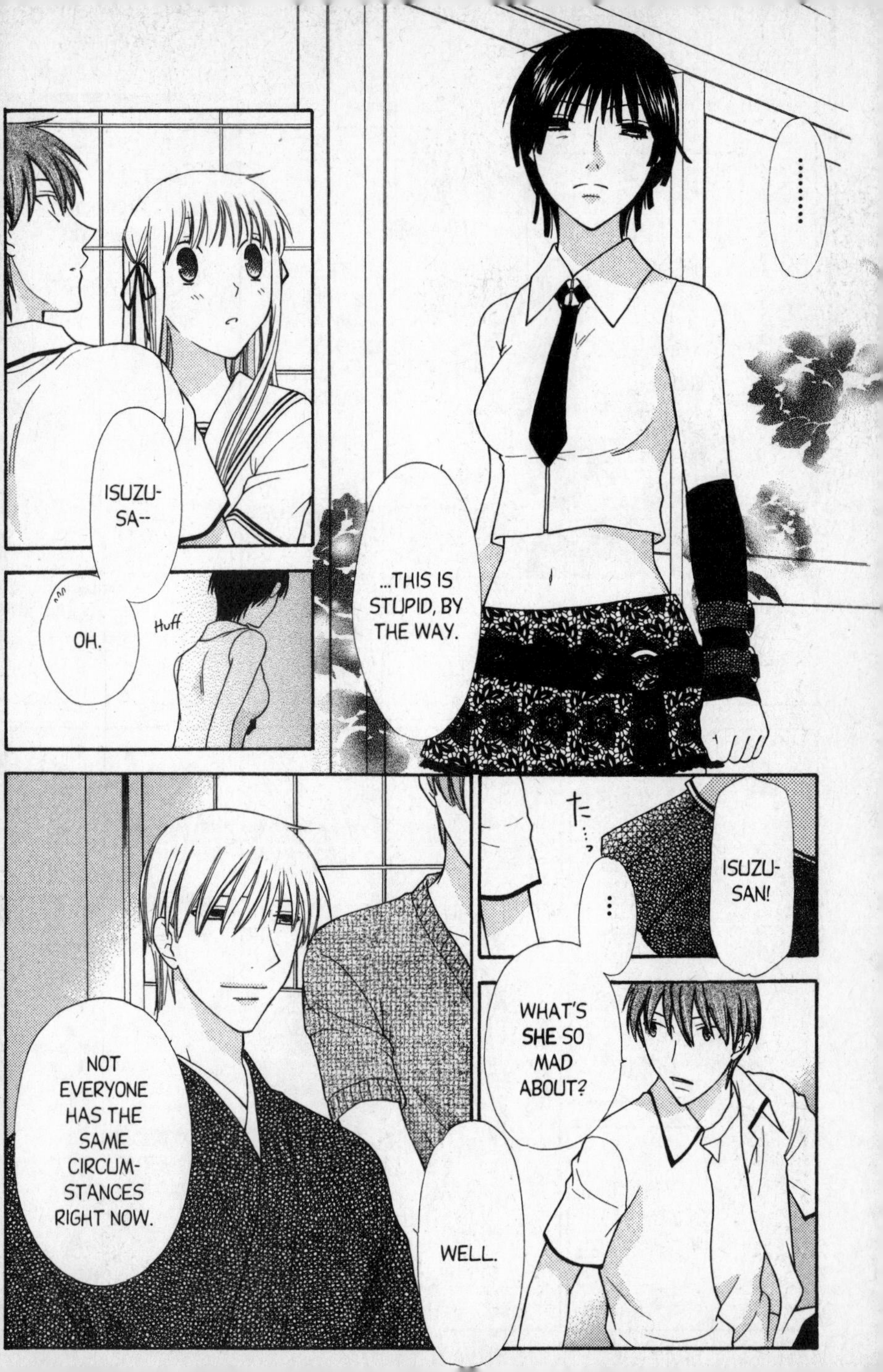
......
...THIS IS STUPID, BY THE WAY.
ISUZU-SA--
OH.
Huff
ISUZU-SAN!
...
WHAT'S SHE SO MAD ABOUT?
WELL.
NOT EVERYONE HAS THE SAME CIRCUM-STANCES RIGHT NOW.

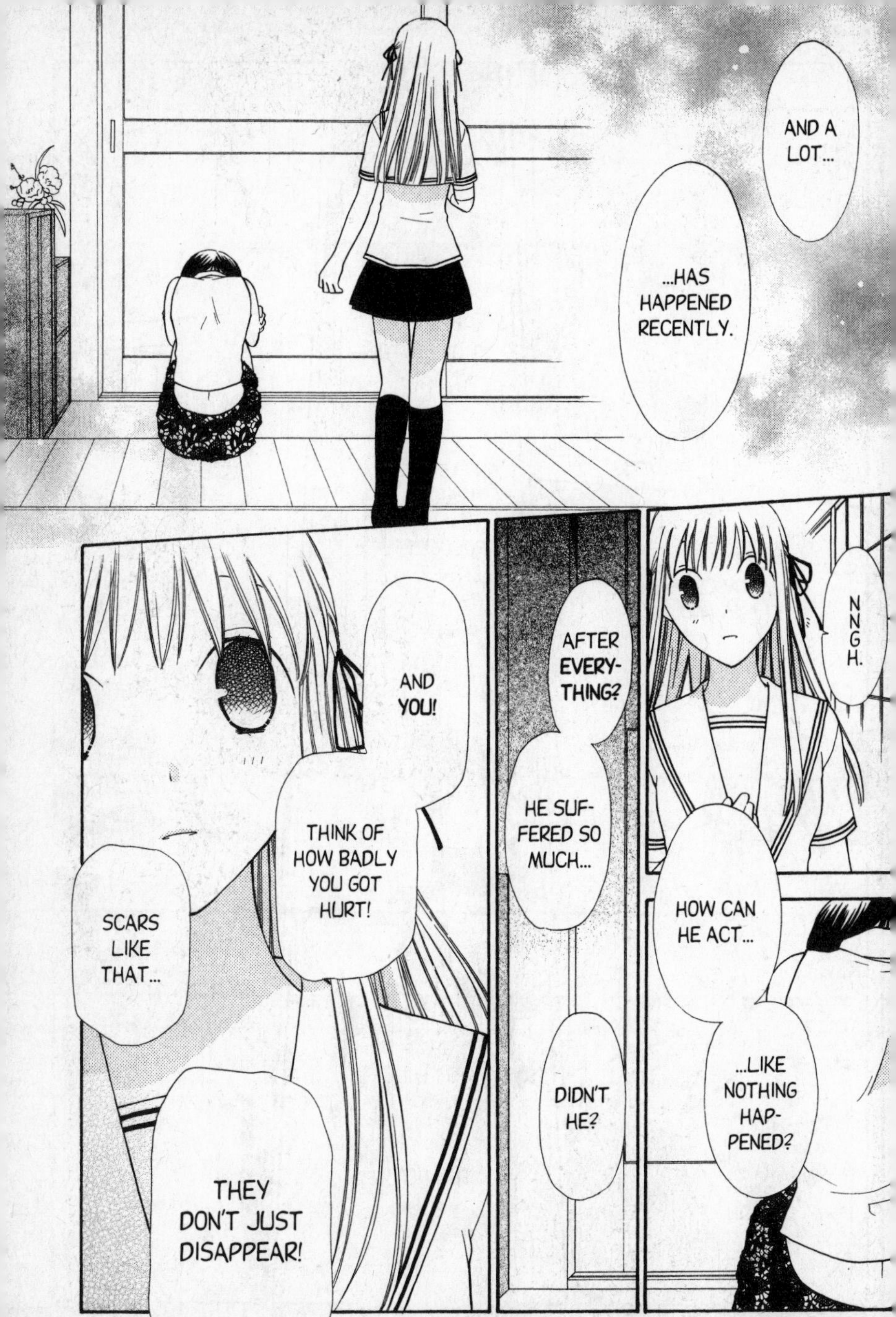
AND A LOT...
...HAS HAPPENED RECENTLY.
NNGH.
HOW CAN HE ACT...
...LIKE NOTHING HAPPENED?
AFTER EVERYTHING?
HE SUFFERED SO MUCH...
DIDN'T HE?
AND YOU!
THINK OF HOW BADLY YOU GOT HURT!
SCARS LIKE THAT...
THEY DON'T JUST DISAPPEAR!

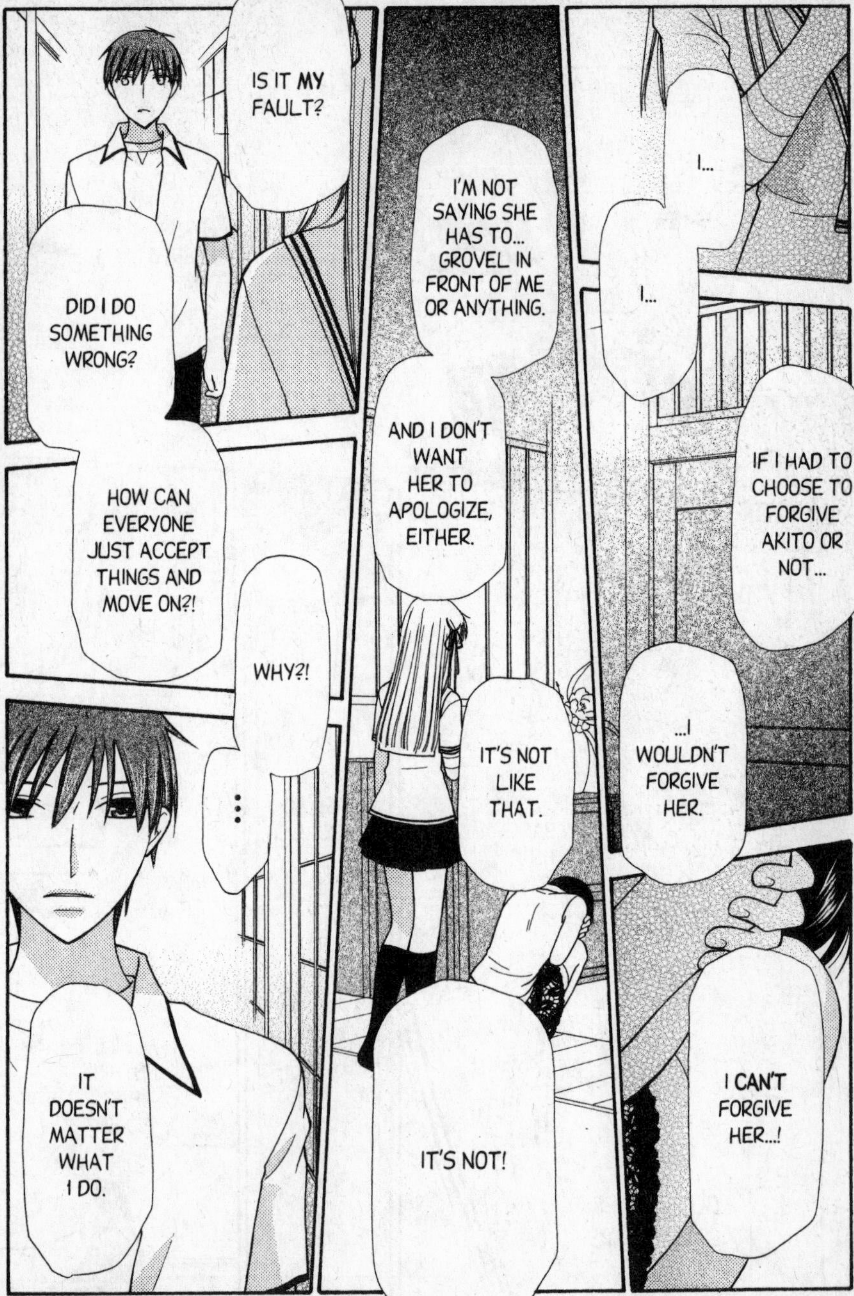
I...
I...
IF I HAD TO CHOOSE TO FORGIVE AKITO OR NOT...
...I WOULDN'T FORGIVE HER.
I CAN'T FORGIVE HER...!
I'M NOT SAYING SHE HAS TO... GROVEL IN FRONT OF ME OR ANYTHING.
AND I DON'T WANT HER TO APOLOGIZE, EITHER.
IT'S NOT LIKE THAT.
IT'S NOT!
IS IT MY FAULT?
DID I DO SOMETHING WRONG?
HOW CAN EVERYONE JUST ACCEPT THINGS AND MOVE ON?!
WHY?!
...
IT DOESN'T MATTER WHAT I DO.

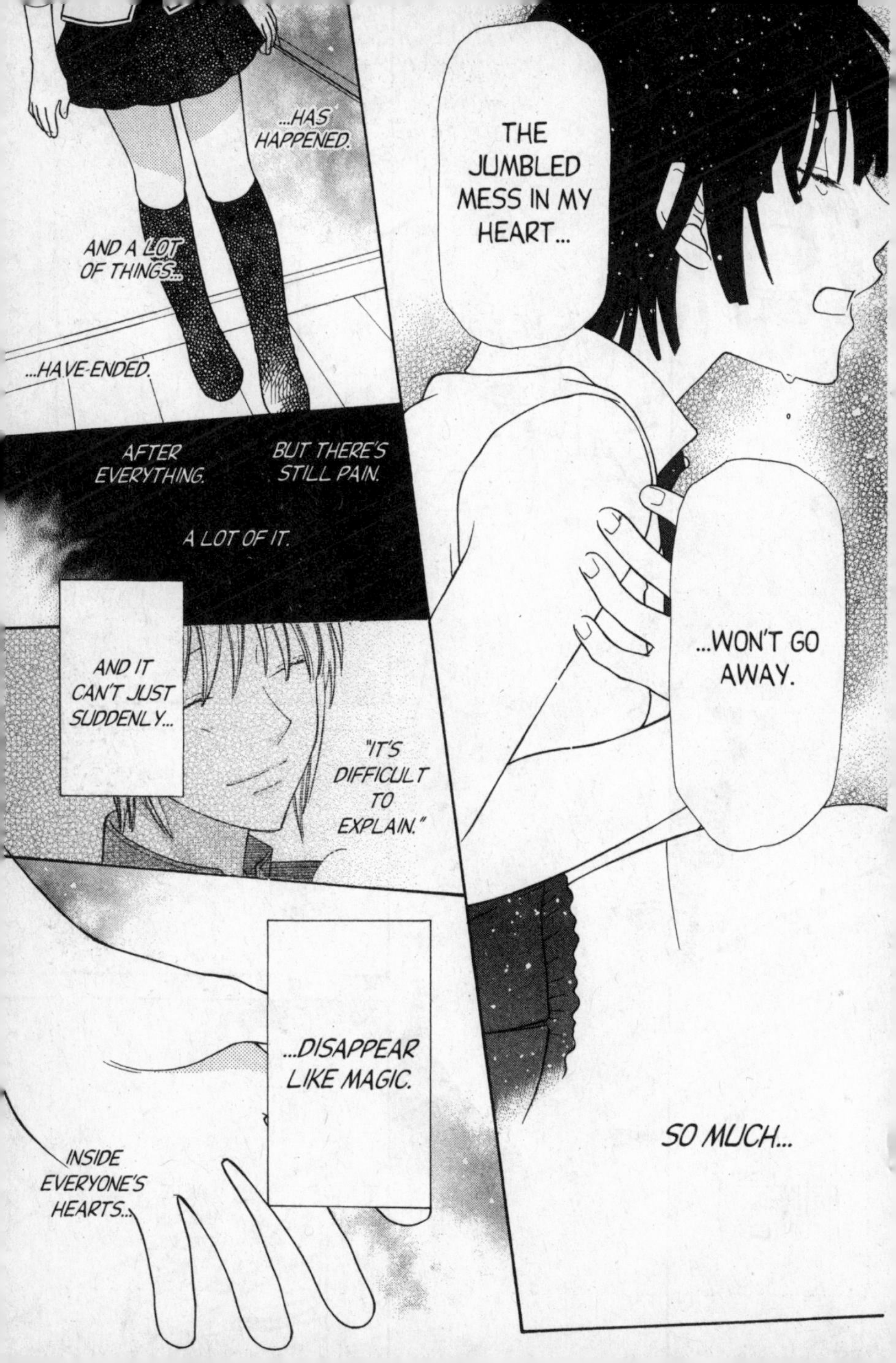
THE JUMBLED MESS IN MY HEART...
...WON'T GO AWAY.
SO MUCH...
...HAS HAPPENED.
AND A LOT OF THINGS...
...HAVE ENDED.
BUT THERE'S STILL PAIN.
AFTER EVERYTHING.
A LOT OF IT.
"IT'S DIFFICULT TO EXPLAIN."
AND IT CAN'T JUST SUDDENLY...
...DISAPPEAR LIKE MAGIC.
INSIDE EVERYONE'S HEARTS...

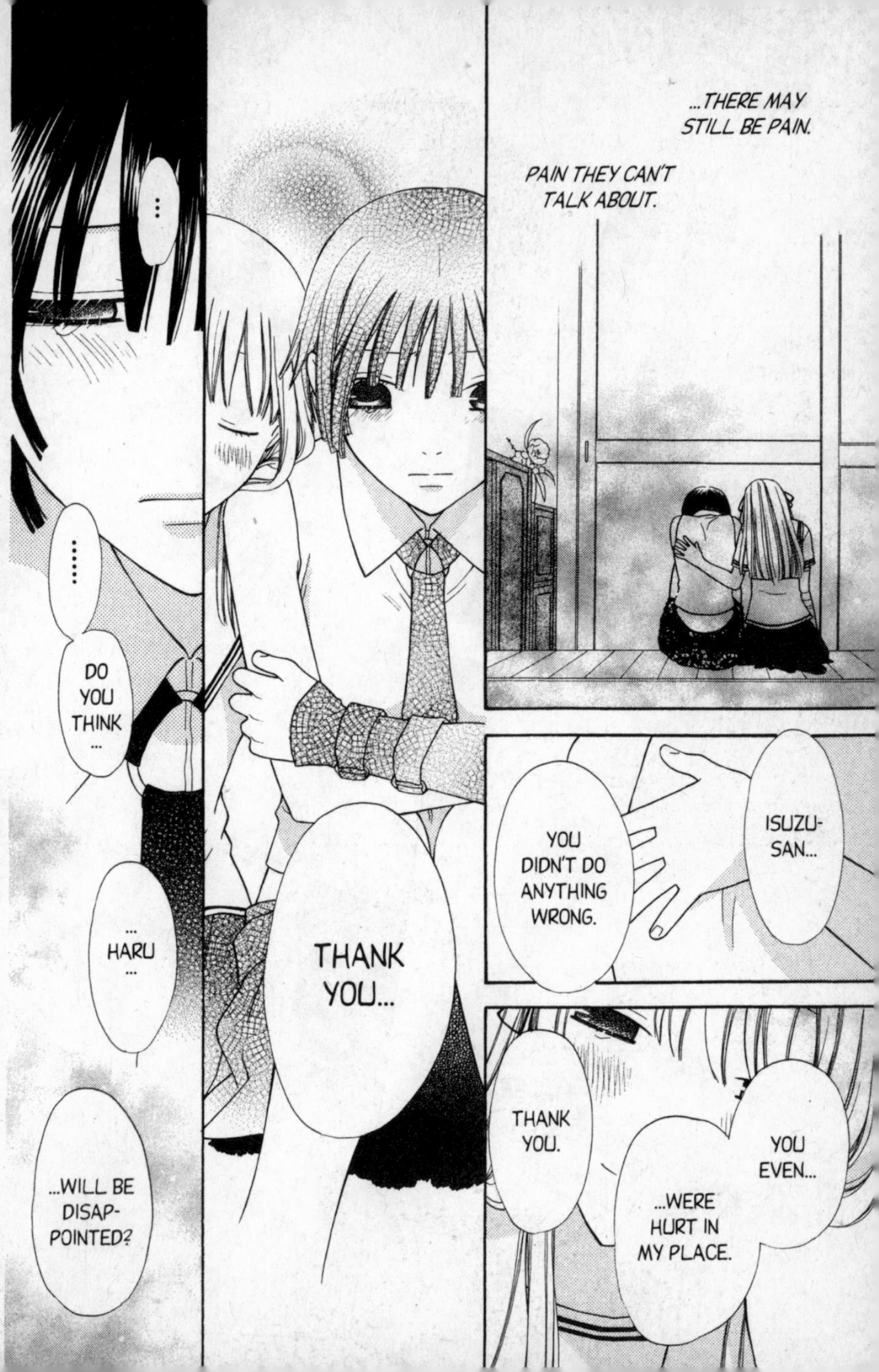
...THERE MAY STILL BE PAIN.
PAIN THEY CAN'T TALK ABOUT.
ISUZU-SAN...
YOU DIDN'T DO ANYTHING WRONG.
YOU EVEN...
...WERE HURT IN MY PLACE.
THANK YOU.
THANK YOU...
...
......
DO YOU THINK...
...HARU...
...WILL BE DISAP-POINTED?

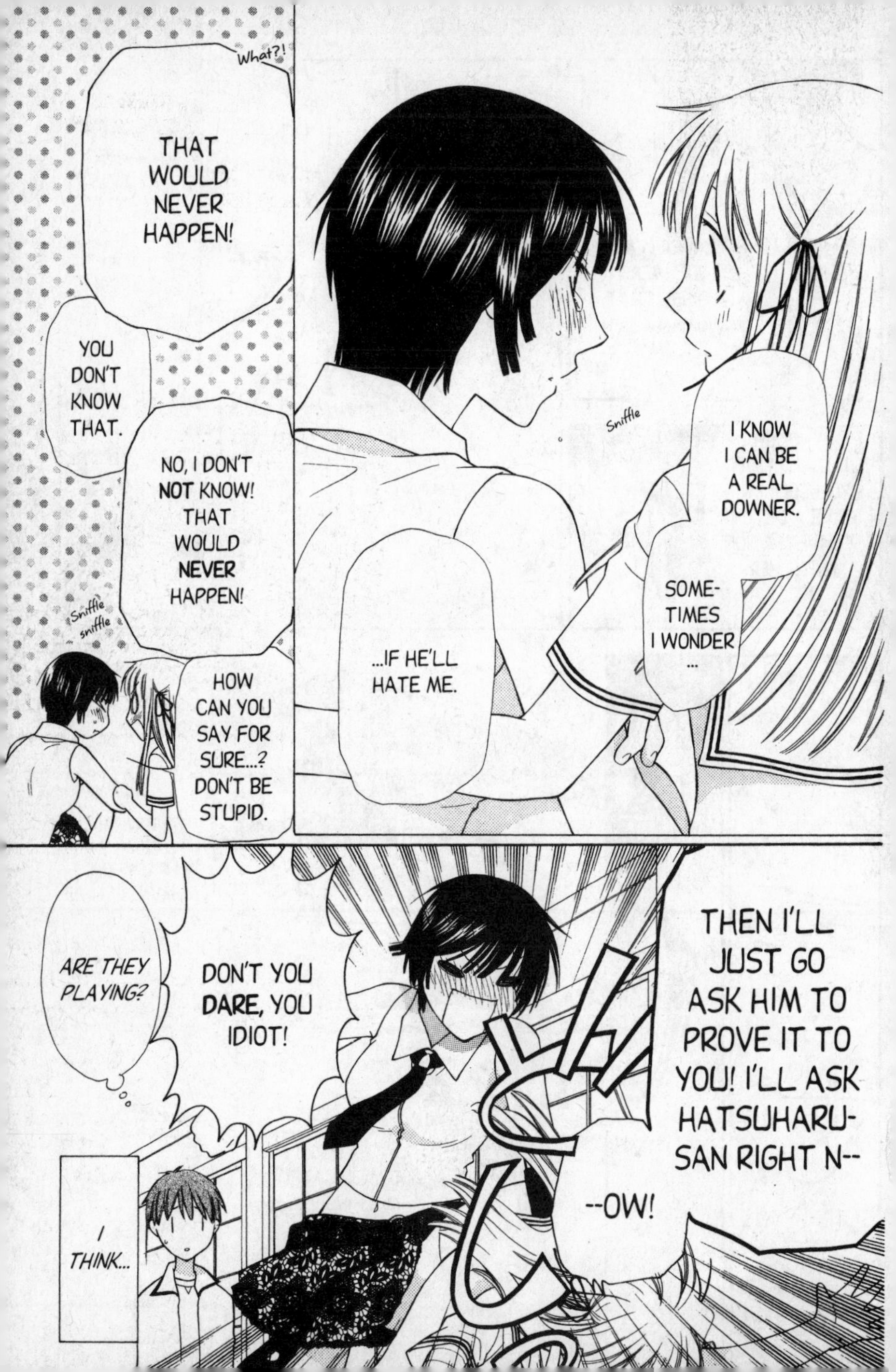

Sniffle
I KNOW I CAN BE A REAL DOWNER.
SOME-TIMES I WONDER ...
...IF HE'LL HATE ME.
What?!
THAT WOULD NEVER HAPPEN!
YOU DON'T KNOW THAT.
NO, I DON'T **NOT** KNOW! THAT WOULD **NEVER** HAPPEN!
Sniffle sniffle
HOW CAN YOU SAY FOR SURE...? DON'T BE STUPID.
THEN I'LL JUST GO ASK HIM TO PROVE IT TO YOU! I'LL ASK HATSUHARU-SAN RIGHT N--
--OW!
DON'T YOU **DARE,** YOU IDIOT!
ARE THEY PLAYING?
I THINK...

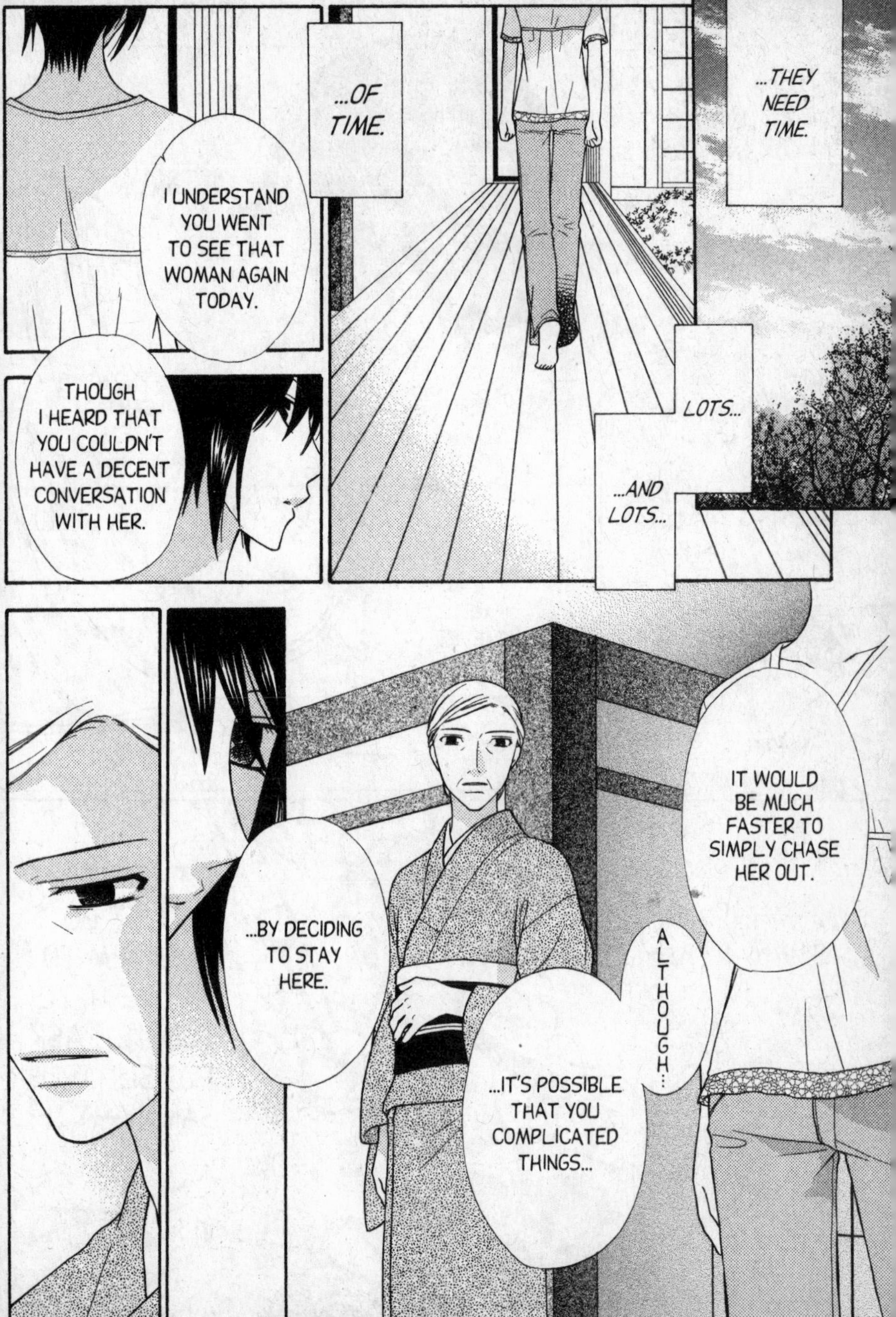
...THEY NEED TIME.
LOTS...
...AND LOTS...
...OF TIME.
I UNDERSTAND YOU WENT TO SEE THAT WOMAN AGAIN TODAY.
THOUGH I HEARD THAT YOU COULDN'T HAVE A DECENT CONVERSATION WITH HER.
IT WOULD BE MUCH FASTER TO SIMPLY CHASE HER OUT.
ALTHOUGH...
...IT'S POSSIBLE THAT YOU COMPLICATED THINGS...
...BY DECIDING TO STAY HERE.

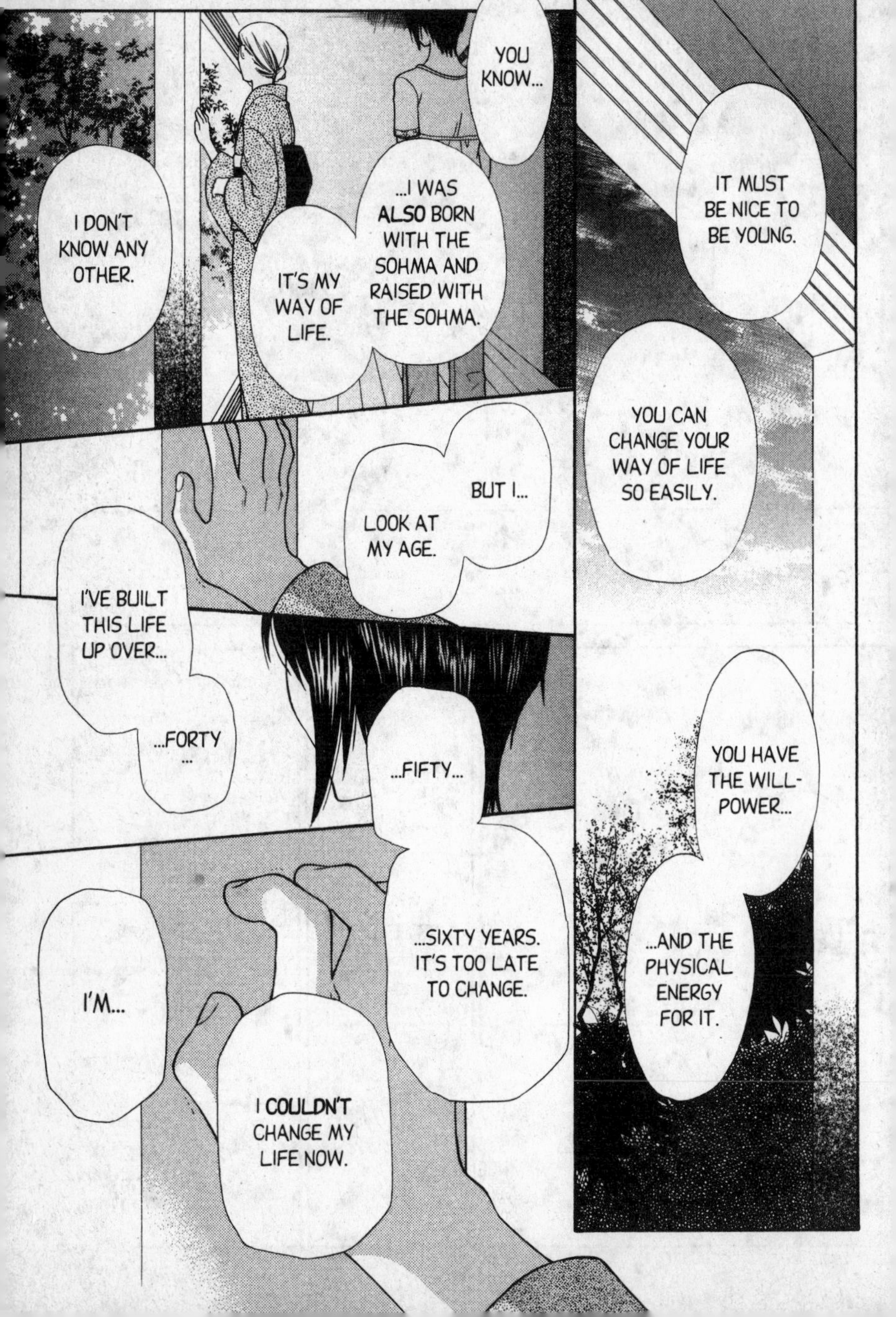
IT MUST BE NICE TO BE YOUNG.
YOU CAN CHANGE YOUR WAY OF LIFE SO EASILY.
YOU HAVE THE WILL-POWER...
...AND THE PHYSICAL ENERGY FOR IT.
YOU KNOW...
...I WAS **ALSO** BORN WITH THE SOHMA AND RAISED WITH THE SOHMA.
IT'S MY WAY OF LIFE.
I DON'T KNOW ANY OTHER.
BUT I...
LOOK AT MY AGE.
I'VE BUILT THIS LIFE UP OVER...
...FORTY ...
...FIFTY...
...SIXTY YEARS. IT'S TOO LATE TO CHANGE.
I'M...
I COULDN'T CHANGE MY LIFE NOW.

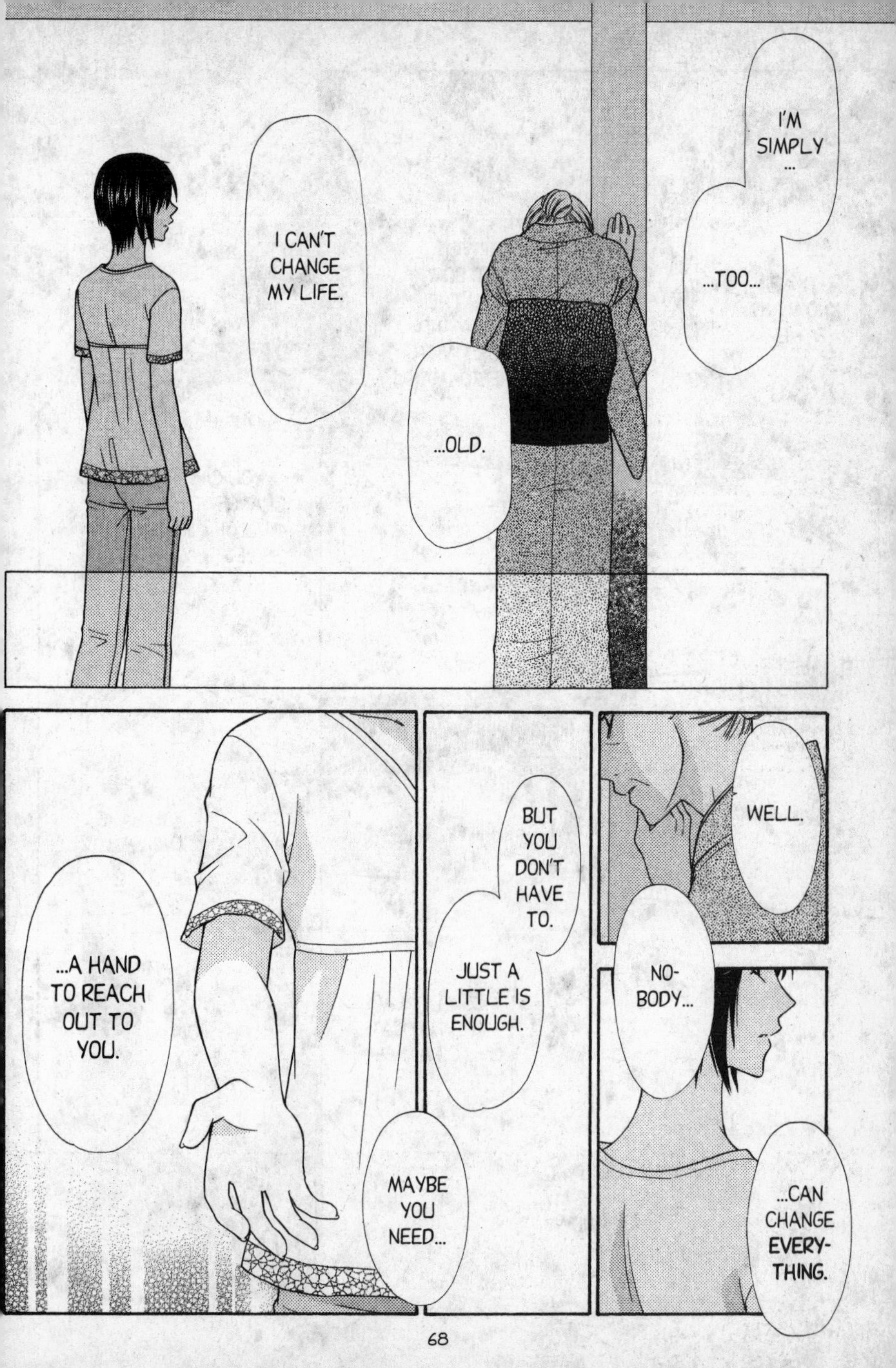
I'M SIMPLY ...
...TOO...
...OLD.
I CAN'T CHANGE MY LIFE.
WELL.
NO-BODY...
...CAN CHANGE EVERY-THING.
BUT YOU DON'T HAVE TO.
JUST A LITTLE IS ENOUGH.
MAYBE YOU NEED...
...A HAND TO REACH OUT TO YOU.

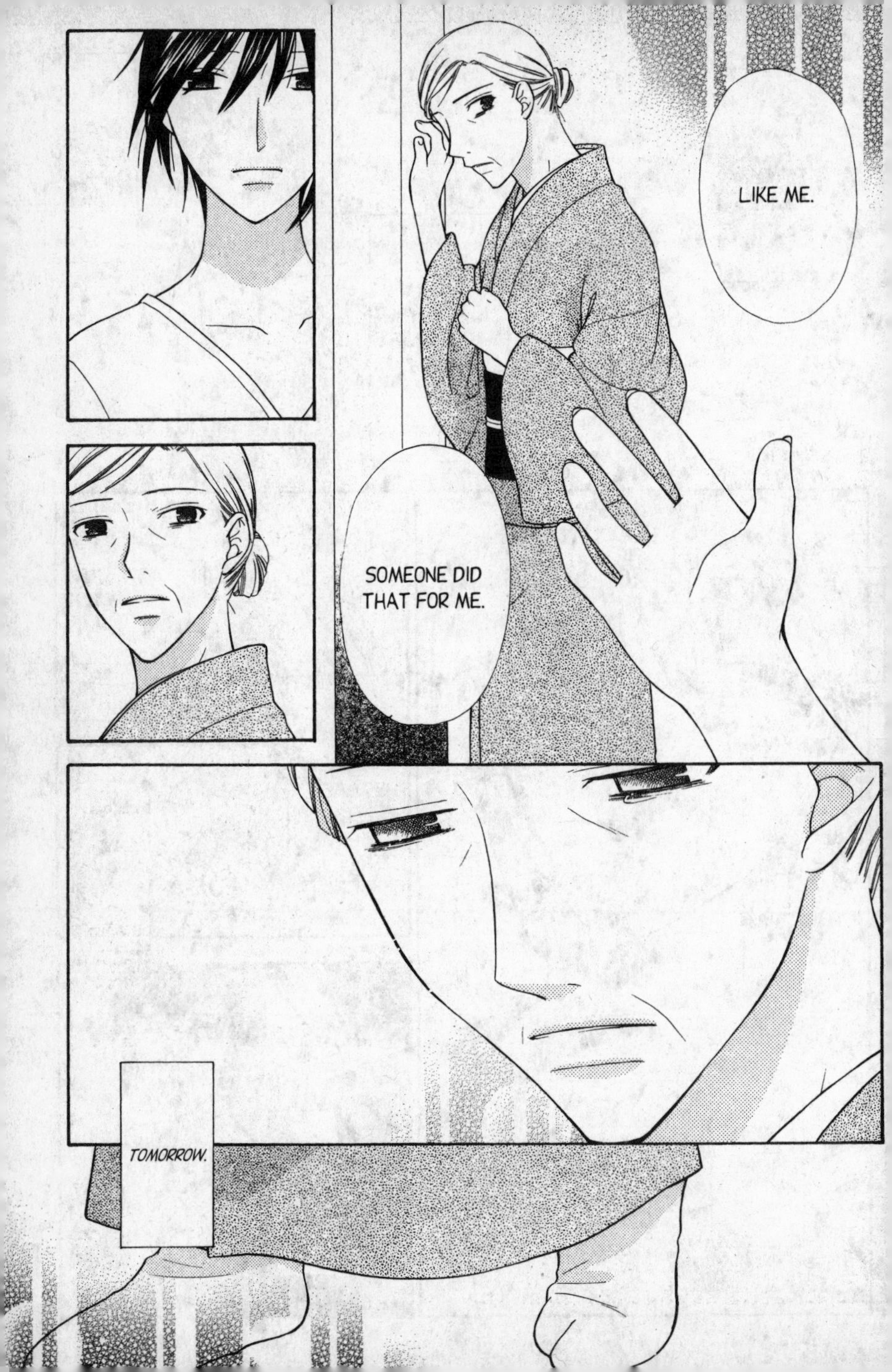
LIKE ME.
SOMEONE DID THAT FOR ME.
TOMORROW.

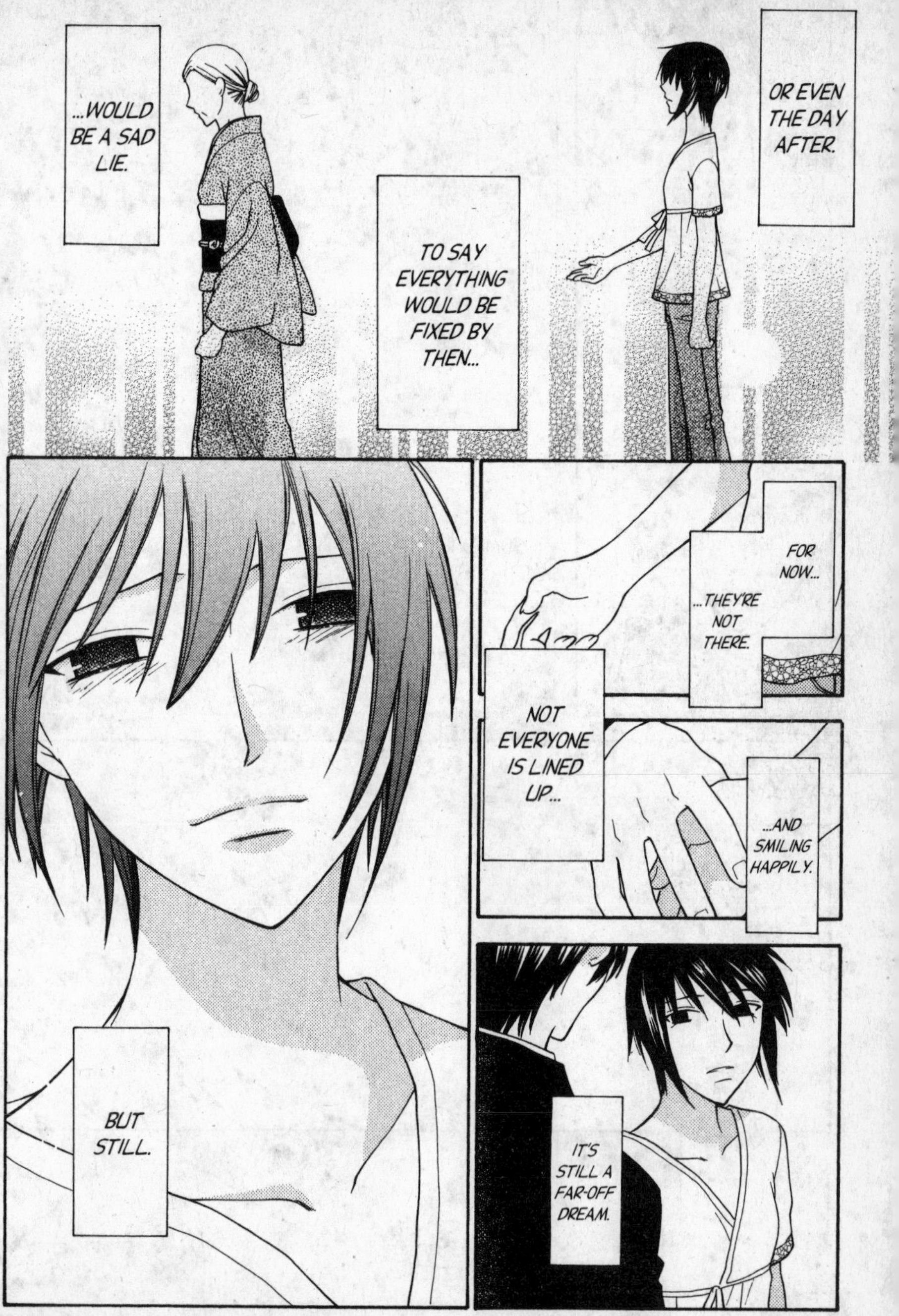
OR EVEN THE DAY AFTER.
TO SAY EVERYTHING WOULD BE FIXED BY THEN...
...WOULD BE A SAD LIE.
FOR NOW...
...THEY'RE NOT THERE.
NOT EVERYONE IS LINED UP...
...AND SMILING HAPPILY.
IT'S STILL A FAR-OFF DREAM.
BUT STILL.

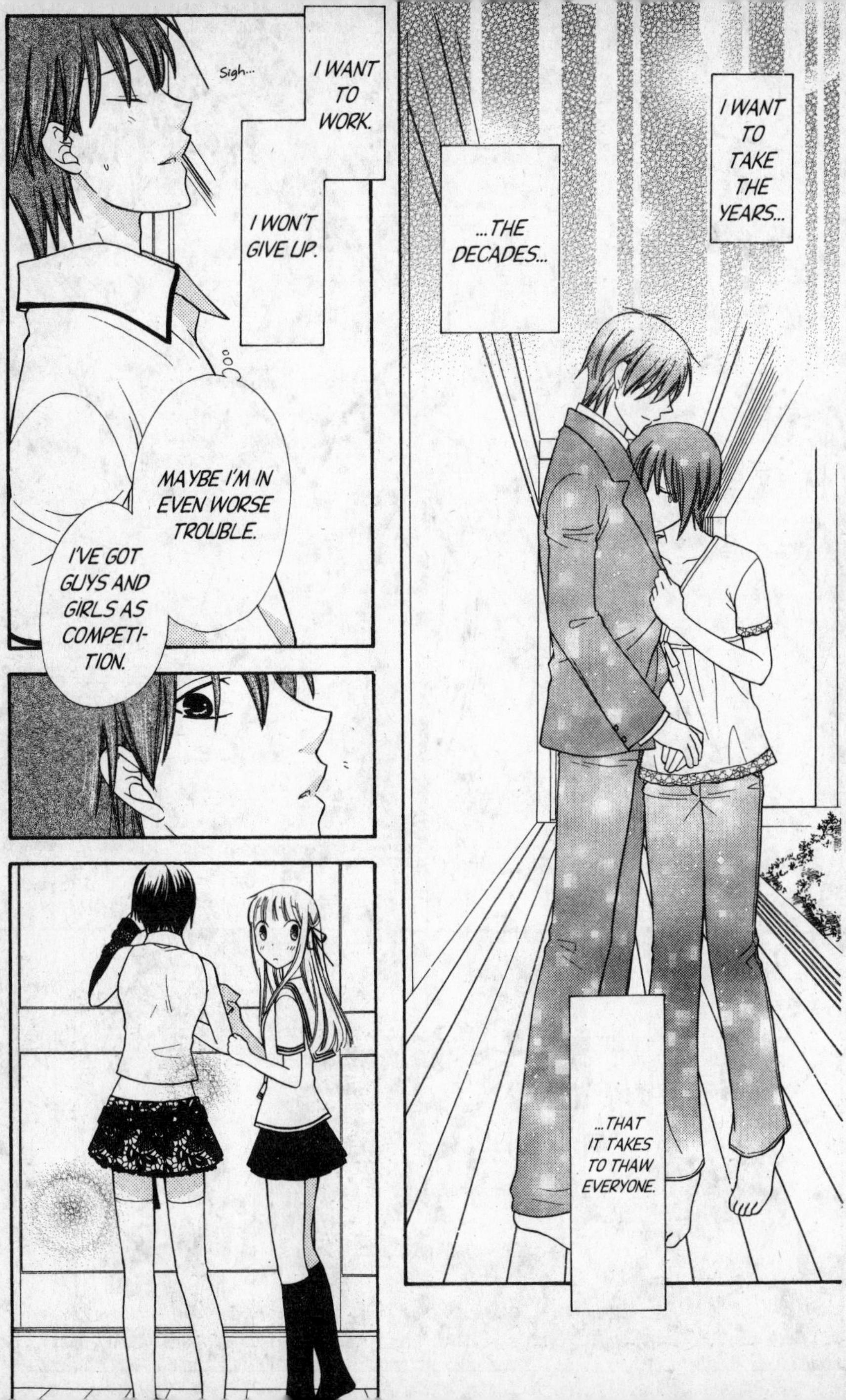
I WANT TO TAKE THE YEARS...
...THE DECADES...
...THAT IT TAKES TO THAW EVERYONE.
I WANT TO WORK.
Sigh...
I WON'T GIVE UP.
MAYBE I'M IN EVEN WORSE TROUBLE.
I'VE GOT GUYS AND GIRLS AS COMPETI-TION.

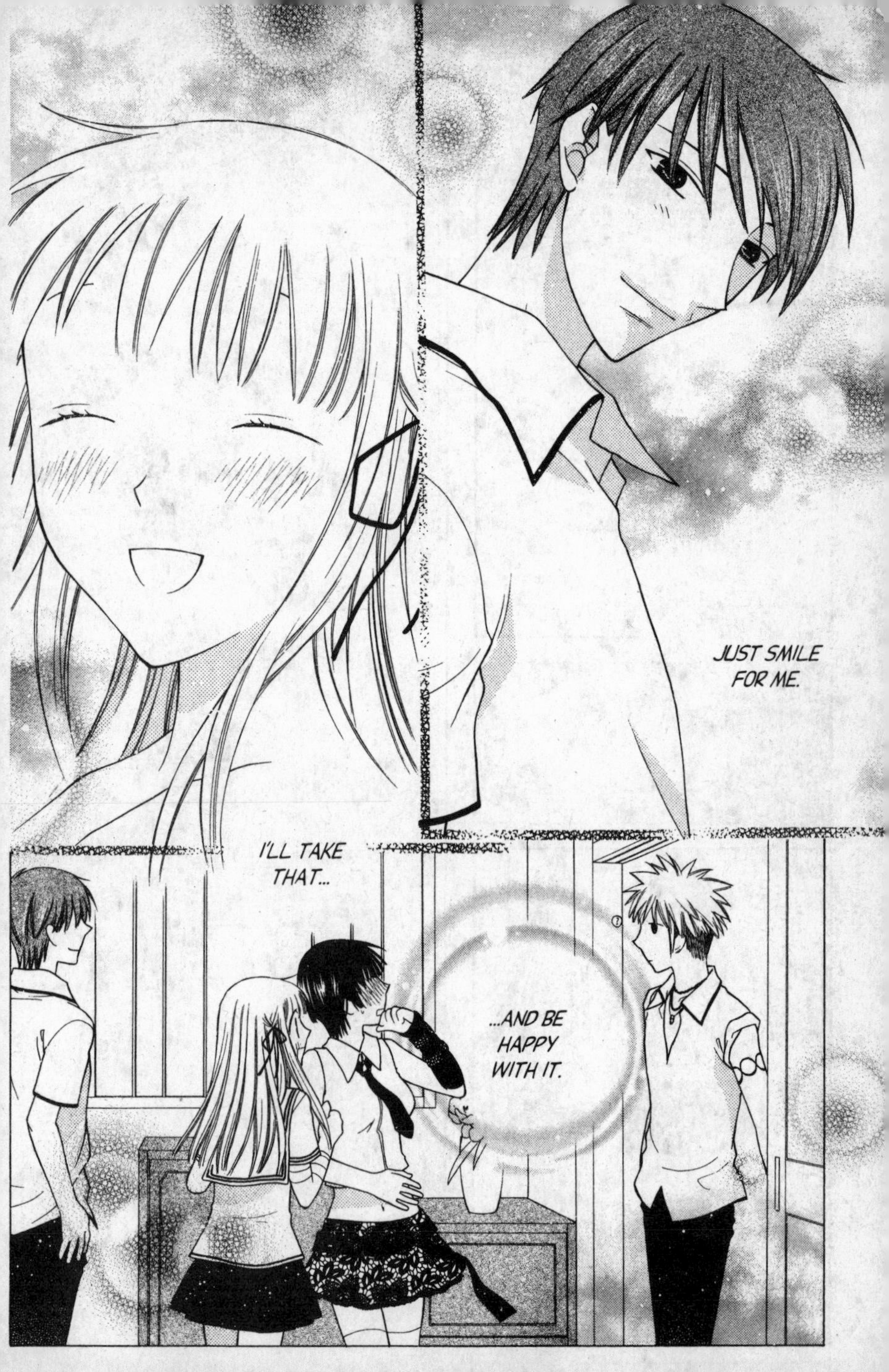
JUST SMILE FOR ME.
I'LL TAKE THAT...
...AND BE HAPPY WITH IT.

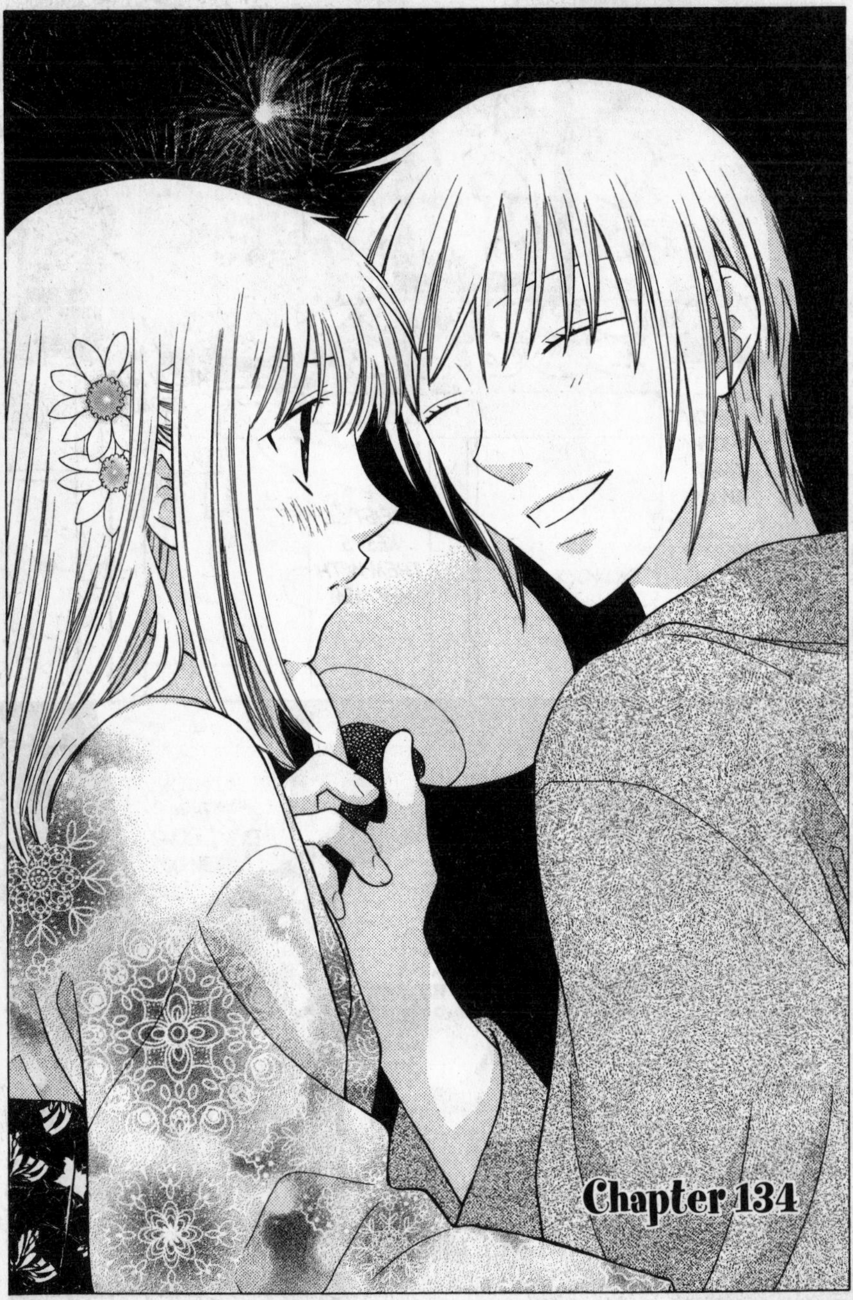
Chapter 134

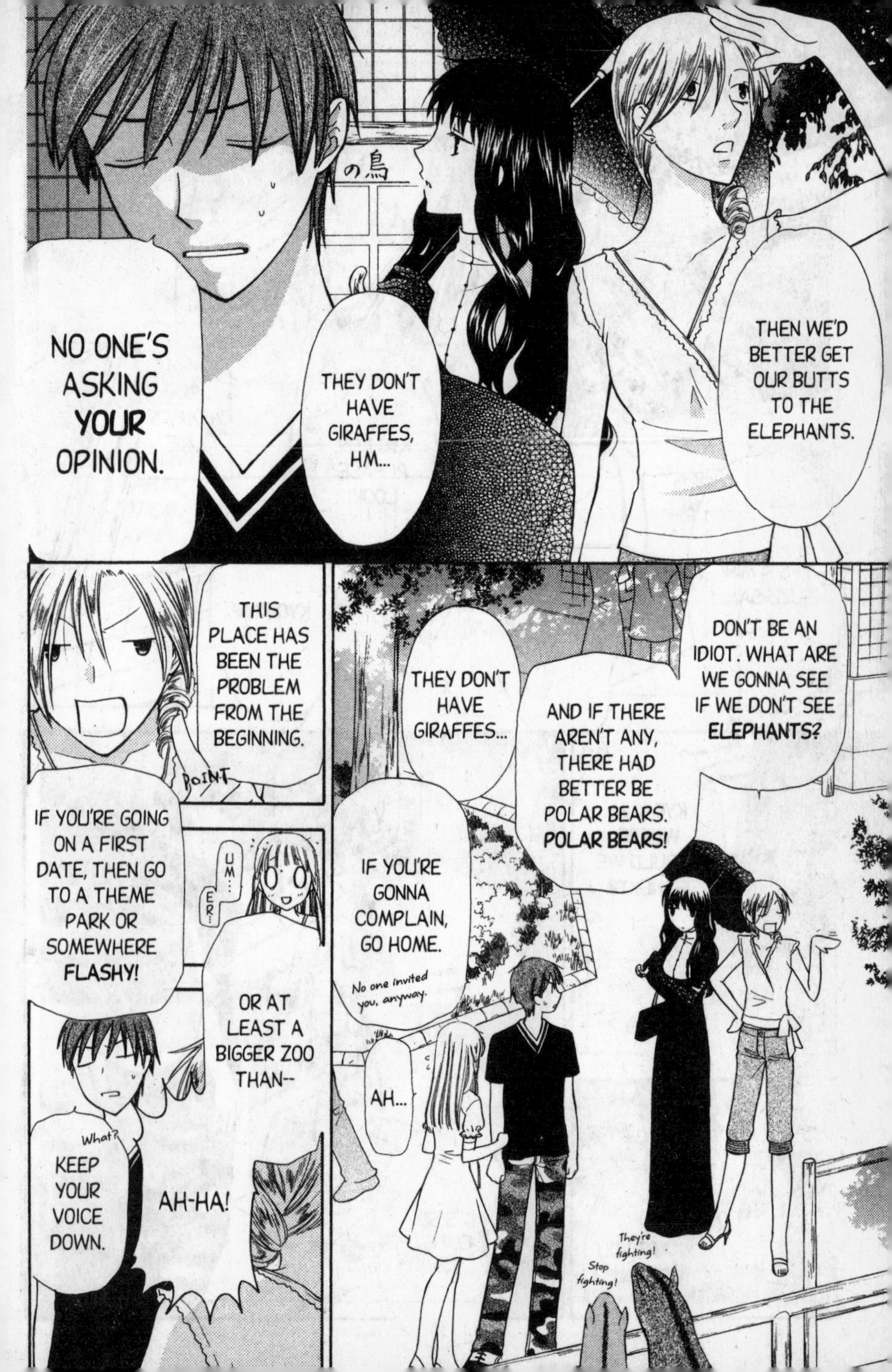
THEN WE'D BETTER GET OUR BUTTS TO THE ELEPHANTS.
の鳥
THEY DON'T HAVE GIRAFFES, HM...
NO ONE'S ASKING YOUR OPINION.
DON'T BE AN IDIOT. WHAT ARE WE GONNA SEE IF WE DON'T SEE ELEPHANTS?
AND IF THERE AREN'T ANY, THERE HAD BETTER BE POLAR BEARS. POLAR BEARS!
THEY DON'T HAVE GIRAFFES...
IF YOU'RE GONNA COMPLAIN, GO HOME.
No one invited you, anyway.
AH...
They're fighting!
Stop fighting!
THIS PLACE HAS BEEN THE PROBLEM FROM THE BEGINNING.
POINT
IF YOU'RE GOING ON A FIRST DATE, THEN GO TO A THEME PARK OR SOMEWHERE FLASHY!
UM... ER...
OR AT LEAST A BIGGER ZOO THAN--
AH-HA!
What?
KEEP YOUR VOICE DOWN.

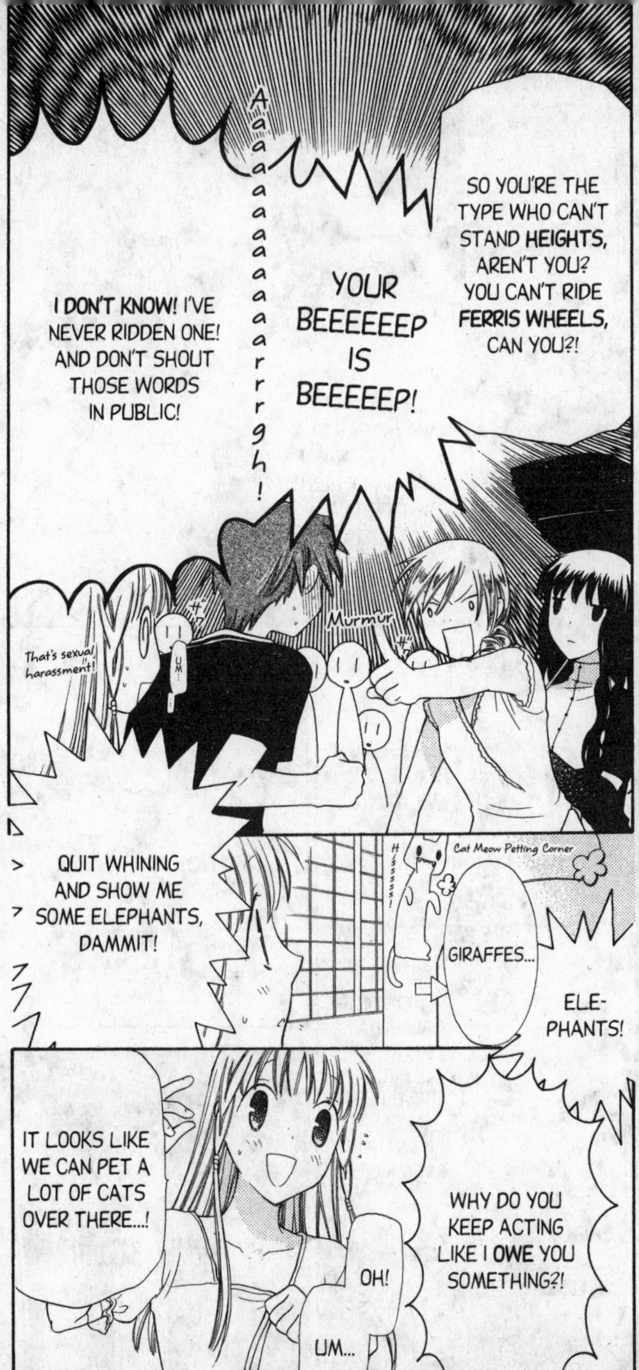
SO YOU'RE THE TYPE WHO CAN'T STAND HEIGHTS, AREN'T YOU? YOU CAN'T RIDE FERRIS WHEELS, CAN YOU?!
YOUR BEEEEEEP IS BEEEEEP!
Aaaaaaaaaaaaarrrgh!
I DON'T KNOW! I'VE NEVER RIDDEN ONE! AND DON'T SHOUT THOSE WORDS IN PUBLIC!
Murmur
That's sexual harassment!
UM...
ELE-PHANTS!
GIRAFFES...
Cat Meow Petting Corner
Hissssss!
QUIT WHINING AND SHOW ME SOME ELEPHANTS, DAMMIT!
WHY DO YOU KEEP ACTING LIKE I OWE YOU SOMETHING?!
UM...
OH!
IT LOOKS LIKE WE CAN PET A LOT OF CATS OVER THERE...!

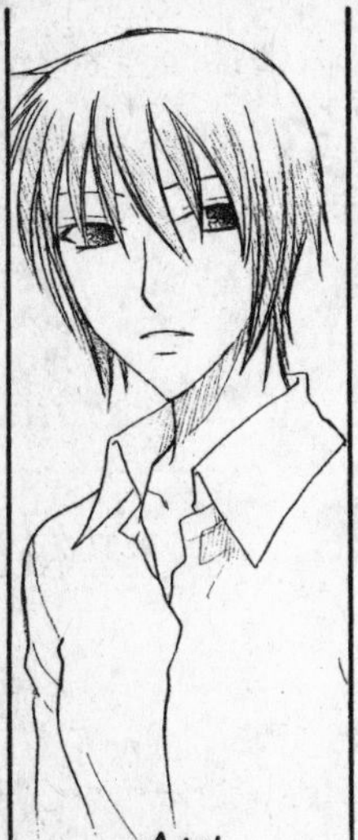

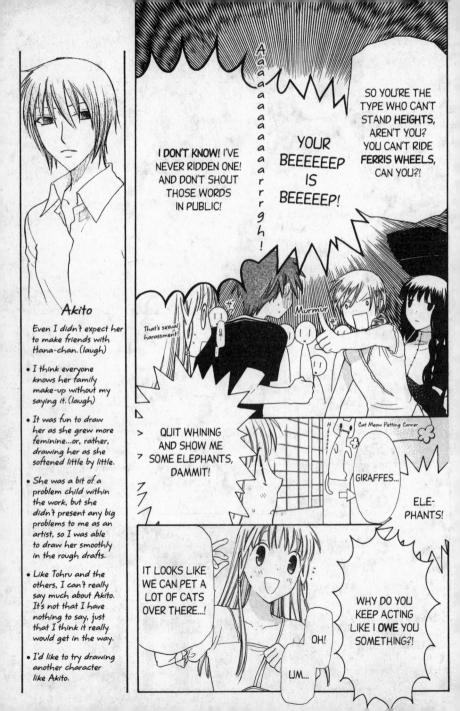

Akito

Even I didn't expect her to make friends with Hana-chan. (laugh)

- I think everyone knows her family make-up without my saying it. (laugh)
- It was fun to draw her as she grew more feminine...or, rather, drawing her as she softened little by little.
- She was a bit of a problem child within the work, but she didn't present any big problems to me as an artist, so I was able to draw her smoothly in the rough drafts.
- Like Tohru and the others, I can't really say much about Akito. It's not that I have nothing to say, just that I think it really would get in the way.
- I'd like to try drawing another character like Akito.

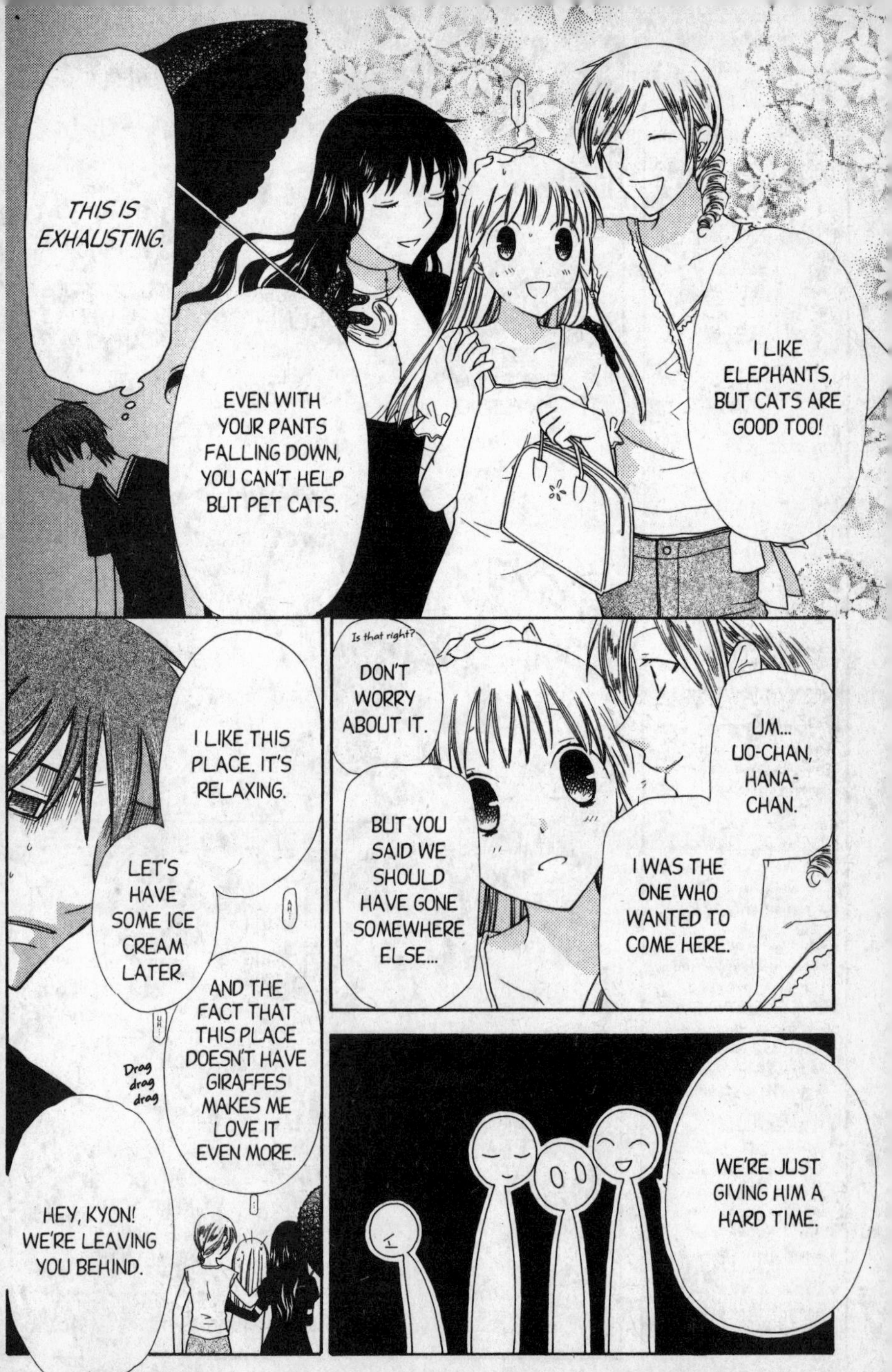
YES...
I LIKE ELEPHANTS, BUT CATS ARE GOOD TOO!
EVEN WITH YOUR PANTS FALLING DOWN, YOU CAN'T HELP BUT PET CATS.
THIS IS EXHAUSTING.
UM... UO-CHAN, HANA-CHAN.
I WAS THE ONE WHO WANTED TO COME HERE.
DON'T WORRY ABOUT IT.
Is that right?
BUT YOU SAID WE SHOULD HAVE GONE SOMEWHERE ELSE...
WE'RE JUST GIVING HIM A HARD TIME.
I LIKE THIS PLACE. IT'S RELAXING.
AH...
LET'S HAVE SOME ICE CREAM LATER.
AND THE FACT THAT THIS PLACE DOESN'T HAVE GIRAFFES MAKES ME LOVE IT EVEN MORE.
UH...
Drag drag drag
HEY, KYON! WE'RE LEAVING YOU BEHIND.

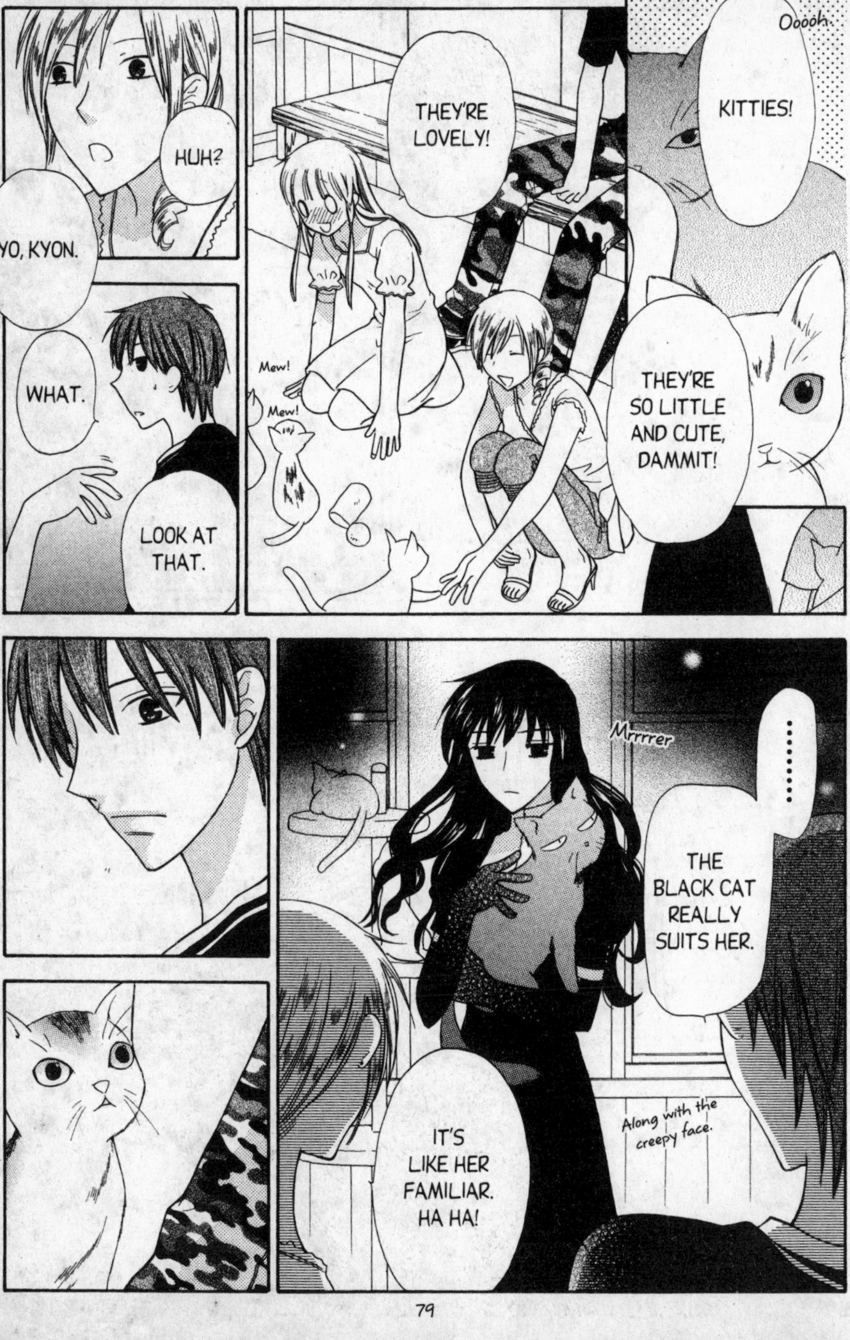
Ooooh
KITTIES!
THEY'RE SO LITTLE AND CUTE, DAMMIT!
THEY'RE LOVELY!
Mew!
Mew!
HUH?
YO, KYON.
WHAT.
LOOK AT THAT.
Mrrrrer
......
THE BLACK CAT REALLY SUITS HER.
Along with the creepy face.
IT'S LIKE HER FAMILIAR. HA HA!

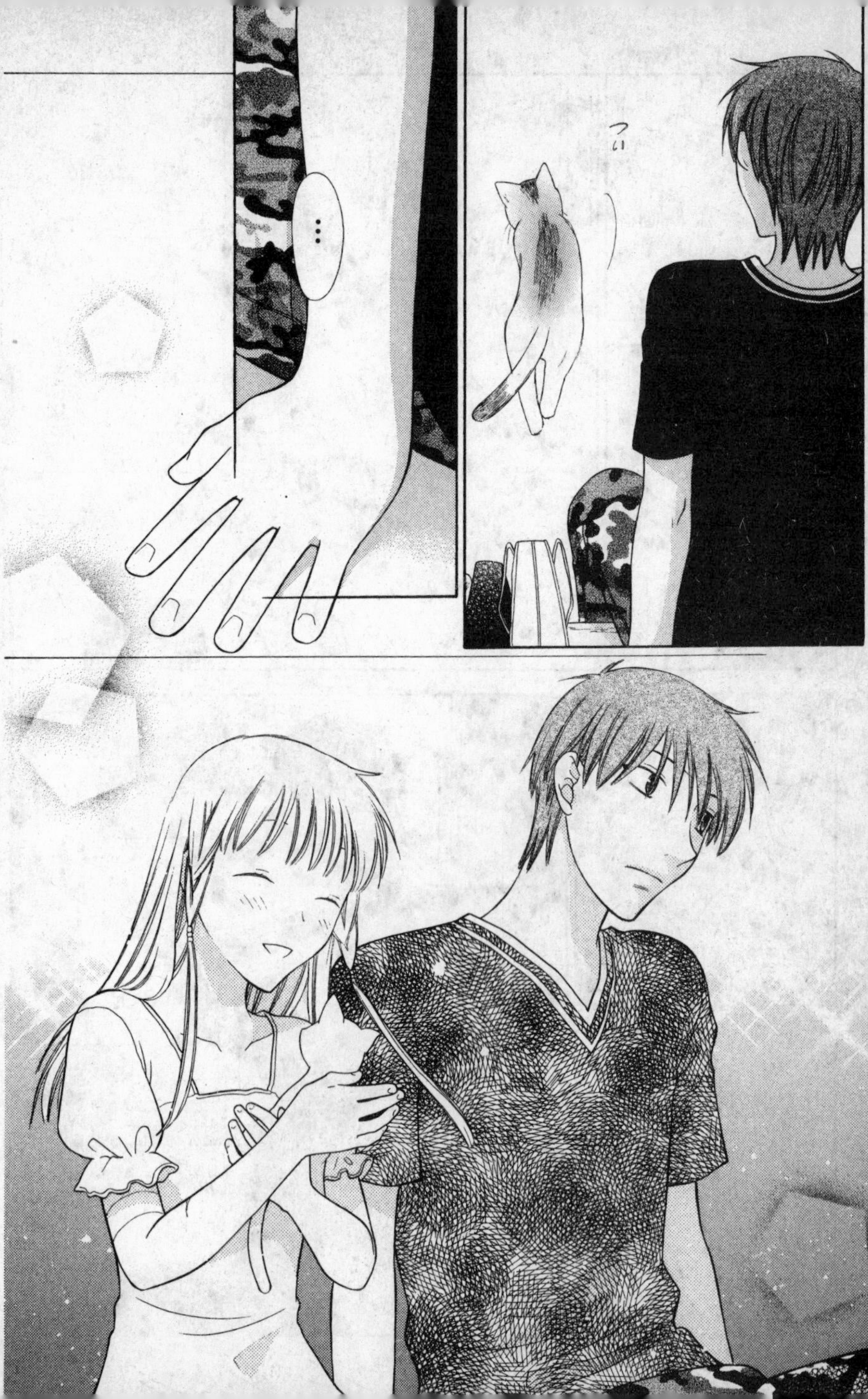
...

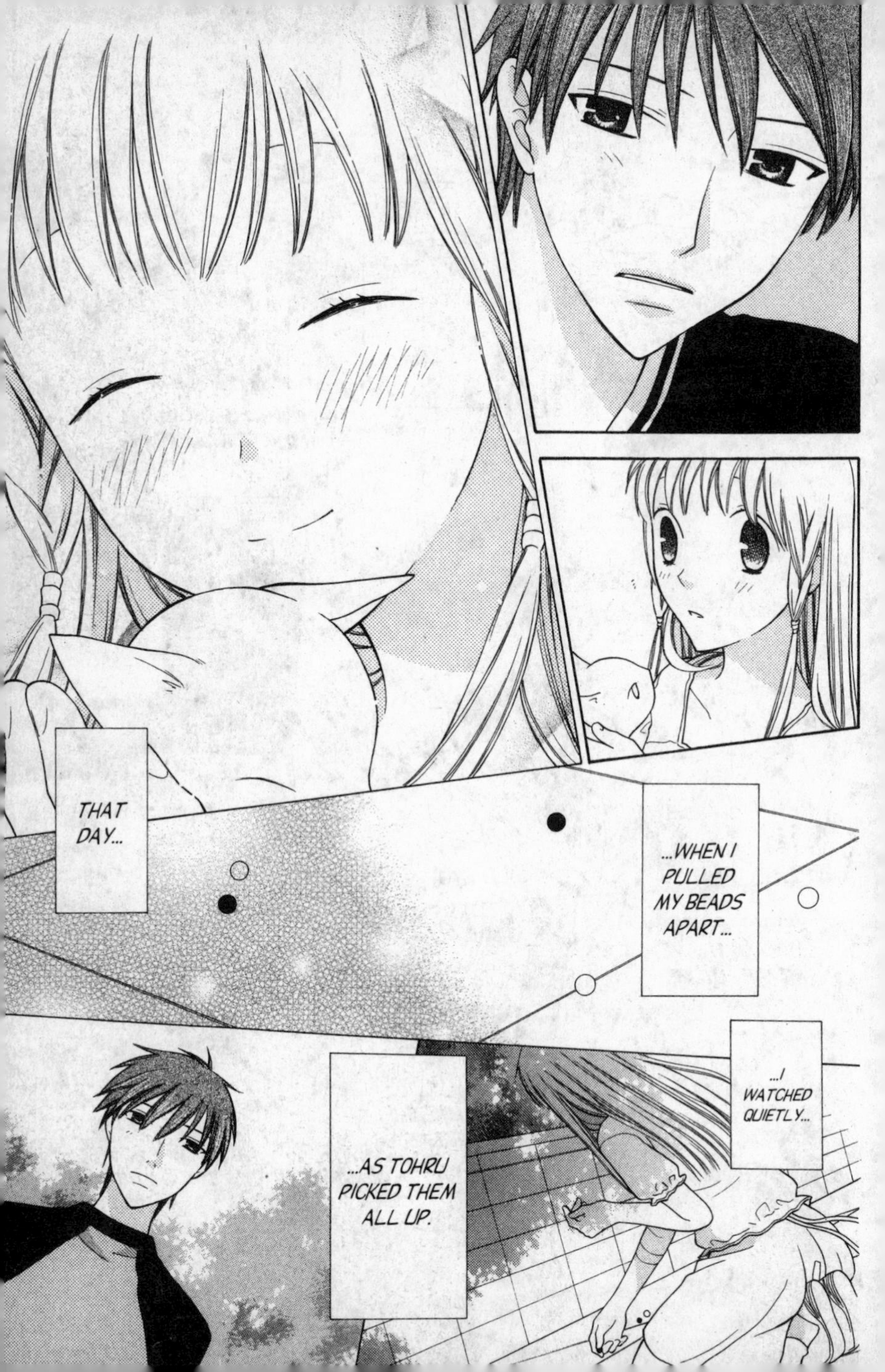
THAT DAY...
...WHEN I PULLED MY BEADS APART...
...I WATCHED QUIETLY...
...AS TOHRU PICKED THEM ALL UP.

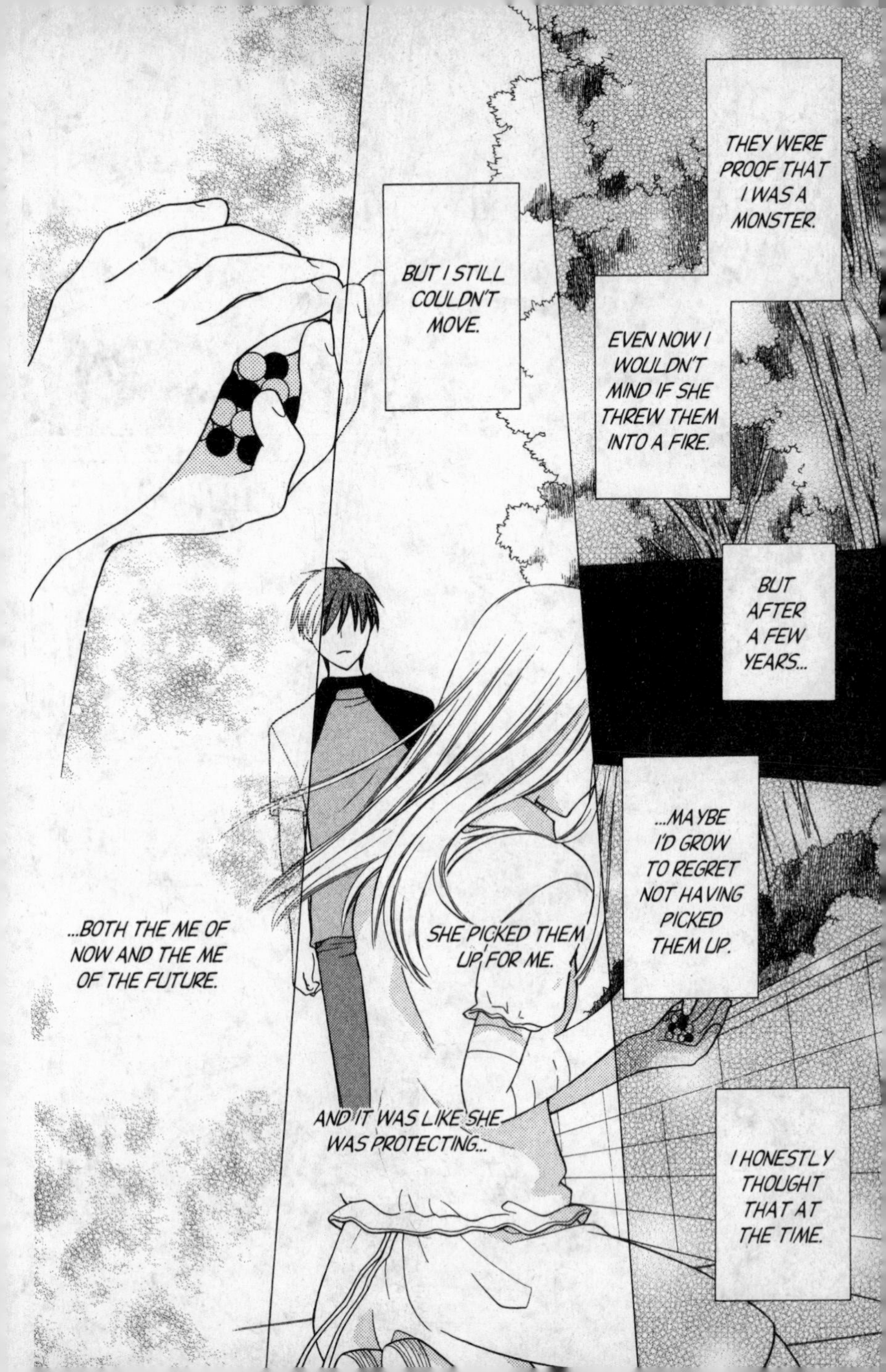
THEY WERE PROOF THAT I WAS A MONSTER.
EVEN NOW I WOULDN'T MIND IF SHE THREW THEM INTO A FIRE.
BUT AFTER A FEW YEARS...
...MAYBE I'D GROW TO REGRET NOT HAVING PICKED THEM UP.
I HONESTLY THOUGHT THAT AT THE TIME.
BUT I STILL COULDN'T MOVE.
SHE PICKED THEM UP FOR ME.
AND IT WAS LIKE SHE WAS PROTECTING...
...BOTH THE ME OF NOW AND THE ME OF THE FUTURE.

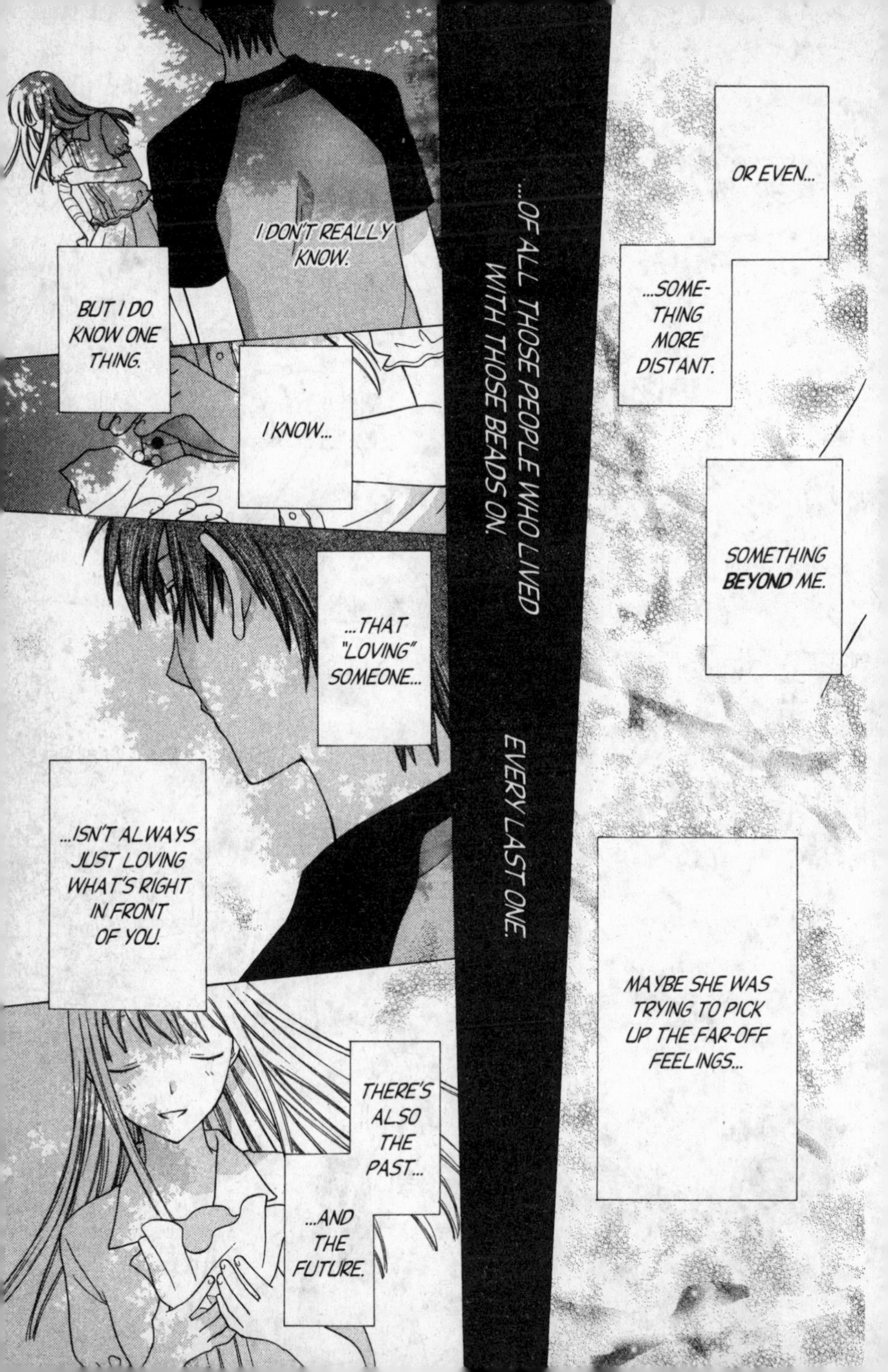
OR EVEN...
...SOMETHING MORE DISTANT.
SOMETHING BEYOND ME.
MAYBE SHE WAS TRYING TO PICK UP THE FAR-OFF FEELINGS...
...OF ALL THOSE PEOPLE WHO LIVED WITH THOSE BEADS ON.
EVERY LAST ONE.
I DON'T REALLY KNOW.
BUT I DO KNOW ONE THING.
I KNOW...
...THAT "LOVING" SOMEONE...
...ISN'T ALWAYS JUST LOVING WHAT'S RIGHT IN FRONT OF YOU.
THERE'S ALSO THE PAST...
...AND THE FUTURE.

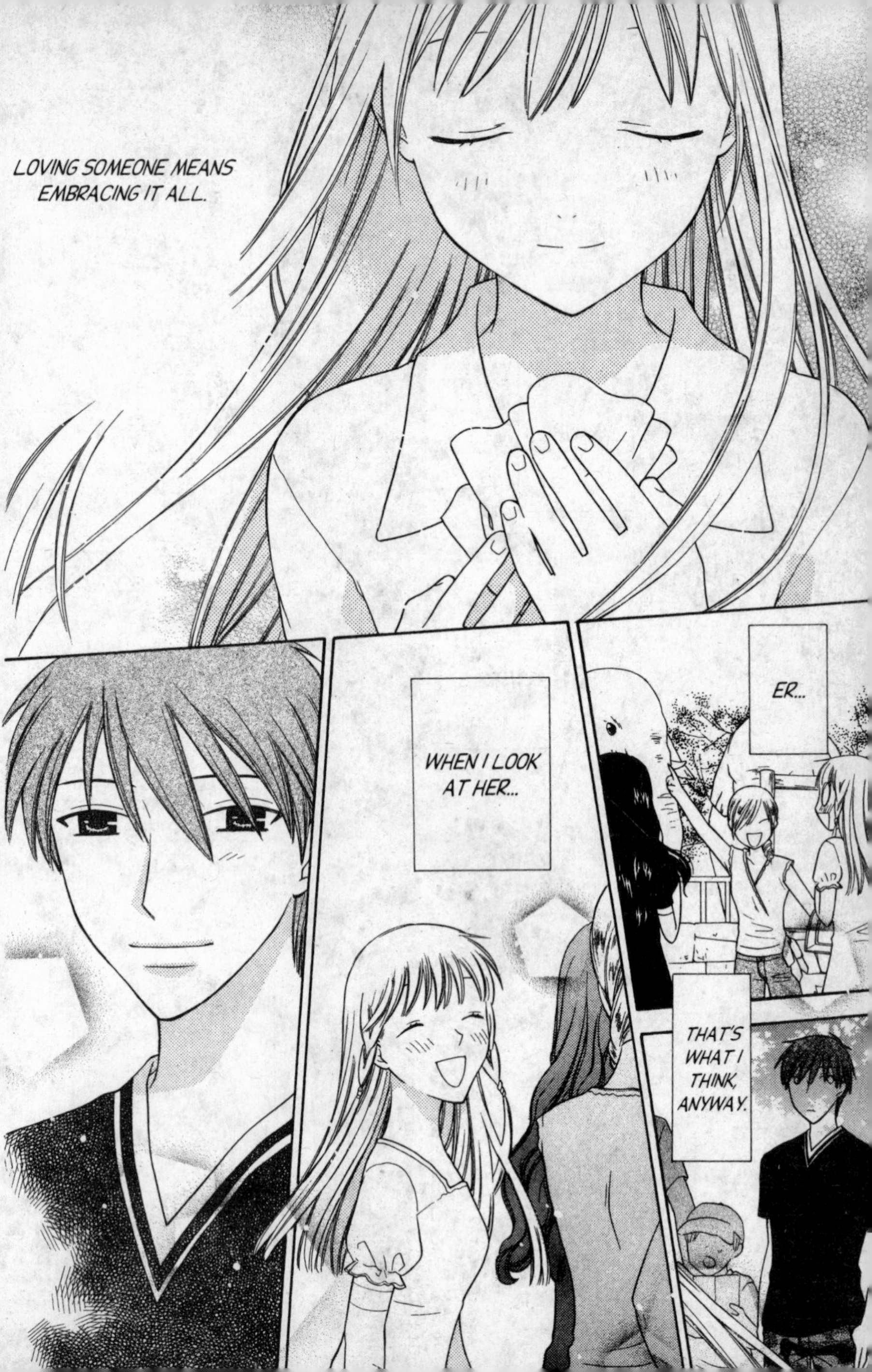
LOVING SOMEONE MEANS EMBRACING IT ALL.
ER...
THAT'S WHAT I THINK, ANYWAY.
WHEN I LOOK AT HER...

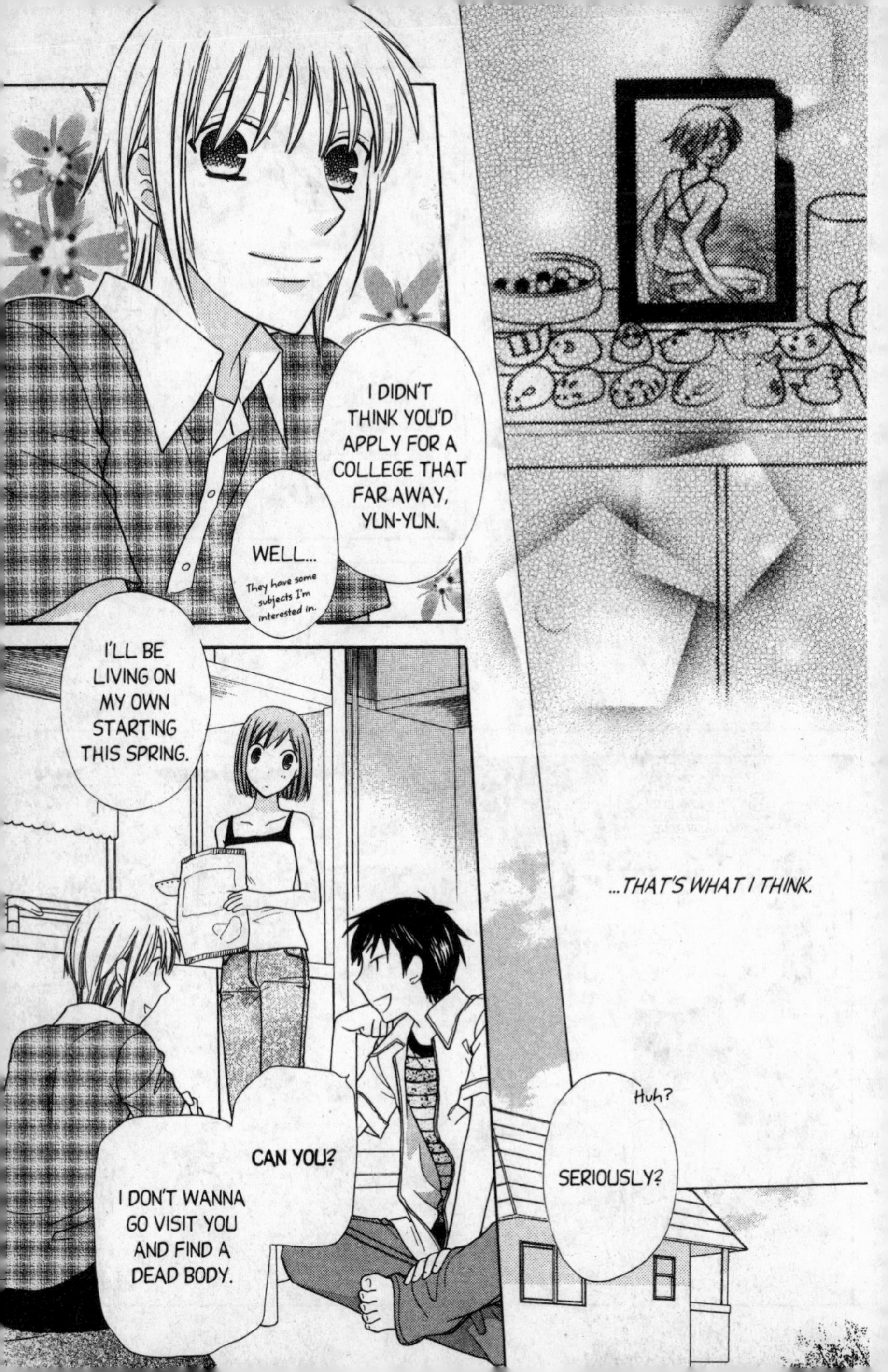
...THAT'S WHAT I THINK.
I DIDN'T THINK YOU'D APPLY FOR A COLLEGE THAT FAR AWAY, YUN-YUN.
WELL... They have some subjects I'm interested in.
I'LL BE LIVING ON MY OWN STARTING THIS SPRING.
Huh? SERIOUSLY?
CAN YOU?
I DON'T WANNA GO VISIT YOU AND FIND A DEAD BODY.

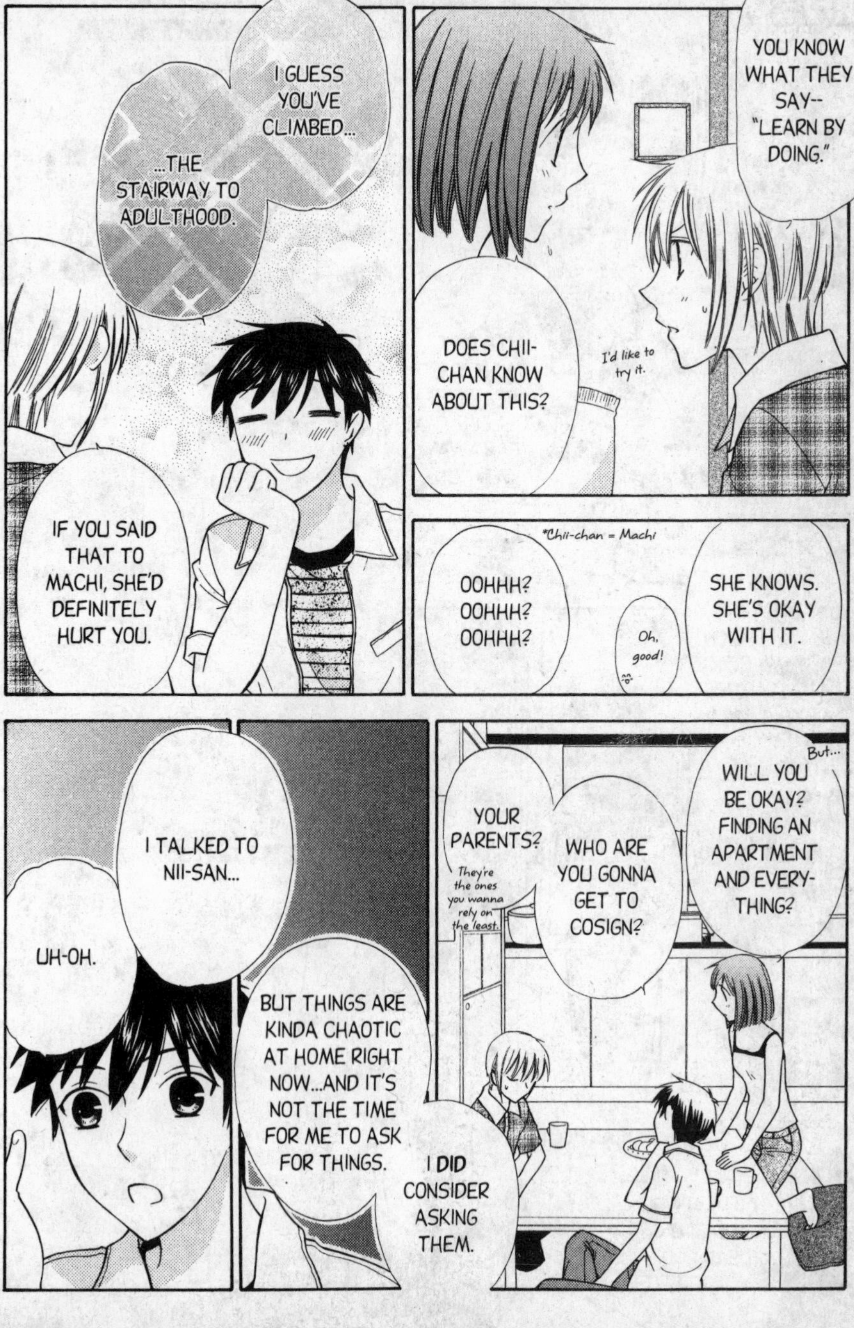
YOU KNOW WHAT THEY SAY-- "LEARN BY DOING."
I'd like to try it.
DOES CHII-CHAN KNOW ABOUT THIS?
SHE KNOWS. SHE'S OKAY WITH IT.
Oh, good!
OOHHH? OOHHH? OOHHH?
*Chii-chan = Machi
I GUESS YOU'VE CLIMBED...
...THE STAIRWAY TO ADULTHOOD.
IF YOU SAID THAT TO MACHI, SHE'D DEFINITELY HURT YOU.
But...
WILL YOU BE OKAY? FINDING AN APARTMENT AND EVERY-THING?
WHO ARE YOU GONNA GET TO COSIGN?
YOUR PARENTS?
They're the ones you wanna rely on the least.
I DID CONSIDER ASKING THEM.
BUT THINGS ARE KINDA CHAOTIC AT HOME RIGHT NOW...AND IT'S NOT THE TIME FOR ME TO ASK FOR THINGS.
I TALKED TO NII-SAN...
UH-OH.

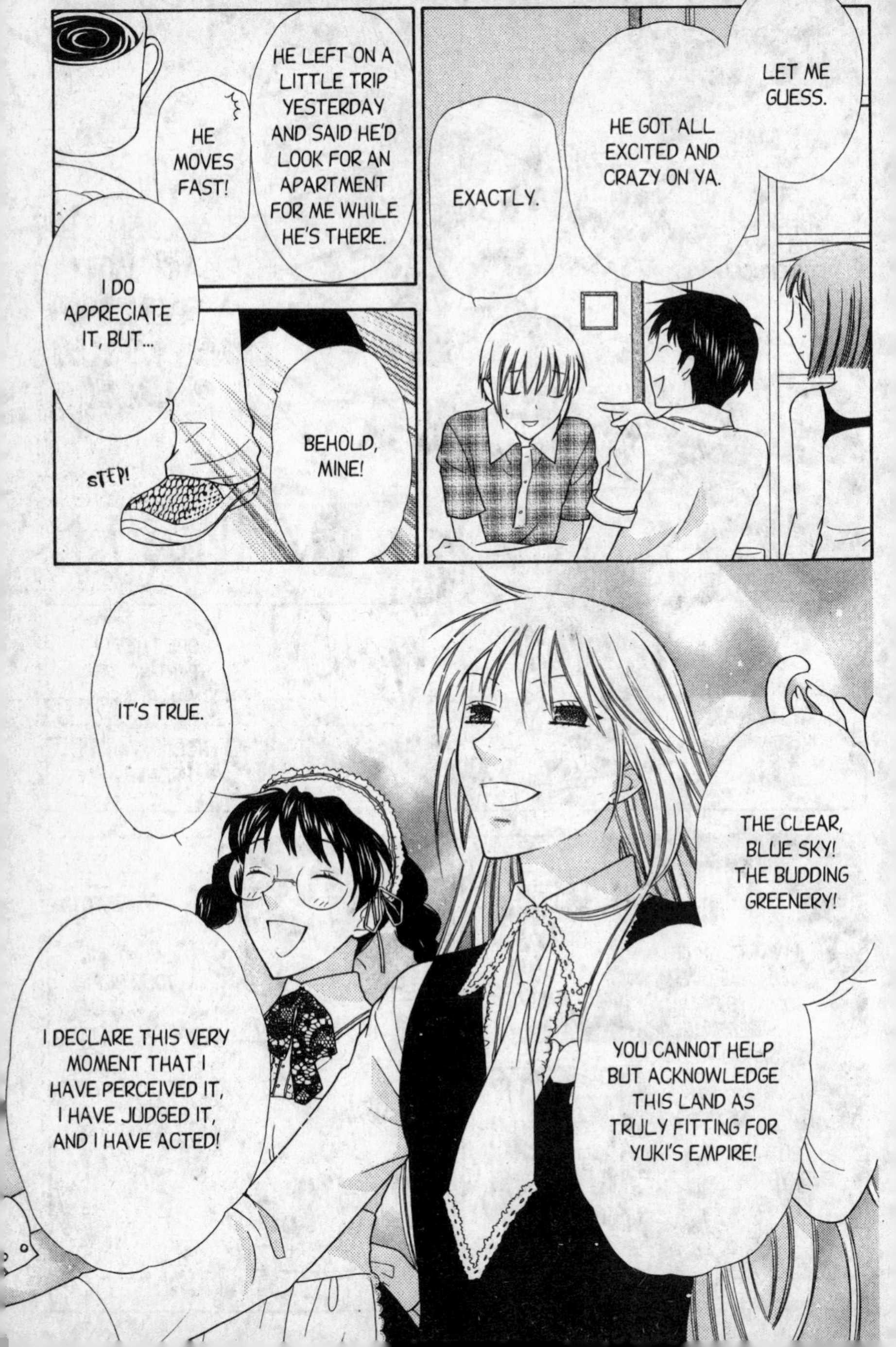
LET ME GUESS.
HE GOT ALL EXCITED AND CRAZY ON YA.
EXACTLY.
HE LEFT ON A LITTLE TRIP YESTERDAY AND SAID HE'D LOOK FOR AN APARTMENT FOR ME WHILE HE'S THERE.
HE MOVES FAST!
I DO APPRECIATE IT, BUT...
BEHOLD, MINE!
STEP!
THE CLEAR, BLUE SKY! THE BUDDING GREENERY!
YOU CANNOT HELP BUT ACKNOWLEDGE THIS LAND AS TRULY FITTING FOR YUKI'S EMPIRE!
IT'S TRUE.
I DECLARE THIS VERY MOMENT THAT I HAVE PERCEIVED IT, I HAVE JUDGED IT, AND I HAVE ACTED!

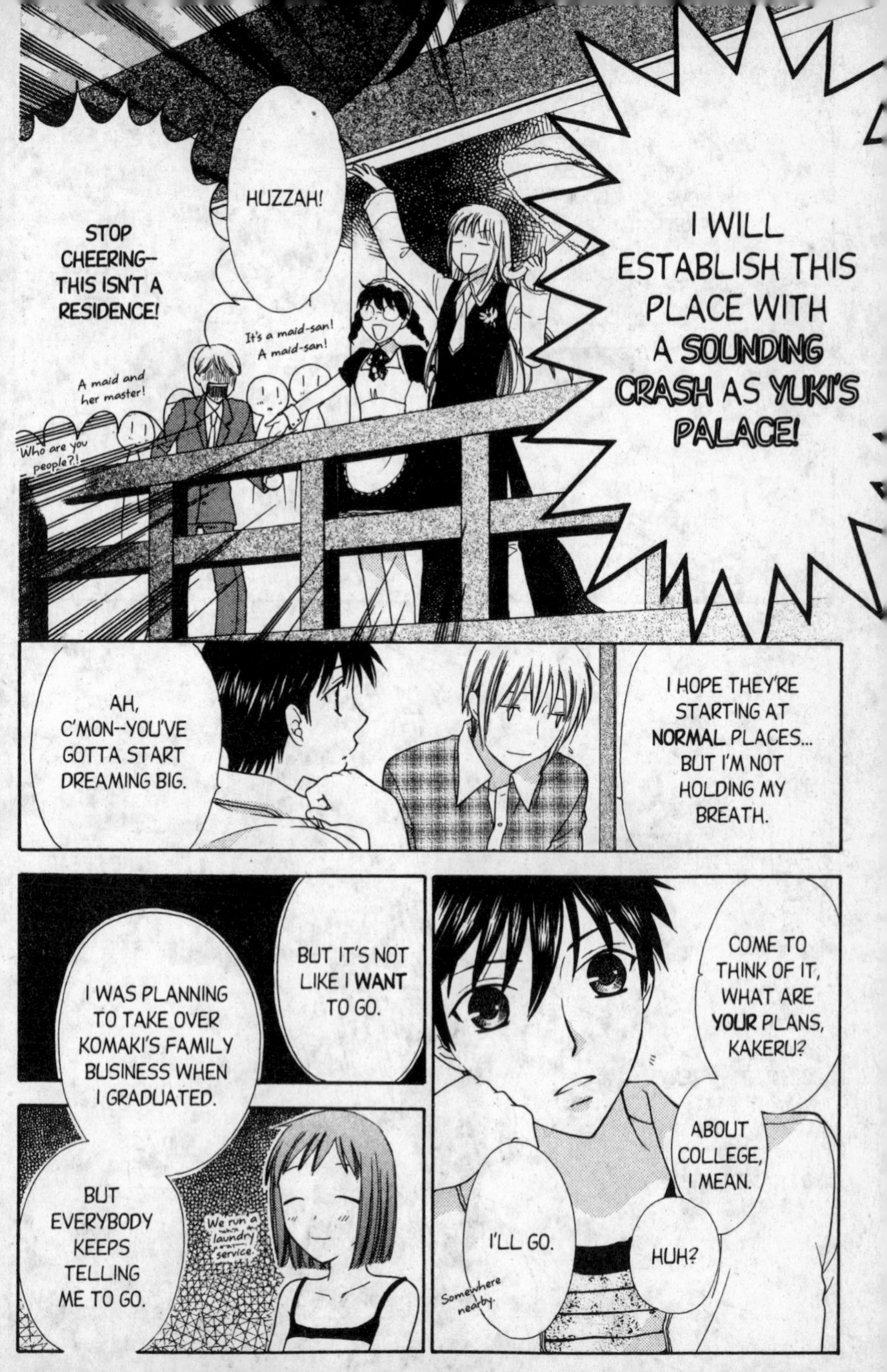
I WILL ESTABLISH THIS PLACE WITH A SOUNDING CRASH AS YUKI'S PALACE!
HUZZAH!
It's a maid-san! A maid-san!
STOP CHEERING— THIS ISN'T A RESIDENCE!
A maid and her master!
Who are you people?!
I HOPE THEY'RE STARTING AT NORMAL PLACES... BUT I'M NOT HOLDING MY BREATH.
AH, C'MON--YOU'VE GOTTA START DREAMING BIG.
COME TO THINK OF IT, WHAT ARE YOUR PLANS, KAKERU?
ABOUT COLLEGE, I MEAN.
HUH?
I'LL GO.
Somewhere nearby.
BUT IT'S NOT LIKE I WANT TO GO.
I WAS PLANNING TO TAKE OVER KOMAKI'S FAMILY BUSINESS WHEN I GRADUATED.
We run a laundry service.
BUT EVERYBODY KEEPS TELLING ME TO GO.

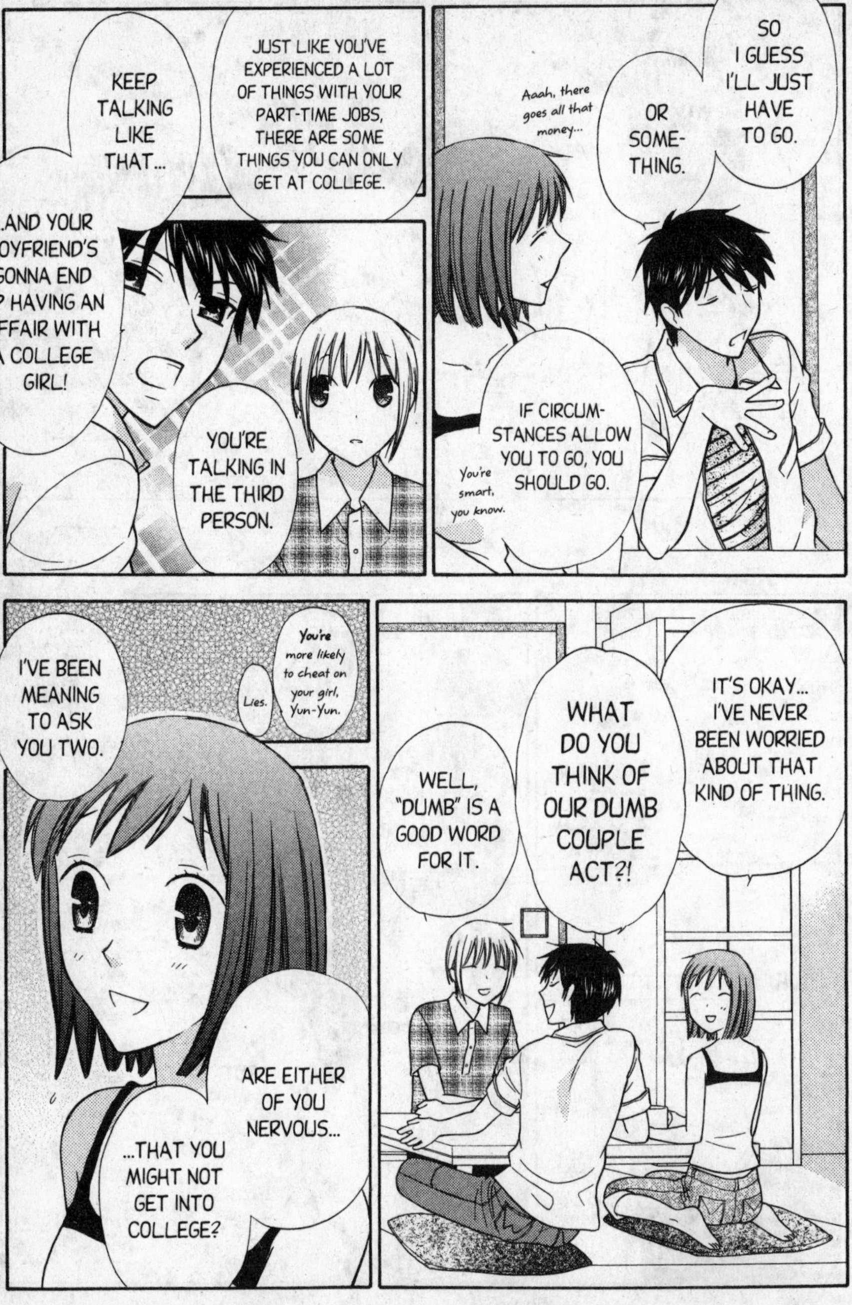
SO I GUESS I'LL JUST HAVE TO GO.
OR SOME-THING.
Aaah, there goes all that money...
IF CIRCUM-STANCES ALLOW YOU TO GO, YOU SHOULD GO.
You're smart, you know.
JUST LIKE YOU'VE EXPERIENCED A LOT OF THINGS WITH YOUR PART-TIME JOBS, THERE ARE SOME THINGS YOU CAN ONLY GET AT COLLEGE.
KEEP TALKING LIKE THAT...
...AND YOUR BOYFRIEND'S GONNA END UP HAVING AN AFFAIR WITH A COLLEGE GIRL!
YOU'RE TALKING IN THE THIRD PERSON.
IT'S OKAY... I'VE NEVER BEEN WORRIED ABOUT THAT KIND OF THING.
WHAT DO YOU THINK OF OUR DUMB COUPLE ACT?!
WELL, "DUMB" IS A GOOD WORD FOR IT.
You're more likely to cheat on your girl, Yun-Yun.
Lies.
I'VE BEEN MEANING TO ASK YOU TWO.
ARE EITHER OF YOU NERVOUS...
...THAT YOU MIGHT NOT GET INTO COLLEGE?

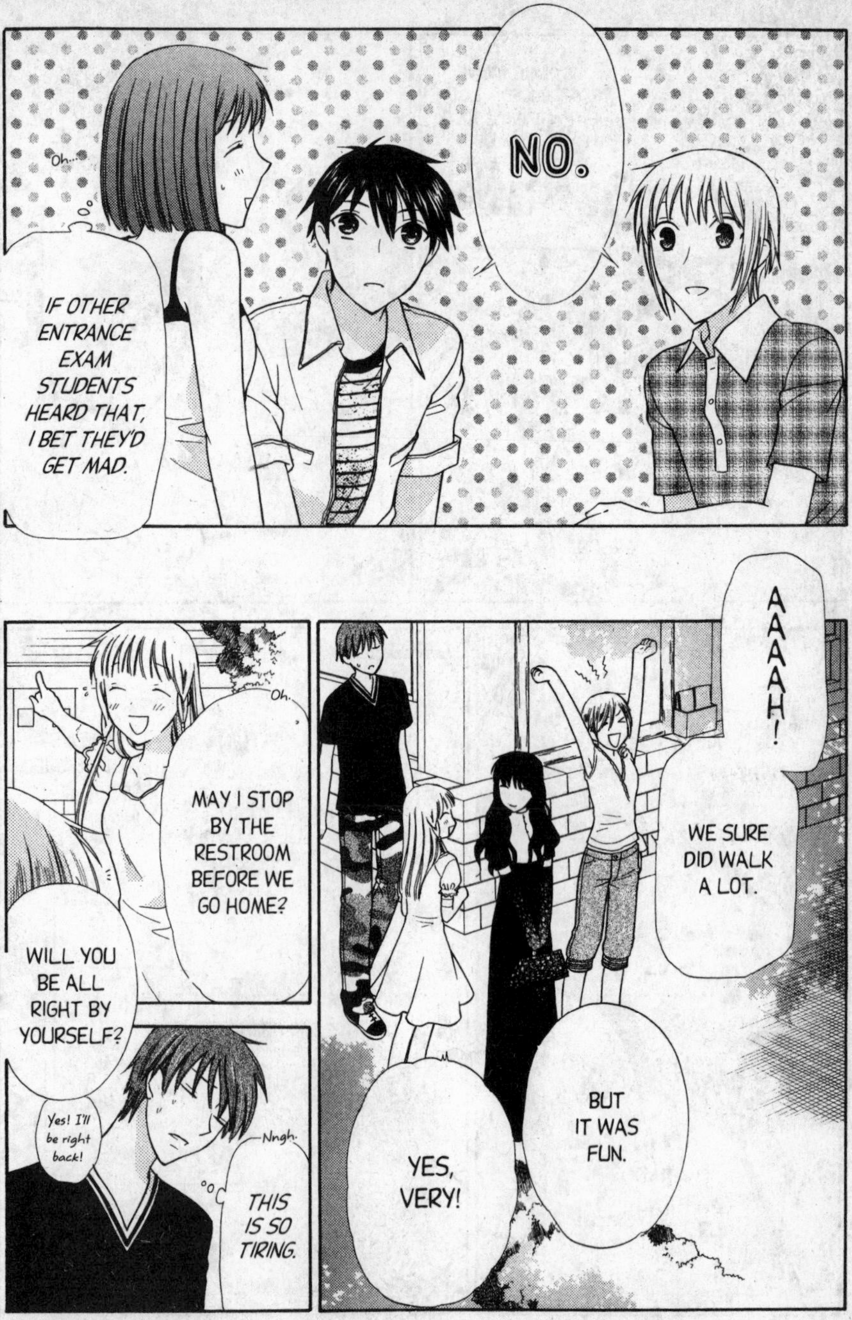
NO.
Oh...
IF OTHER ENTRANCE EXAM STUDENTS HEARD THAT, I BET THEY'D GET MAD.
AAAAH!
WE SURE DID WALK A LOT.
BUT IT WAS FUN.
YES, VERY!
Oh.
MAY I STOP BY THE RESTROOM BEFORE WE GO HOME?
WILL YOU BE ALL RIGHT BY YOURSELF?
Yes! I'll be right back!
Nngh.
THIS IS SO TIRING.

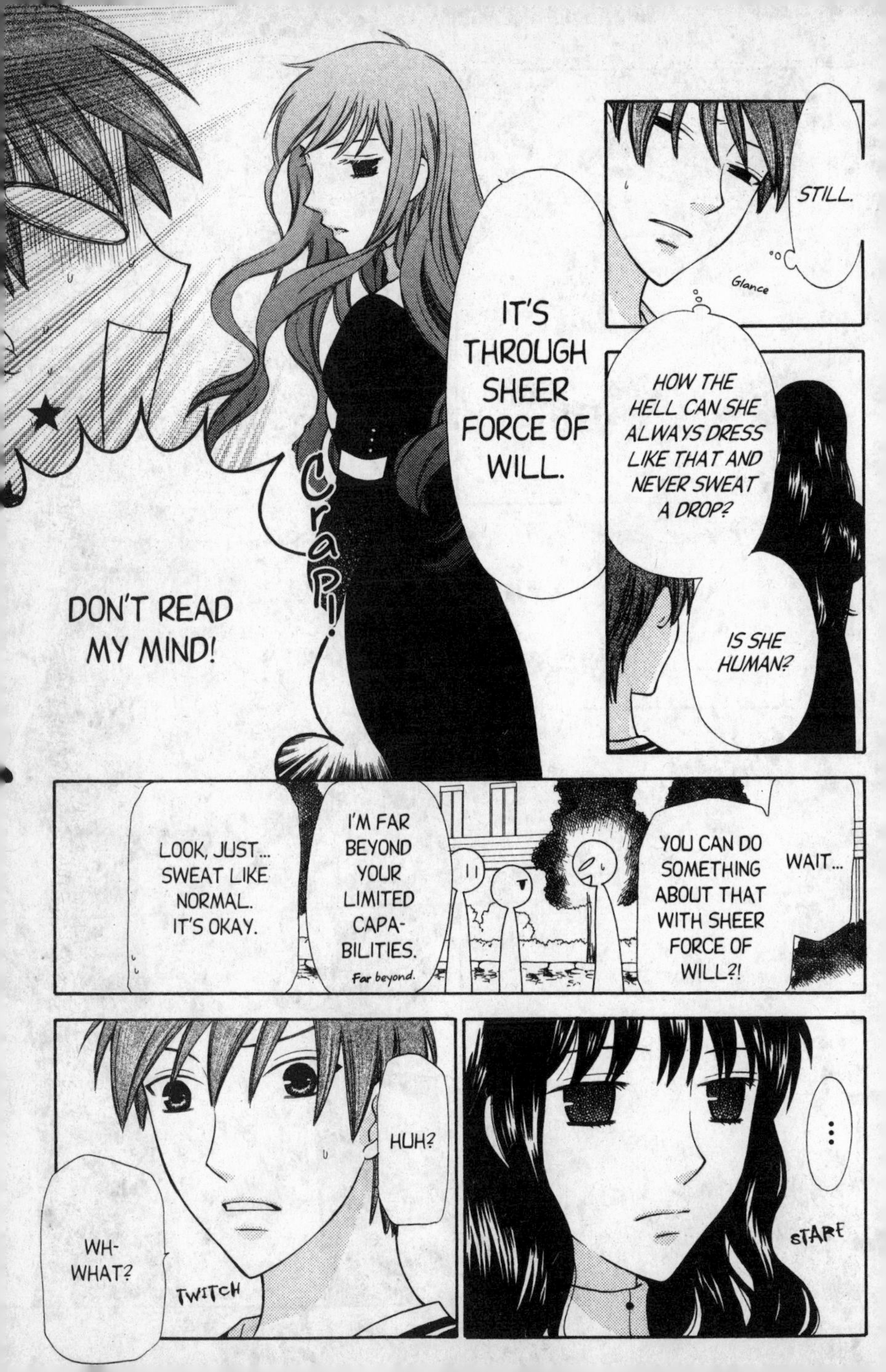
STILL.
Glance
HOW THE HELL CAN SHE ALWAYS DRESS LIKE THAT AND NEVER SWEAT A DROP?
IS SHE HUMAN?
IT'S THROUGH SHEER FORCE OF WILL.
Crap!
DON'T READ MY MIND!
WAIT...
YOU CAN DO SOMETHING ABOUT THAT WITH SHEER FORCE OF WILL?!
I'M FAR BEYOND YOUR LIMITED CAPA-BILITIES.
Far beyond.
LOOK, JUST... SWEAT LIKE NORMAL. IT'S OKAY.
...
STARE
HUH?
WH-WHAT?
TWITCH

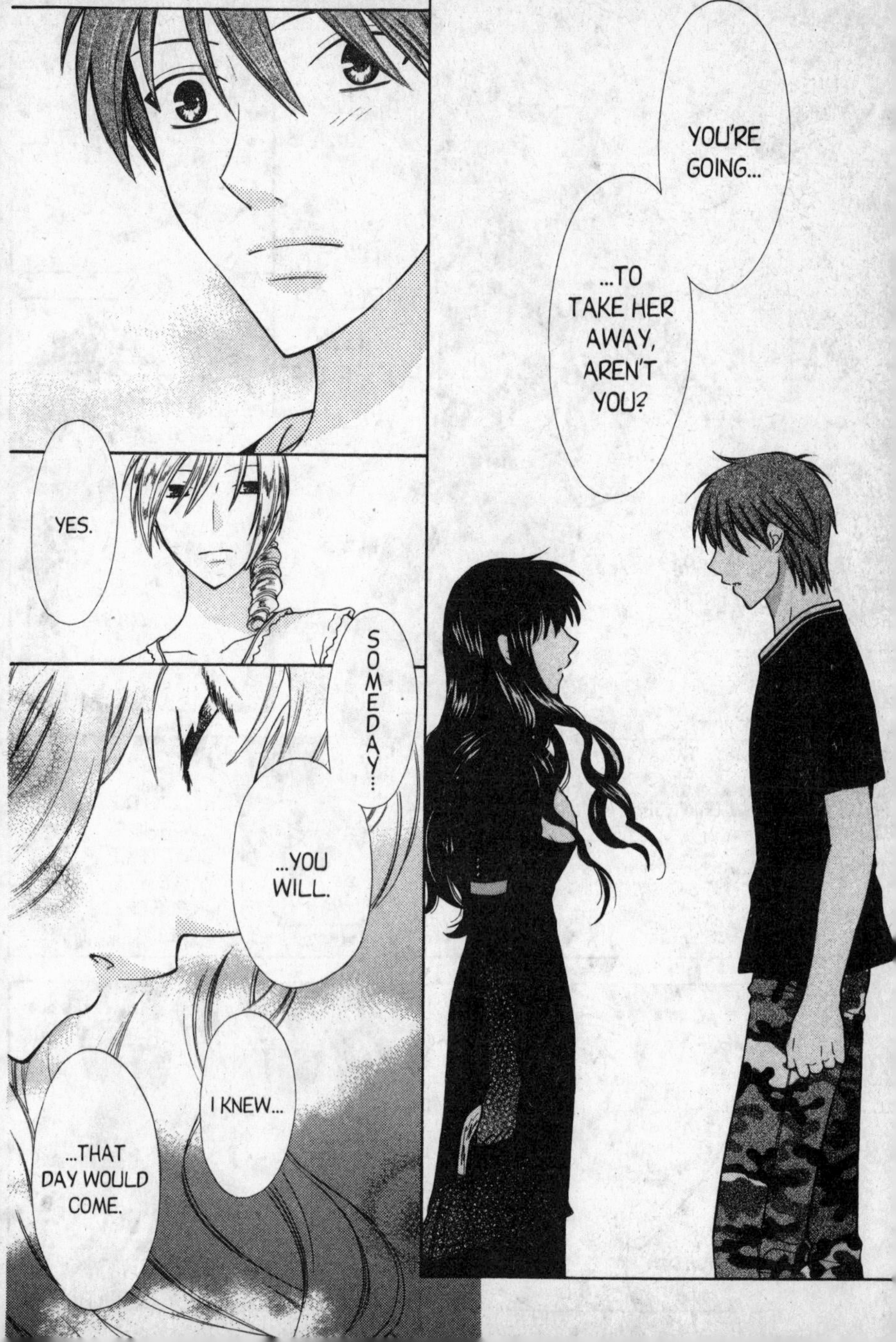
YOU'RE GOING...
...TO TAKE HER AWAY, AREN'T YOU?
YES.
SOMEDAY...
...YOU WILL.
I KNEW...
...THAT DAY WOULD COME.

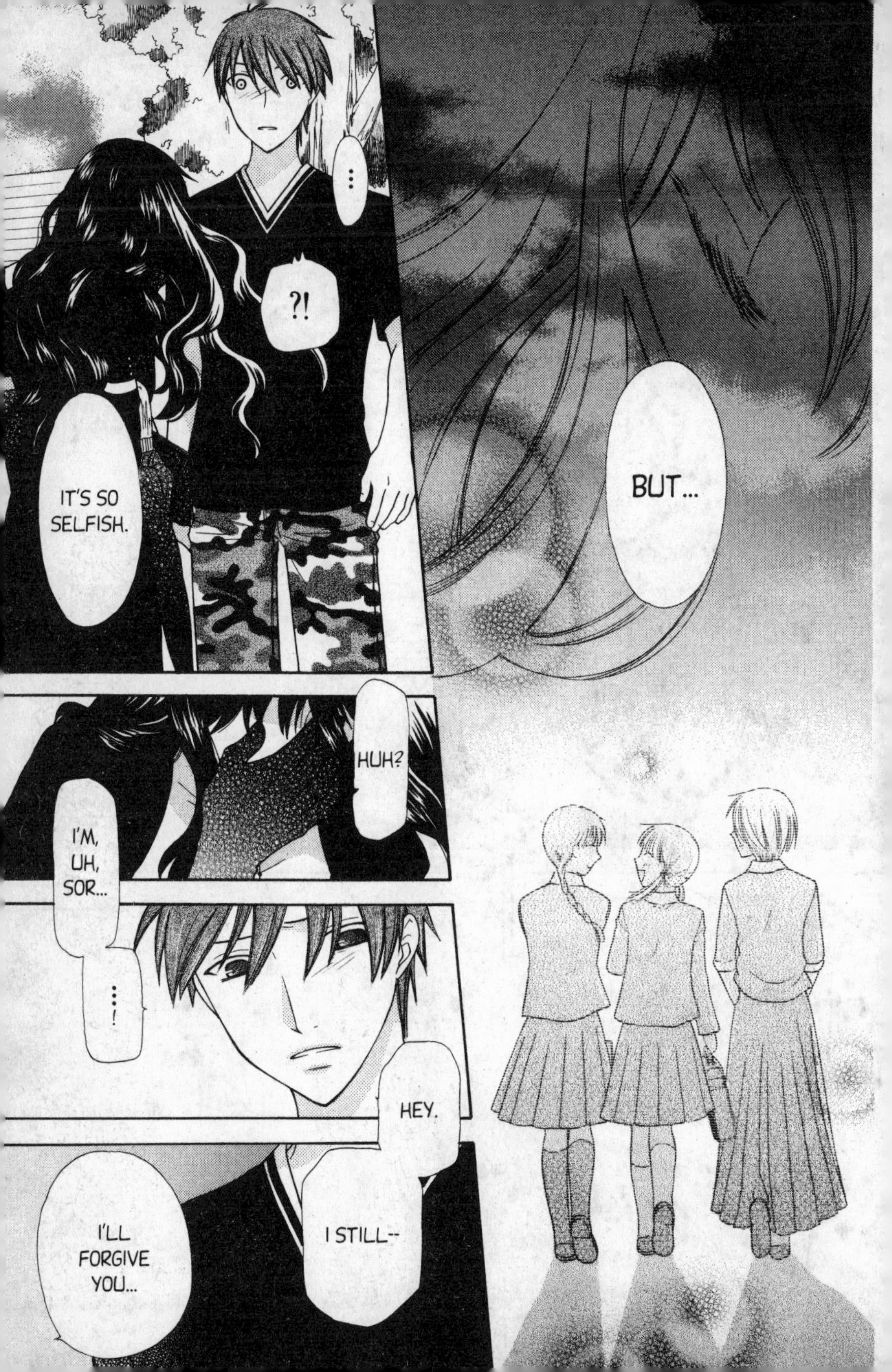
BUT...
...
?!
IT'S SO SELFISH.
HUH?
I'M, UH, SOR...
...!
HEY.
I STILL--
I'LL FORGIVE YOU...

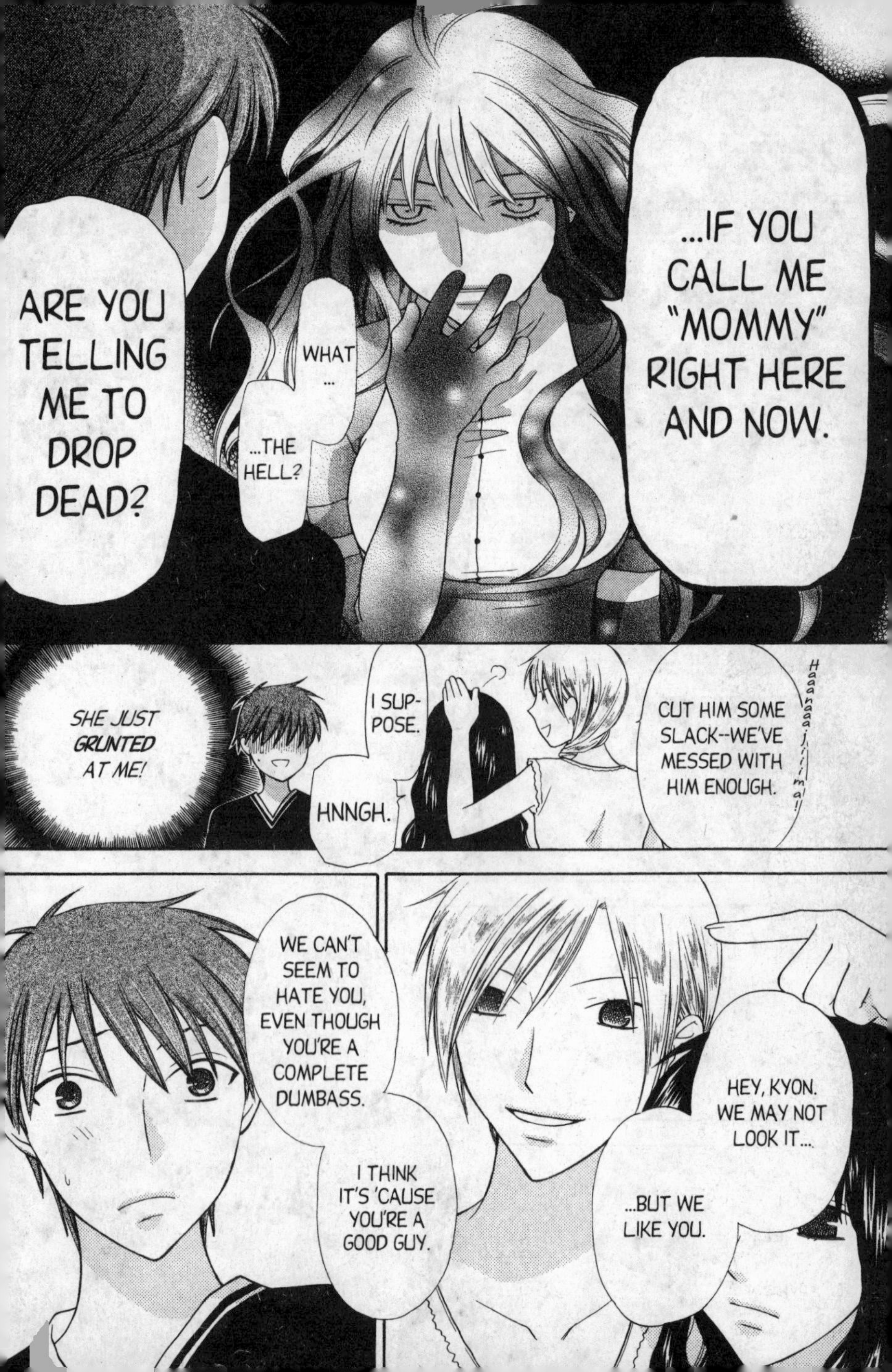
...IF YOU CALL ME "MOMMY" RIGHT HERE AND NOW.
WHAT ... ...THE HELL?
ARE YOU TELLING ME TO DROP DEAD?
CUT HIM SOME SLACK--WE'VE MESSED WITH HIM ENOUGH.
I SUP-POSE.
HNNGH.
SHE JUST GRUNTED AT ME!
HEY, KYON. WE MAY NOT LOOK IT...
...BUT WE LIKE YOU.
WE CAN'T SEEM TO HATE YOU, EVEN THOUGH YOU'RE A COMPLETE DUMBASS.
I THINK IT'S 'CAUSE YOU'RE A GOOD GUY.

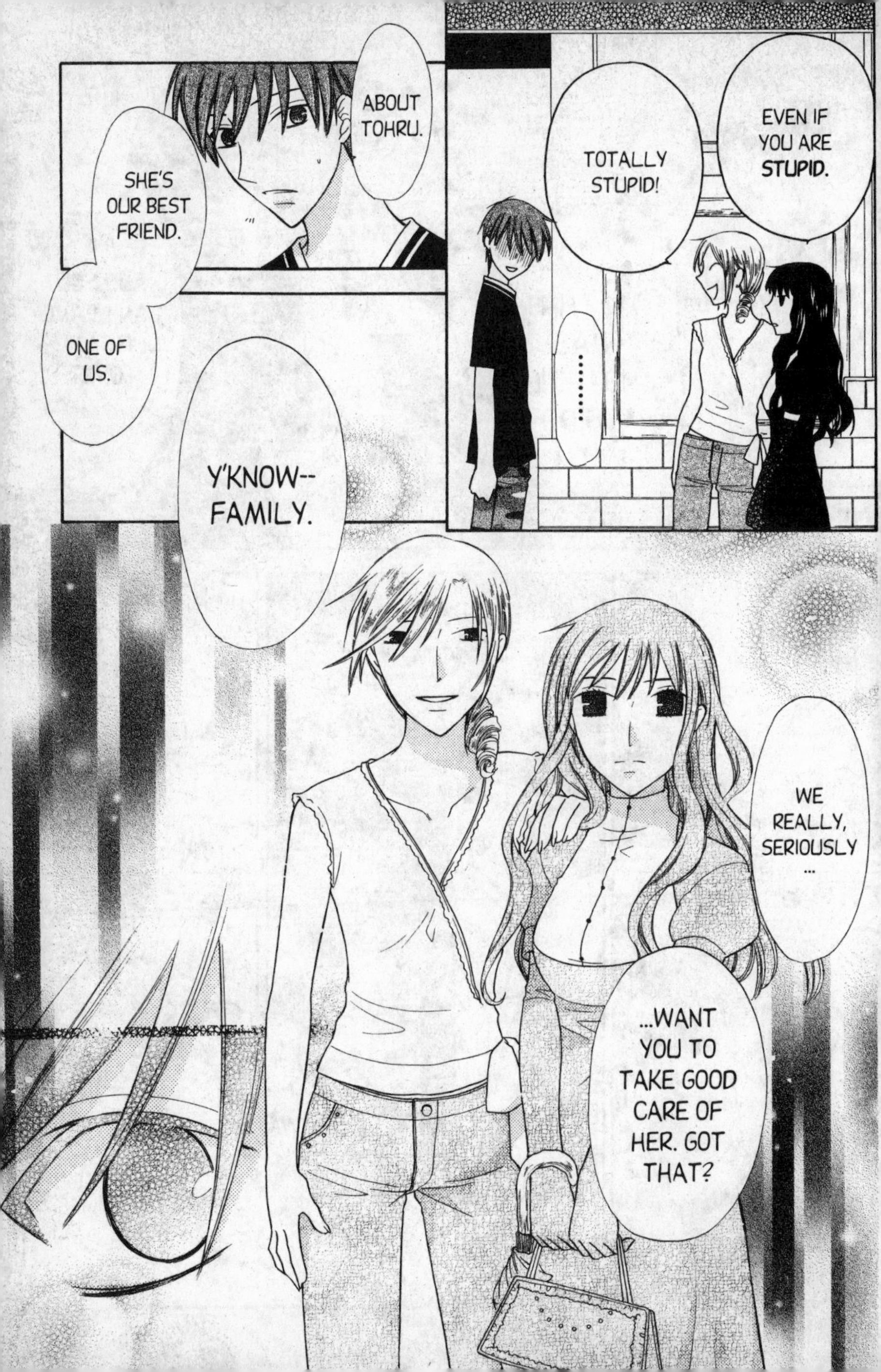
EVEN IF YOU ARE **STUPID.**
TOTALLY **STUPID!**
....
ABOUT TOHRU.
SHE'S OUR BEST FRIEND.
ONE OF US.
Y'KNOW-- FAMILY.
WE REALLY, SERIOUSLY ...
...WANT YOU TO TAKE GOOD CARE OF HER. GOT THAT?

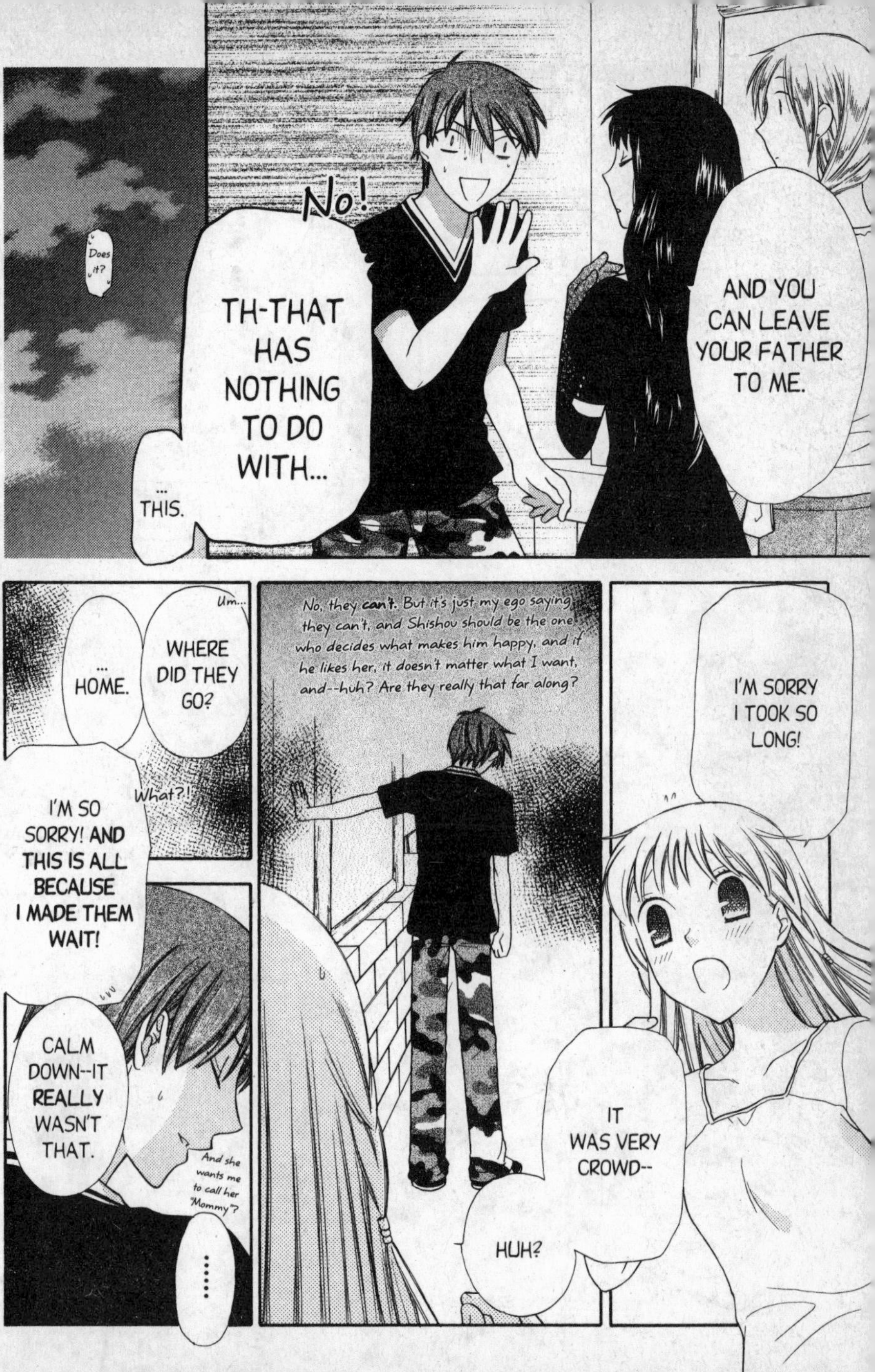
AND YOU CAN LEAVE YOUR FATHER TO ME.
No!
TH-THAT HAS NOTHING TO DO WITH...
... THIS.
Does it?
I'M SORRY I TOOK SO LONG!
IT WAS VERY CROWD--
HUH?
No, they **can't**. But it's just my ego saying they can't, and Shishou should be the one who decides what makes him happy, and if he likes her, it doesn't matter what I want, and--huh? Are they really that far along?
Um...
WHERE DID THEY GO?
... HOME.
What?!
I'M SO SORRY! AND THIS IS ALL BECAUSE I MADE THEM WAIT!
CALM DOWN--IT **REALLY** WASN'T THAT.
And she wants me to call her "Mommy"?
......

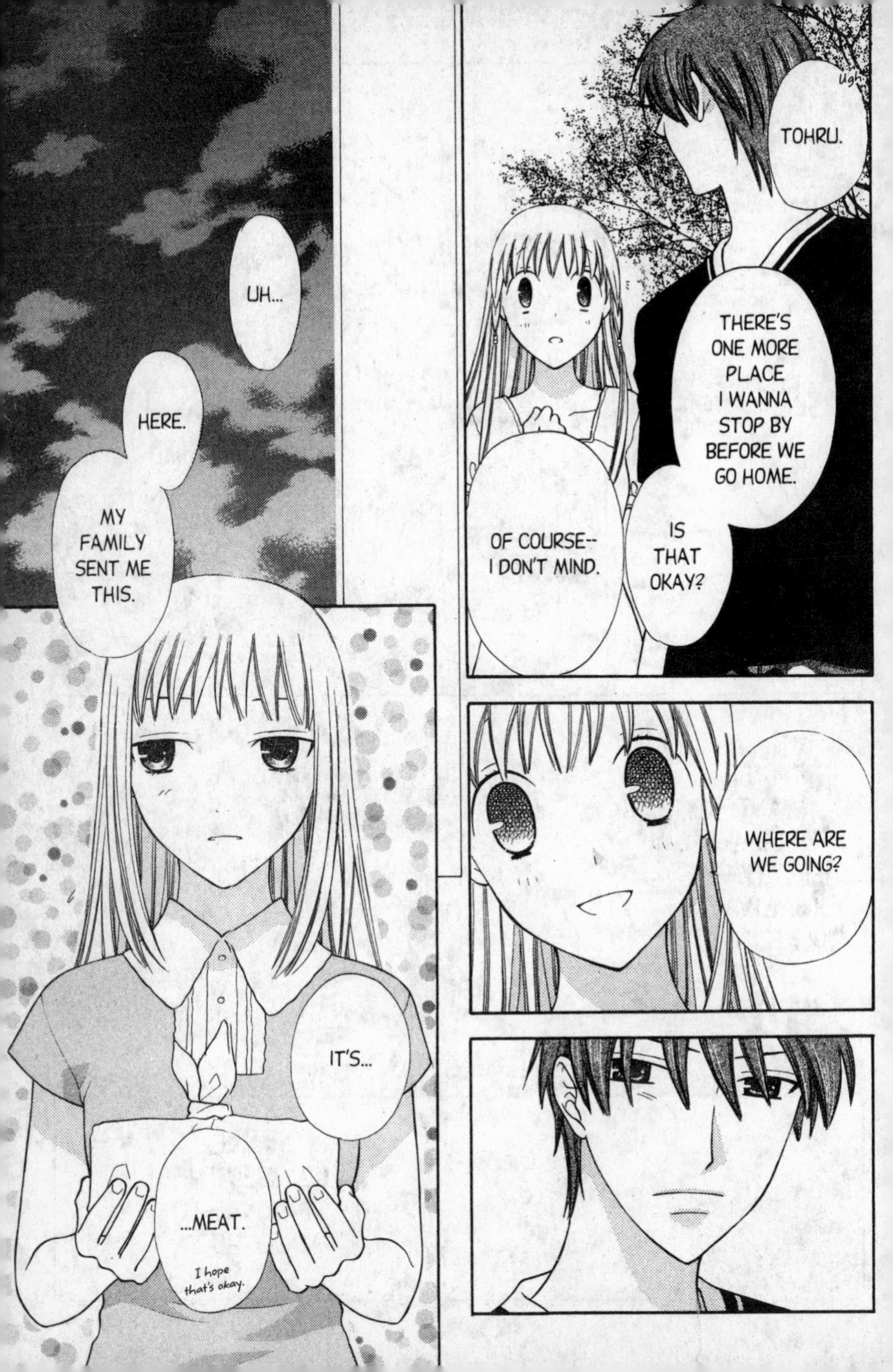
Ugh
TOHRU.
THERE'S ONE MORE PLACE I WANNA STOP BY BEFORE WE GO HOME.
IS THAT OKAY?
OF COURSE-- I DON'T MIND.
WHERE ARE WE GOING?
UH...
HERE.
MY FAMILY SENT ME THIS.
IT'S...
...MEAT.
I hope that's okay.

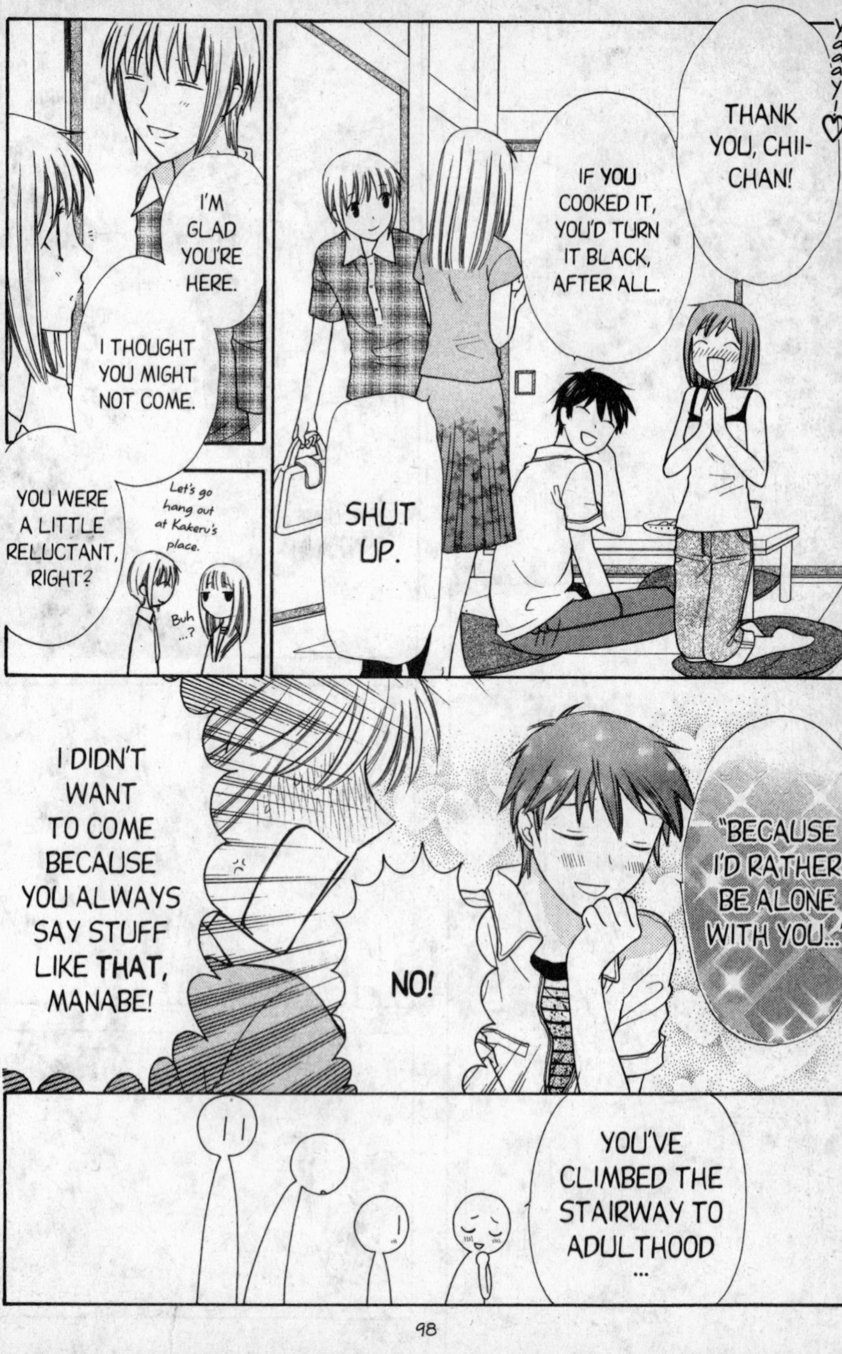

Yaaay!♡
THANK YOU, CHII-CHAN!
IF YOU COOKED IT, YOU'D TURN IT BLACK, AFTER ALL.
SHUT UP.
I'M GLAD YOU'RE HERE.
I THOUGHT YOU MIGHT NOT COME.
YOU WERE A LITTLE RELUCTANT, RIGHT?
Let's go hang out at Kakeru's place.
Buh ...?
"BECAUSE I'D RATHER BE ALONE WITH YOU..."
NO!
I DIDN'T WANT TO COME BECAUSE YOU ALWAYS SAY STUFF LIKE THAT, MANABE!
YOU'VE CLIMBED THE STAIRWAY TO ADULTHOOD ...

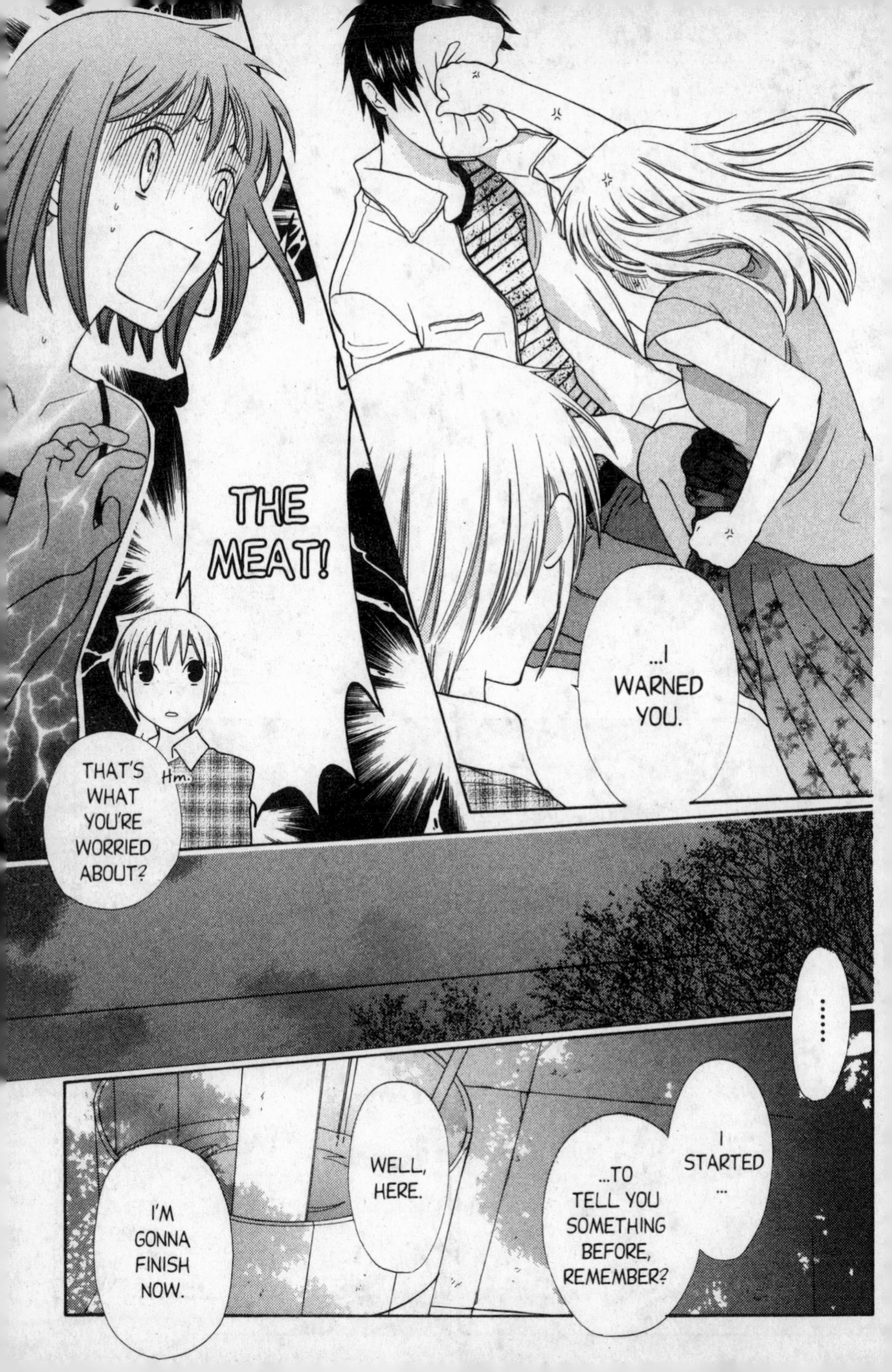
THE MEAT!
...I WARNED YOU.
Hm.
THAT'S WHAT YOU'RE WORRIED ABOUT?
......
I STARTED...
...TO TELL YOU SOMETHING BEFORE, REMEMBER?
WELL, HERE.
I'M GONNA FINISH NOW.

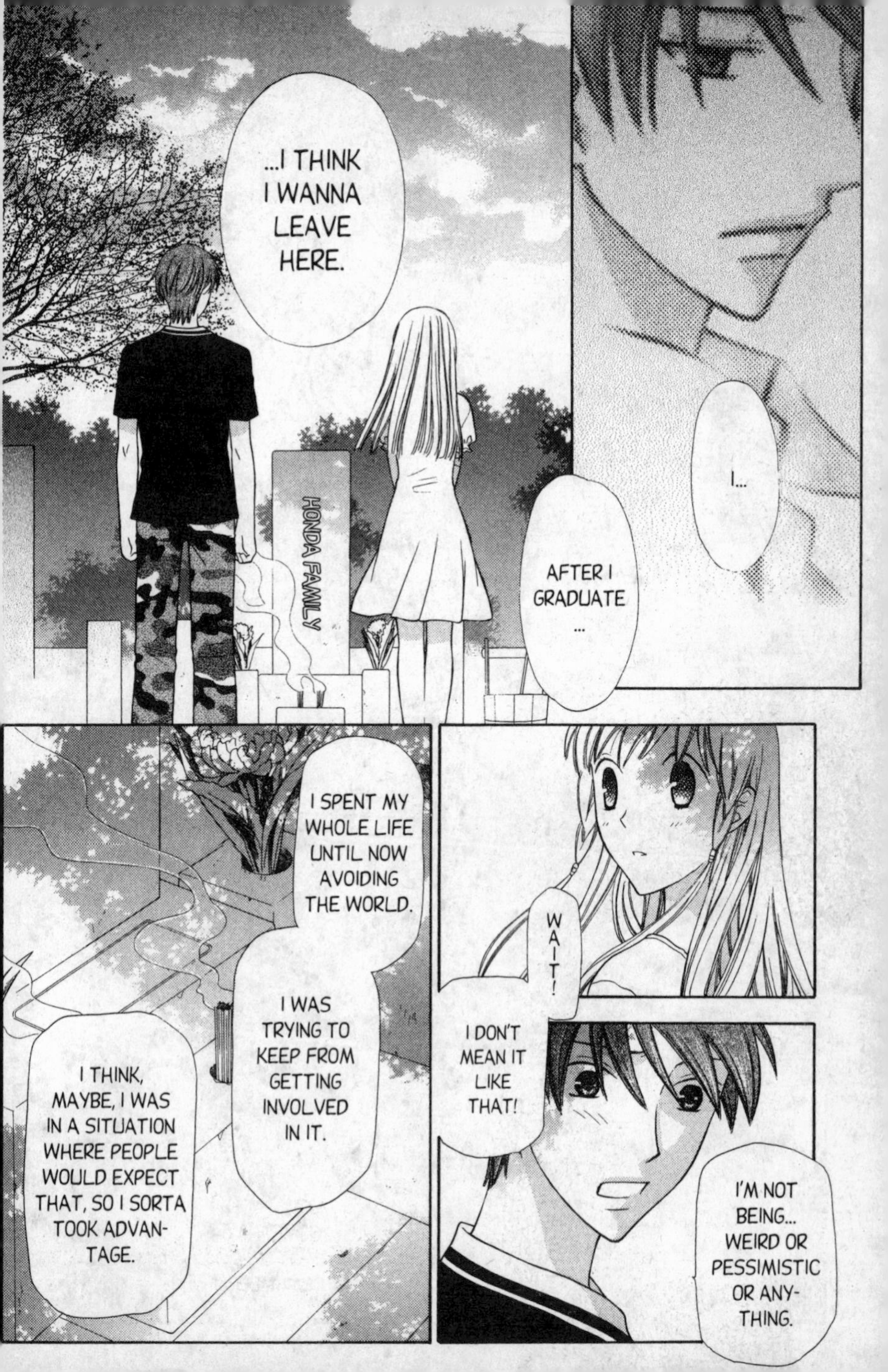
I...
AFTER I GRADUATE ...
...I THINK I WANNA LEAVE HERE.
HONDA FAMILY
WAIT!
I DON'T MEAN IT LIKE THAT!
I'M NOT BEING... WEIRD OR PESSIMISTIC OR ANY-THING.
I SPENT MY WHOLE LIFE UNTIL NOW AVOIDING THE WORLD.
I WAS TRYING TO KEEP FROM GETTING INVOLVED IN IT.
I THINK, MAYBE, I WAS IN A SITUATION WHERE PEOPLE WOULD EXPECT THAT, SO I SORTA TOOK ADVAN-TAGE.

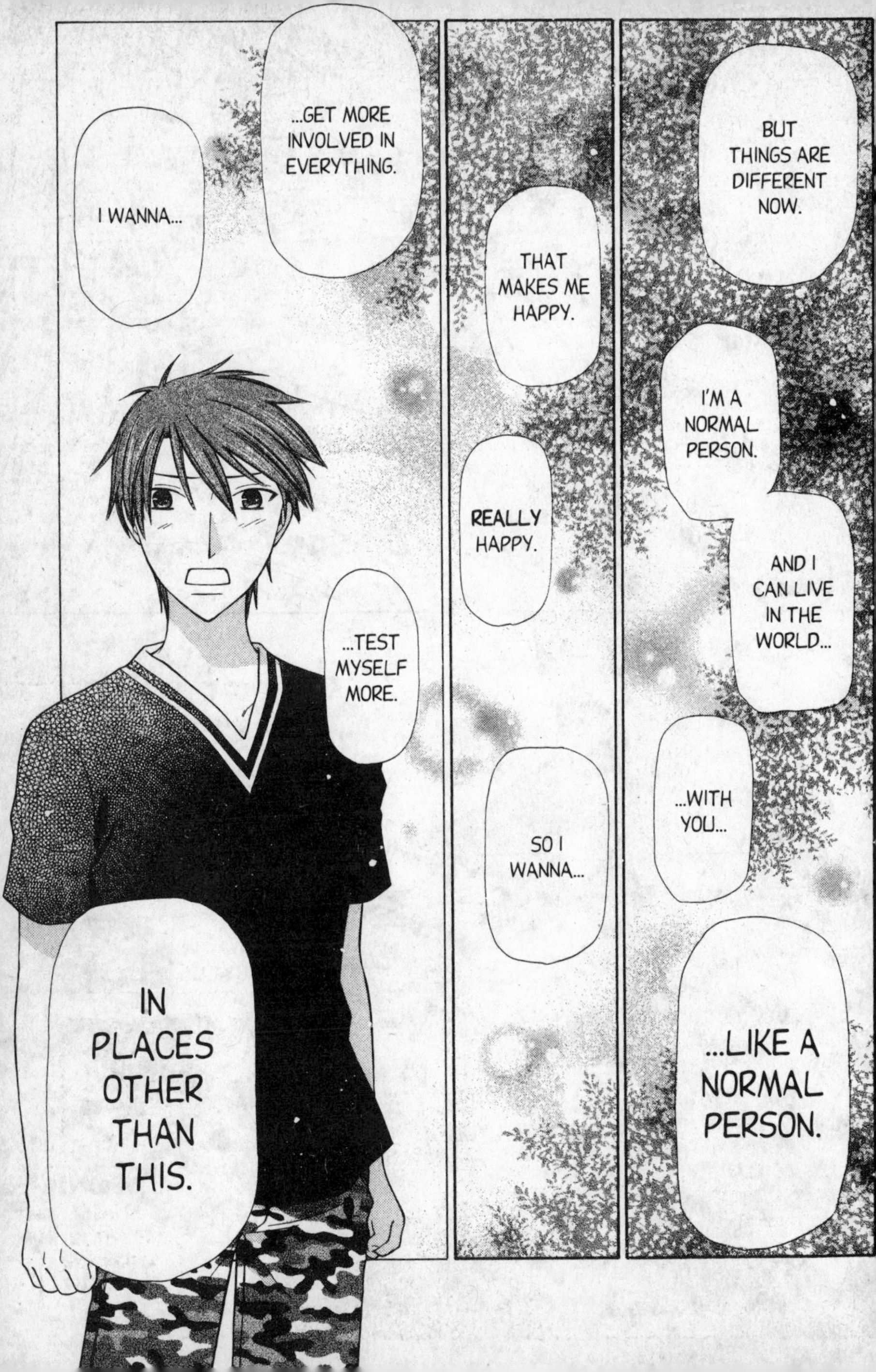
BUT THINGS ARE DIFFERENT NOW.
I'M A NORMAL PERSON.
AND I CAN LIVE IN THE WORLD...
...WITH YOU...
...LIKE A NORMAL PERSON.
THAT MAKES ME HAPPY.
REALLY HAPPY.
SO I WANNA...
...GET MORE INVOLVED IN EVERYTHING.
I WANNA...
...TEST MYSELF MORE.
IN PLACES OTHER THAN THIS.

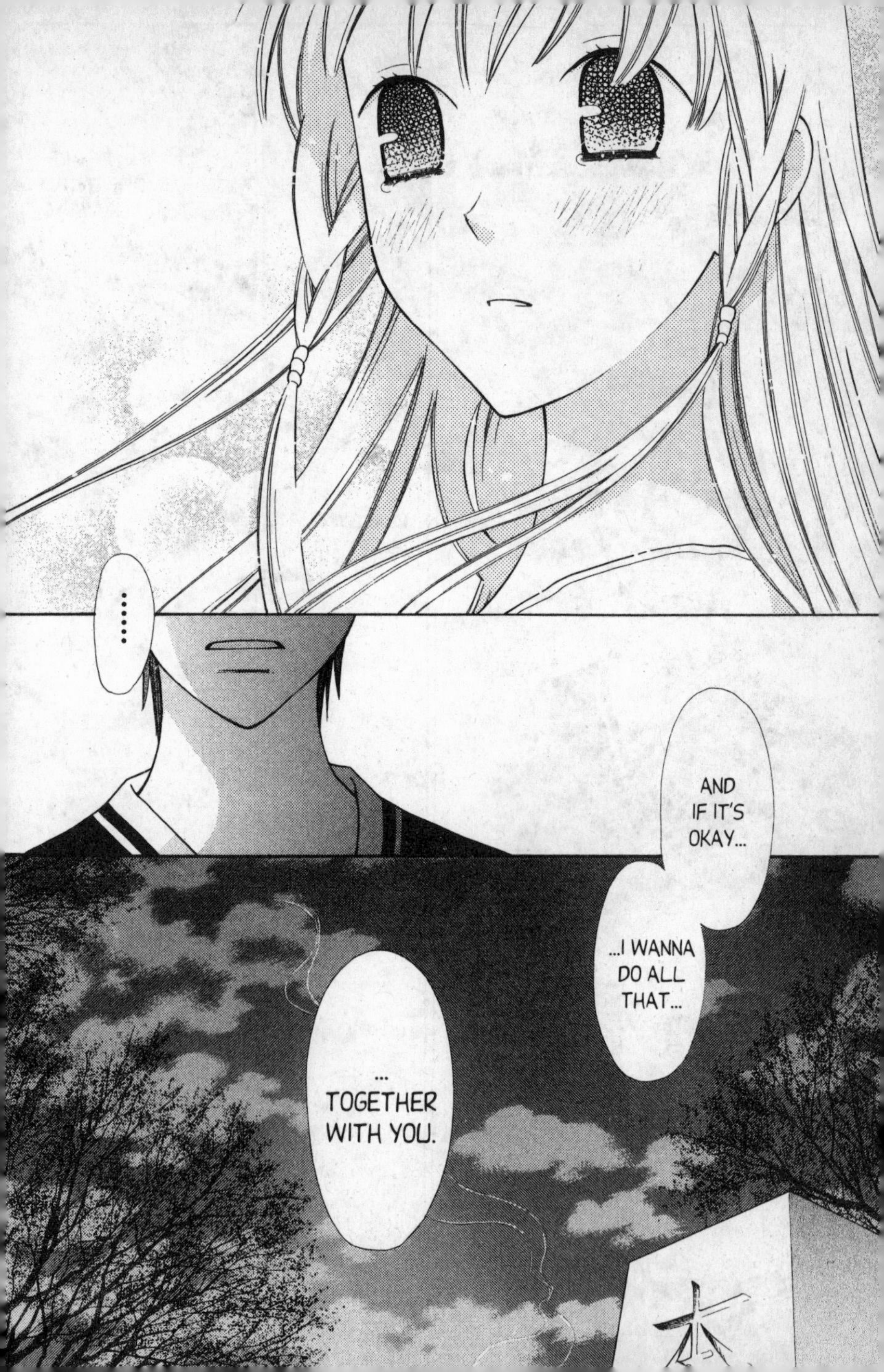
......
AND IF IT'S OKAY...
...I WANNA DO ALL THAT...
...TOGETHER WITH YOU.

Chapter 135

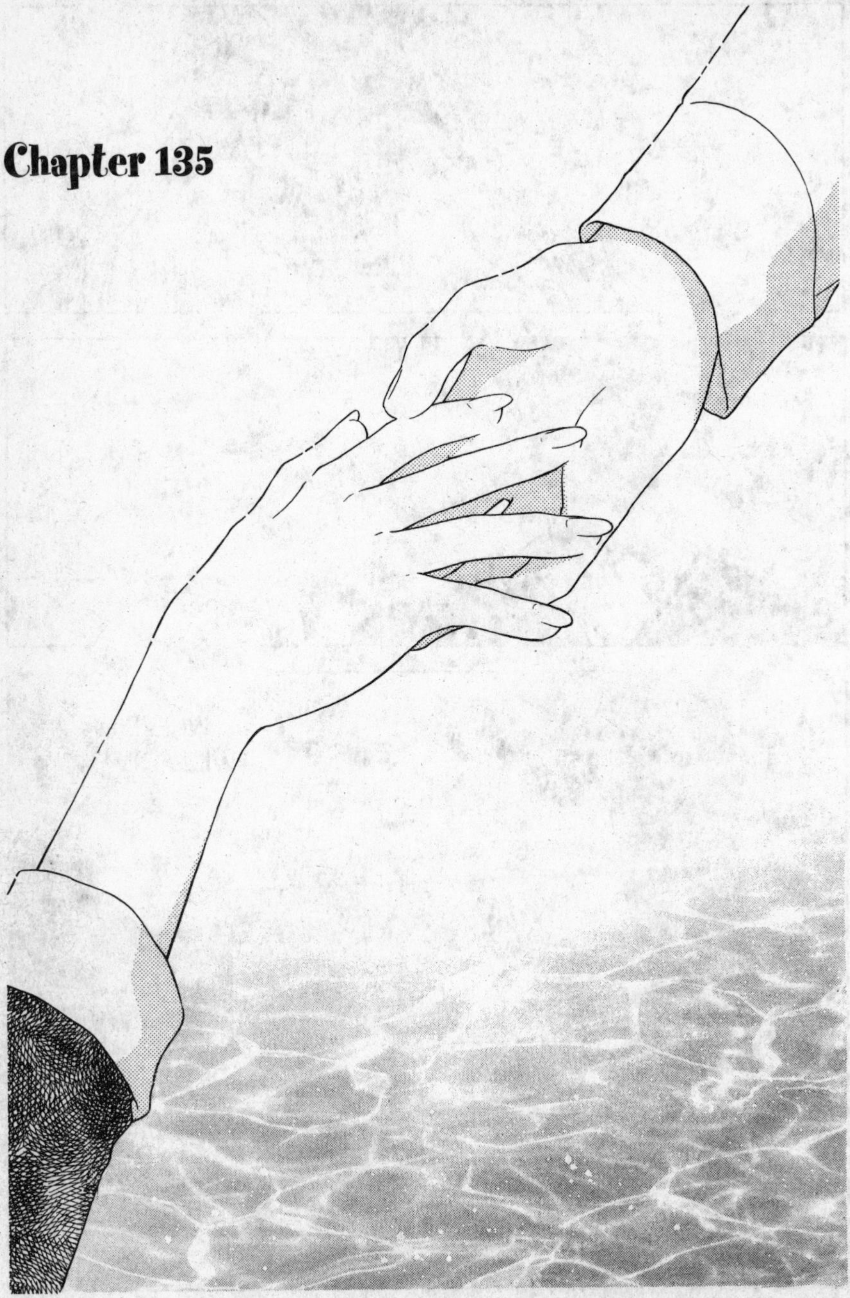

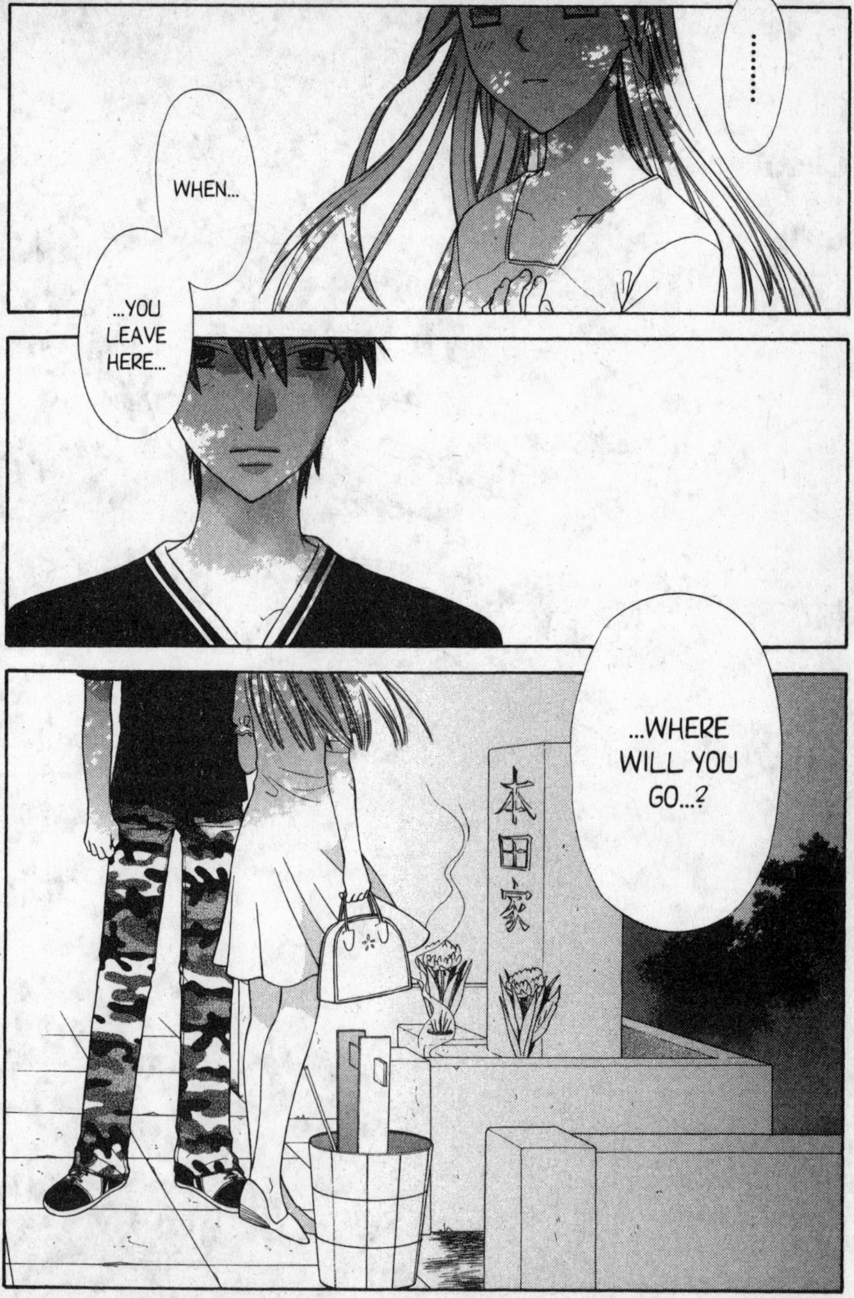
......
WHEN...
...YOU LEAVE HERE...
...WHERE WILL YOU GO...?
本田家

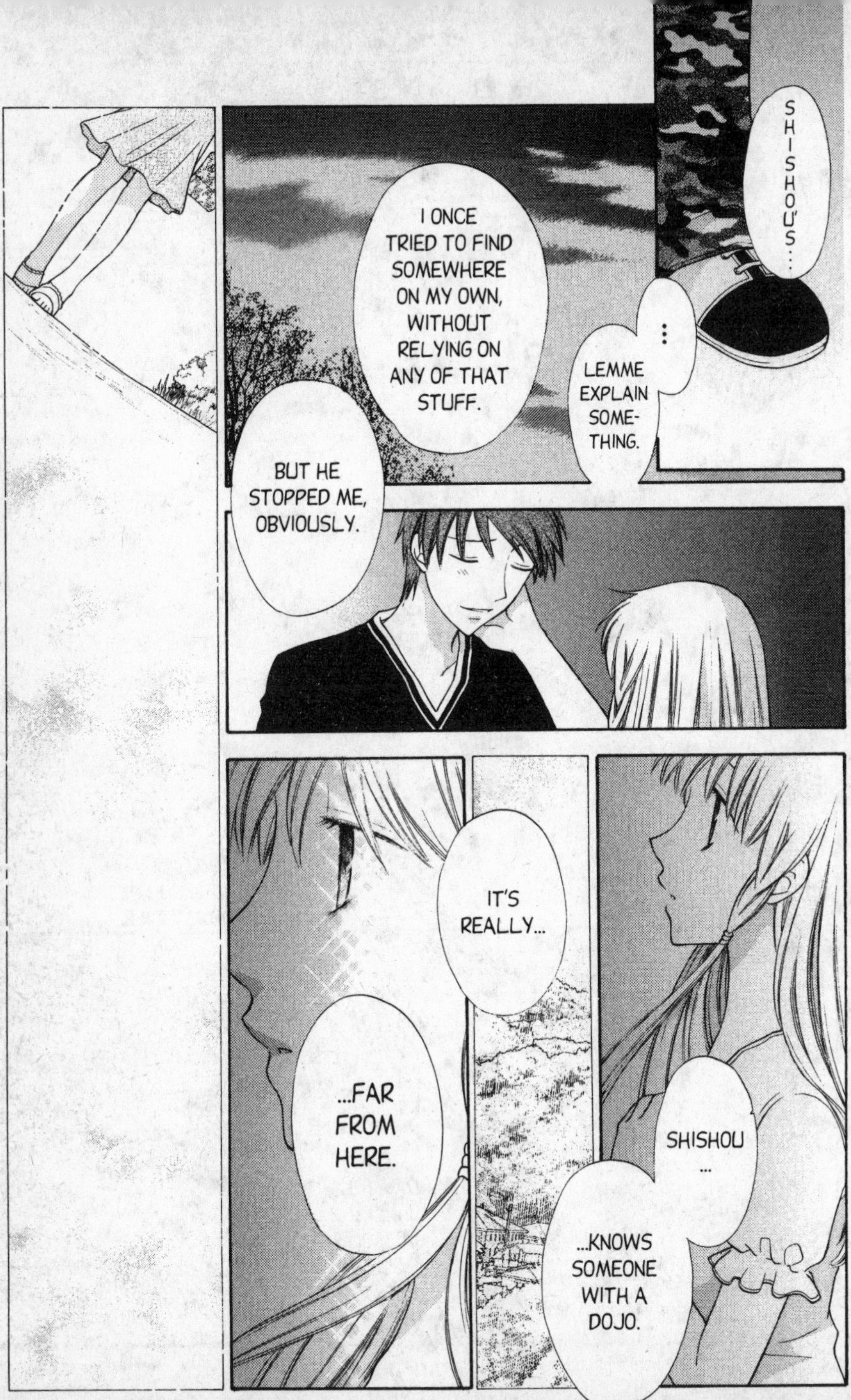
SHISHOU'S...
...
LEMME EXPLAIN SOME-THING.
I ONCE TRIED TO FIND SOMEWHERE ON MY OWN, WITHOUT RELYING ON ANY OF THAT STUFF.
BUT HE STOPPED ME, OBVIOUSLY.
SHISHOU...
...KNOWS SOMEONE WITH A DOJO.
IT'S REALLY...
...FAR FROM HERE.

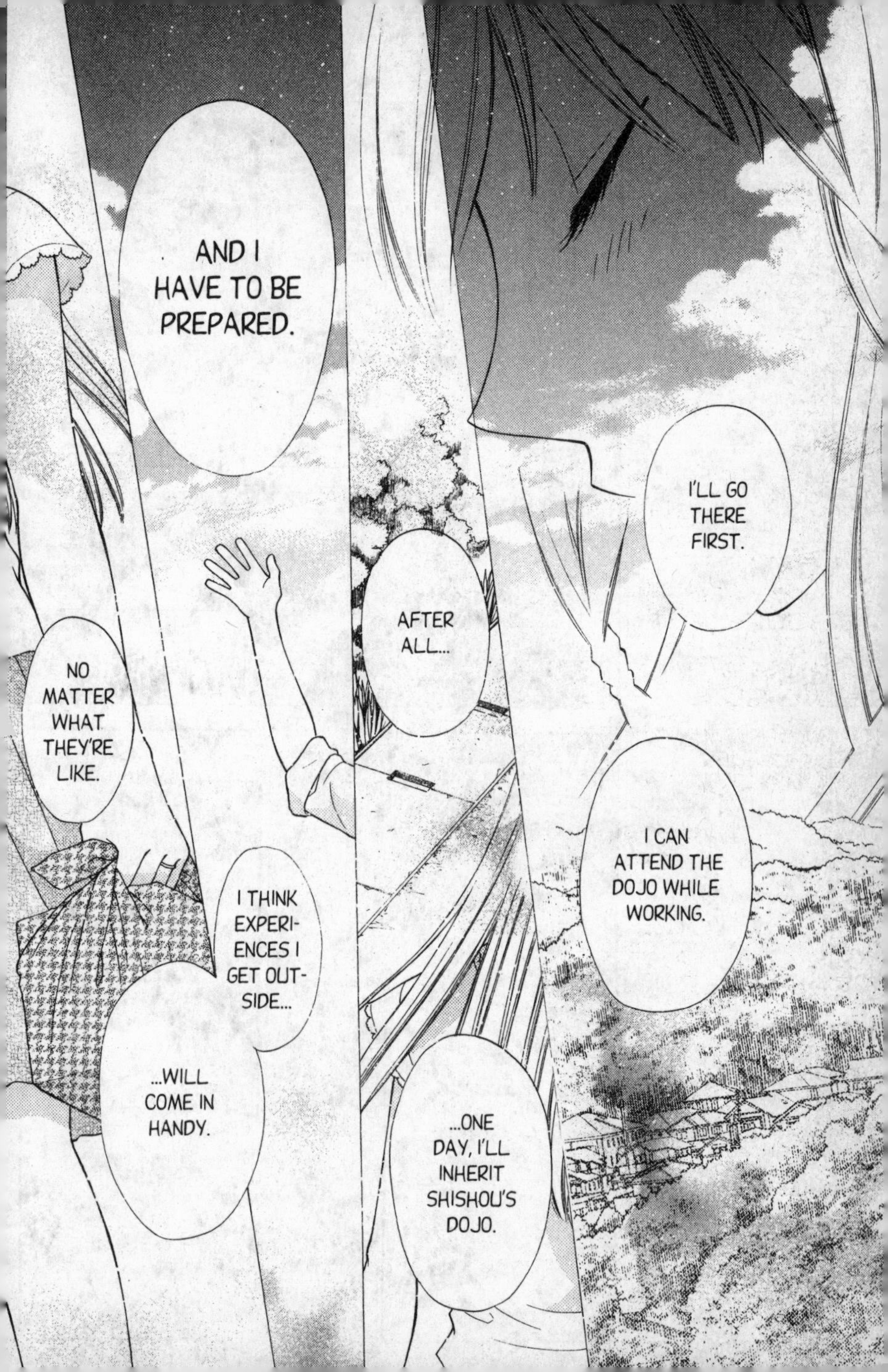

I'LL GO THERE FIRST.
I CAN ATTEND THE DOJO WHILE WORKING.
AFTER ALL...
...ONE DAY, I'LL INHERIT SHISHOU'S DOJO.
AND I HAVE TO BE PREPARED.
NO MATTER WHAT THEY'RE LIKE.
I THINK EXPERI- ENCES I GET OUT- SIDE...
...WILL COME IN HANDY.

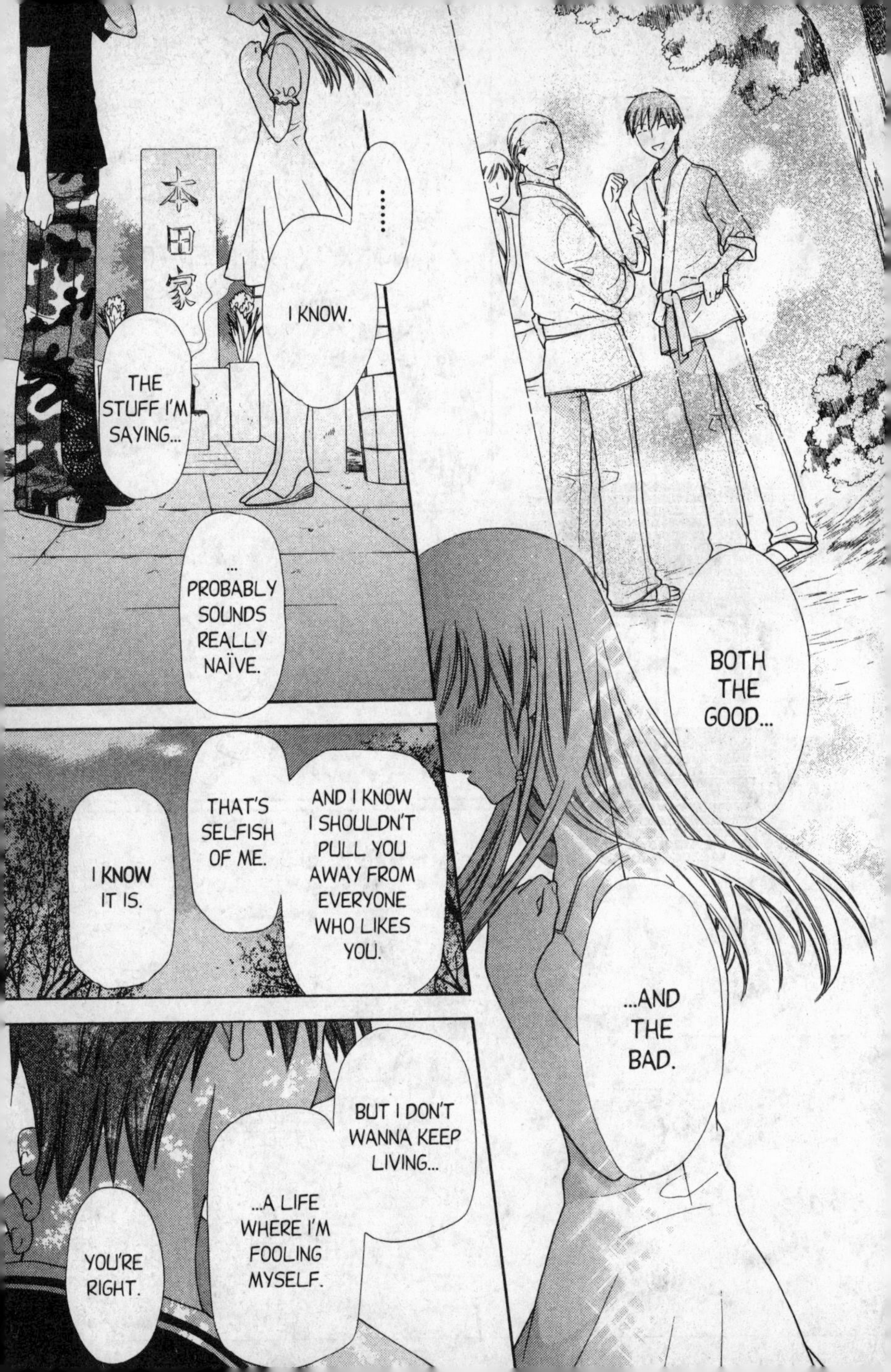
BOTH THE GOOD...
...AND THE BAD.
......
I KNOW.
本田家
THE STUFF I'M SAYING...
...PROBABLY SOUNDS REALLY NAÏVE.
AND I KNOW I SHOULDN'T PULL YOU AWAY FROM EVERYONE WHO LIKES YOU.
THAT'S SELFISH OF ME.
I KNOW IT IS.
BUT I DON'T WANNA KEEP LIVING...
...A LIFE WHERE I'M FOOLING MYSELF.
YOU'RE RIGHT.

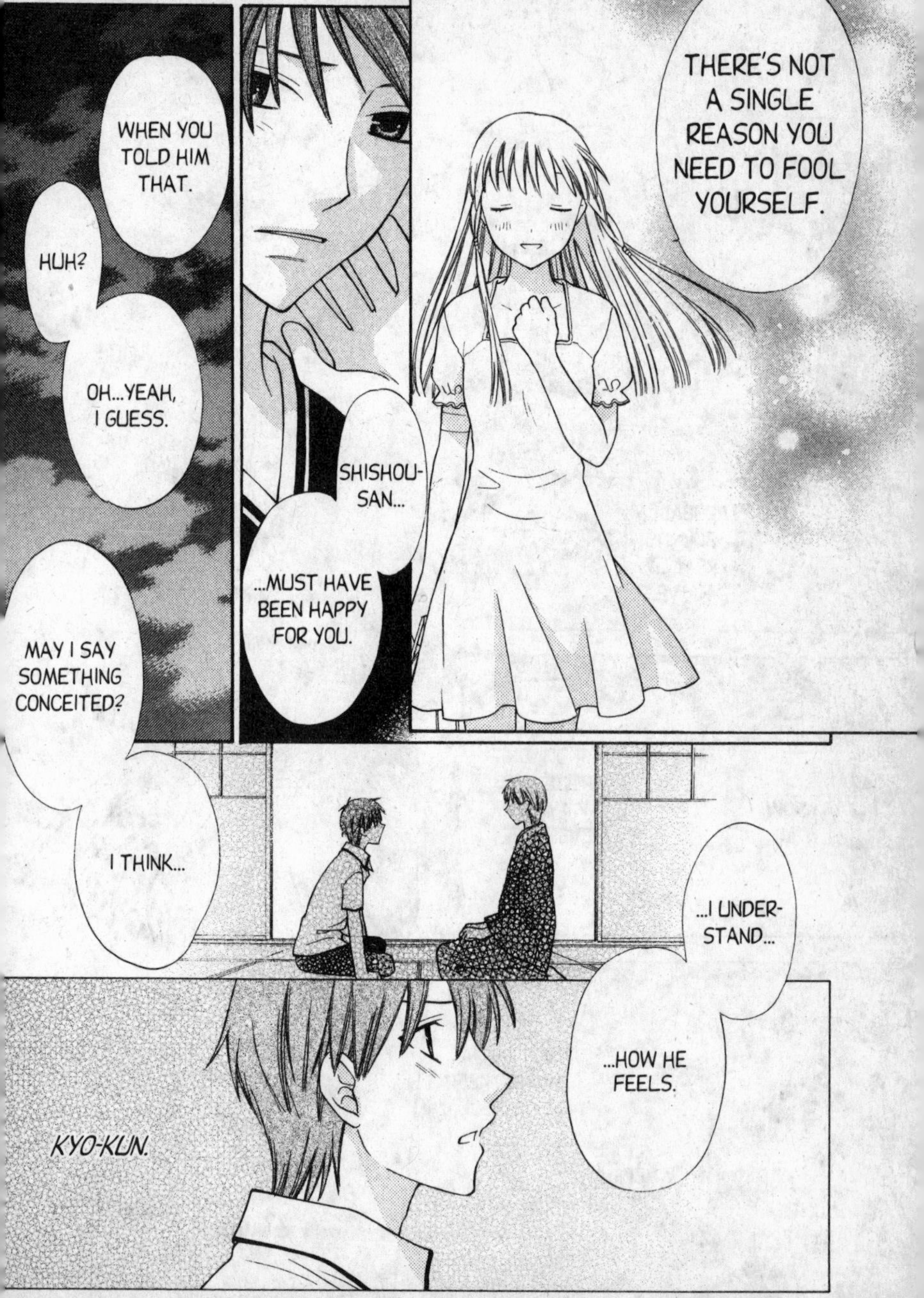
THERE'S NOT A SINGLE REASON YOU NEED TO FOOL YOURSELF.
SHISHOU-SAN...
...MUST HAVE BEEN HAPPY FOR YOU.
WHEN YOU TOLD HIM THAT.
HUH?
OH...YEAH, I GUESS.
MAY I SAY SOMETHING CONCEITED?
I THINK...
...I UNDERSTAND...
...HOW HE FEELS.
KYO-KUN.

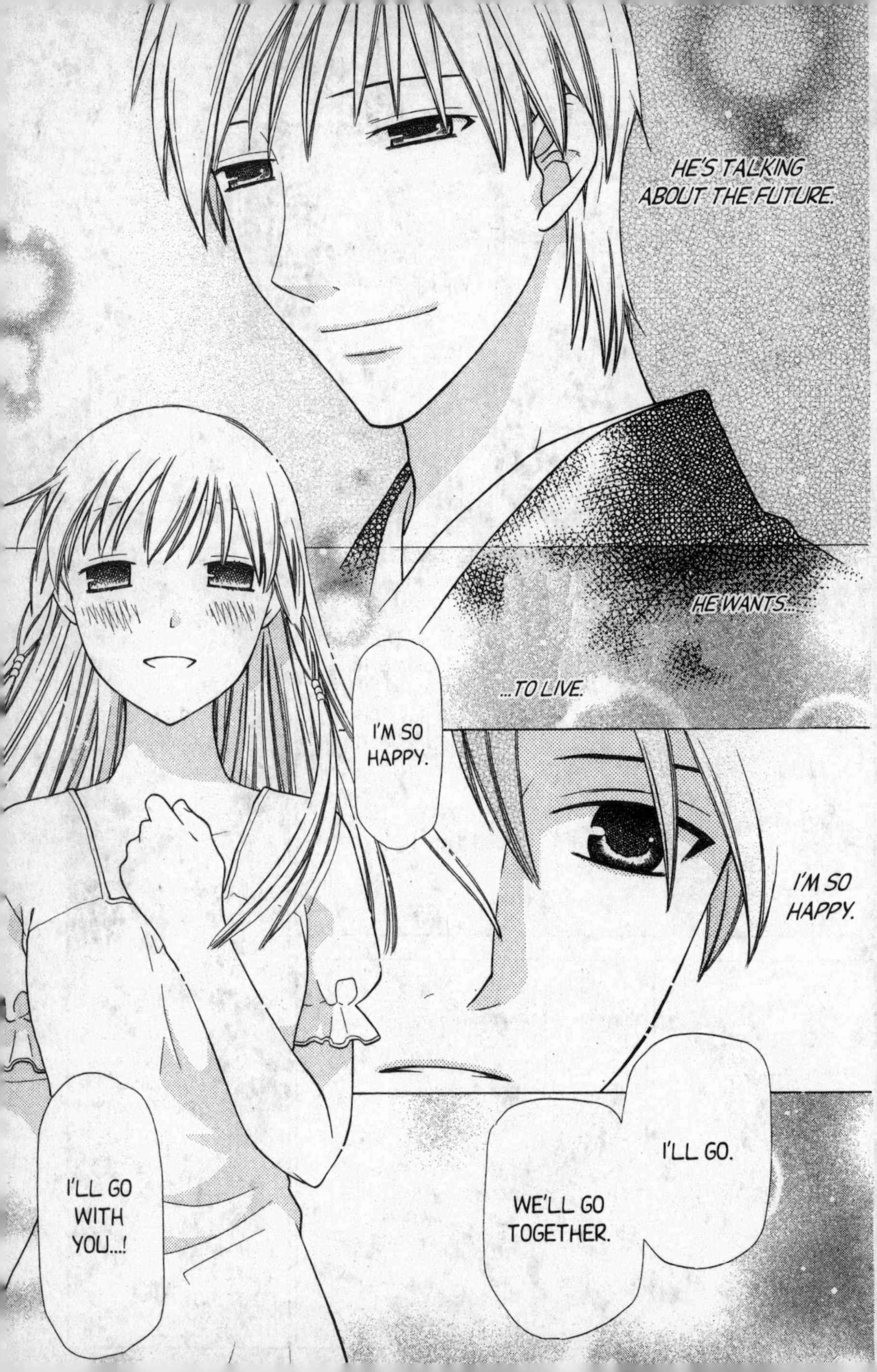
HE'S TALKING ABOUT THE FUTURE.
HE WANTS...
...TO LIVE.
I'M SO HAPPY.
I'M SO HAPPY.
I'LL GO.
WE'LL GO TOGETHER.
I'LL GO WITH YOU...!

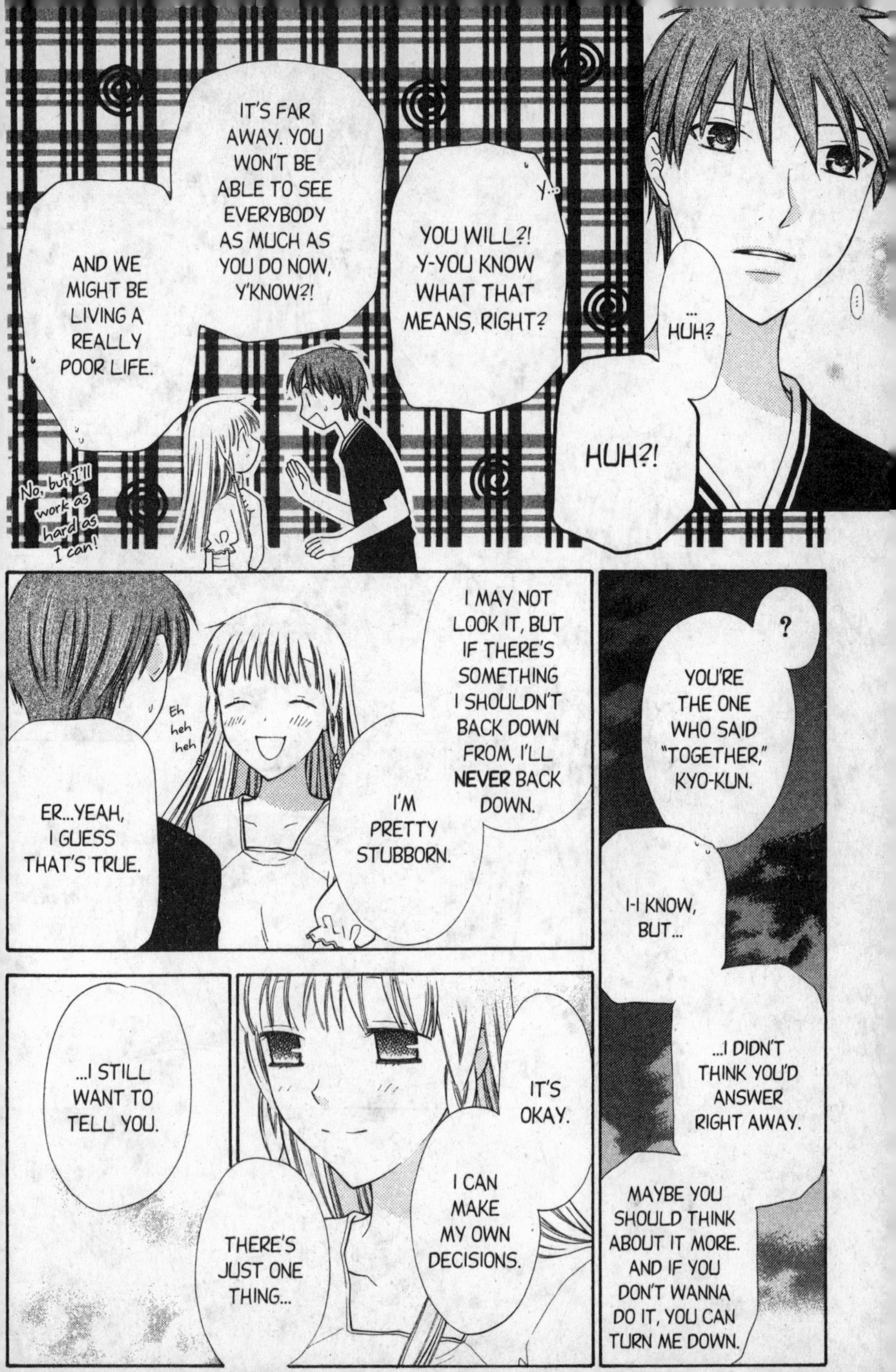
...HUH?
HUH?!
Y...
YOU WILL?! Y-YOU KNOW WHAT THAT MEANS, RIGHT?
IT'S FAR AWAY. YOU WON'T BE ABLE TO SEE EVERYBODY AS MUCH AS YOU DO NOW, Y'KNOW?!
AND WE MIGHT BE LIVING A REALLY POOR LIFE.
No, but I'll work as hard as I can!
?
YOU'RE THE ONE WHO SAID "TOGETHER," KYO-KUN.
I-I KNOW, BUT...
...I DIDN'T THINK YOU'D ANSWER RIGHT AWAY.
MAYBE YOU SHOULD THINK ABOUT IT MORE. AND IF YOU DON'T WANNA DO IT, YOU CAN TURN ME DOWN.
I MAY NOT LOOK IT, BUT IF THERE'S SOMETHING I SHOULDN'T BACK DOWN FROM, I'LL **NEVER** BACK DOWN.
I'M PRETTY STUBBORN.
Eh heh heh
ER...YEAH, I GUESS THAT'S TRUE.
IT'S OKAY.
I CAN MAKE MY OWN DECISIONS.
THERE'S JUST ONE THING...
...I STILL WANT TO TELL YOU.

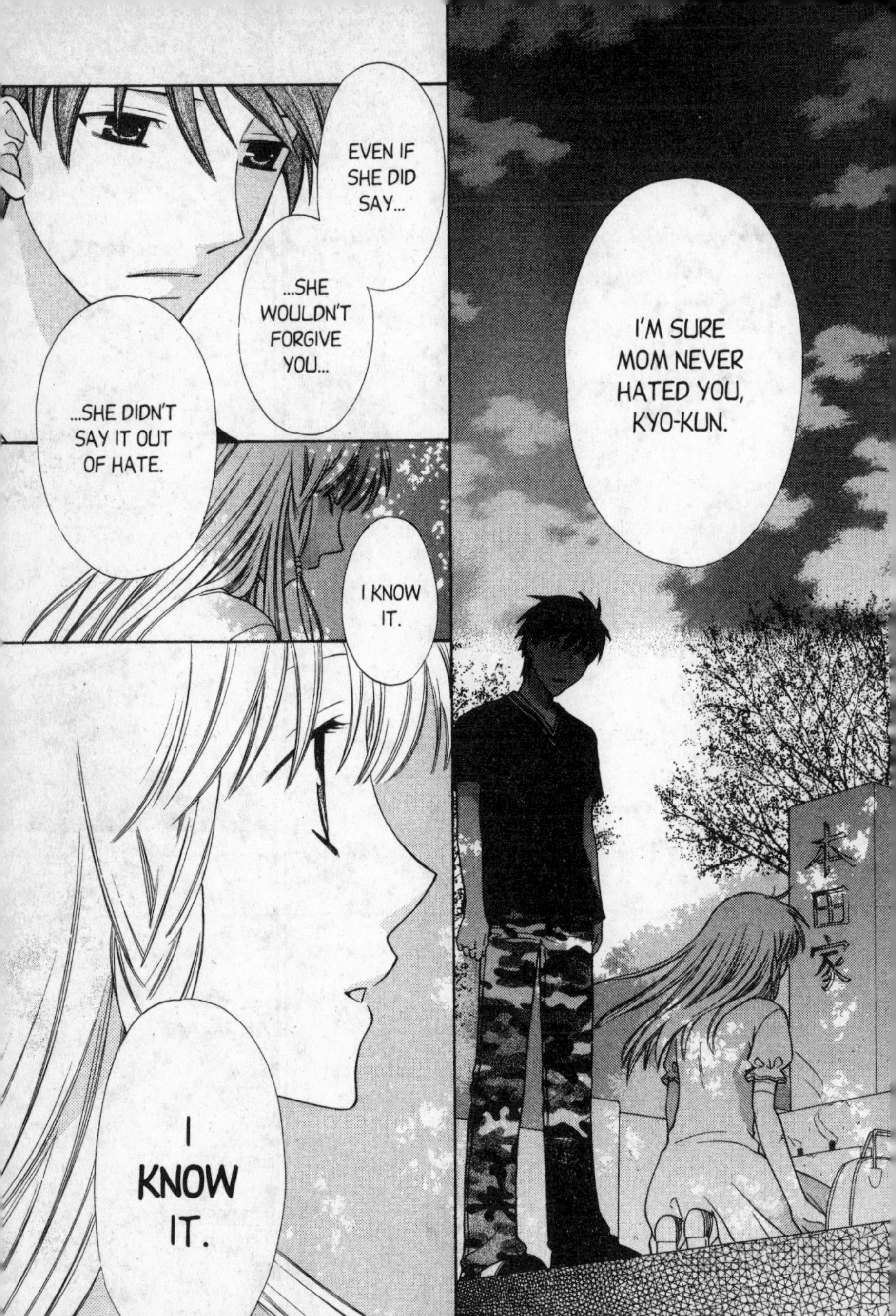
I'M SURE MOM NEVER HATED YOU, KYO-KUN.
本田家
EVEN IF SHE DID SAY...
...SHE WOULDN'T FORGIVE YOU...
...SHE DIDN'T SAY IT OUT OF HATE.
I KNOW IT.
I KNOW IT.

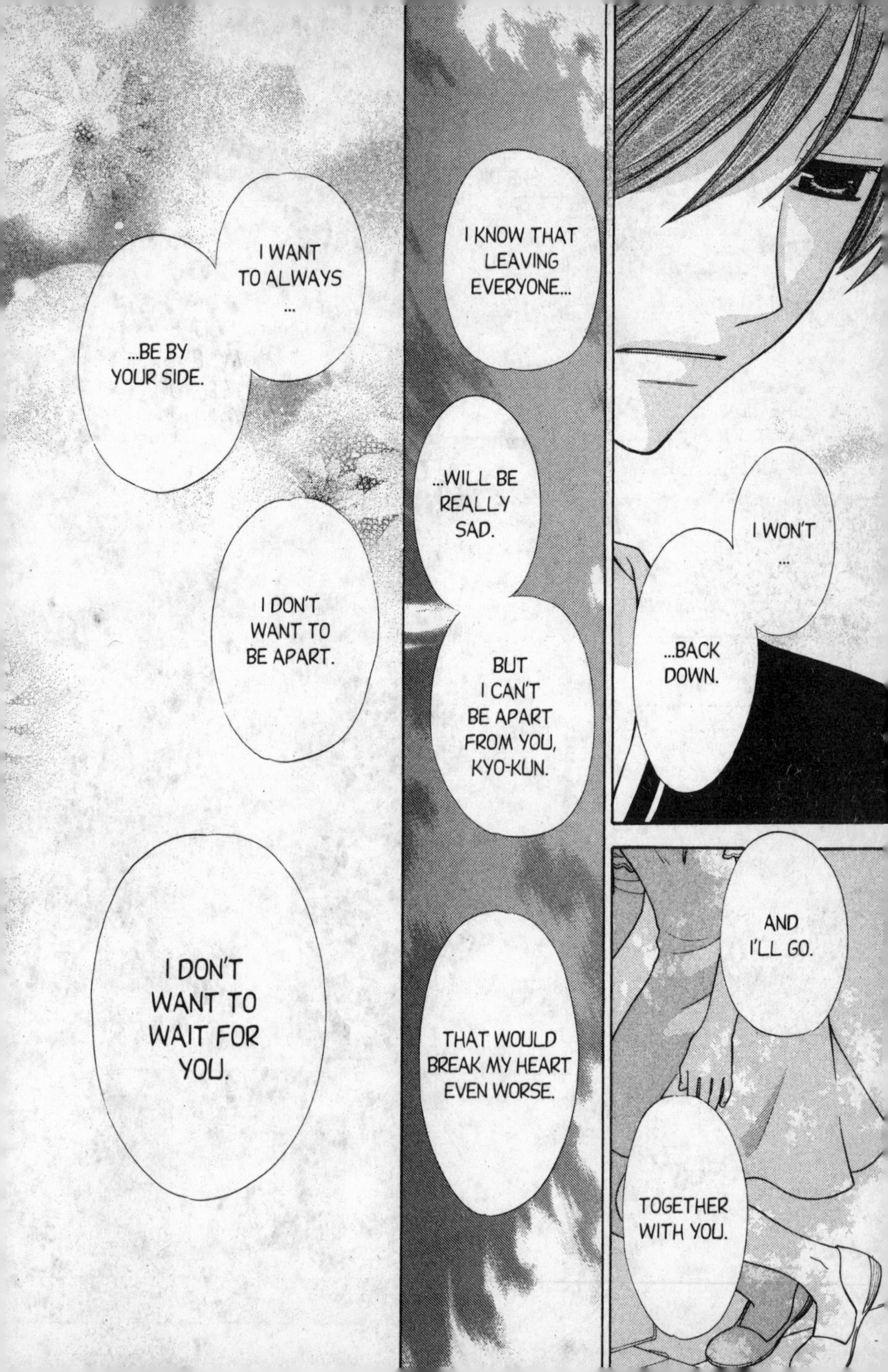
I WON'T
...
...BACK DOWN.
AND I'LL GO.
TOGETHER WITH YOU.
I KNOW THAT LEAVING EVERYONE...
...WILL BE REALLY SAD.
BUT I CAN'T BE APART FROM YOU, KYO-KUN.
THAT WOULD BREAK MY HEART EVEN WORSE.
I WANT TO ALWAYS
...
...BE BY YOUR SIDE.
I DON'T WANT TO BE APART.
I DON'T WANT TO WAIT FOR YOU.

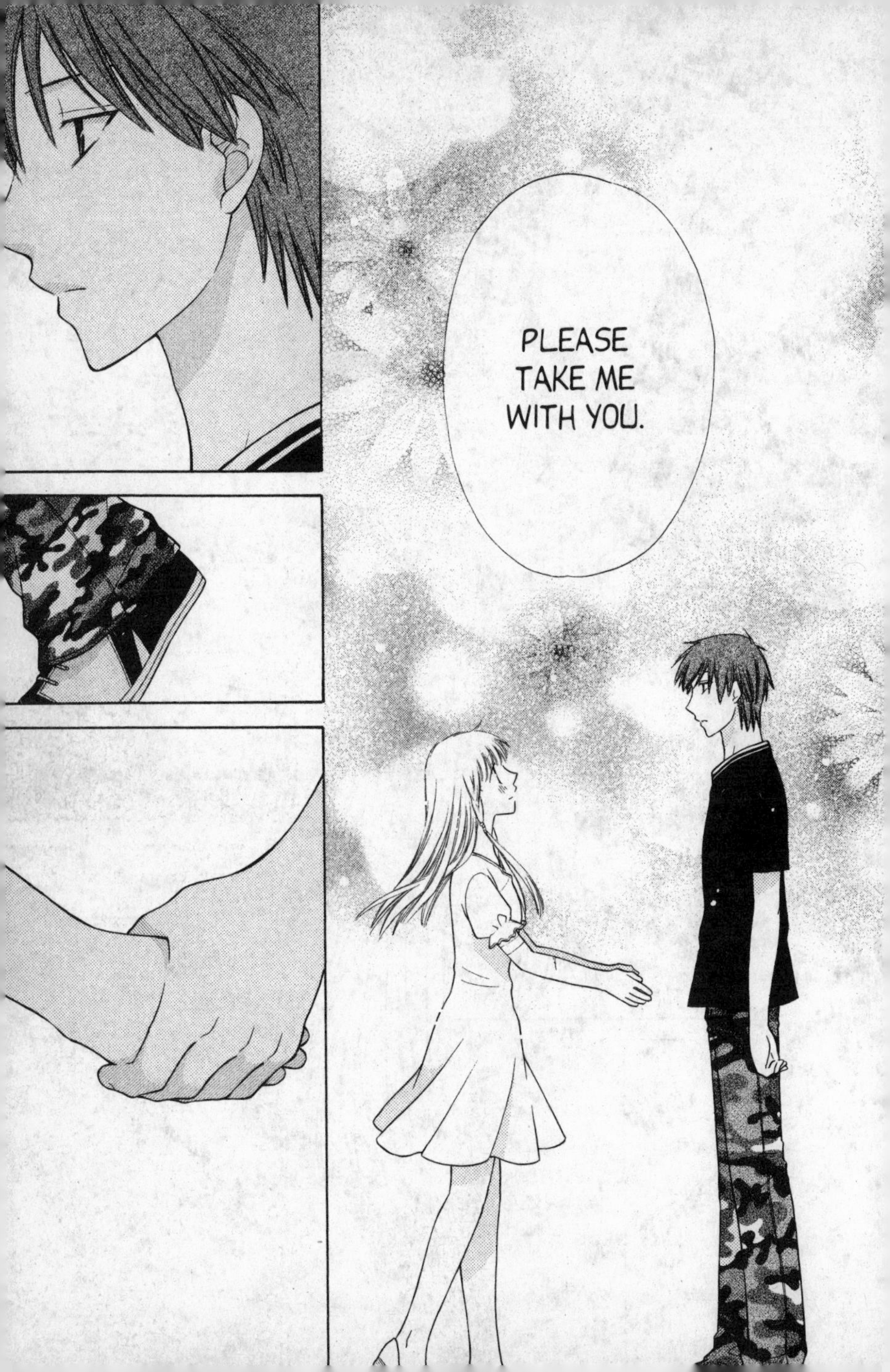
PLEASE TAKE ME WITH YOU.

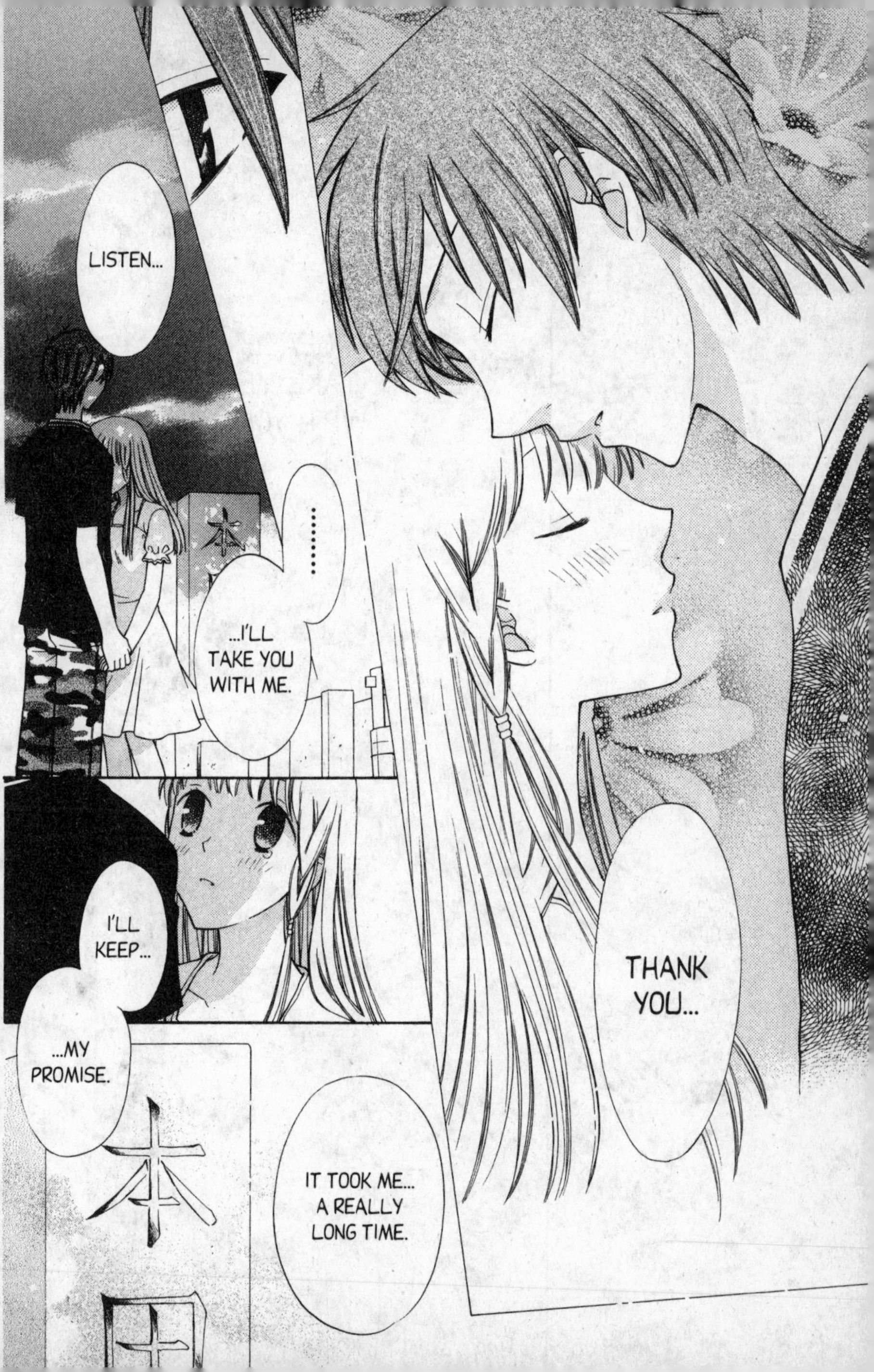
THANK YOU...
IT TOOK ME... A REALLY LONG TIME.
LISTEN...
......
...I'LL TAKE YOU WITH ME.
I'LL KEEP...
...MY PROMISE.

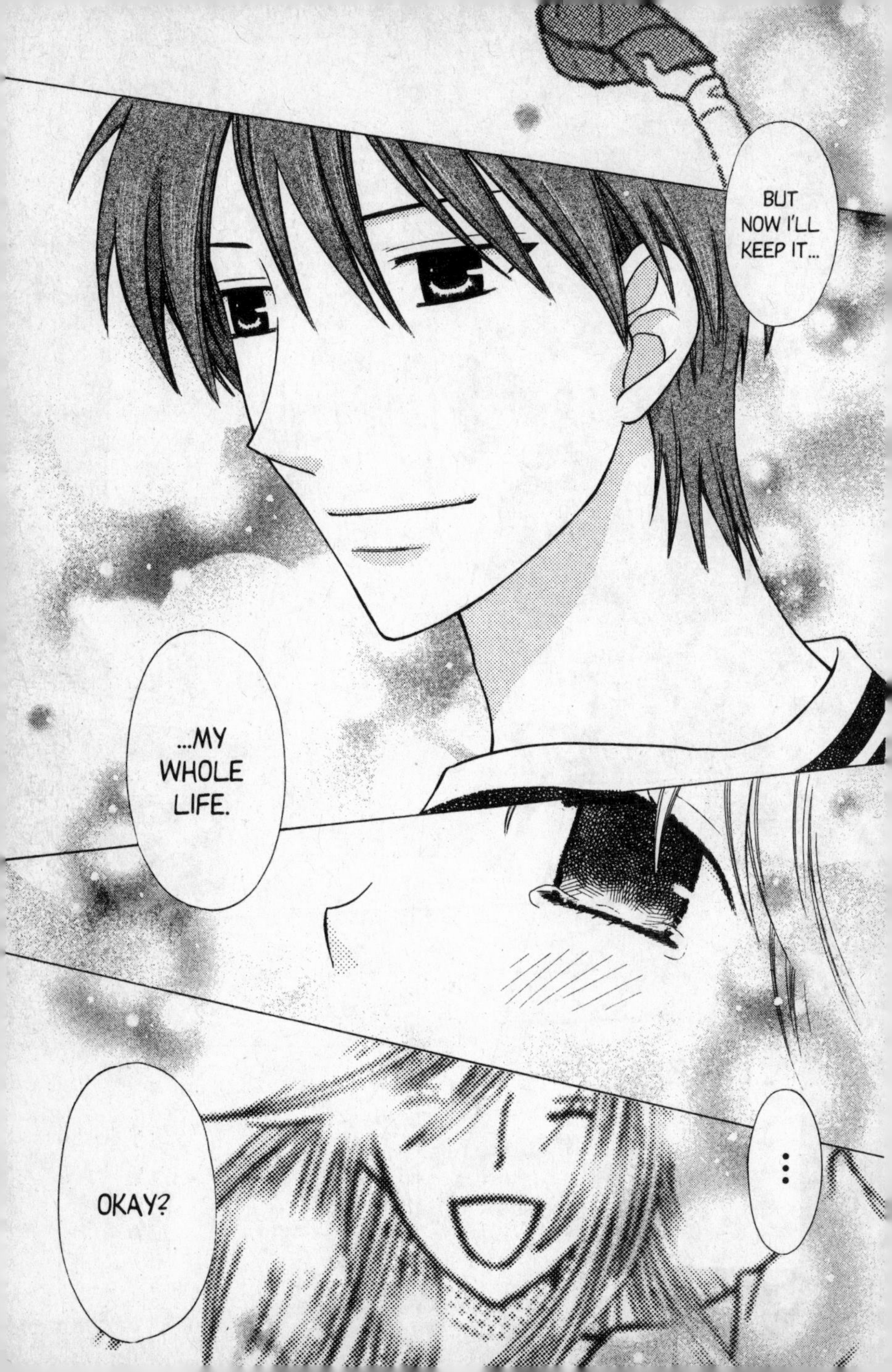
BUT NOW I'LL KEEP IT...
...MY WHOLE LIFE.
...
OKAY?

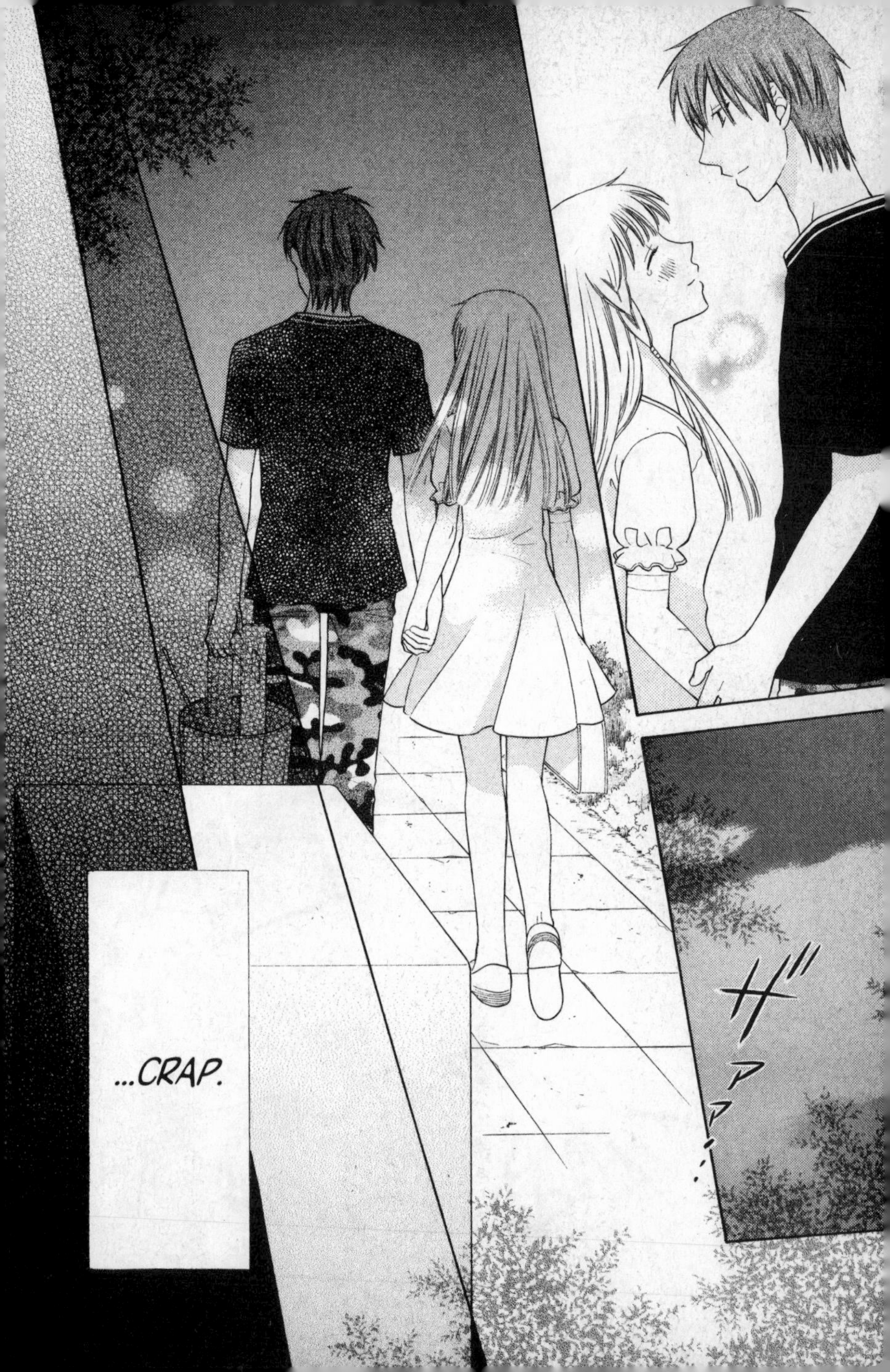
ザアア…
...CRAP.

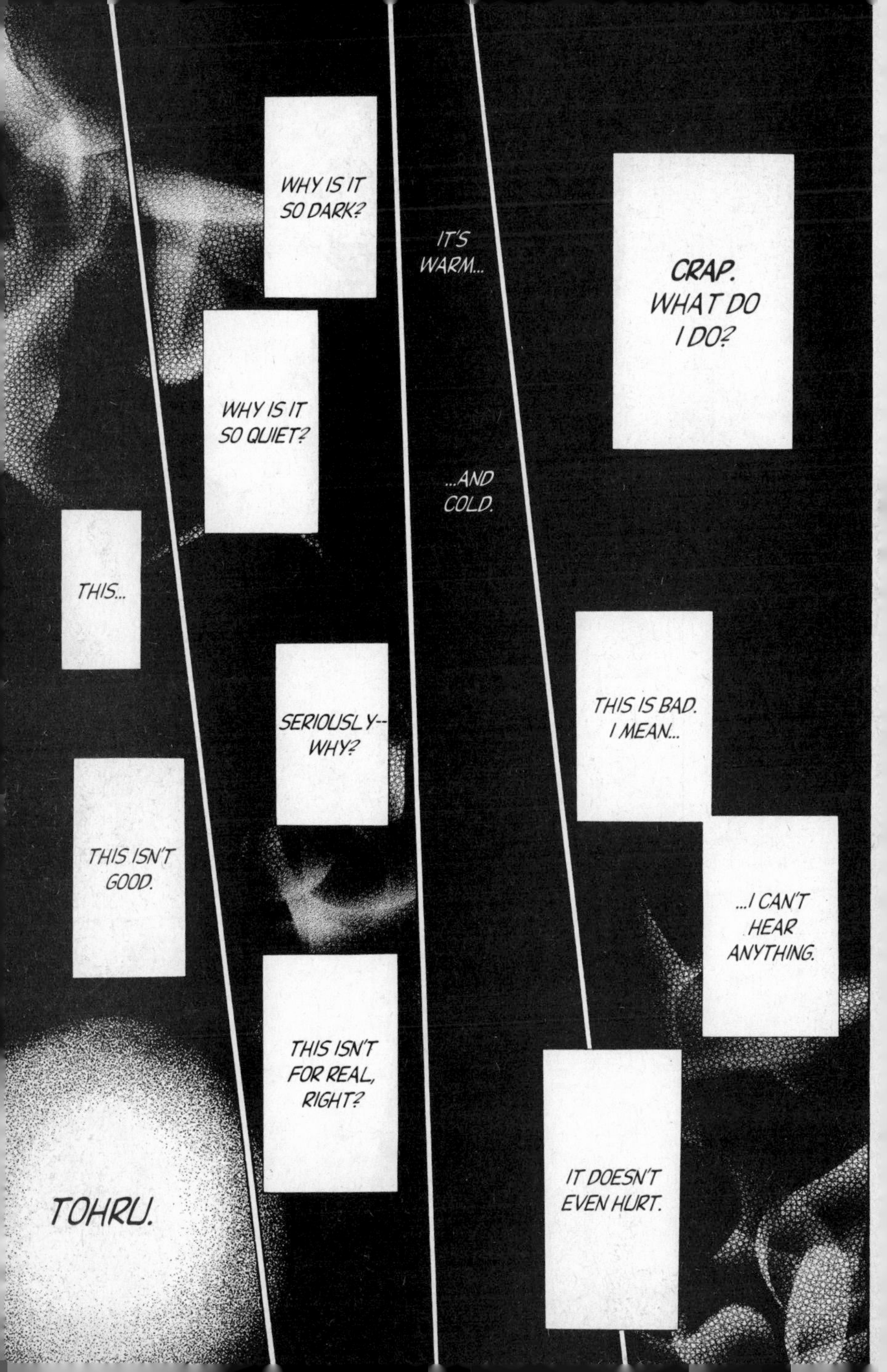
CRAP. WHAT DO I DO?
THIS IS BAD. I MEAN...
...I CAN'T HEAR ANYTHING.
IT DOESN'T EVEN HURT.
IT'S WARM...
...AND COLD.
WHY IS IT SO DARK?
WHY IS IT SO QUIET?
SERIOUSLY--WHY?
THIS ISN'T FOR REAL, RIGHT?
THIS...
THIS ISN'T GOOD.
TOHRU.

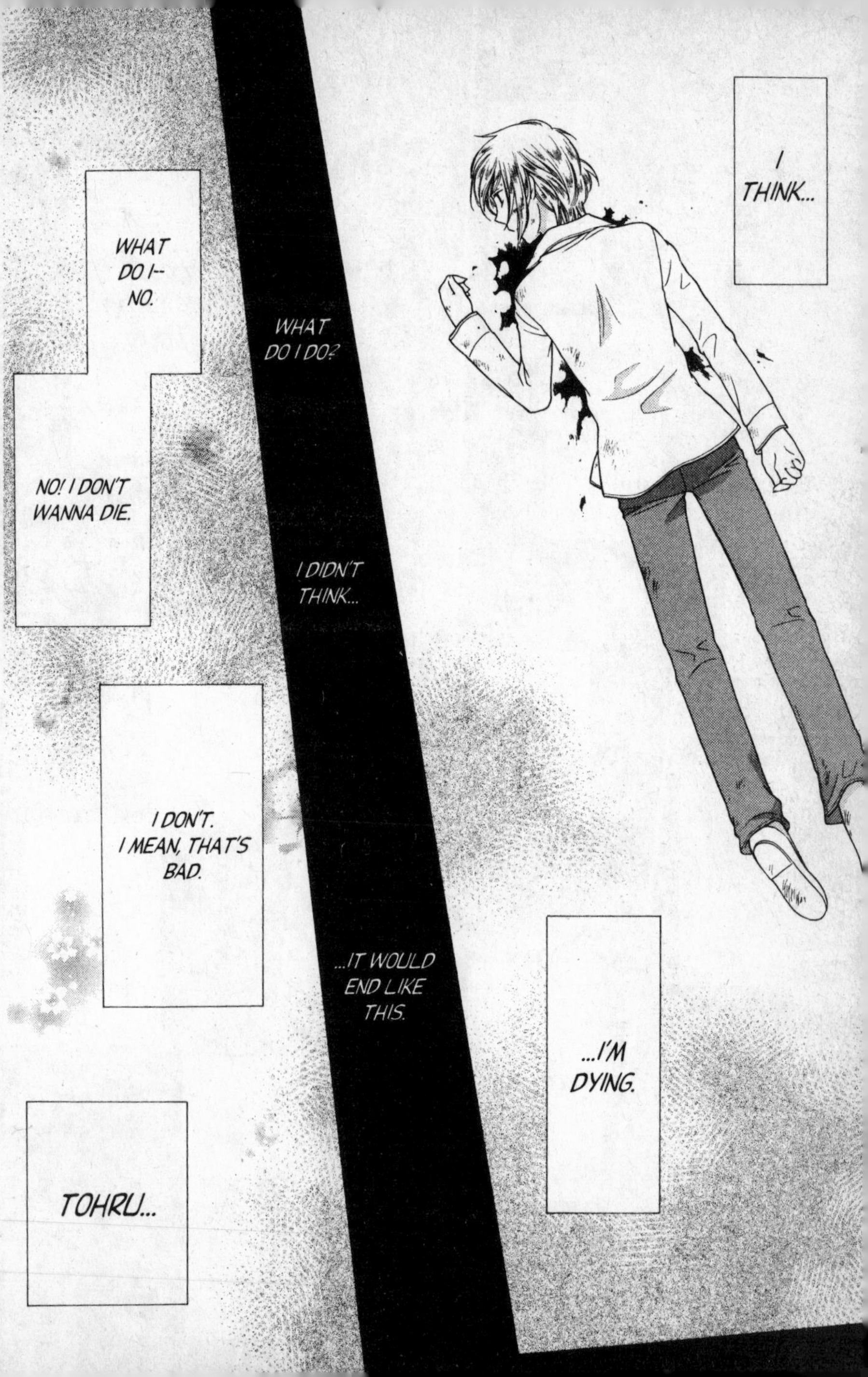
I THINK...
...I'M DYING.
WHAT DO I DO?
I DIDN'T THINK...
...IT WOULD END LIKE THIS.
WHAT DO I-- NO.
NO! I DON'T WANNA DIE.
I DON'T. I MEAN, THAT'S BAD.
TOHRU...

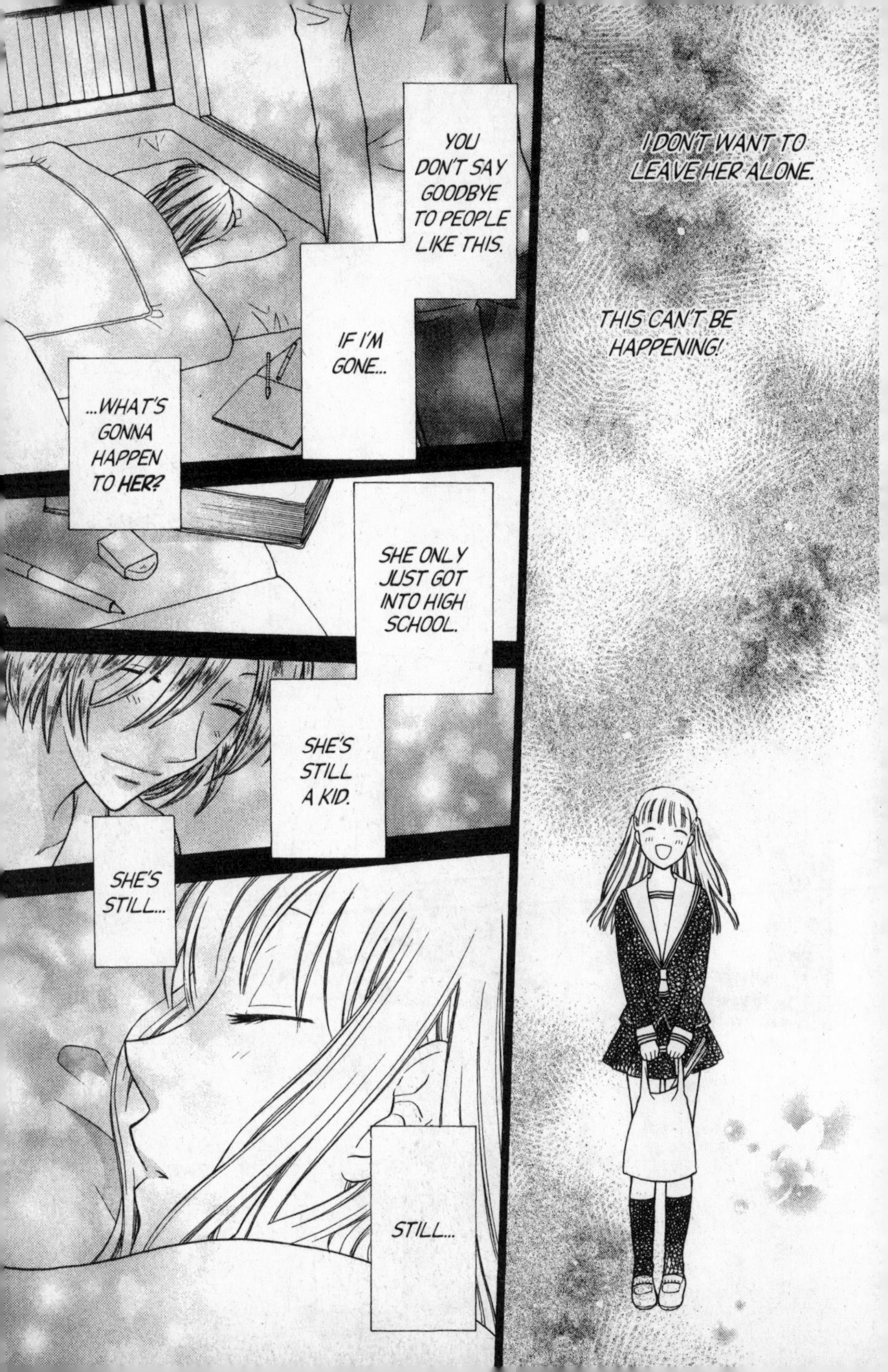
I DON'T WANT TO LEAVE HER ALONE.
THIS CAN'T BE HAPPENING!
YOU DON'T SAY GOODBYE TO PEOPLE LIKE THIS.
IF I'M GONE...
...WHAT'S GONNA HAPPEN TO HER?
SHE ONLY JUST GOT INTO HIGH SCHOOL.
SHE'S STILL A KID.
SHE'S STILL...
STILL...

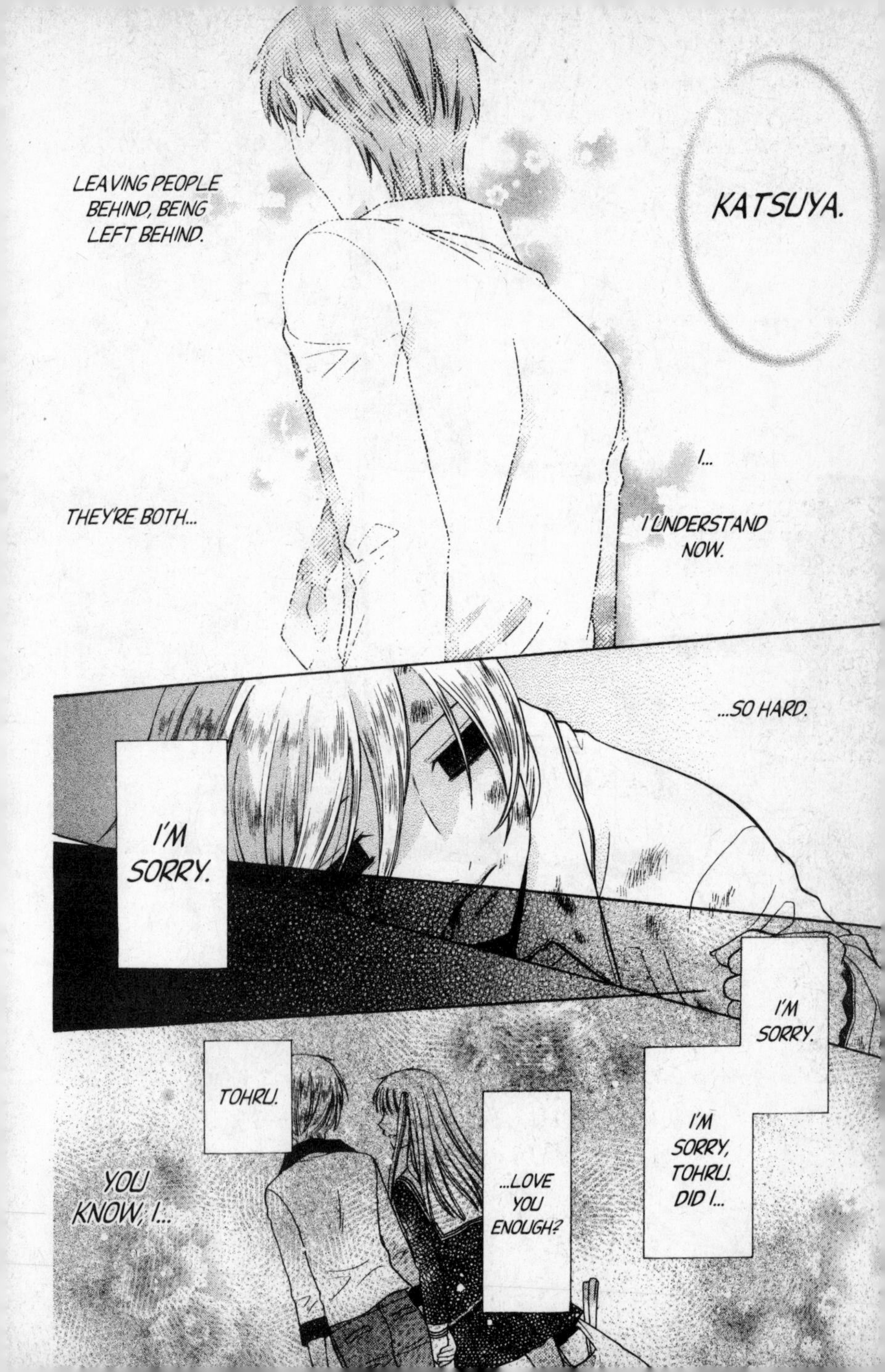
KATSUYA.
I...
I UNDERSTAND NOW.
LEAVING PEOPLE BEHIND, BEING LEFT BEHIND.
THEY'RE BOTH...
...SO HARD.
I'M SORRY.
I'M SORRY.
I'M SORRY, TOHRU. DID I...
...LOVE YOU ENOUGH?
TOHRU.
YOU KNOW, I...

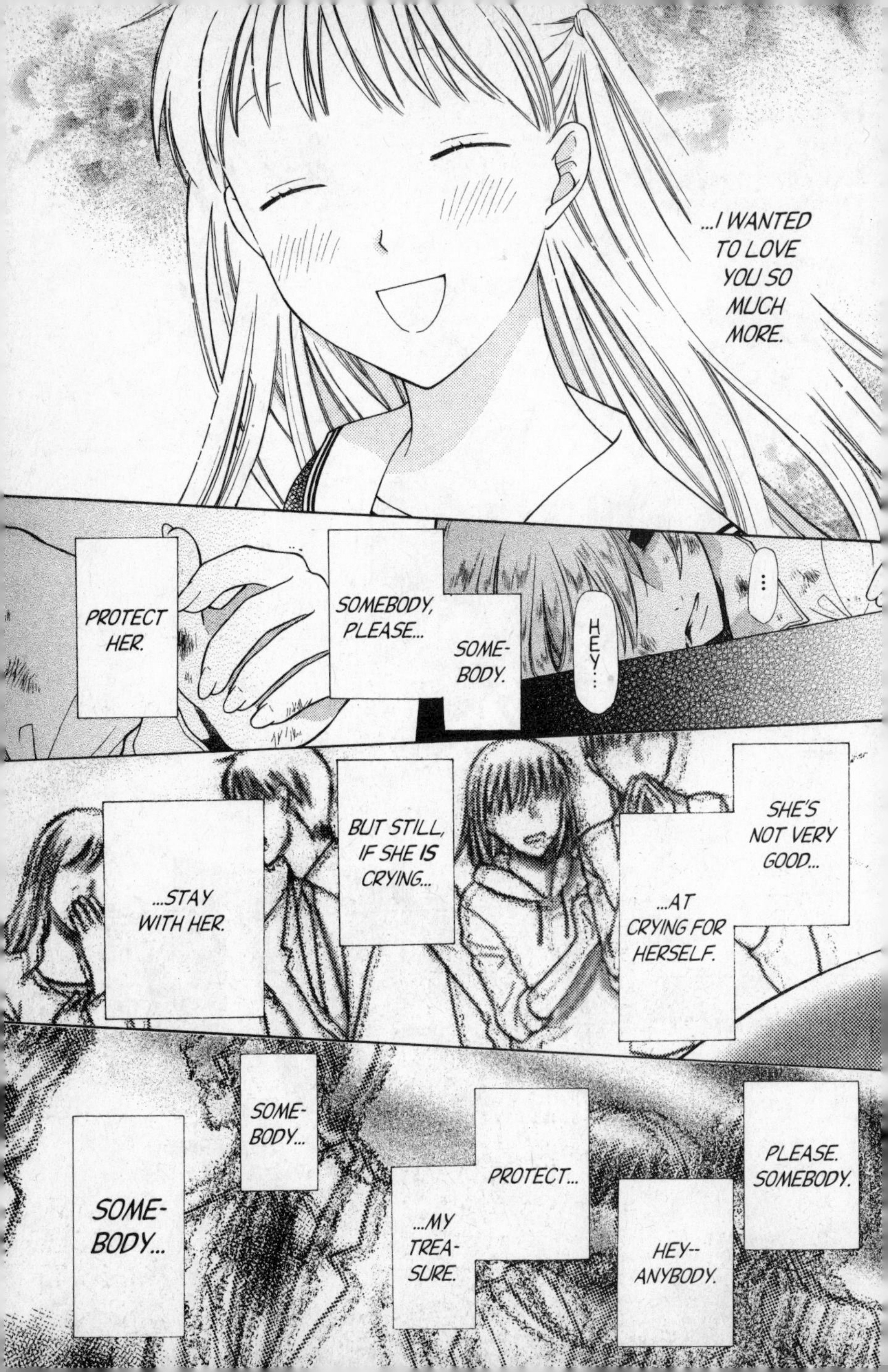
...I WANTED TO LOVE YOU SO MUCH MORE.
...
HEY...
SOME-BODY.
SOMEBODY, PLEASE...
PROTECT HER.
SHE'S NOT VERY GOOD...
...AT CRYING FOR HERSELF.
BUT STILL, IF SHE IS CRYING...
...STAY WITH HER.
PLEASE. SOMEBODY.
HEY-- ANYBODY.
PROTECT...
...MY TREA-SURE.
SOME-BODY...
SOME-BODY...

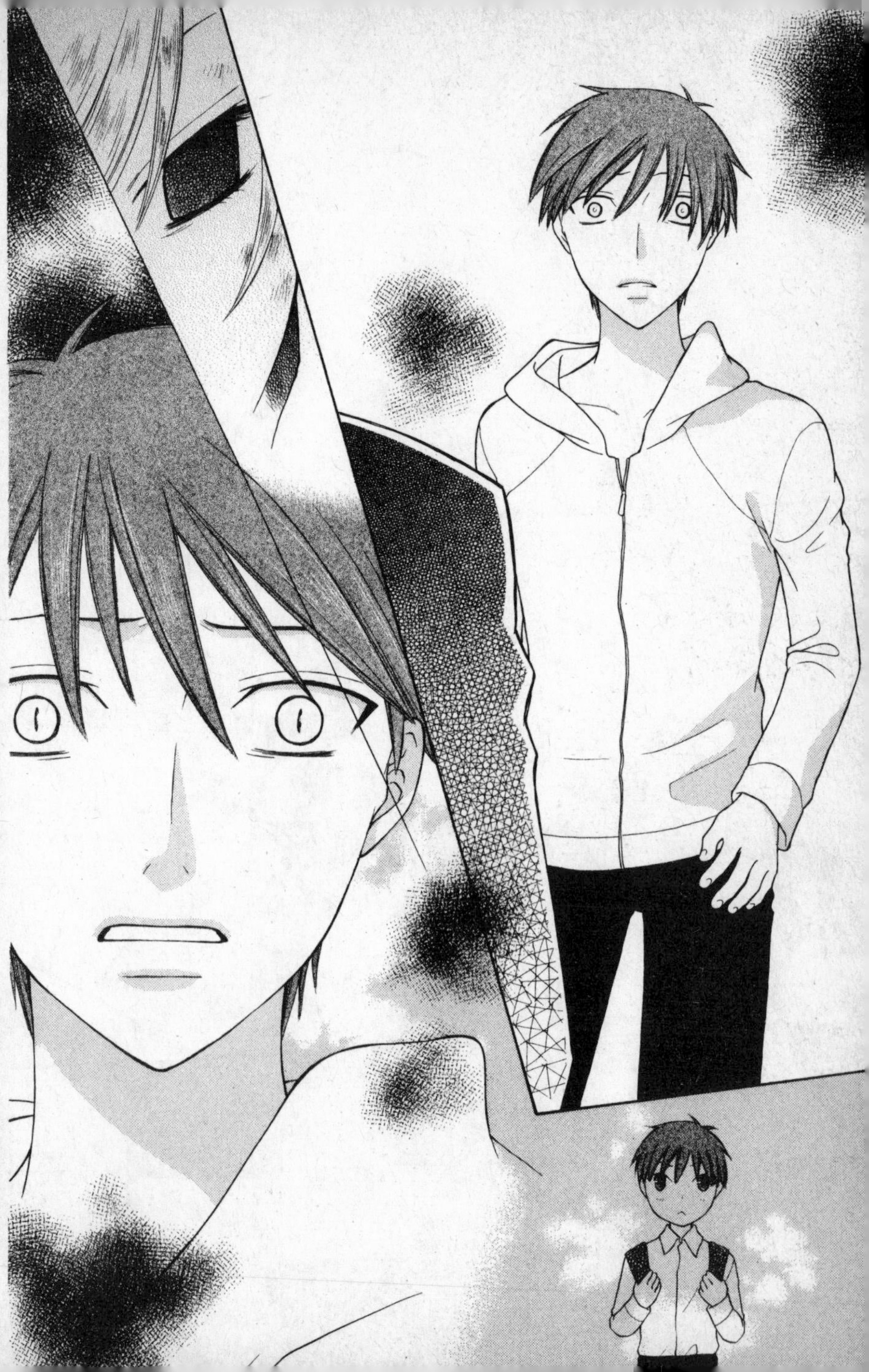

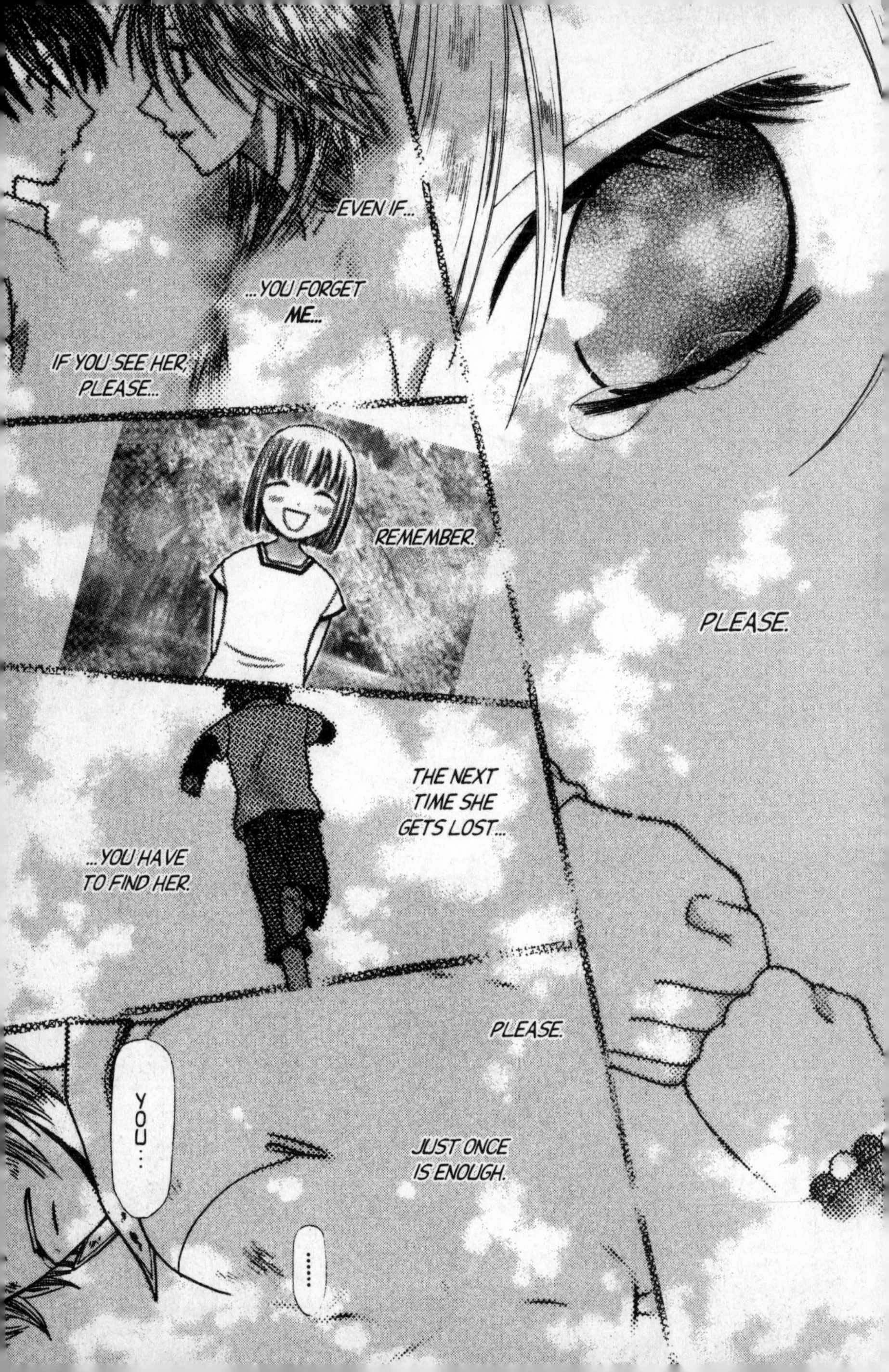

EVEN IF...
...YOU FORGET ME...
IF YOU SEE HER, PLEASE...
REMEMBER.
PLEASE.
THE NEXT TIME SHE GETS LOST...
...YOU HAVE TO FIND HER.
PLEASE.
JUST ONCE IS ENOUGH.
YOU...
......

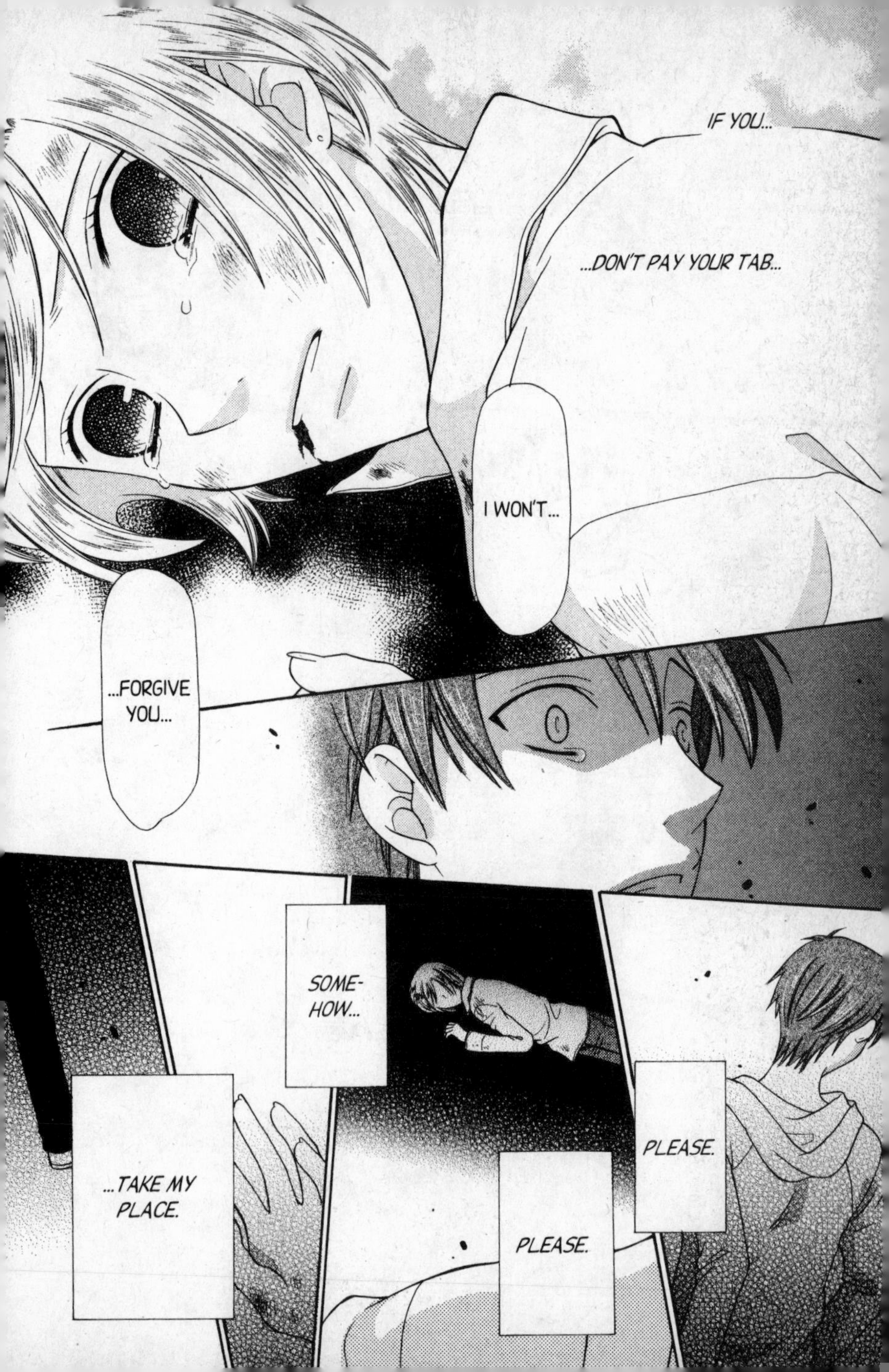
IF YOU...
...DON'T PAY YOUR TAB...
I WON'T...
...FORGIVE YOU...
PLEASE.
PLEASE.
SOME-HOW...
...TAKE MY PLACE.

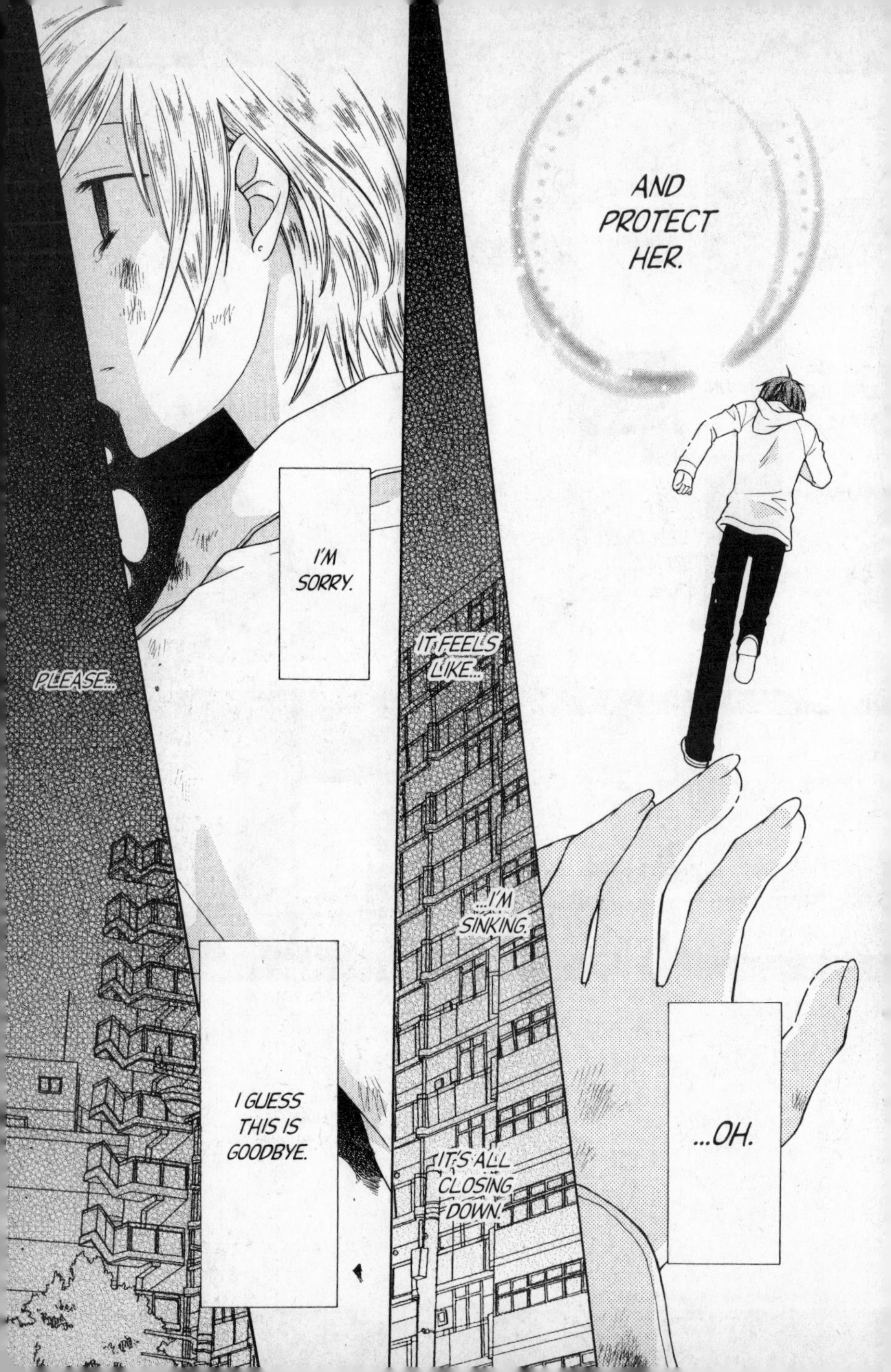
AND PROTECT HER.
...OH.
IT FEELS LIKE...
...I'M SINKING.
IT'S ALL CLOSING DOWN.
I'M SORRY.
PLEASE...
I GUESS THIS IS GOODBYE.

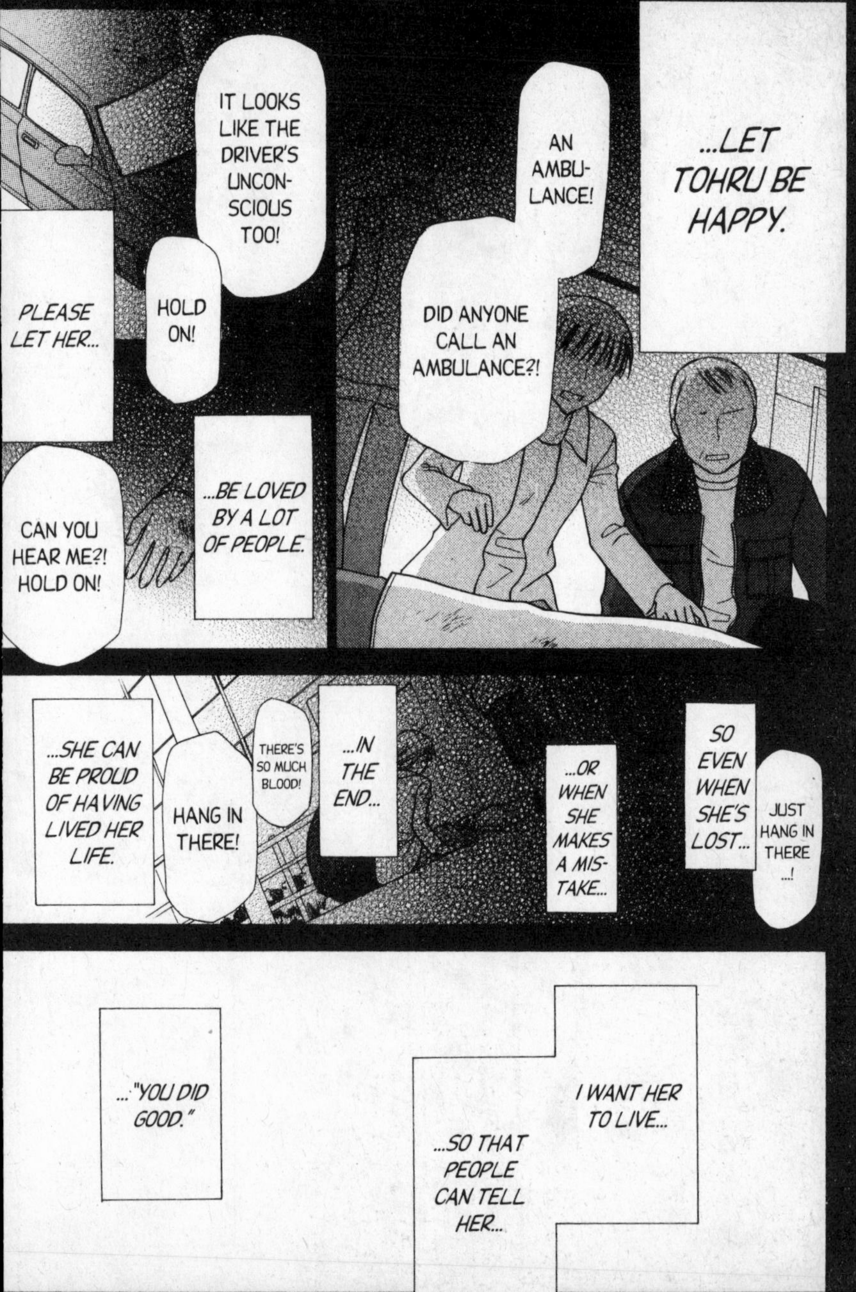
...LET TOHRU BE HAPPY.
AN AMBU-LANCE!
DID ANYONE CALL AN AMBULANCE?!
IT LOOKS LIKE THE DRIVER'S UNCON-SCIOUS TOO!
HOLD ON!
PLEASE LET HER...
...BE LOVED BY A LOT OF PEOPLE.
CAN YOU HEAR ME?! HOLD ON!
SO EVEN WHEN SHE'S LOST...
JUST HANG IN THERE ...!
...OR WHEN SHE MAKES A MIS-TAKE...
...IN THE END...
THERE'S SO MUCH BLOOD!
HANG IN THERE!
...SHE CAN BE PROUD OF HAVING LIVED HER LIFE.
I WANT HER TO LIVE...
...SO THAT PEOPLE CAN TELL HER...
..."YOU DID GOOD."

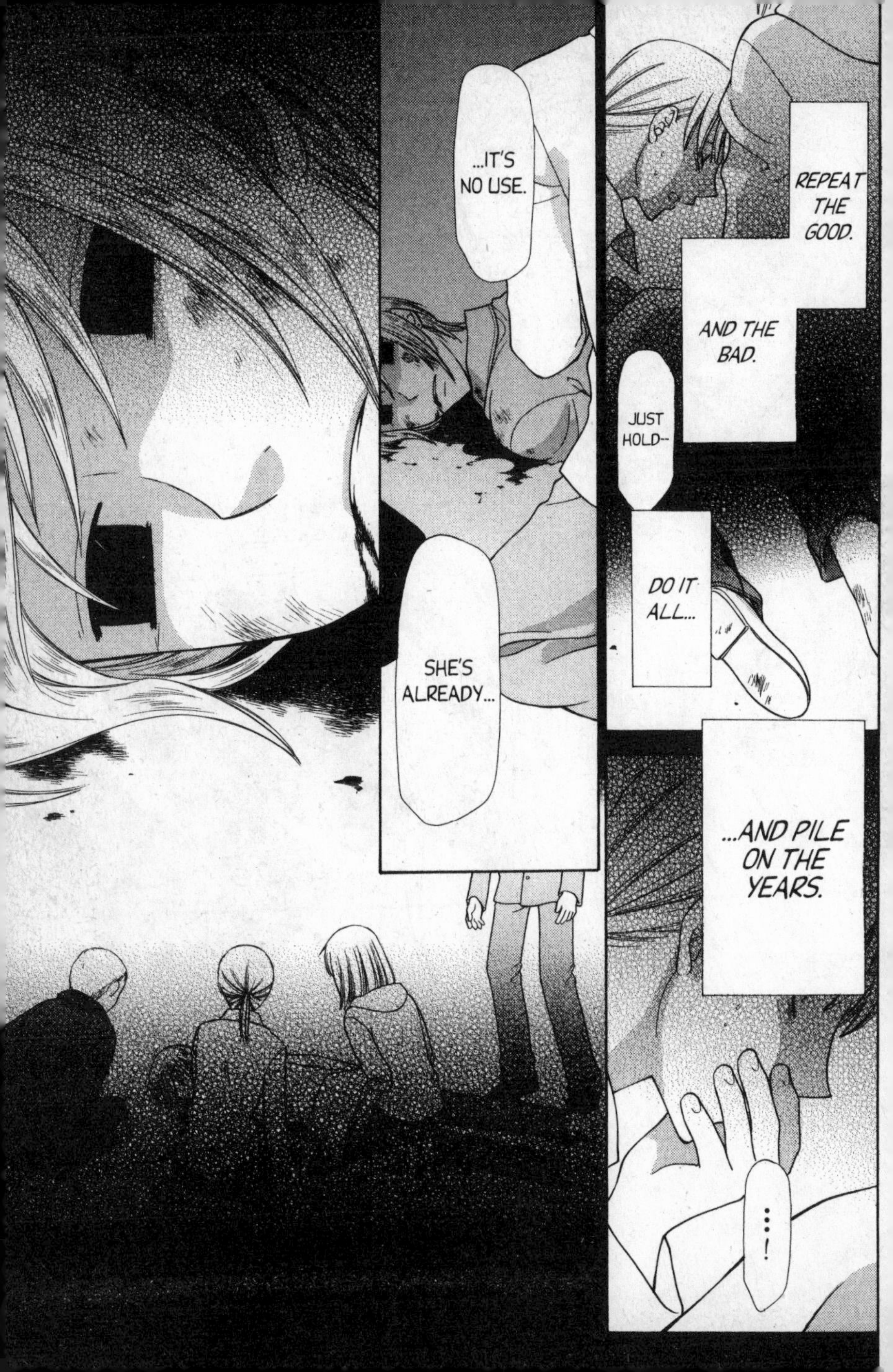
REPEAT THE GOOD.
AND THE BAD.
JUST HOLD--
DO IT ALL...
...AND PILE ON THE YEARS.
...!
...IT'S NO USE.
SHE'S ALREADY...

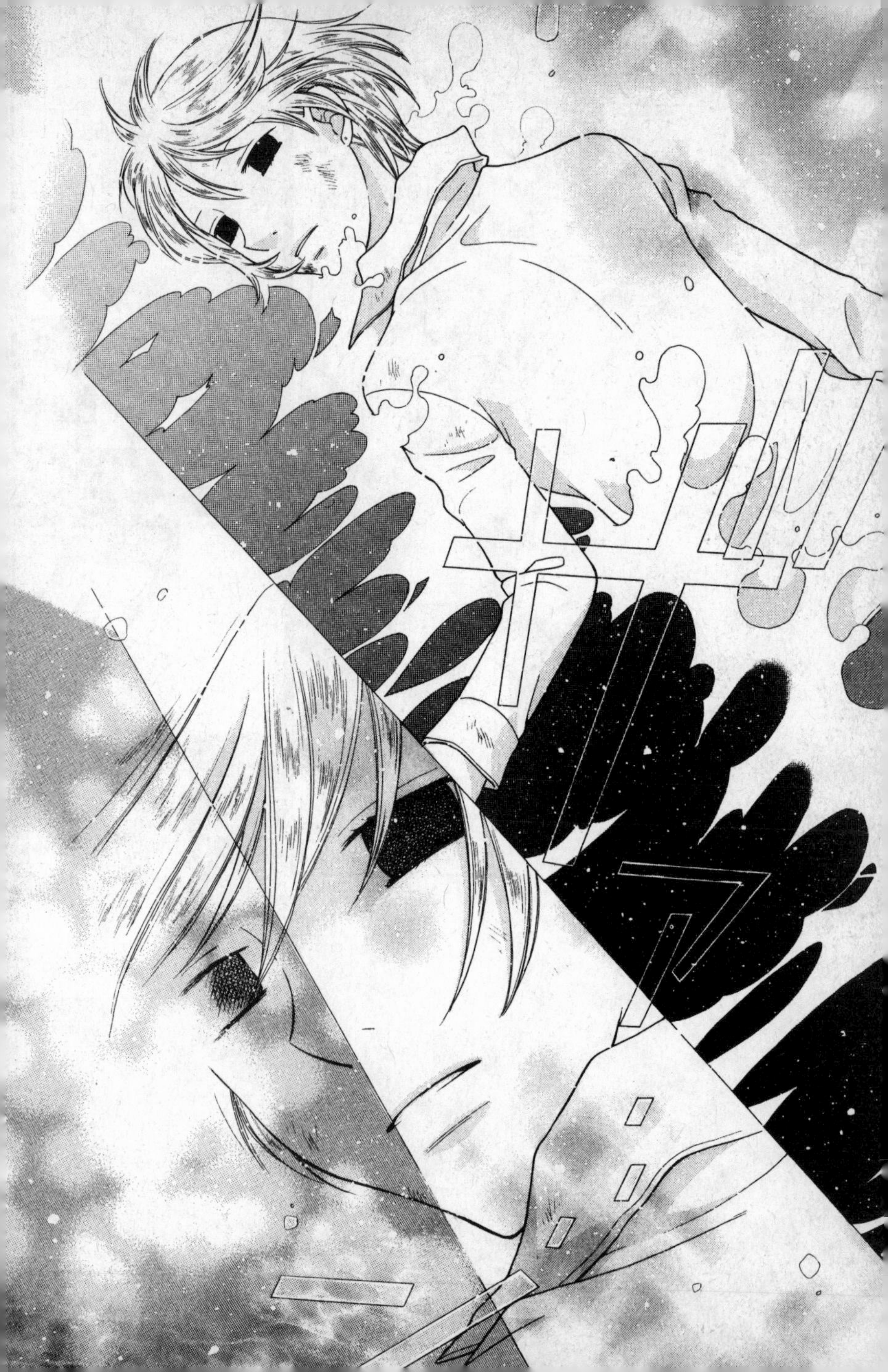

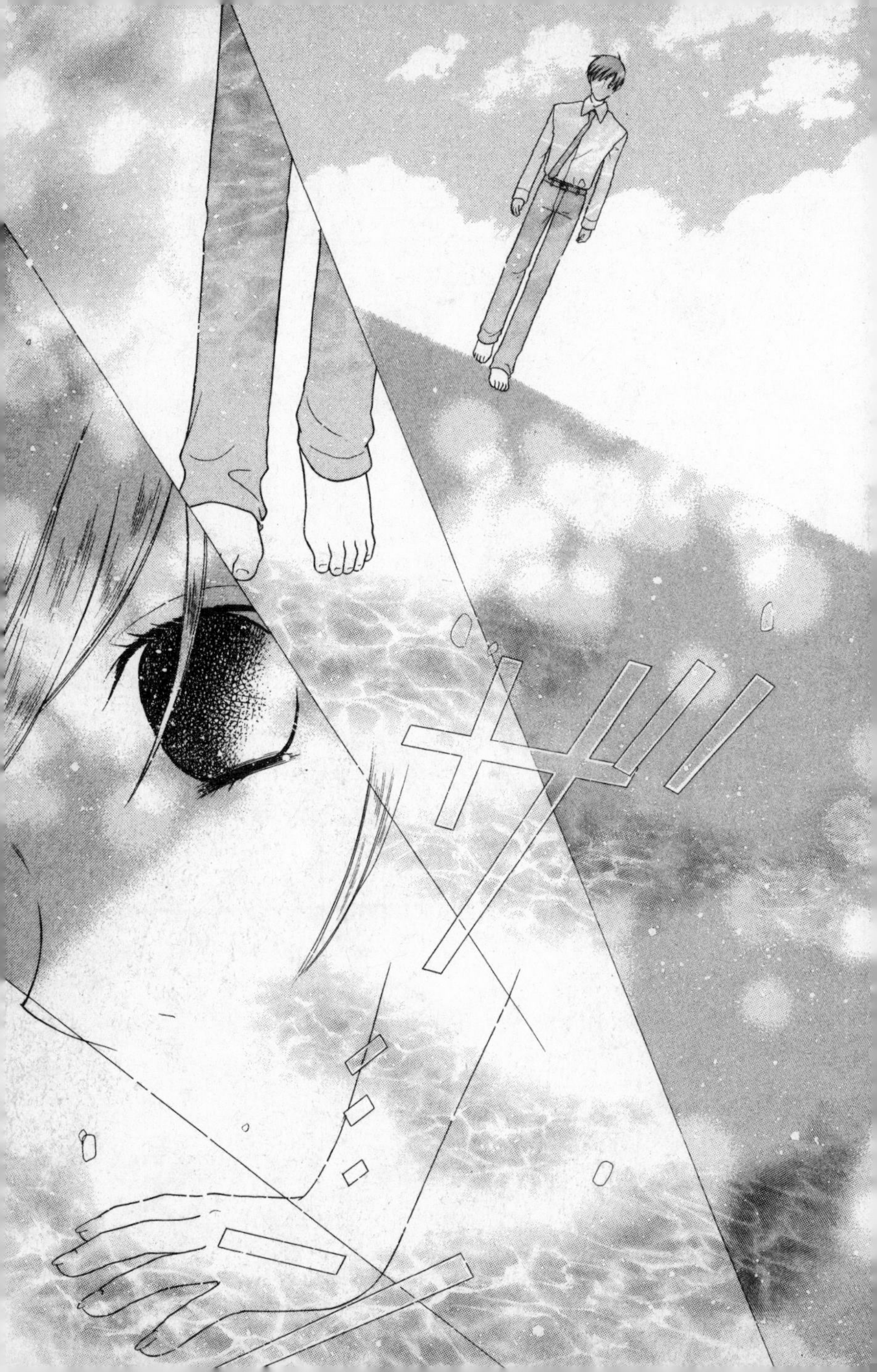

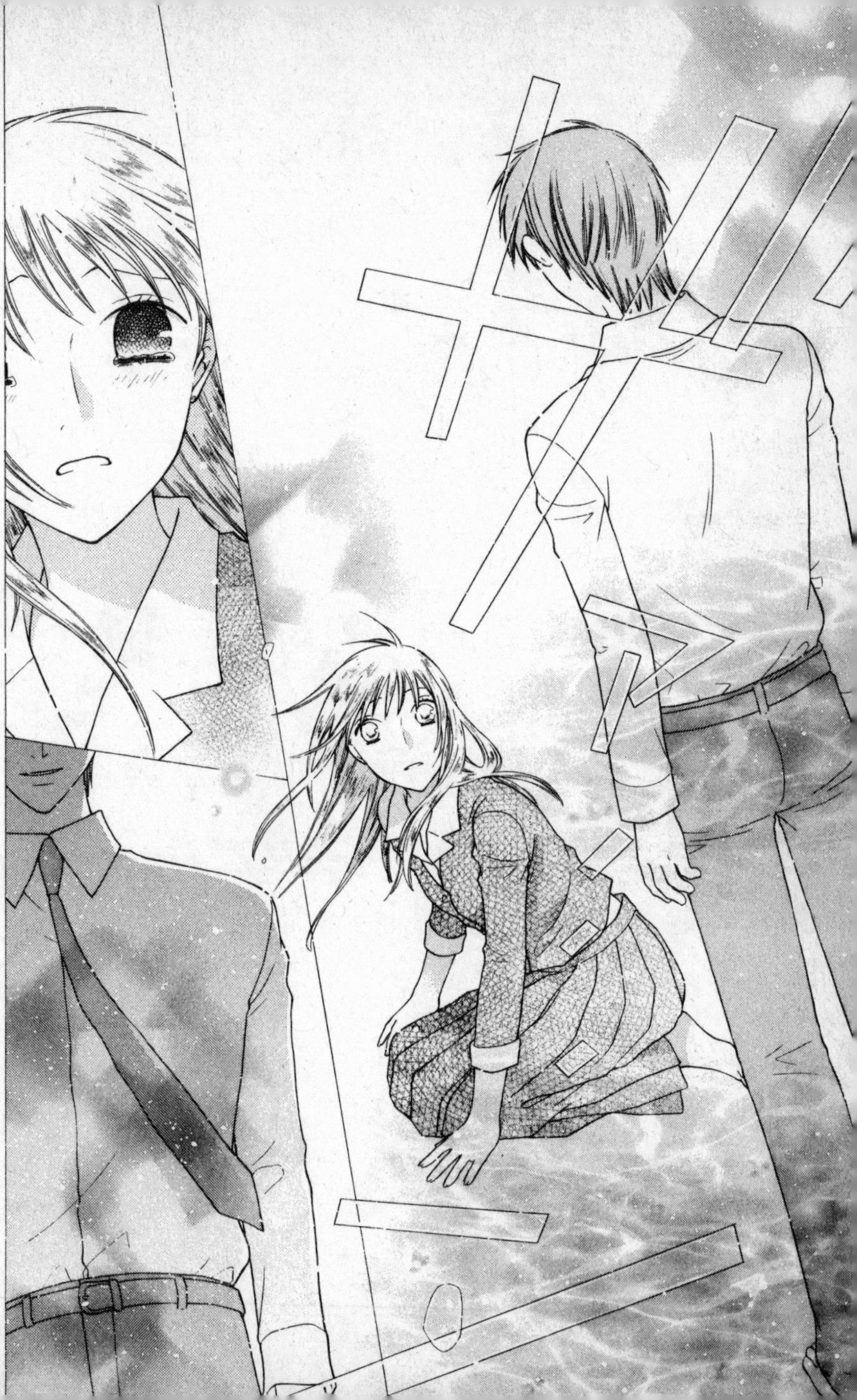

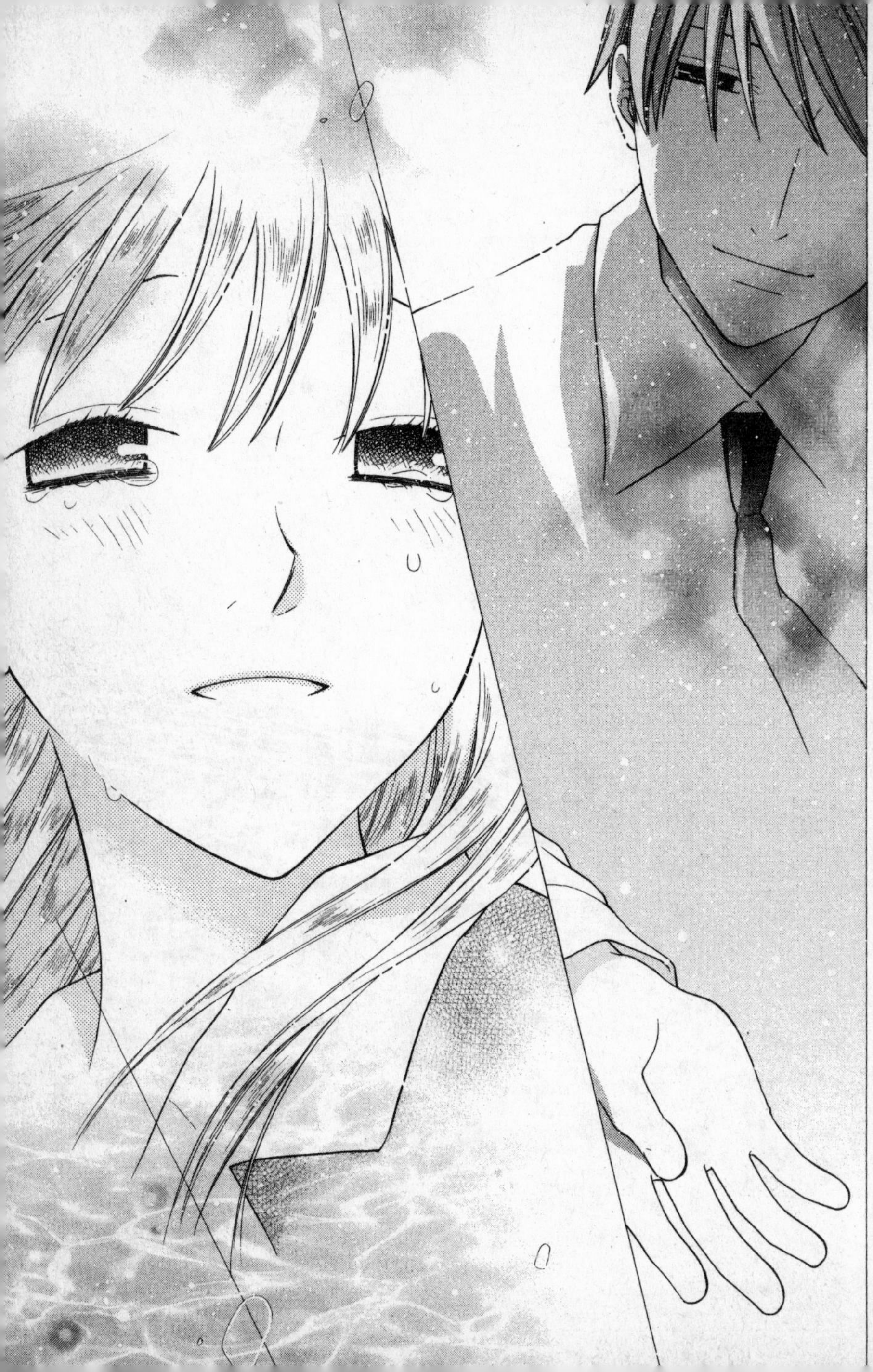

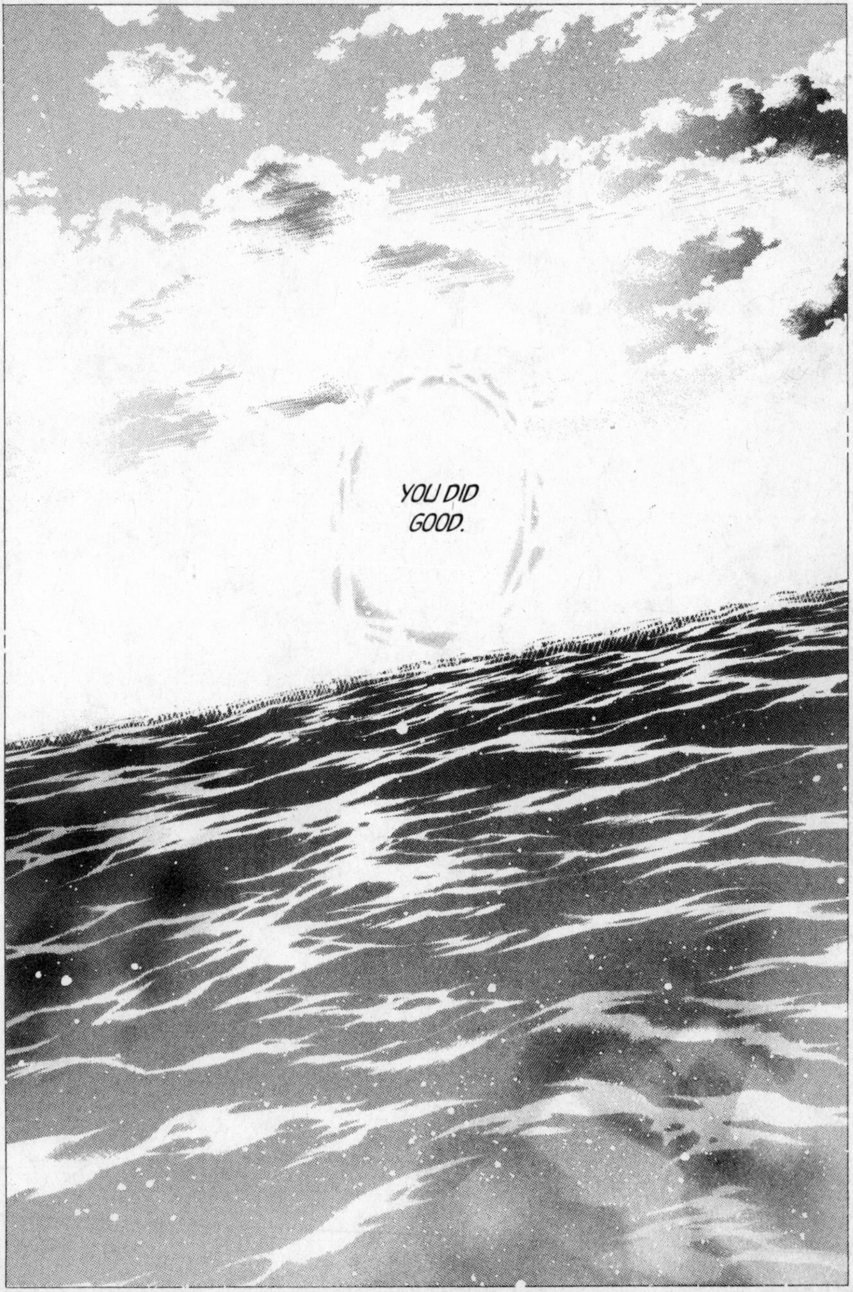
YOU DID GOOD.

Kyo is a type of character I hadn't drawn much in the past, so when I started the series, I was nervous about whether or not I could draw him well. But before I knew it, he was a powerful force that pulled Furuba along. Thank you. I feel like he'll be a kind father.

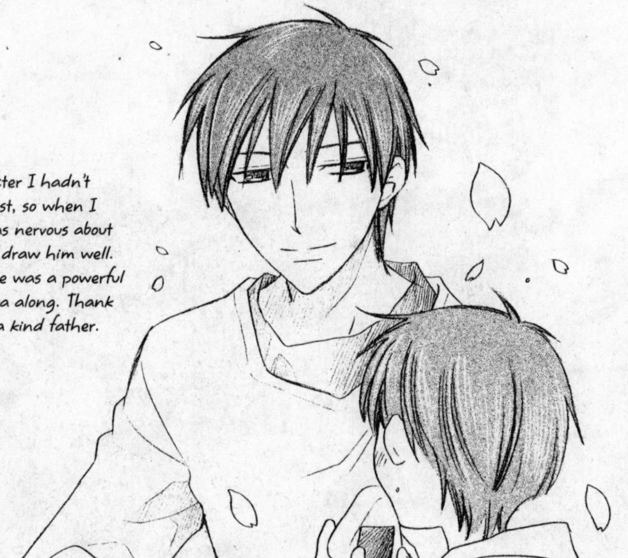

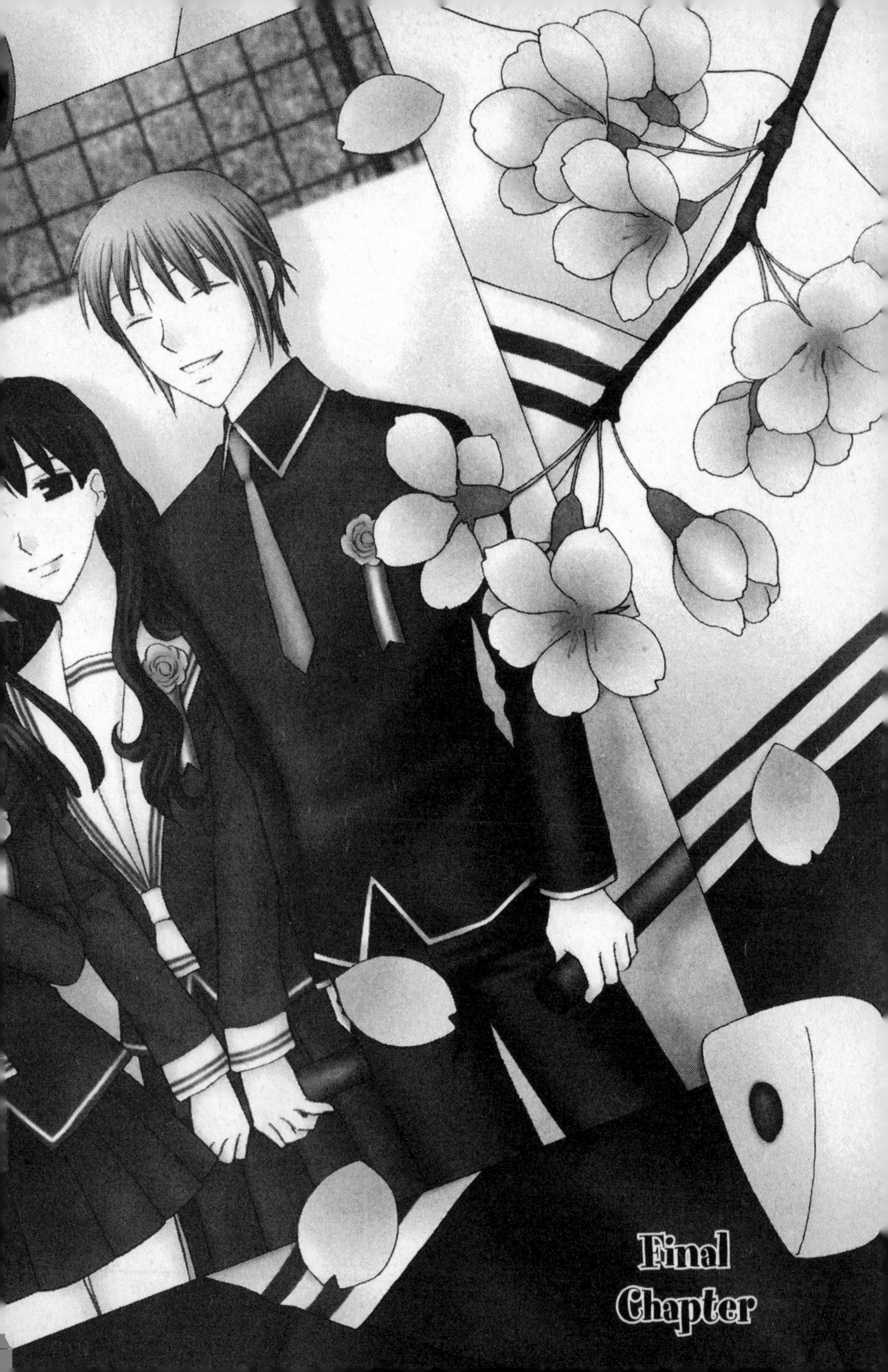
Final
Chapter

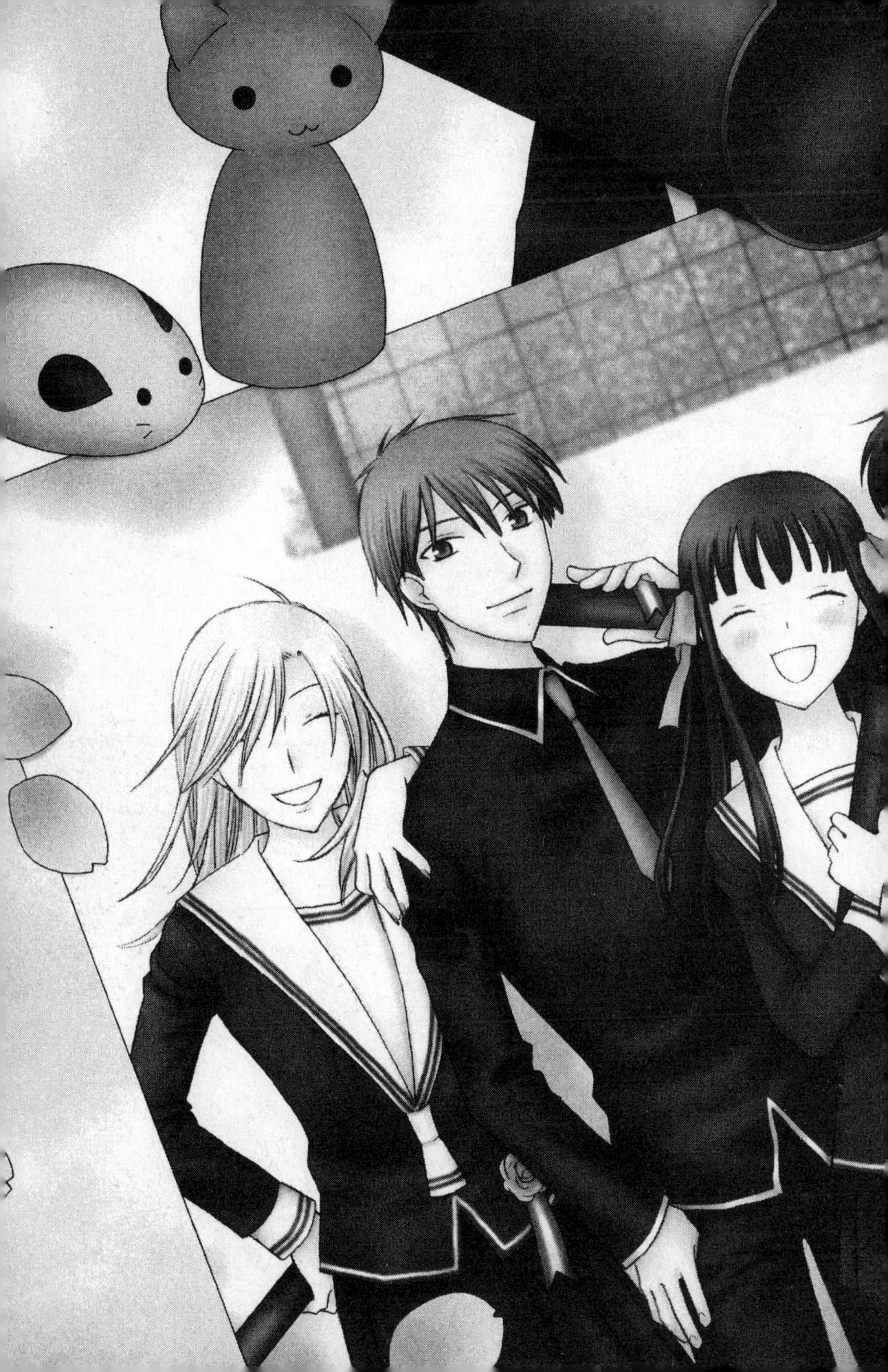

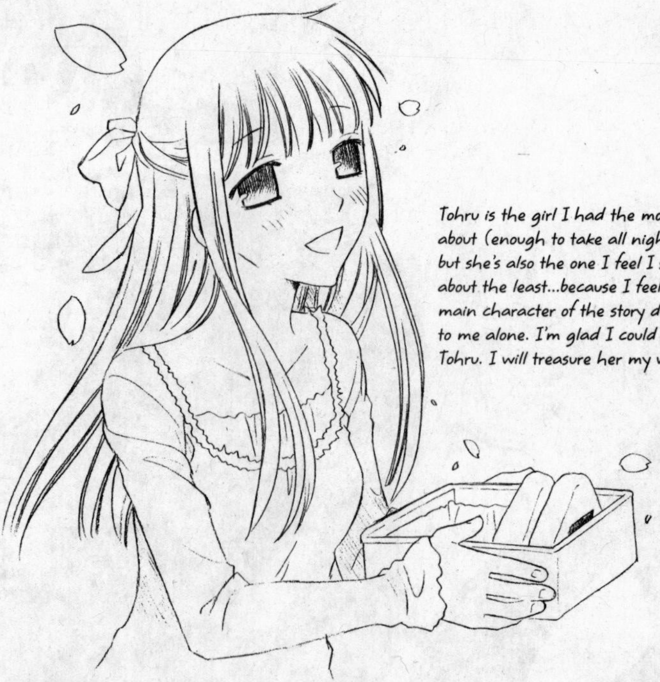

Tohru is the girl I had the most to say about (enough to take all night-- (laugh), but she's also the one I feel I should talk about the least...because I feel like the main character of the story doesn't belong to me alone. I'm glad I could give birth to Tohru. I will treasure her my whole life.

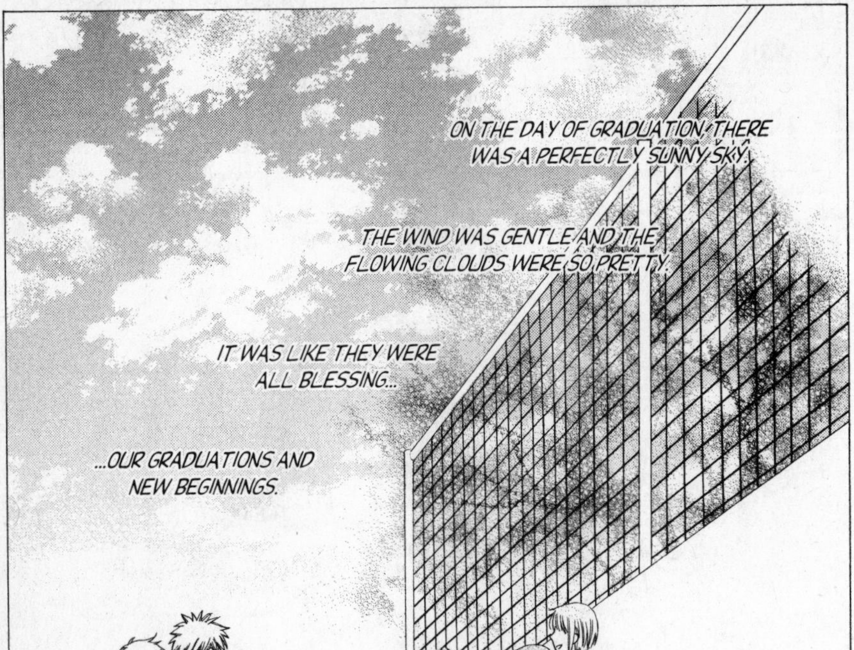
ON THE DAY OF GRADUATION, THERE WAS A PERFECTLY SUNNY SKY.
THE WIND WAS GENTLE AND THE FLOWING CLOUDS WERE SO PRETTY.
IT WAS LIKE THEY WERE ALL BLESSING...
...OUR GRADUATIONS AND NEW BEGINNINGS.

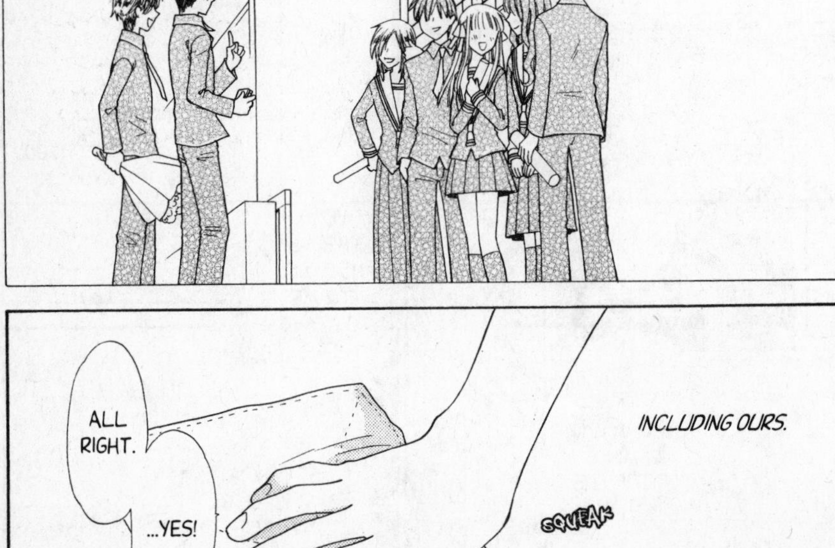
INCLUDING OURS.
ALL RIGHT.
SQUEAK
...YES!

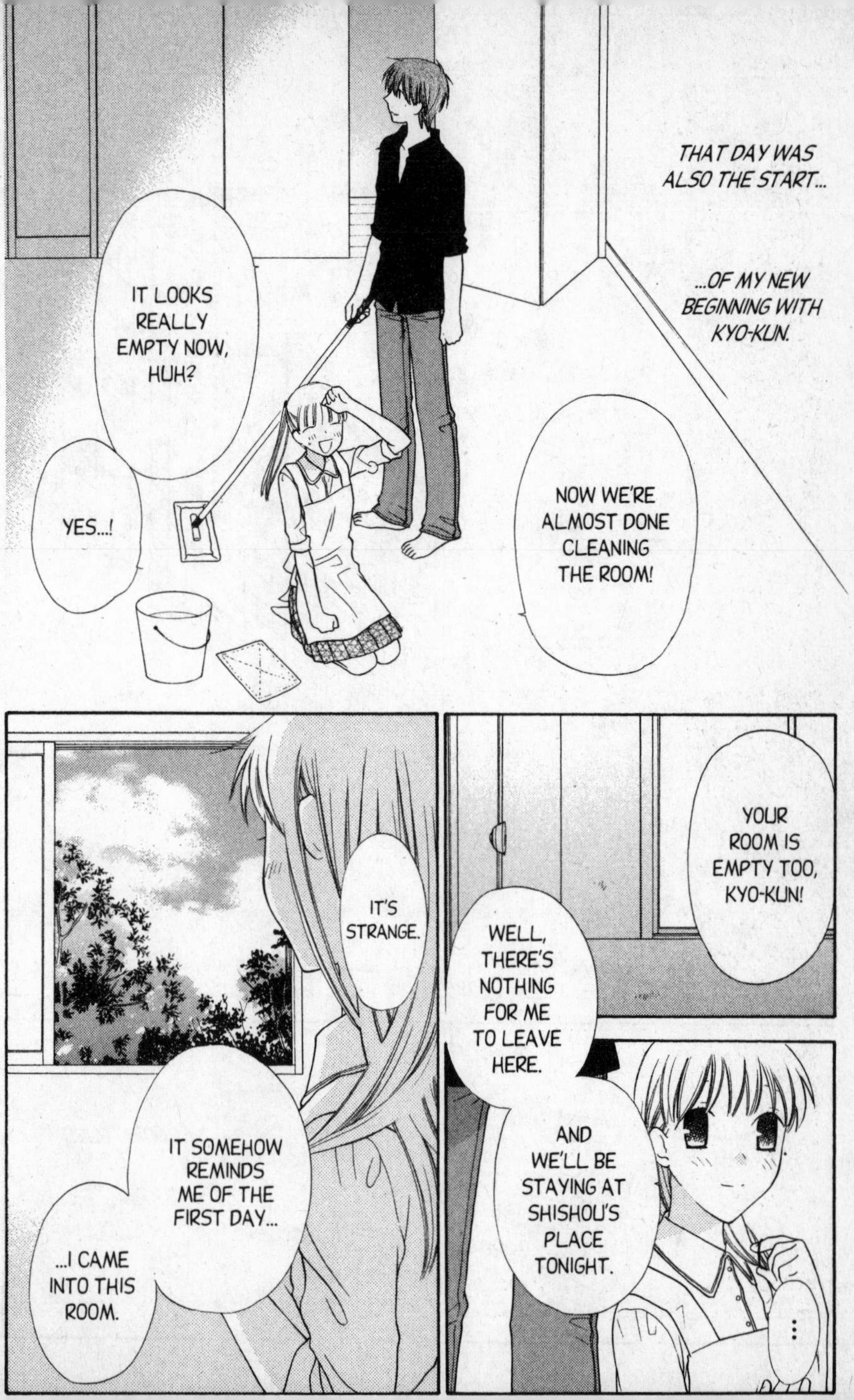
THAT DAY WAS ALSO THE START...
...OF MY NEW BEGINNING WITH KYO-KUN.
NOW WE'RE ALMOST DONE CLEANING THE ROOM!
IT LOOKS REALLY EMPTY NOW, HUH?
YES...!
YOUR ROOM IS EMPTY TOO, KYO-KUN!
WELL, THERE'S NOTHING FOR ME TO LEAVE HERE.
...
AND WE'LL BE STAYING AT SHISHOU'S PLACE TONIGHT.
IT'S STRANGE.
IT SOMEHOW REMINDS ME OF THE FIRST DAY...
...I CAME INTO THIS ROOM.

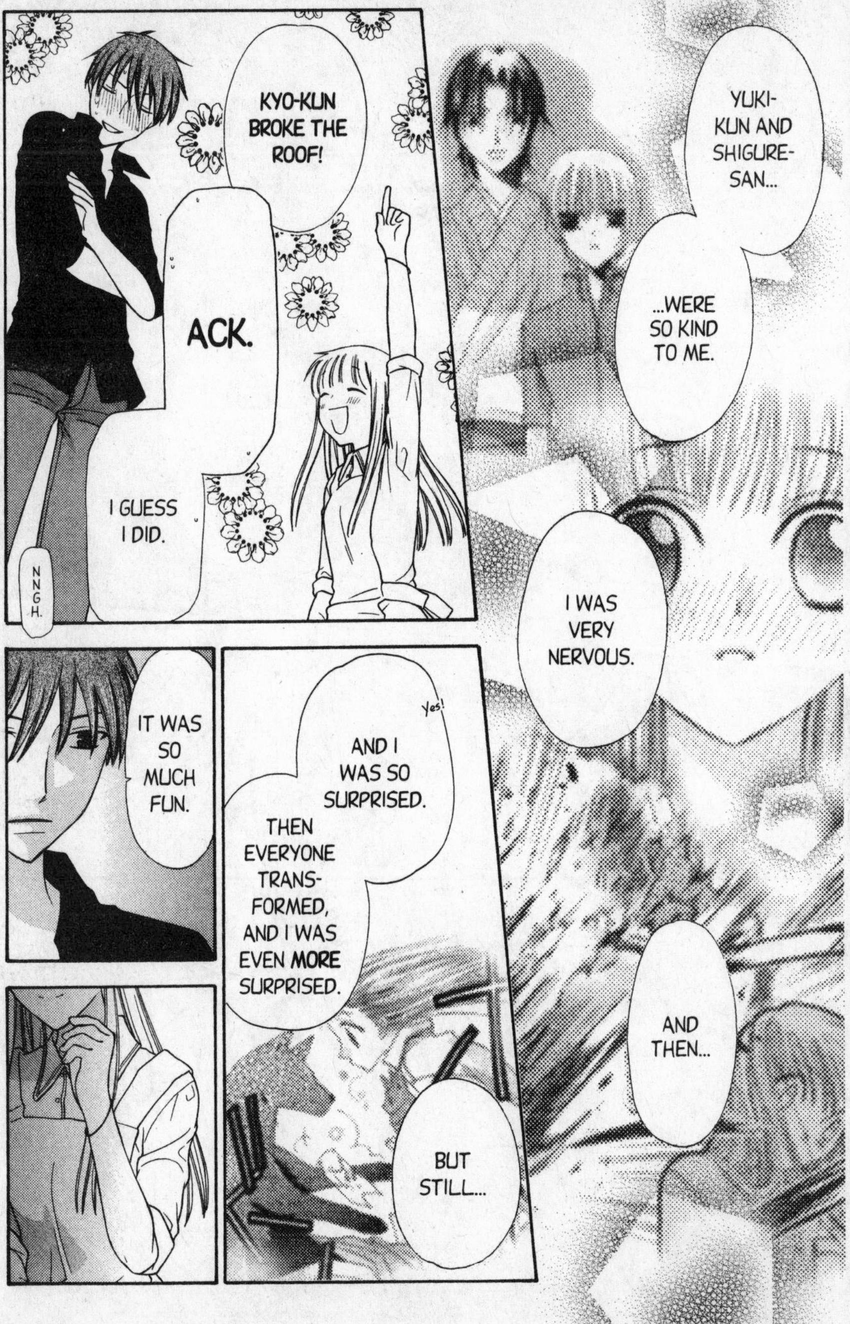

YUKI-KUN AND SHIGURE-SAN...
...WERE SO KIND TO ME.
I WAS VERY NERVOUS.
AND THEN...
KYO-KUN BROKE THE ROOF!
ACK.
I GUESS I DID.
NNGH.
Yes!
AND I WAS SO SURPRISED.
THEN EVERYONE TRANSFORMED, AND I WAS EVEN **MORE** SURPRISED.
BUT STILL...
IT WAS SO MUCH FUN.

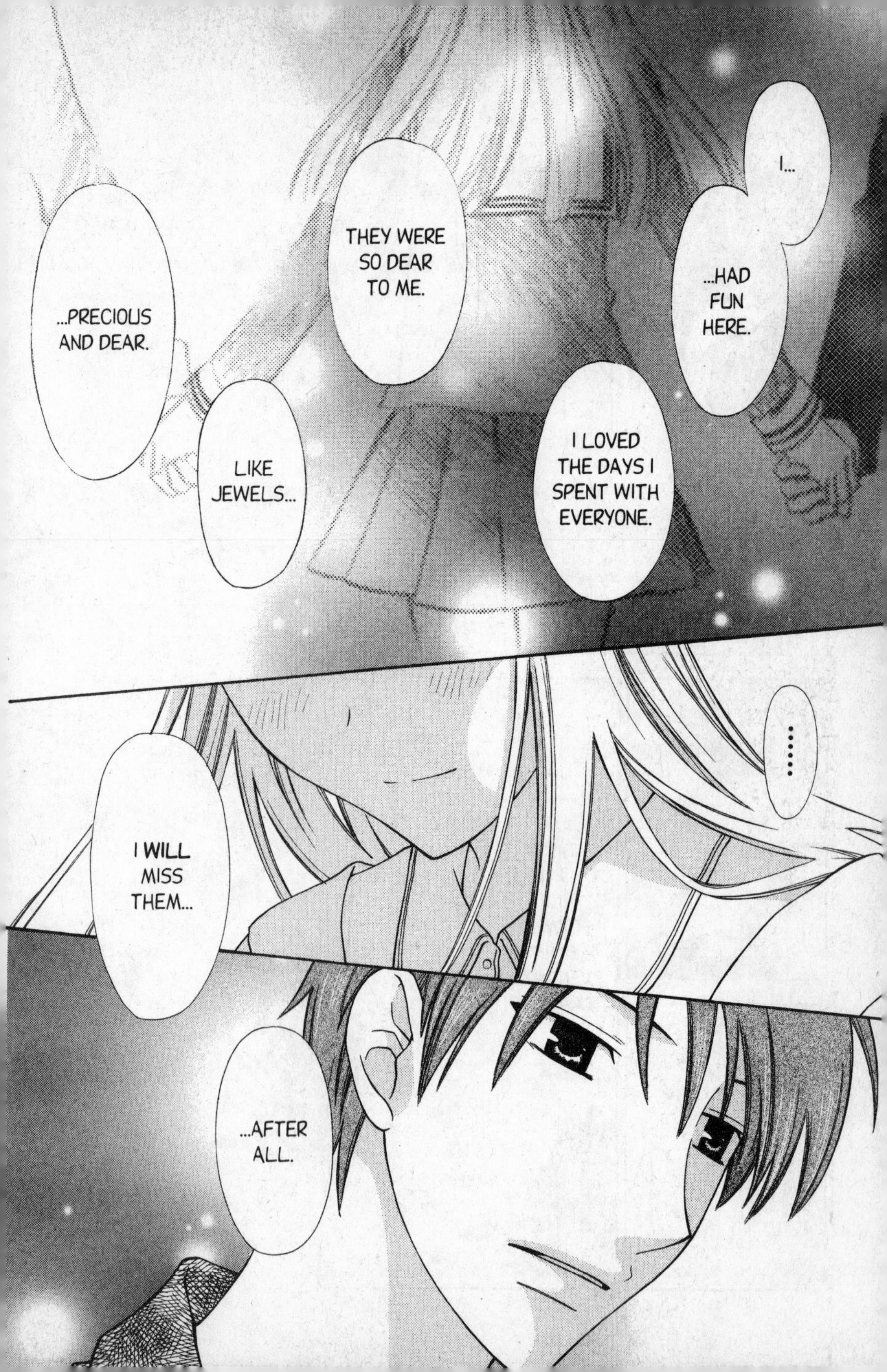
I...
...HAD FUN HERE.
I LOVED THE DAYS I SPENT WITH EVERYONE.
THEY WERE SO DEAR TO ME.
LIKE JEWELS...
...PRECIOUS AND DEAR.
......
I WILL MISS THEM...
...AFTER ALL..

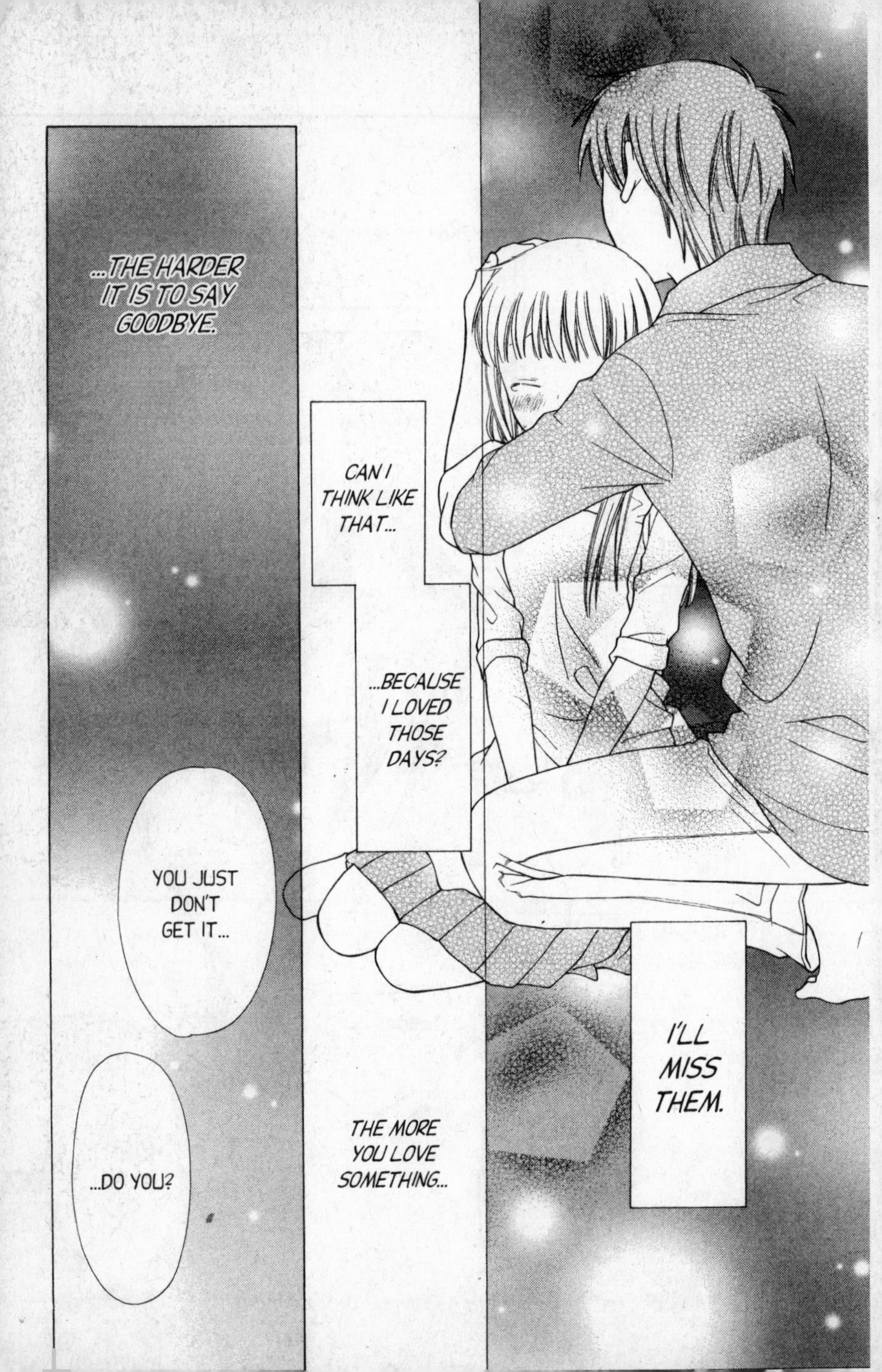
CAN I THINK LIKE THAT...
...BECAUSE I LOVED THOSE DAYS?
I'LL MISS THEM.
THE MORE YOU LOVE SOMETHING...
...THE HARDER IT IS TO SAY GOODBYE.
YOU JUST DON'T GET IT...
...DO YOU?

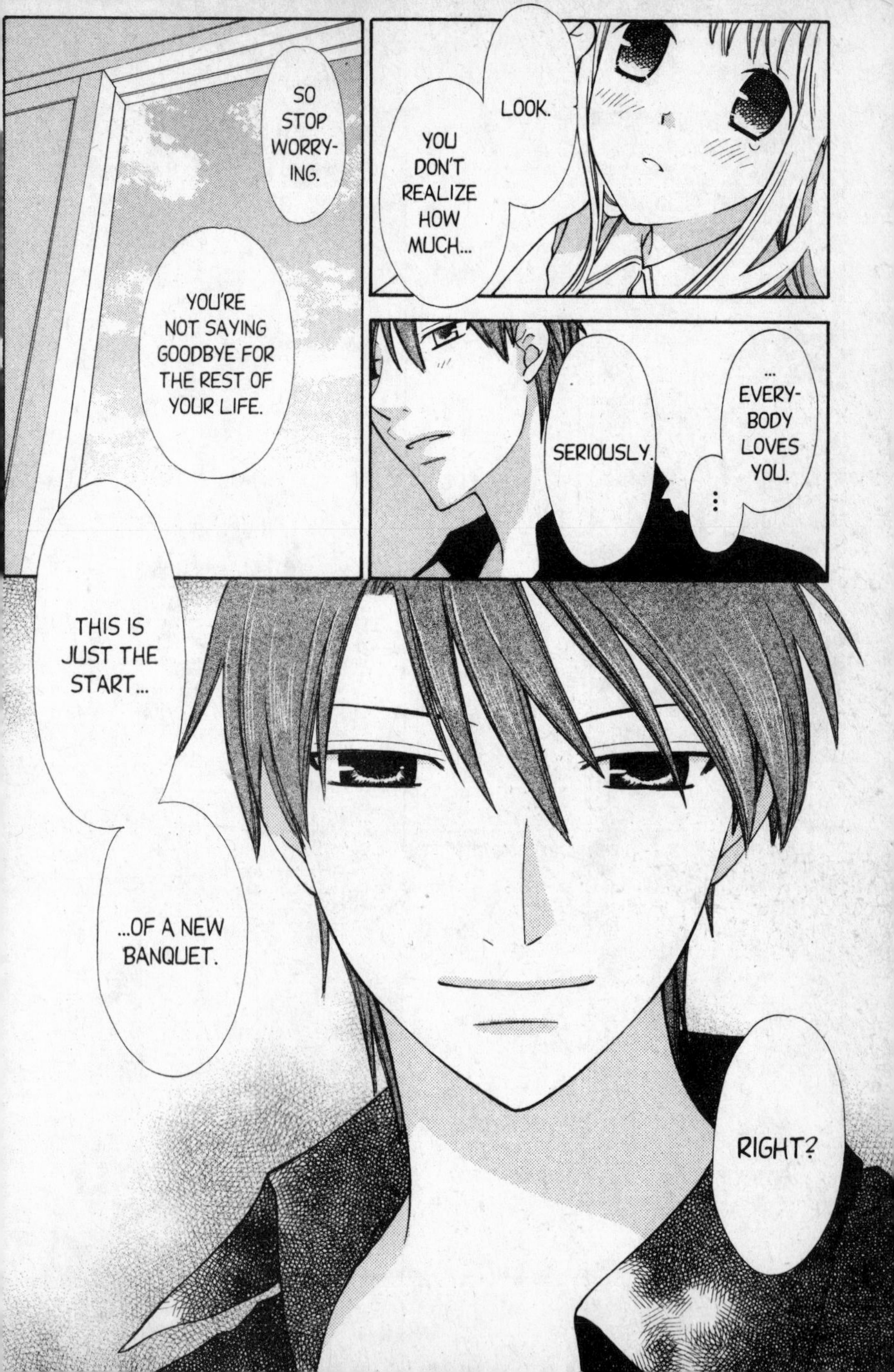
LOOK.
YOU DON'T REALIZE HOW MUCH...
... EVERY-BODY LOVES YOU.
...
SERIOUSLY.
SO STOP WORRY-ING.
YOU'RE NOT SAYING GOODBYE FOR THE REST OF YOUR LIFE.
THIS IS JUST THE START...
...OF A NEW BANQUET.
RIGHT?

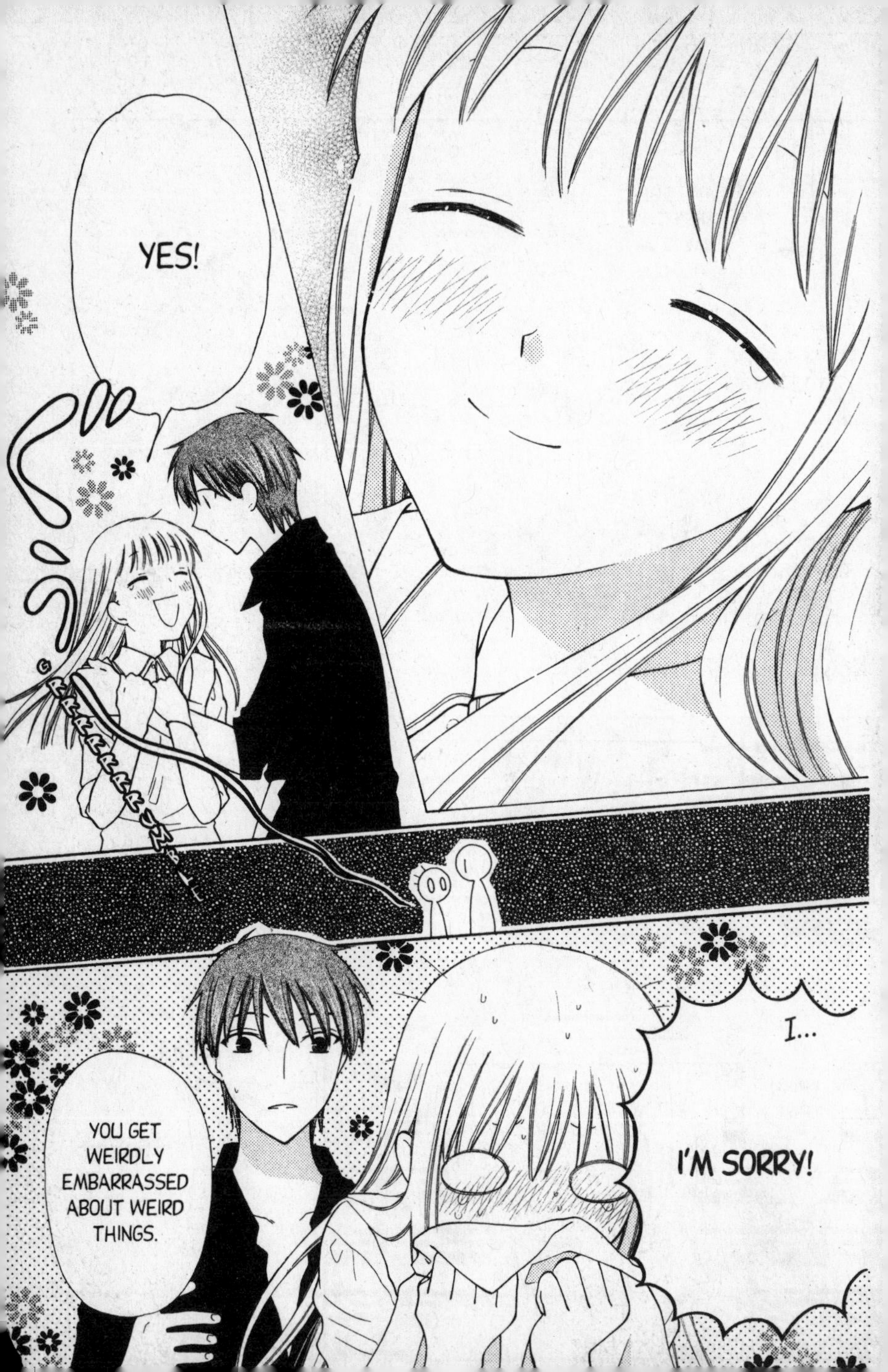
YES!
GRRRRRRRUMBLE
I...
I'M SORRY!
YOU GET WEIRDLY EMBARRASSED ABOUT WEIRD THINGS.

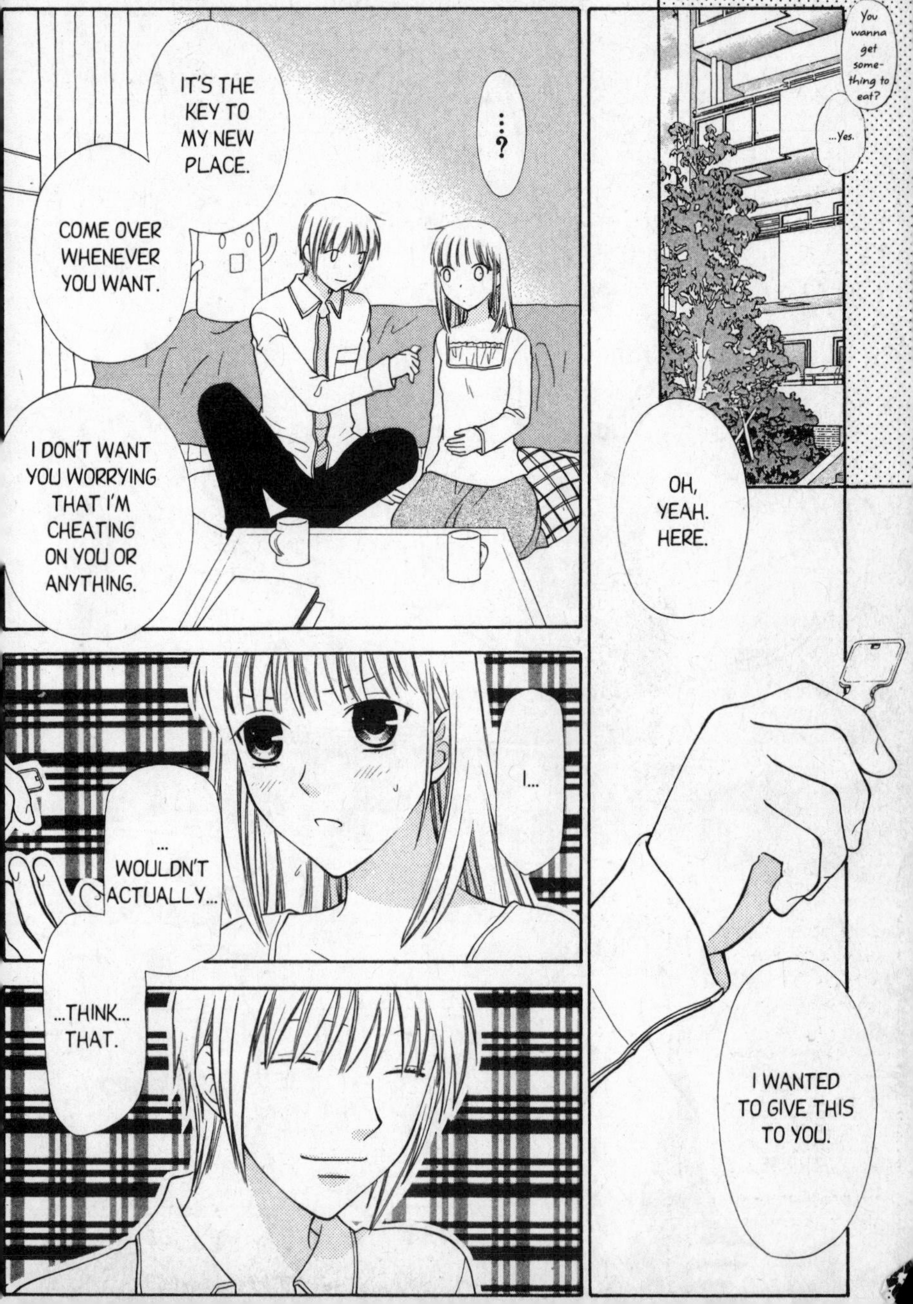
You wanna get some-thing to eat?
...Yes.
OH, YEAH. HERE.
I WANTED TO GIVE THIS TO YOU.
IT'S THE KEY TO MY NEW PLACE.
...?
COME OVER WHENEVER YOU WANT.
I DON'T WANT YOU WORRYING THAT I'M CHEATING ON YOU OR ANYTHING.
I...
... WOULDN'T ACTUALLY...
...THINK... THAT.

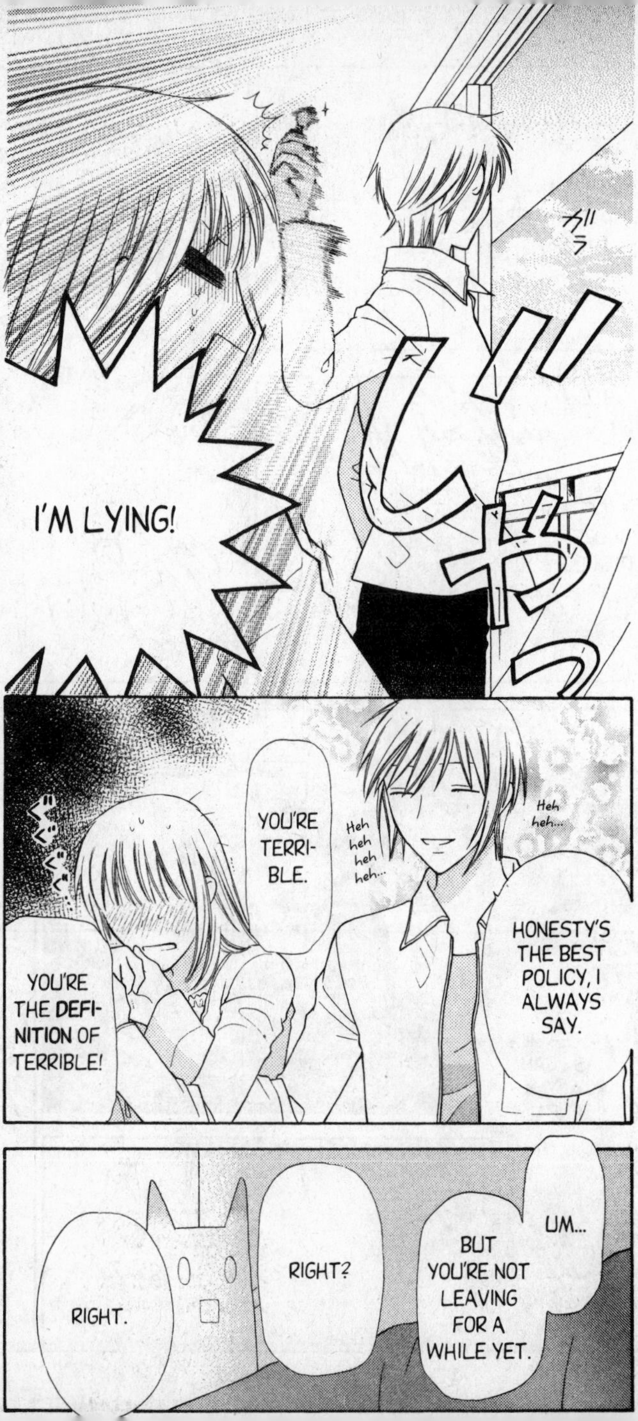
ガラ
じゃっ
I'M LYING!
HONESTY'S THE BEST POLICY, I ALWAYS SAY.
Heh heh...
Heh heh heh heh...
YOU'RE TERRIBLE.
YOU'RE THE DEFINITION OF TERRIBLE!
UM...
BUT YOU'RE NOT LEAVING FOR A WHILE YET.
RIGHT?
RIGHT.

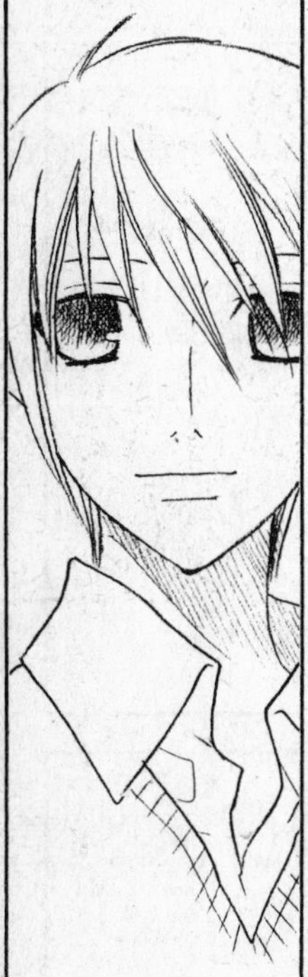

Yuki

I went through a pretty difficult labor giving birth to Yuki, and we both suffered and suffered, but now I honestly believe that it was all worth it. He's gained a little confidence, and got a little mean (laugh). I would have liked to draw Yuki a little more.

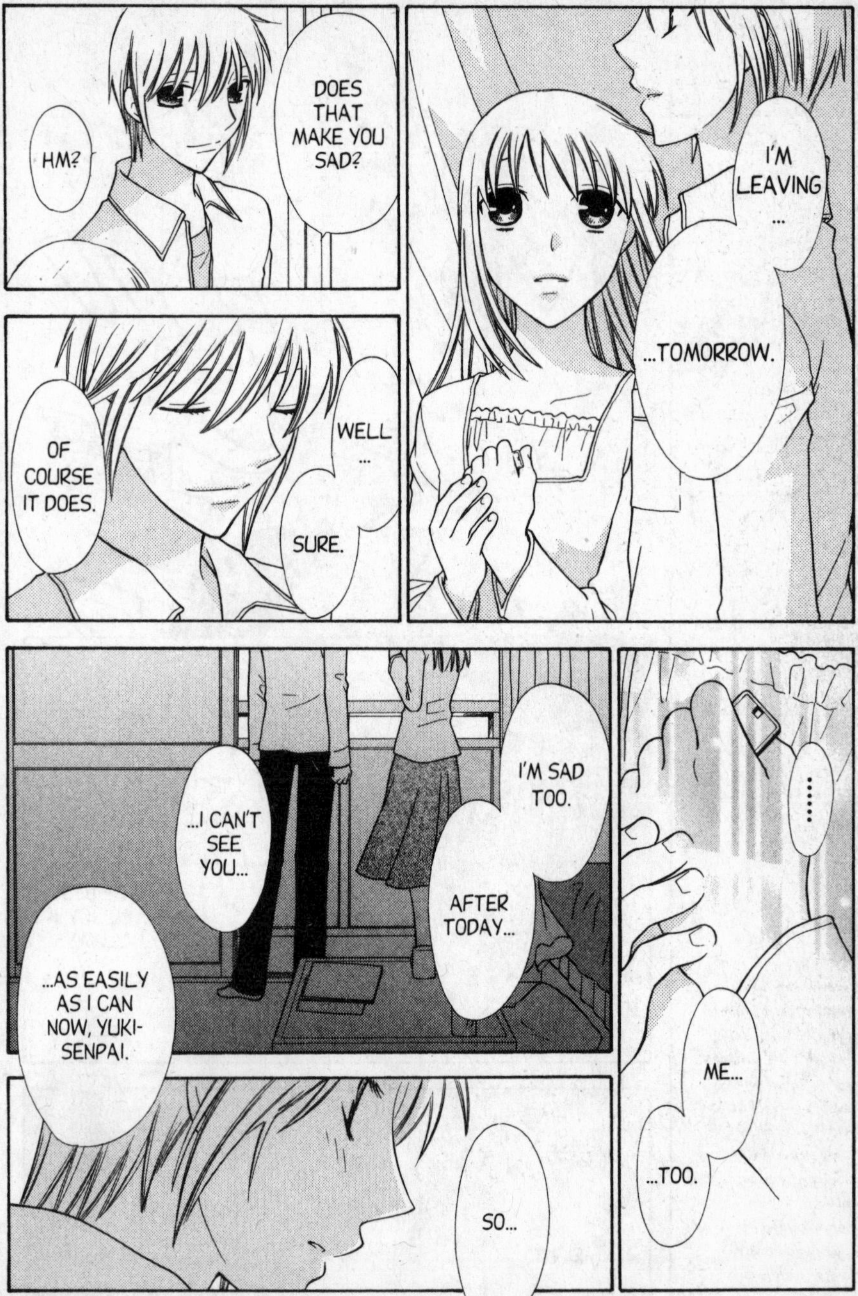
I'M LEAVING ...
...TOMORROW.
HM?
DOES THAT MAKE YOU SAD?
WELL ...
SURE.
OF COURSE IT DOES.
......
ME...
...TOO.
I'M SAD TOO.
AFTER TODAY...
...I CAN'T SEE YOU...
...AS EASILY AS I CAN NOW, YUKI-SENPAI.
SO...

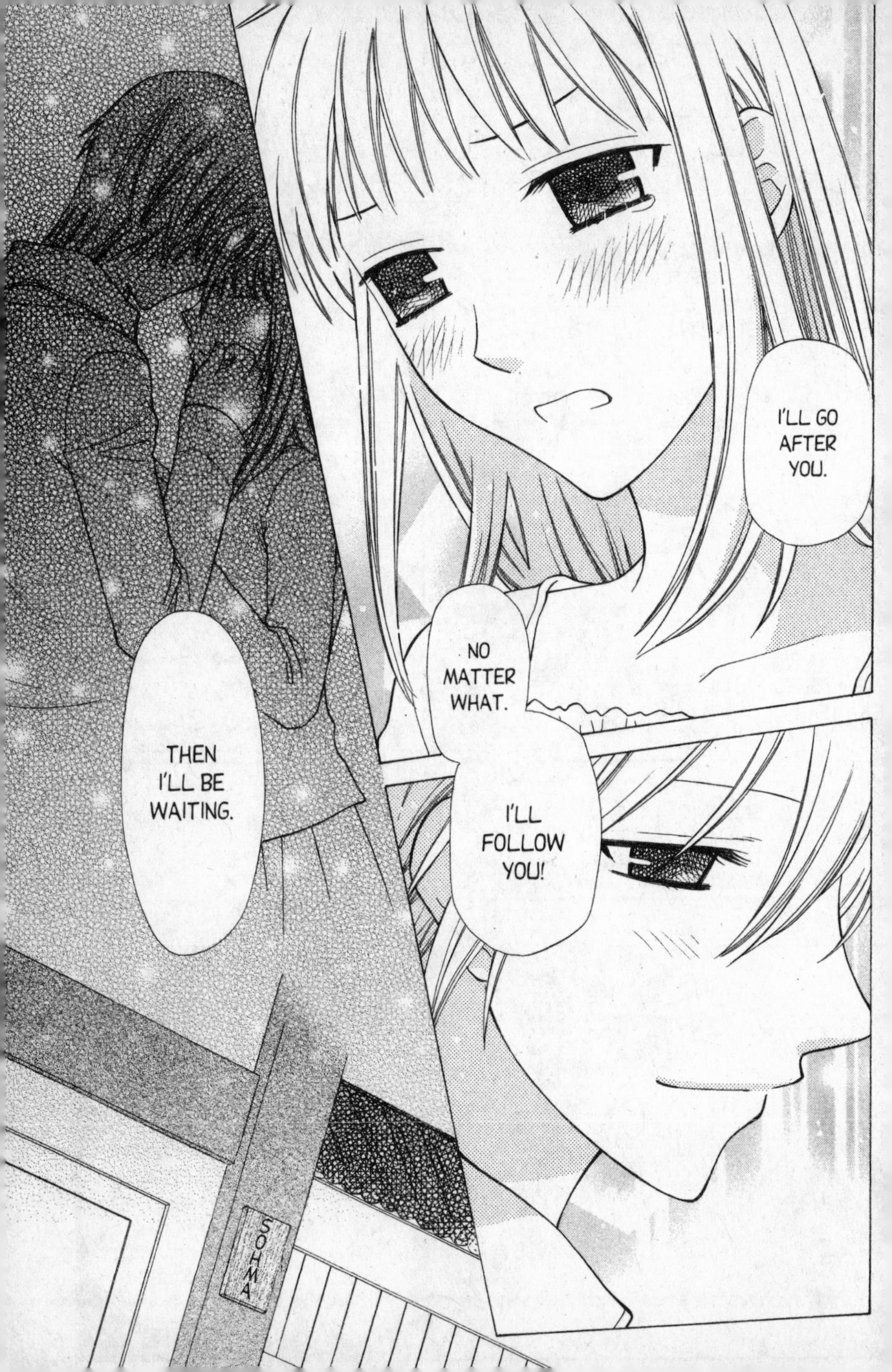
I'LL GO AFTER YOU.
NO MATTER WHAT.
I'LL FOLLOW YOU!
THEN I'LL BE WAITING.
SOHMA

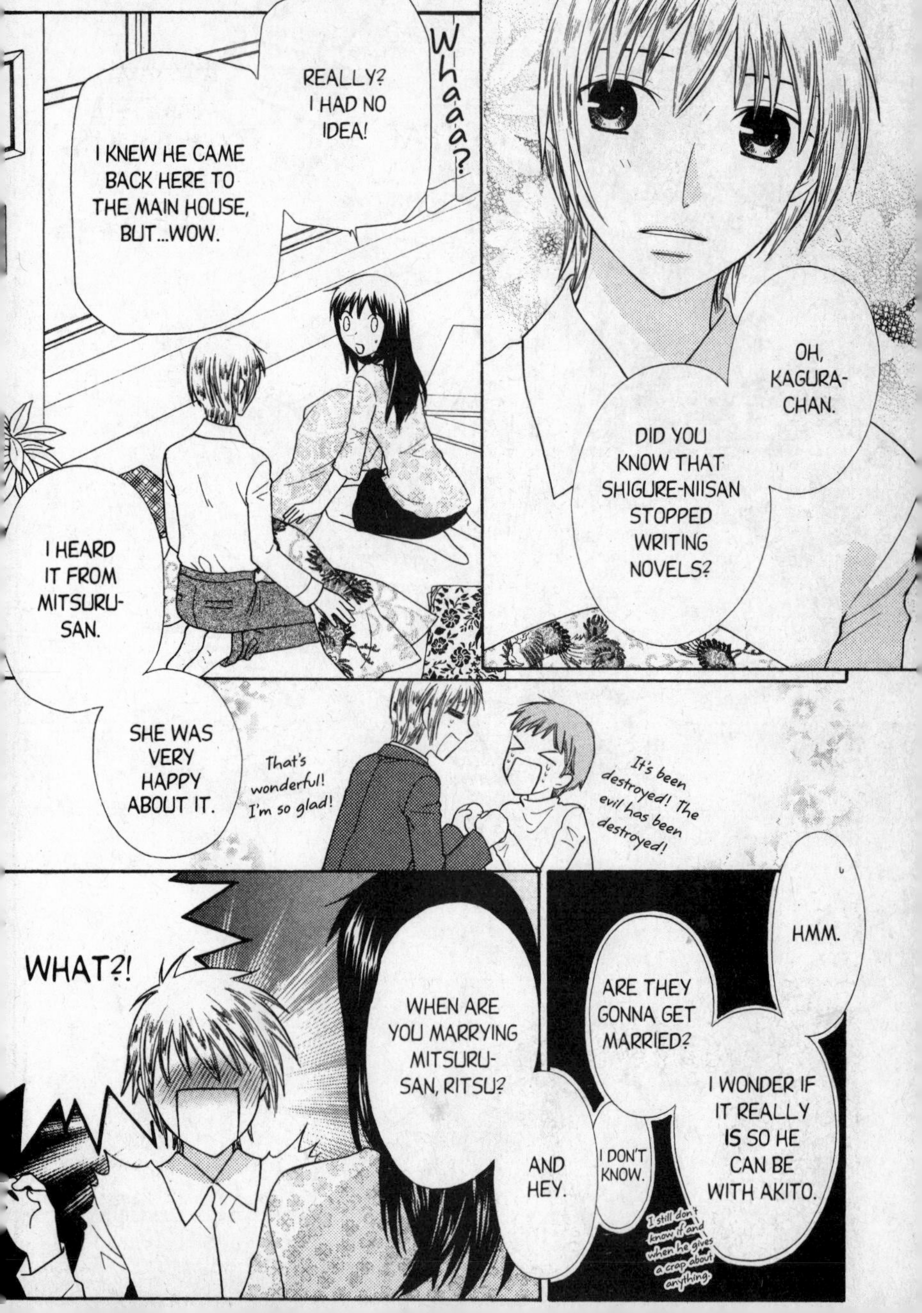

OH, KAGURA-CHAN.
DID YOU KNOW THAT SHIGURE-NIISAN STOPPED WRITING NOVELS?
Whaaa?
REALLY? I HAD NO IDEA!
I KNEW HE CAME BACK HERE TO THE MAIN HOUSE, BUT...WOW.
I HEARD IT FROM MITSURU-SAN.
SHE WAS VERY HAPPY ABOUT IT.
It's been destroyed! The evil has been destroyed!
That's wonderful! I'm so glad!
HMM.
ARE THEY GONNA GET MARRIED?
I WONDER IF IT REALLY IS SO HE CAN BE WITH AKITO.
I DON'T KNOW.
I still don't know if and when he gives a crap about anything.
AND HEY.
WHEN ARE YOU MARRYING MITSURU-SAN, RITSU?
WHAT?!

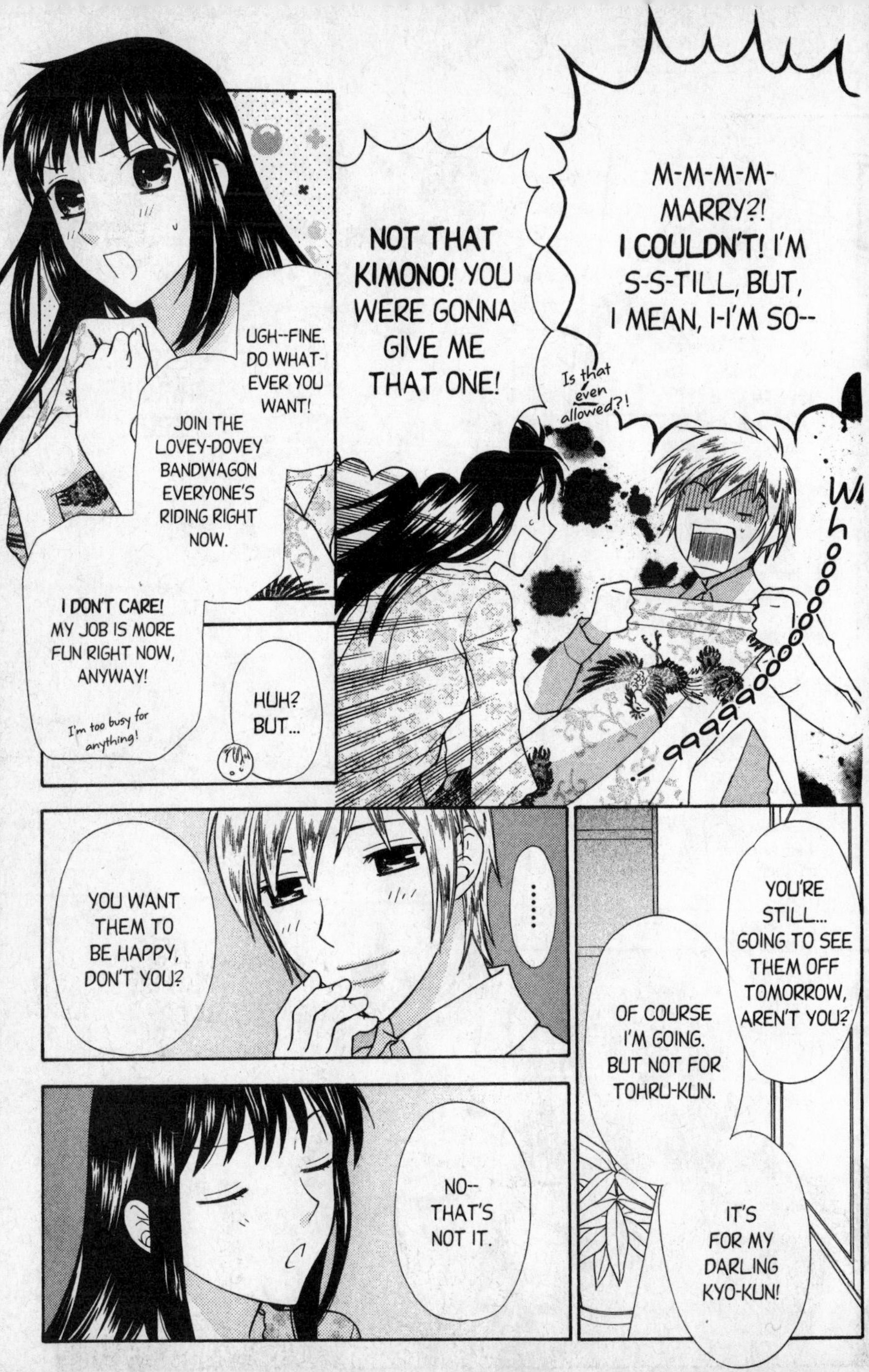
M-M-M-M-MARRY?! I COULDN'T! I'M S-S-TILL, BUT, I MEAN, I-I'M SO--
NOT THAT KIMONO! YOU WERE GONNA GIVE ME THAT ONE!
Is that even allowed?!
Whooooooooooooo--ggggggg--!
UGH--FINE. DO WHAT-EVER YOU WANT!
JOIN THE LOVEY-DOVEY BANDWAGON EVERYONE'S RIDING RIGHT NOW.
HUH? BUT...
I DON'T CARE! MY JOB IS MORE FUN RIGHT NOW, ANYWAY!
I'm too busy for anything!
YOU'RE STILL... GOING TO SEE THEM OFF TOMORROW, AREN'T YOU?
OF COURSE I'M GOING. BUT NOT FOR TOHRU-KUN.
IT'S FOR MY DARLING KYO-KUN!
......
YOU WANT THEM TO BE HAPPY, DON'T YOU?
NO-- THAT'S NOT IT.

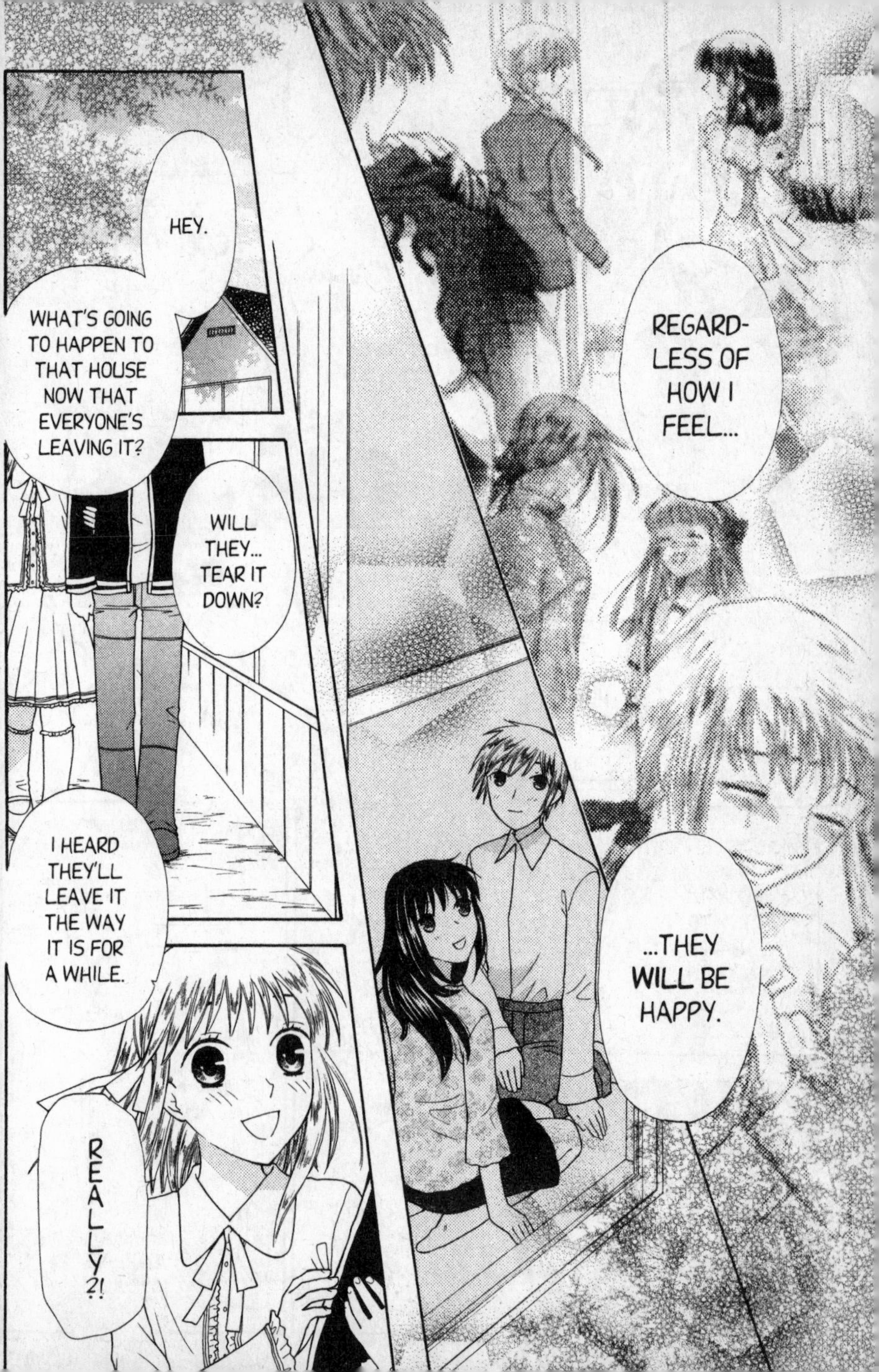
REGARDLESS OF HOW I FEEL...
...THEY WILL BE HAPPY.
HEY.
WHAT'S GOING TO HAPPEN TO THAT HOUSE NOW THAT EVERYONE'S LEAVING IT?
WILL THEY... TEAR IT DOWN?
I HEARD THEY'LL LEAVE IT THE WAY IT IS FOR A WHILE.
REALLY?!

In the End

Maybe I should say something more fitting of a final volume, but thinking about it again, nothing comes to mind. Actually, I've been thinking (more than usual) that I don't want to say anything unnecessary and get in the readers' way. And I won't say much about Tohru, Kyo, or Yuki, either. That's because I've drawn a lot about each of them in the story. But I do talk about them a tiny bit in the bonus manga in the second fanbook. Anyone who's interested, please read it. This is a plug(laugh).

I've always wanted my manga to be like a cuttlefish--the more you bite into it, the better it gets. Of course, that's really difficult to achieve, but it's still one of the things I'm always wishing for. I do know nothing will happen from just wishing, so I'm still working very hard at it every day(laugh). I'll keep working hard. Praying for the day we meet again...

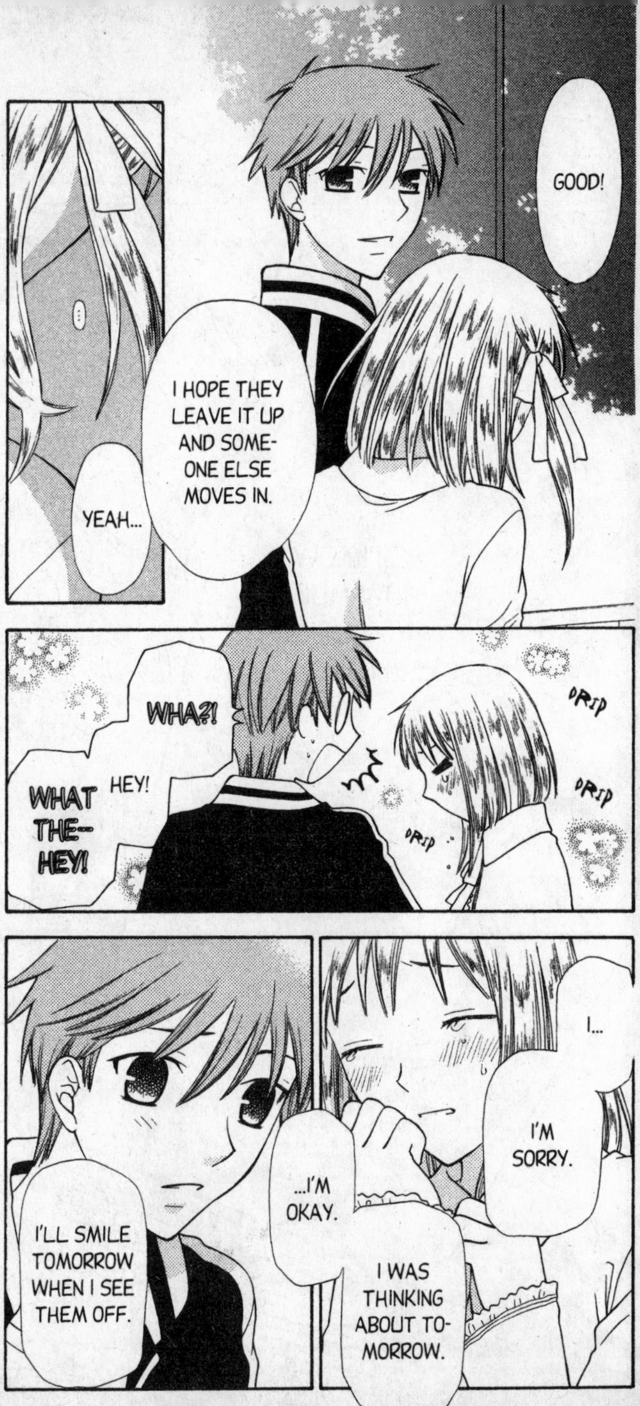
GOOD!
I HOPE THEY LEAVE IT UP AND SOME-ONE ELSE MOVES IN.
...
YEAH...
DRIP
DRIP
DRIP
WHA?!
HEY!
WHAT THE-- HEY!
I...
I'M SORRY.
I WAS THINKING ABOUT TO-MORROW.
...I'M OKAY.
I'LL SMILE TOMORROW WHEN I SEE THEM OFF.

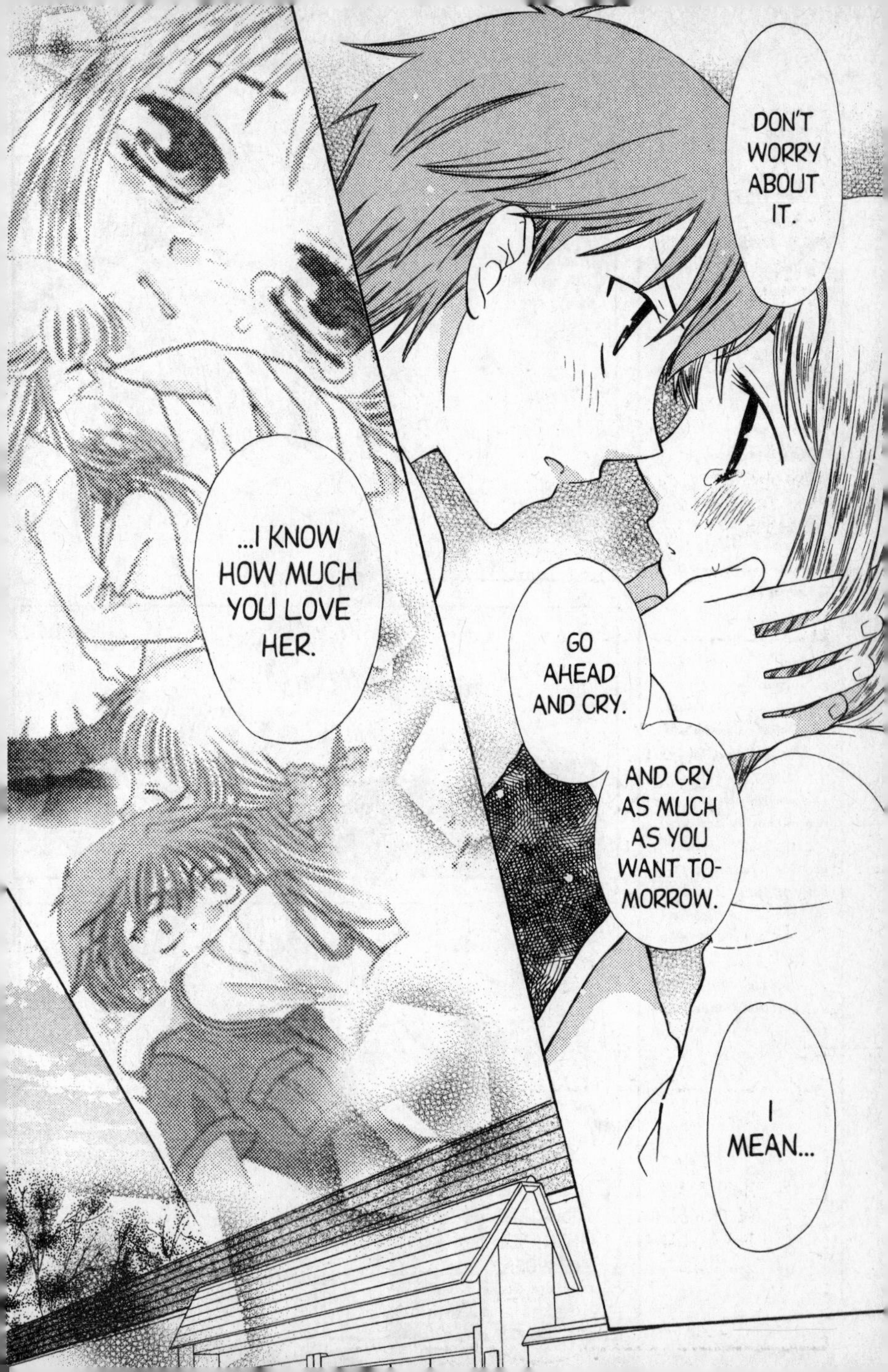
DON'T WORRY ABOUT IT.
GO AHEAD AND CRY.
AND CRY AS MUCH AS YOU WANT TO-MORROW.
I MEAN...
...I KNOW HOW MUCH YOU LOVE HER.

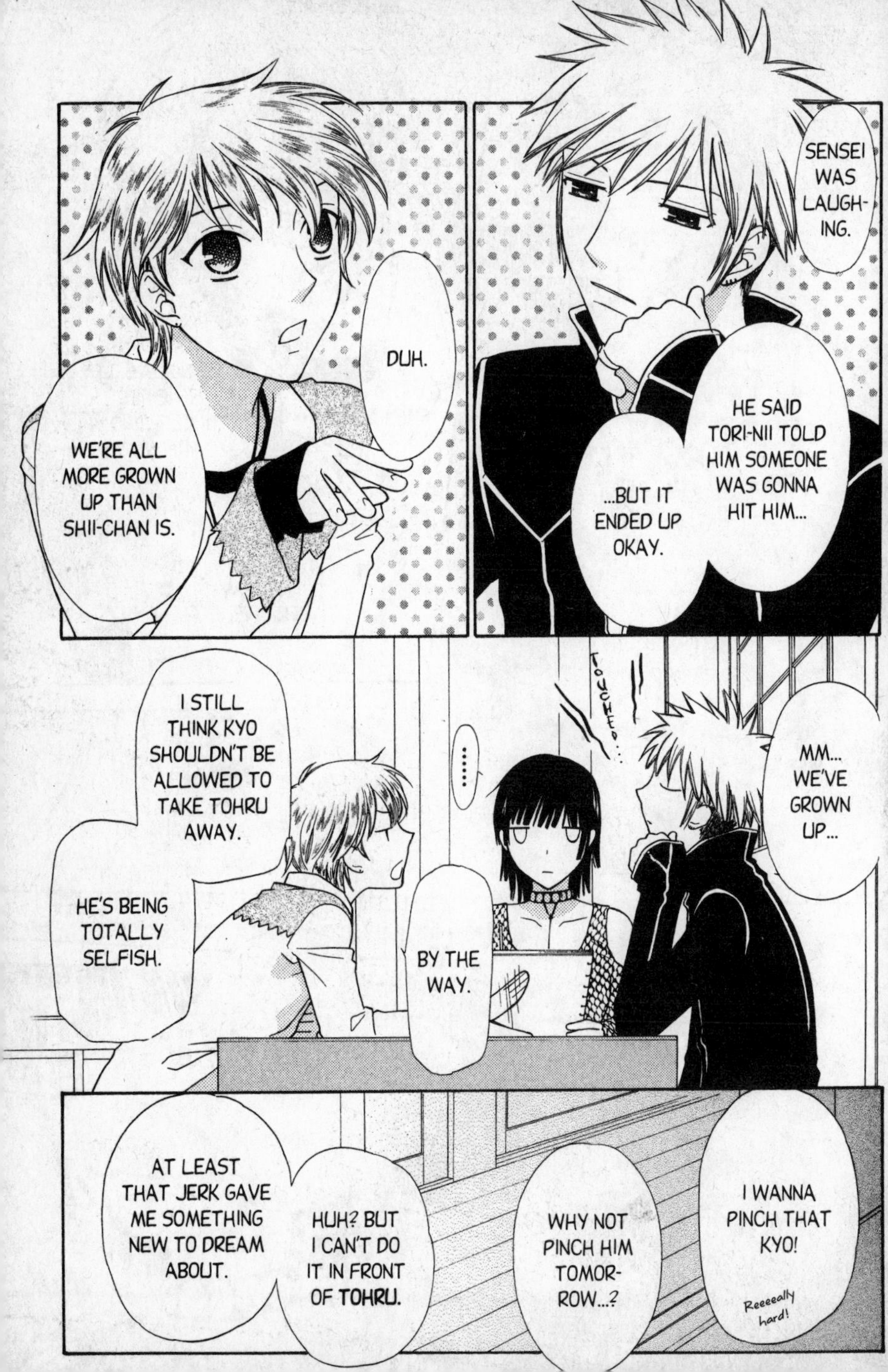
SENSEI WAS LAUGH-ING.
HE SAID TORI-NII TOLD HIM SOMEONE WAS GONNA HIT HIM...
...BUT IT ENDED UP OKAY.
DUH.
WE'RE ALL MORE GROWN UP THAN SHII-CHAN IS.
MM... WE'VE GROWN UP...
TOUCHED...
......
I STILL THINK KYO SHOULDN'T BE ALLOWED TO TAKE TOHRU AWAY.
HE'S BEING TOTALLY SELFISH.
BY THE WAY.
I WANNA PINCH THAT KYO!
Reeeeally hard!
WHY NOT PINCH HIM TOMOR-ROW...?
HUH? BUT I CAN'T DO IT IN FRONT OF TOHRU.
AT LEAST THAT JERK GAVE ME SOMETHING NEW TO DREAM ABOUT.

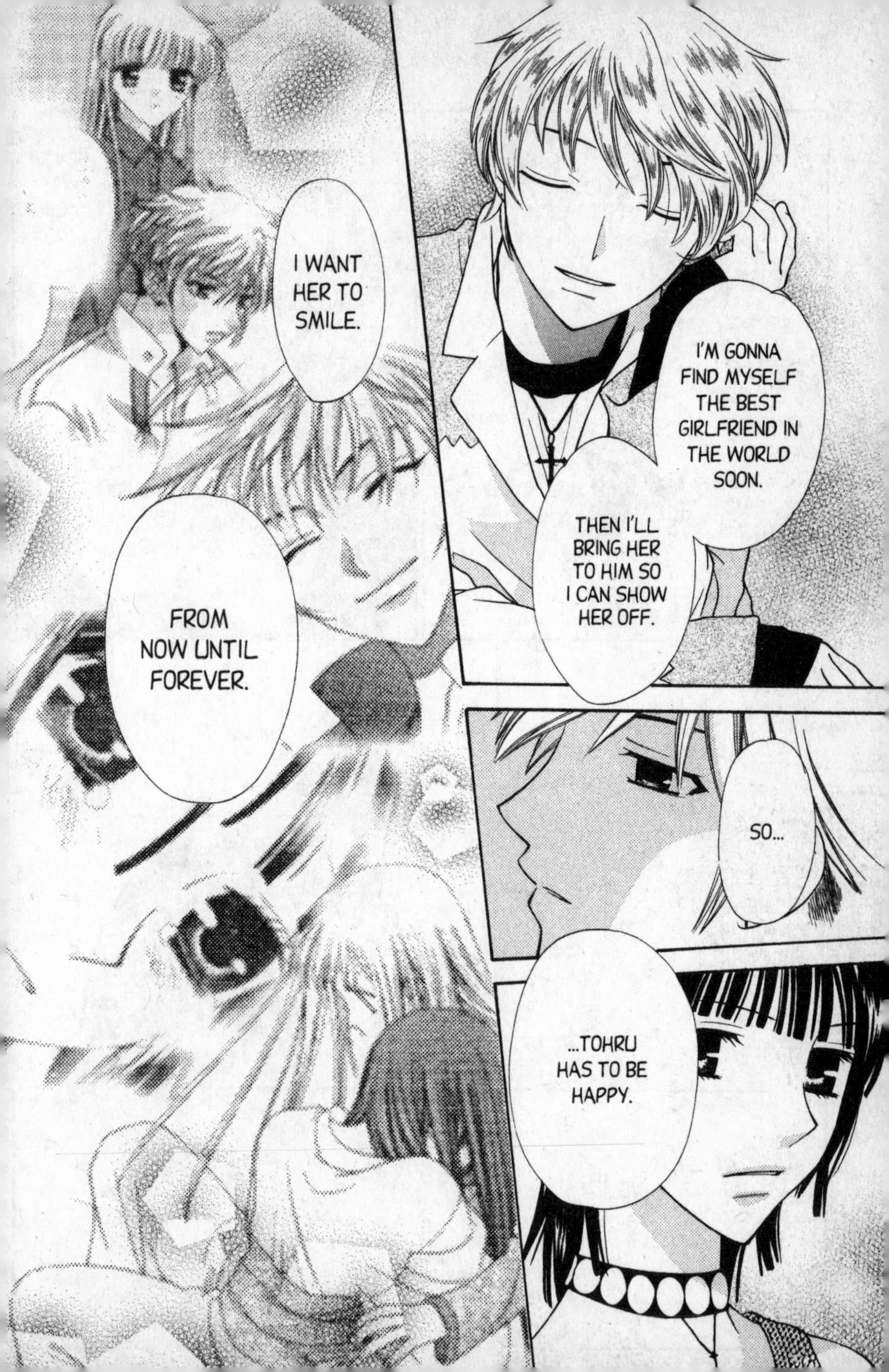
I'M GONNA FIND MYSELF THE BEST GIRLFRIEND IN THE WORLD SOON.
THEN I'LL BRING HER TO HIM SO I CAN SHOW HER OFF.
SO...
...TOHRU HAS TO BE HAPPY.
I WANT HER TO SMILE.
FROM NOW UNTIL FOREVER.

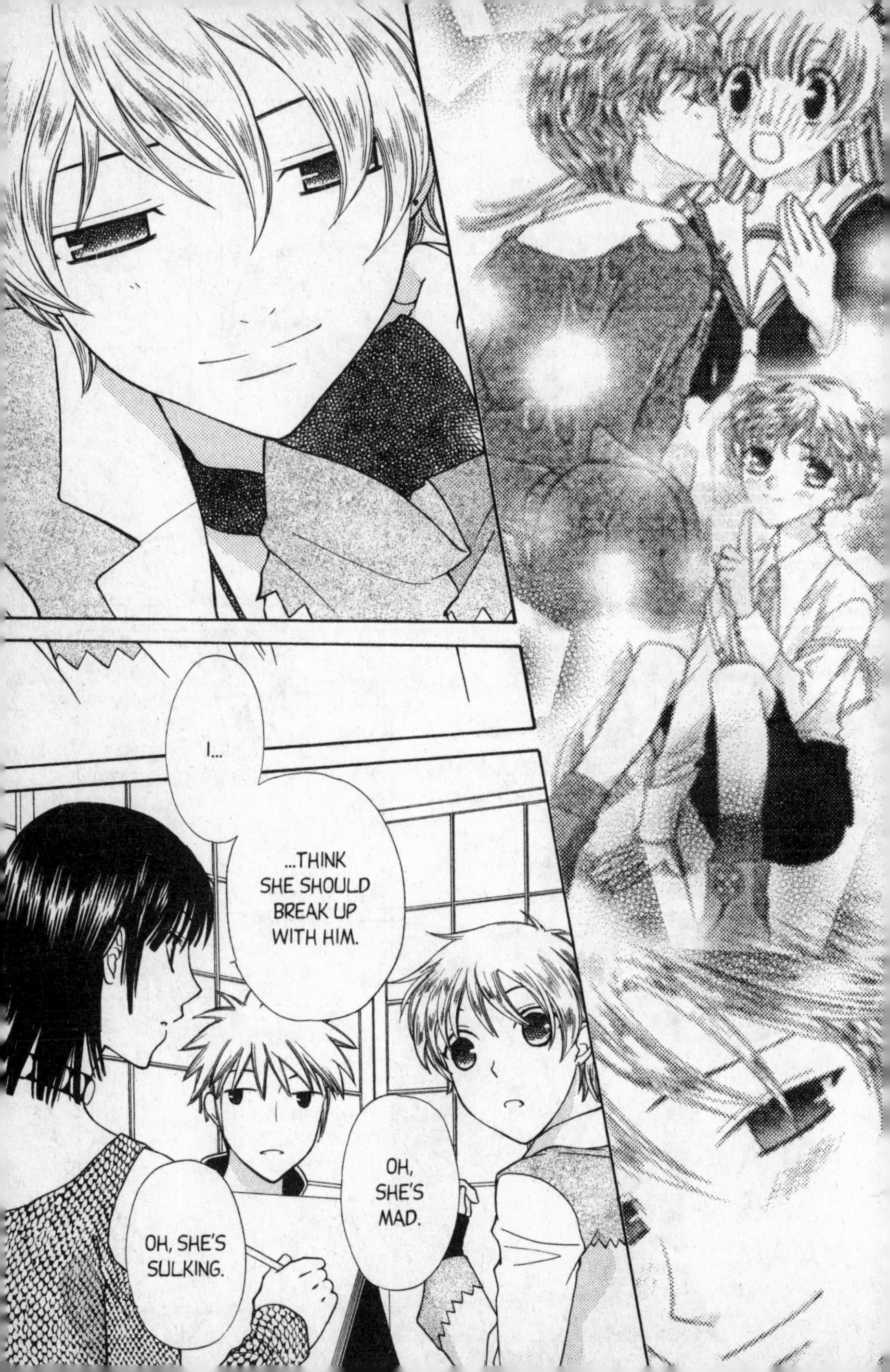
I...
...THINK SHE SHOULD BREAK UP WITH HIM.
OH, SHE'S MAD.
OH, SHE'S SULKING.

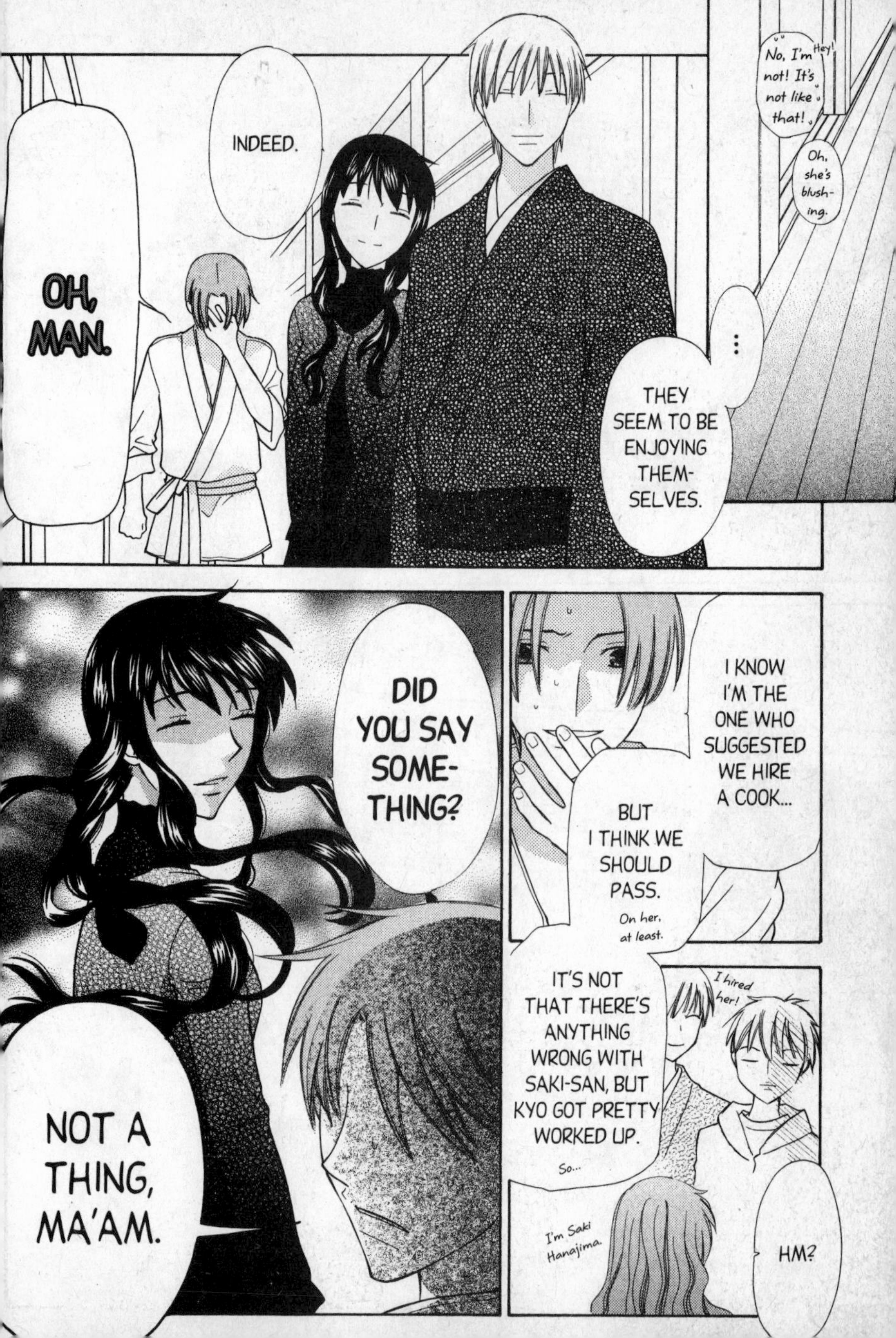
Hey!
No, I'm not! It's not like that!
Oh, she's blush-ing.
...
THEY SEEM TO BE ENJOYING THEM-SELVES.
INDEED.
OH, MAN.
I KNOW I'M THE ONE WHO SUGGESTED WE HIRE A COOK...
BUT I THINK WE SHOULD PASS.
On her, at least.
I hired her!
IT'S NOT THAT THERE'S ANYTHING WRONG WITH SAKI-SAN, BUT KYO GOT PRETTY WORKED UP.
So...
HM?
I'm Saki Hanajima.
DID YOU SAY SOME-THING?
NOT A THING, MA'AM.

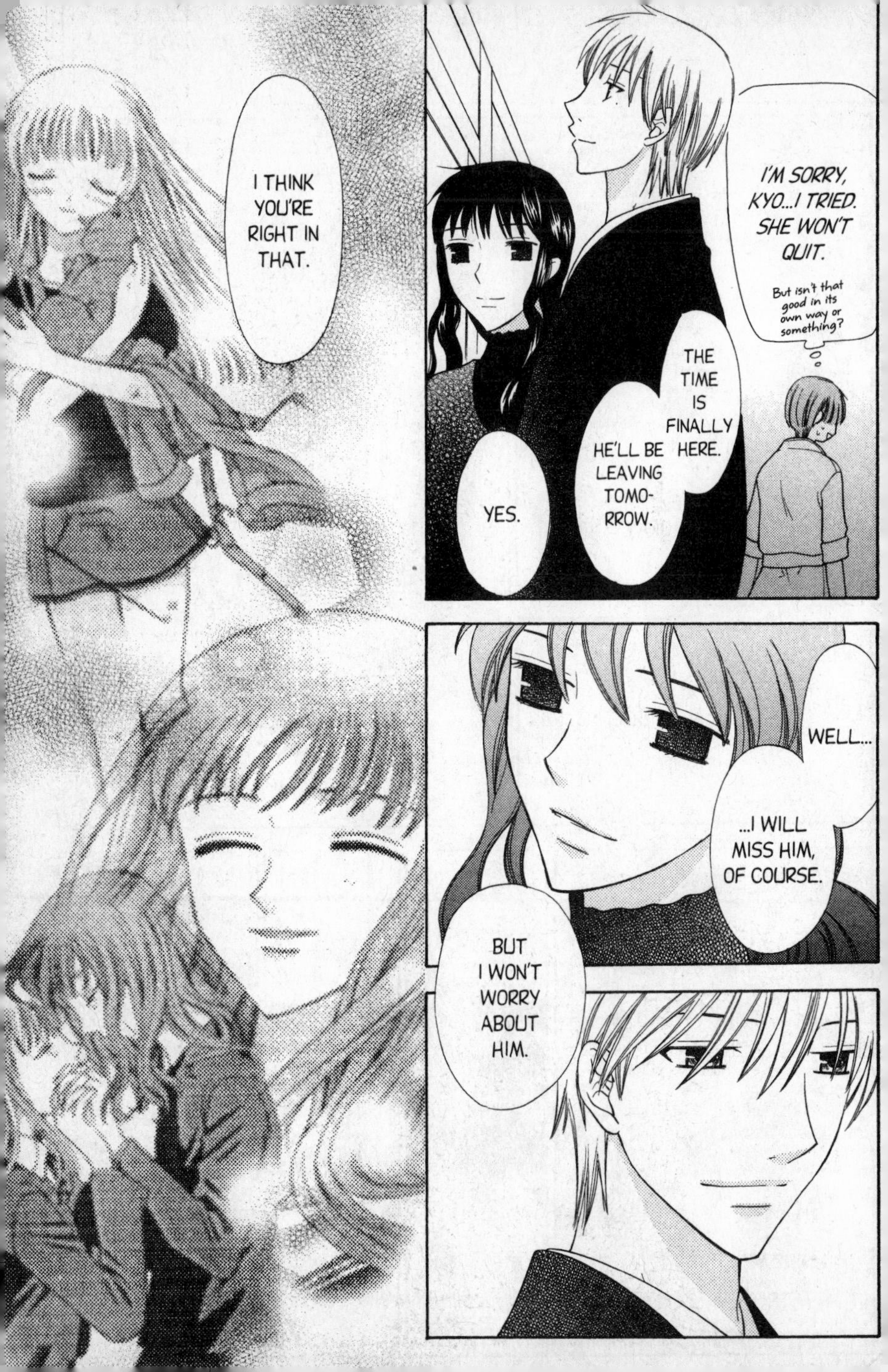
I'M SORRY, KYO...I TRIED. SHE WON'T QUIT.
But isn't that good in its own way or something?
THE TIME IS FINALLY HERE.
HE'LL BE LEAVING TOMORROW.
YES.
WELL...
...I WILL MISS HIM, OF COURSE.
BUT I WON'T WORRY ABOUT HIM.
I THINK YOU'RE RIGHT IN THAT.

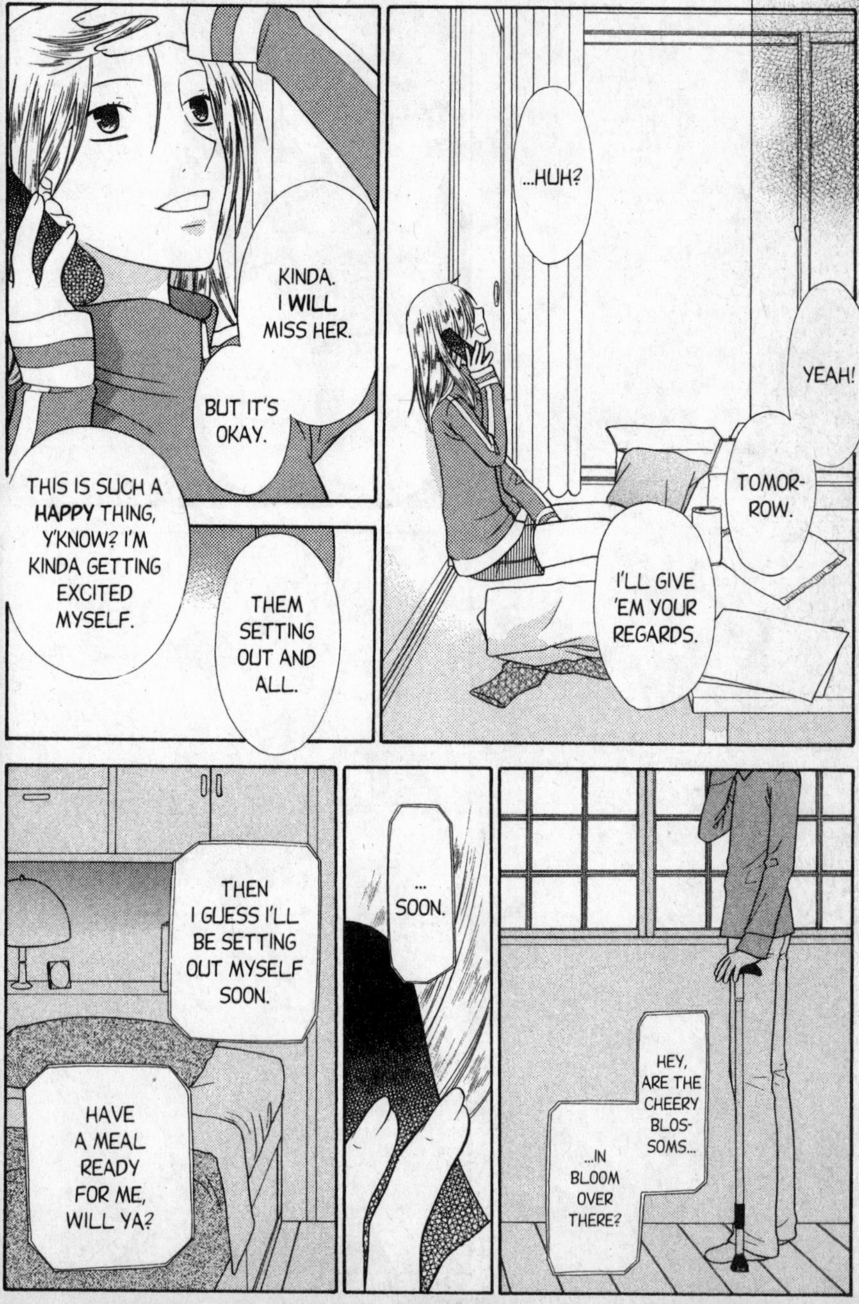
YEAH!
TOMORROW.
I'LL GIVE 'EM YOUR REGARDS.
...HUH?
KINDA. I **WILL** MISS HER.
BUT IT'S OKAY.
THIS IS SUCH A **HAPPY** THING, Y'KNOW? I'M KINDA GETTING EXCITED MYSELF.
THEM SETTING OUT AND ALL.
HEY, ARE THE CHEERY BLOSSOMS...
...IN BLOOM OVER THERE?
... SOON.
THEN I GUESS I'LL BE SETTING OUT MYSELF SOON.
HAVE A MEAL READY FOR ME, WILL YA?

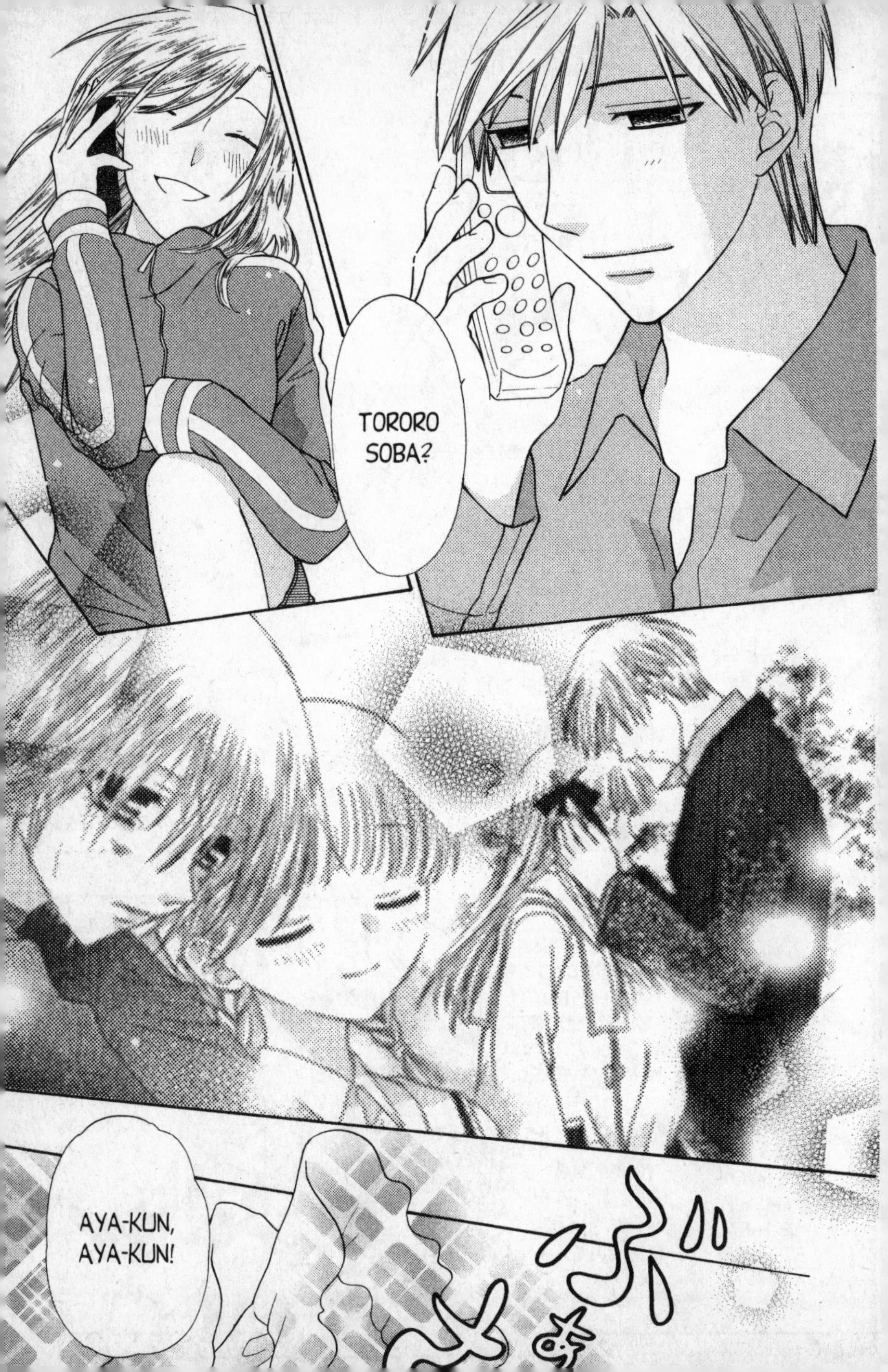
TORORO SOBA?
AYA-KUN, AYA-KUN!

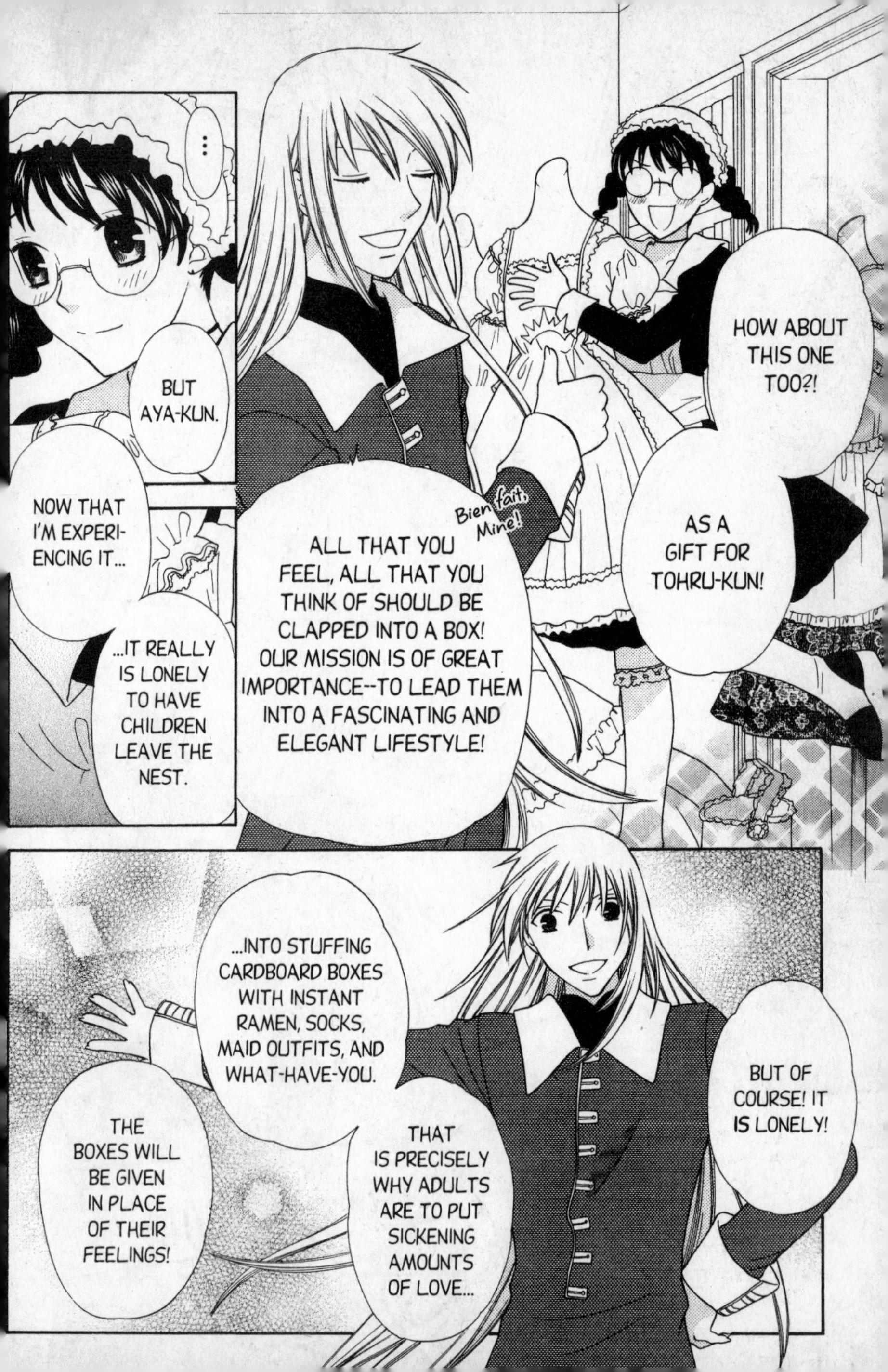
HOW ABOUT THIS ONE TOO?!
AS A GIFT FOR TOHRU-KUN!
Bien fait, Mine!
ALL THAT YOU FEEL, ALL THAT YOU THINK OF SHOULD BE CLAPPED INTO A BOX! OUR MISSION IS OF GREAT IMPORTANCE--TO LEAD THEM INTO A FASCINATING AND ELEGANT LIFESTYLE!
...
BUT AYA-KUN.
NOW THAT I'M EXPERI-ENCING IT...
...IT REALLY IS LONELY TO HAVE CHILDREN LEAVE THE NEST.
BUT OF COURSE! IT IS LONELY!
THAT IS PRECISELY WHY ADULTS ARE TO PUT SICKENING AMOUNTS OF LOVE...
...INTO STUFFING CARDBOARD BOXES WITH INSTANT RAMEN, SOCKS, MAID OUTFITS, AND WHAT-HAVE-YOU.
THE BOXES WILL BE GIVEN IN PLACE OF THEIR FEELINGS!

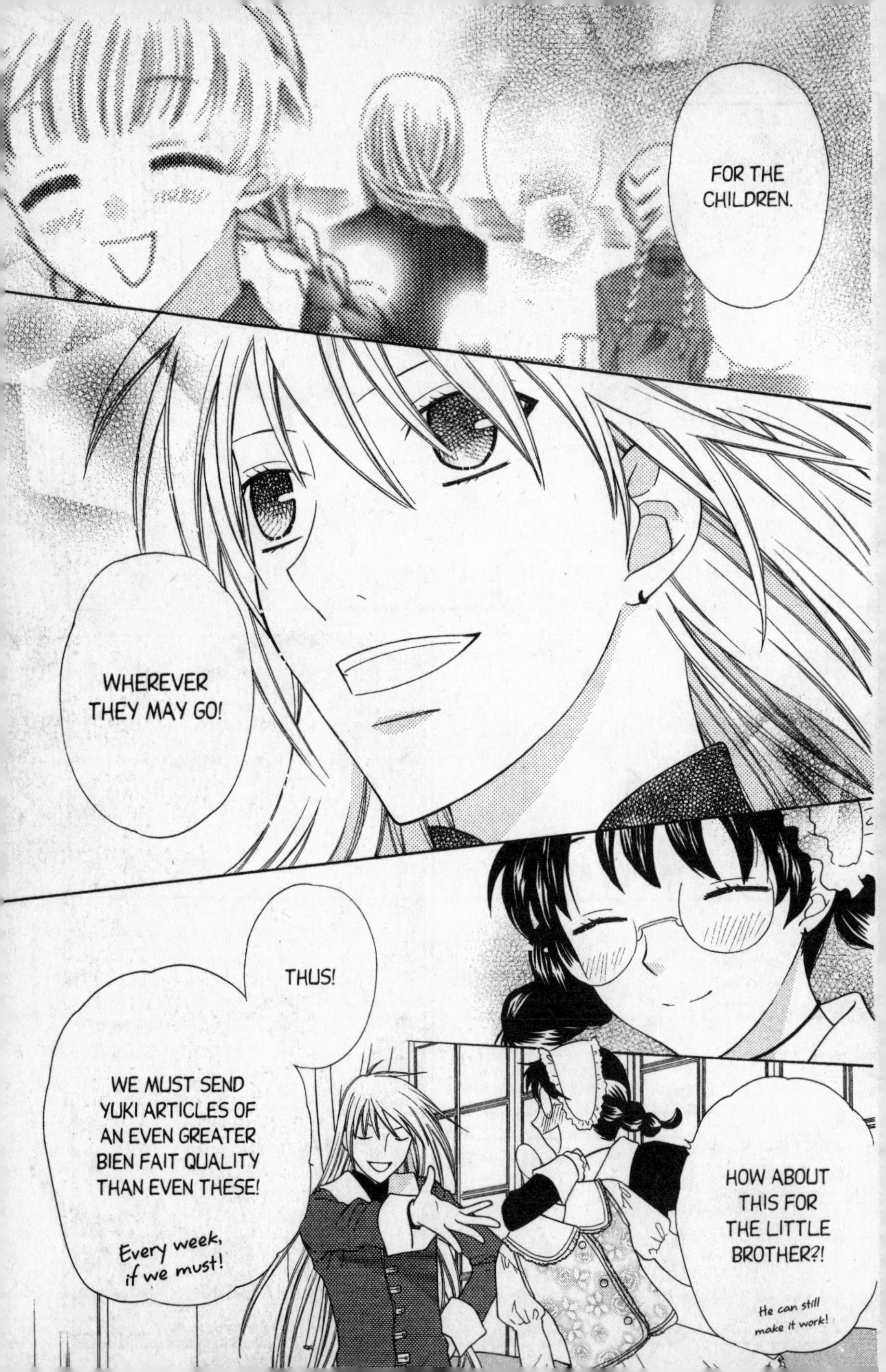
FOR THE CHILDREN.
WHEREVER THEY MAY GO!
THUS!
HOW ABOUT THIS FOR THE LITTLE BROTHER?!
He can still make it work!
WE MUST SEND YUKI ARTICLES OF AN EVEN GREATER BIEN FAIT QUALITY THAN EVEN THESE!
Every week, if we must!

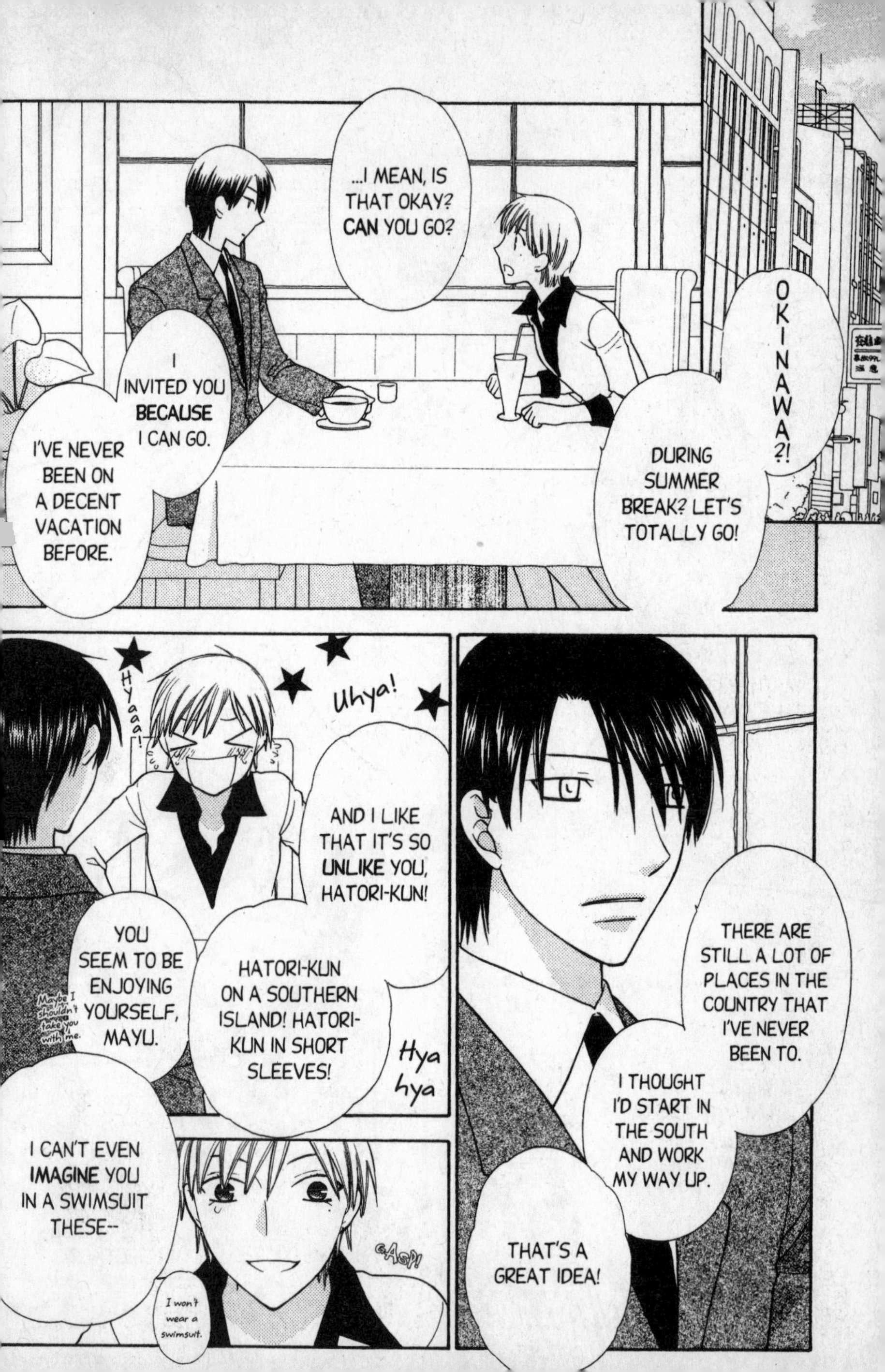
OKINAWA?!
DURING SUMMER BREAK? LET'S TOTALLY GO!
...I MEAN, IS THAT OKAY? CAN YOU GO?
I INVITED YOU BECAUSE I CAN GO.
I'VE NEVER BEEN ON A DECENT VACATION BEFORE.
THERE ARE STILL A LOT OF PLACES IN THE COUNTRY THAT I'VE NEVER BEEN TO.
I THOUGHT I'D START IN THE SOUTH AND WORK MY WAY UP.
THAT'S A GREAT IDEA!
Uhya!
Hyaaa!
AND I LIKE THAT IT'S SO UNLIKE YOU, HATORI-KUN!
HATORI-KUN ON A SOUTHERN ISLAND! HATORI-KUN IN SHORT SLEEVES!
Hya hya
YOU SEEM TO BE ENJOYING YOURSELF, MAYU.
Maybe I shouldn't take you with me.
GASP!
I CAN'T EVEN IMAGINE YOU IN A SWIMSUIT THESE--
I won't wear a swimsuit.

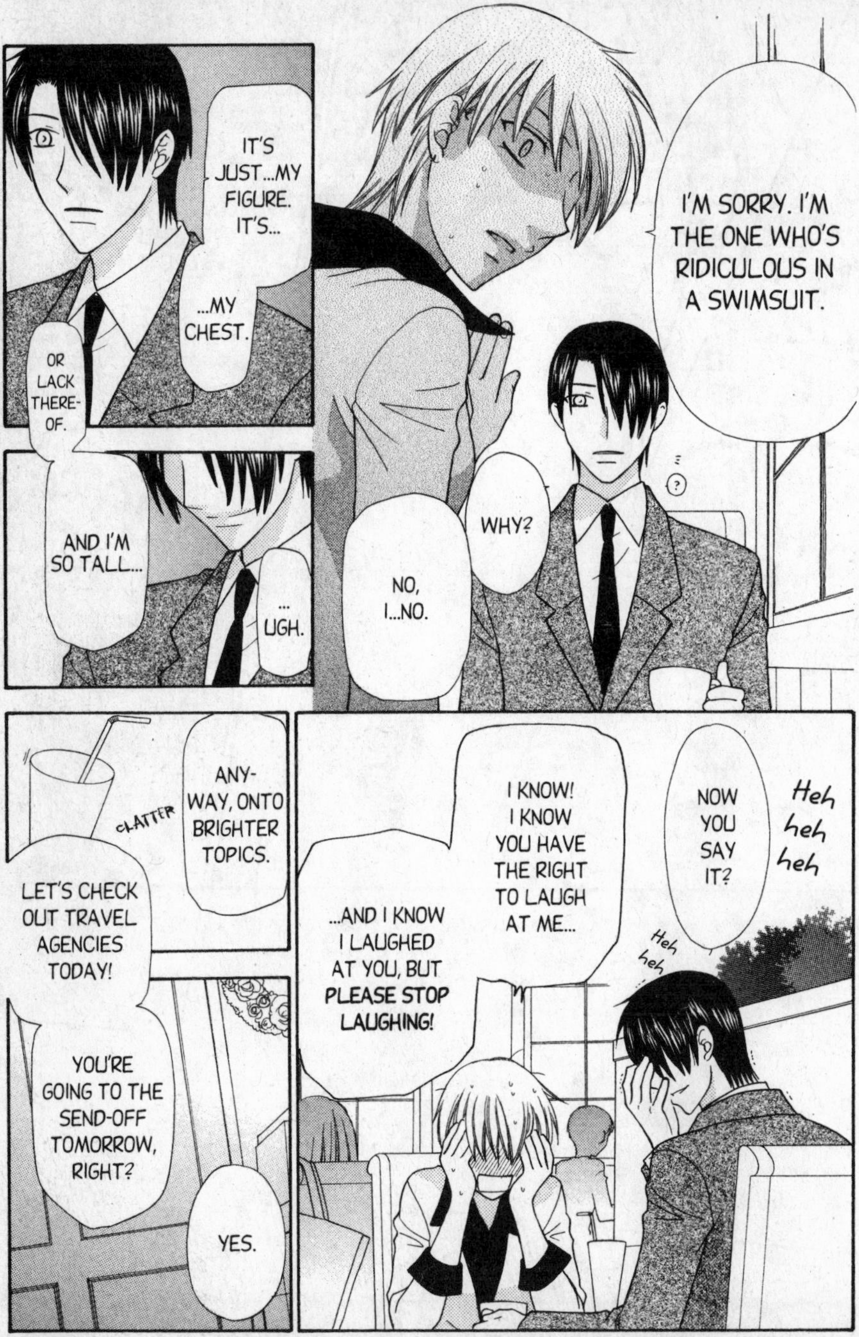
I'M SORRY. I'M THE ONE WHO'S RIDICULOUS IN A SWIMSUIT.
?
WHY?
NO, I...NO.
IT'S JUST...MY FIGURE. IT'S...
...MY CHEST.
OR LACK THERE-OF.
AND I'M SO TALL...
...UGH.
Heh heh heh
NOW YOU SAY IT?
I KNOW! I KNOW YOU HAVE THE RIGHT TO LAUGH AT ME...
...AND I KNOW I LAUGHED AT YOU, BUT PLEASE STOP LAUGHING!
Heh heh
ANY-WAY, ONTO BRIGHTER TOPICS.
CLATTER
LET'S CHECK OUT TRAVEL AGENCIES TODAY!
YOU'RE GOING TO THE SEND-OFF TOMORROW, RIGHT?
YES.

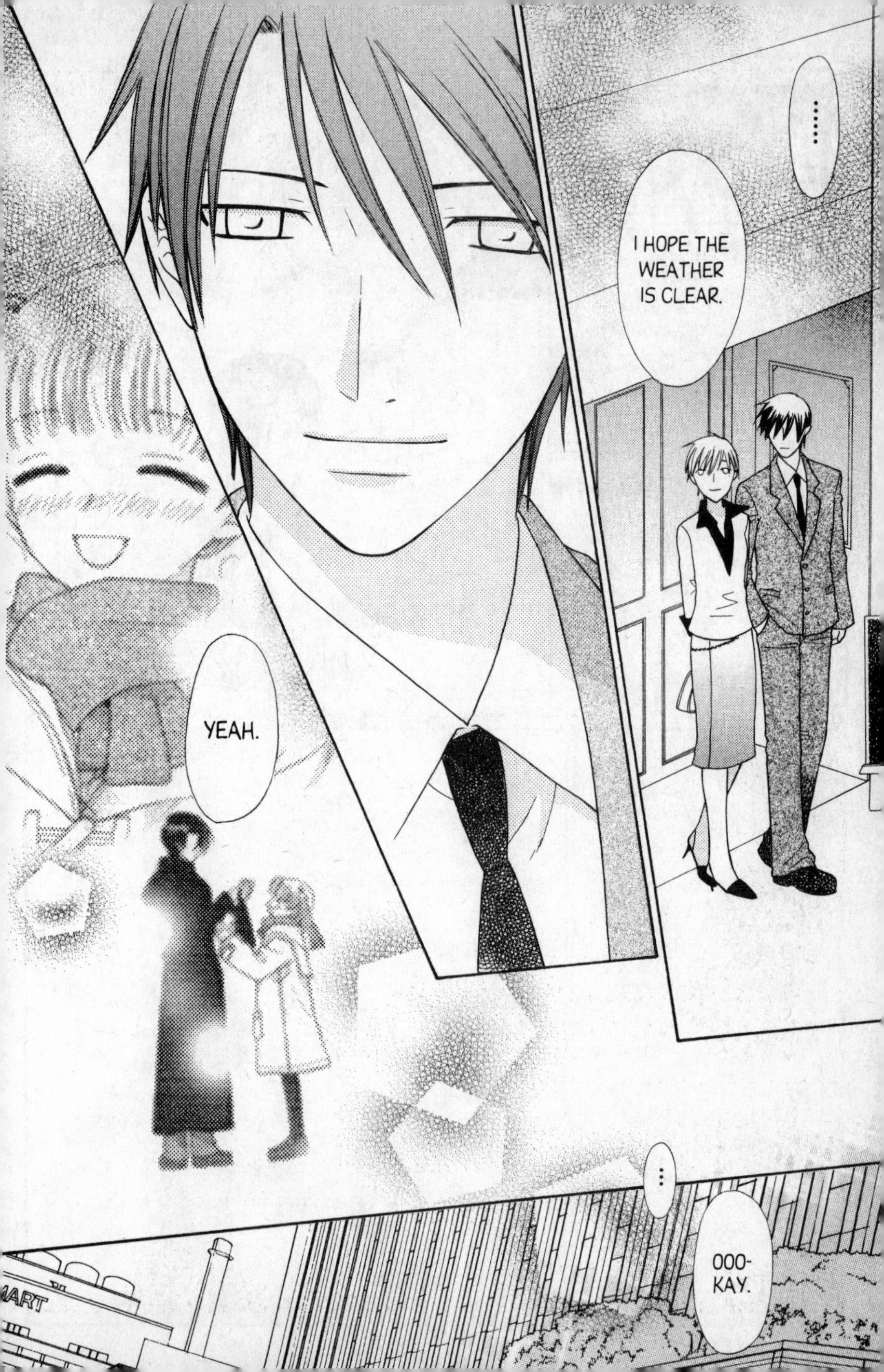
……
I HOPE THE WEATHER IS CLEAR.
YEAH.
…
OOO-KAY.
MART

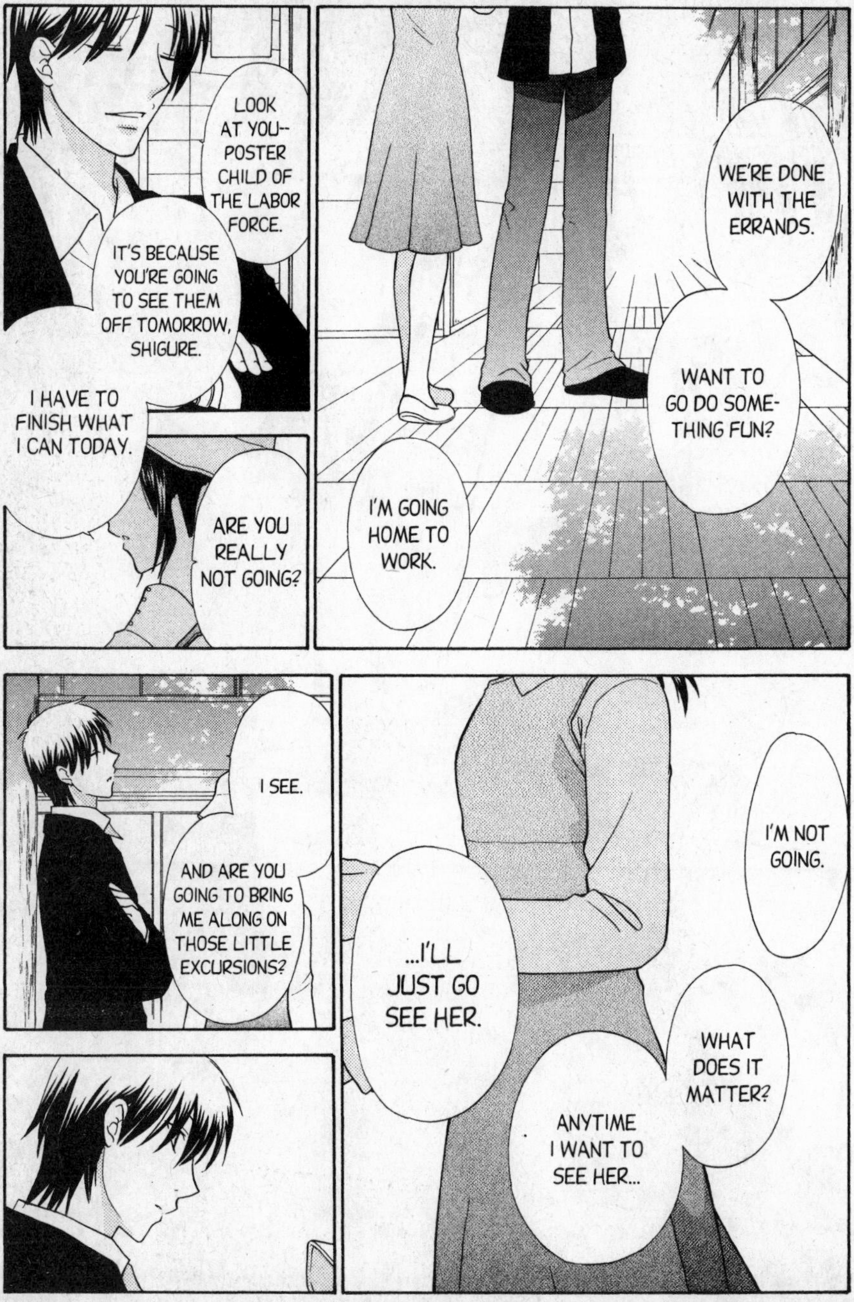

WE'RE DONE WITH THE ERRANDS.
WANT TO GO DO SOME-THING FUN?
I'M GOING HOME TO WORK.
LOOK AT YOU-- POSTER CHILD OF THE LABOR FORCE.
IT'S BECAUSE YOU'RE GOING TO SEE THEM OFF TOMORROW, SHIGURE.
I HAVE TO FINISH WHAT I CAN TODAY.
ARE YOU REALLY NOT GOING?
I'M NOT GOING.
WHAT DOES IT MATTER?
ANYTIME I WANT TO SEE HER...
...I'LL JUST GO SEE HER.
I SEE.
AND ARE YOU GOING TO BRING ME ALONG ON THOSE LITTLE EXCURSIONS?

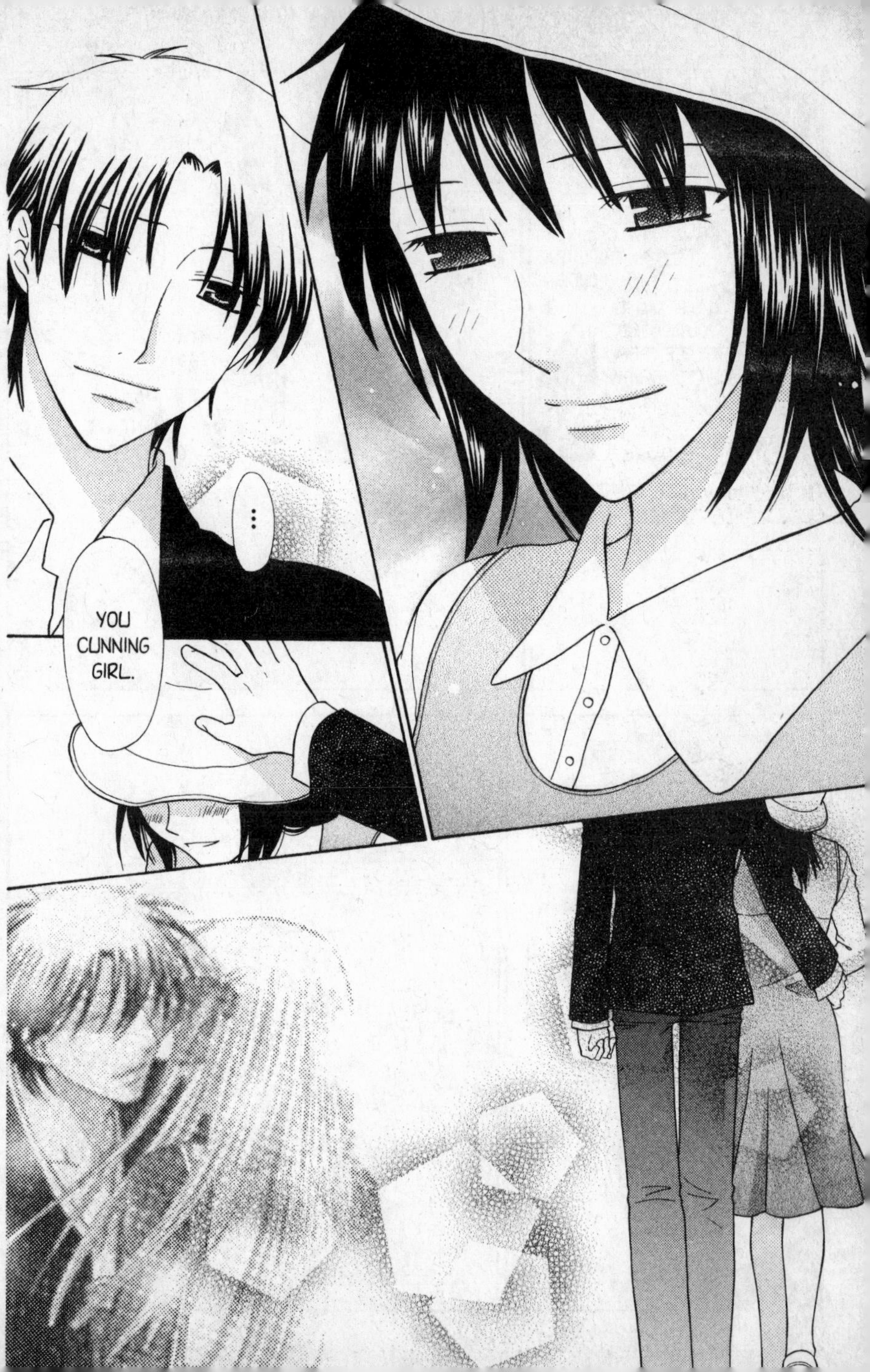
...
YOU CUNNING GIRL.

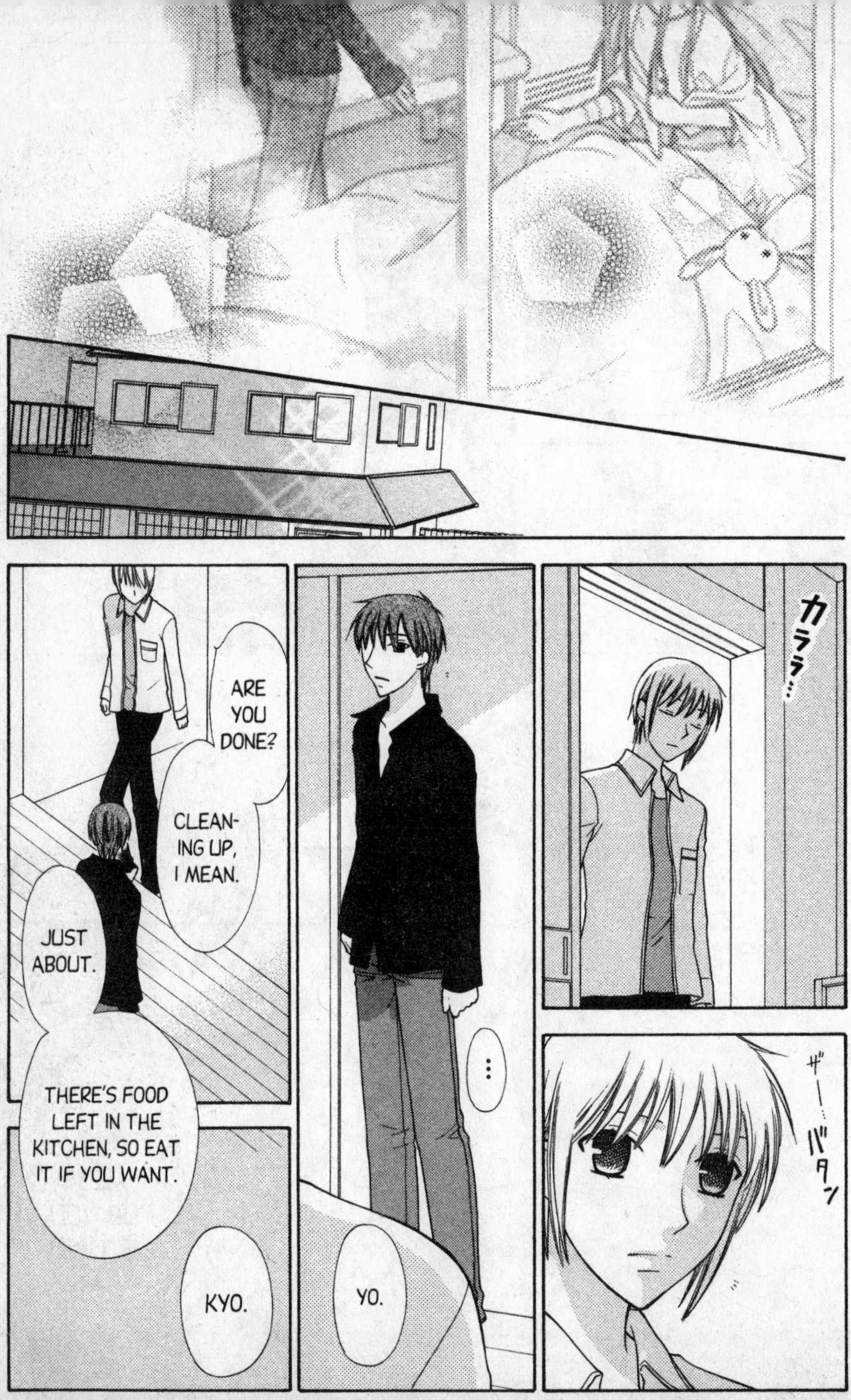
カラララ…
ザー…バタン
…
YO.
ARE YOU DONE?
CLEANING UP, I MEAN.
JUST ABOUT.
THERE'S FOOD LEFT IN THE KITCHEN, SO EAT IT IF YOU WANT.
KYO.

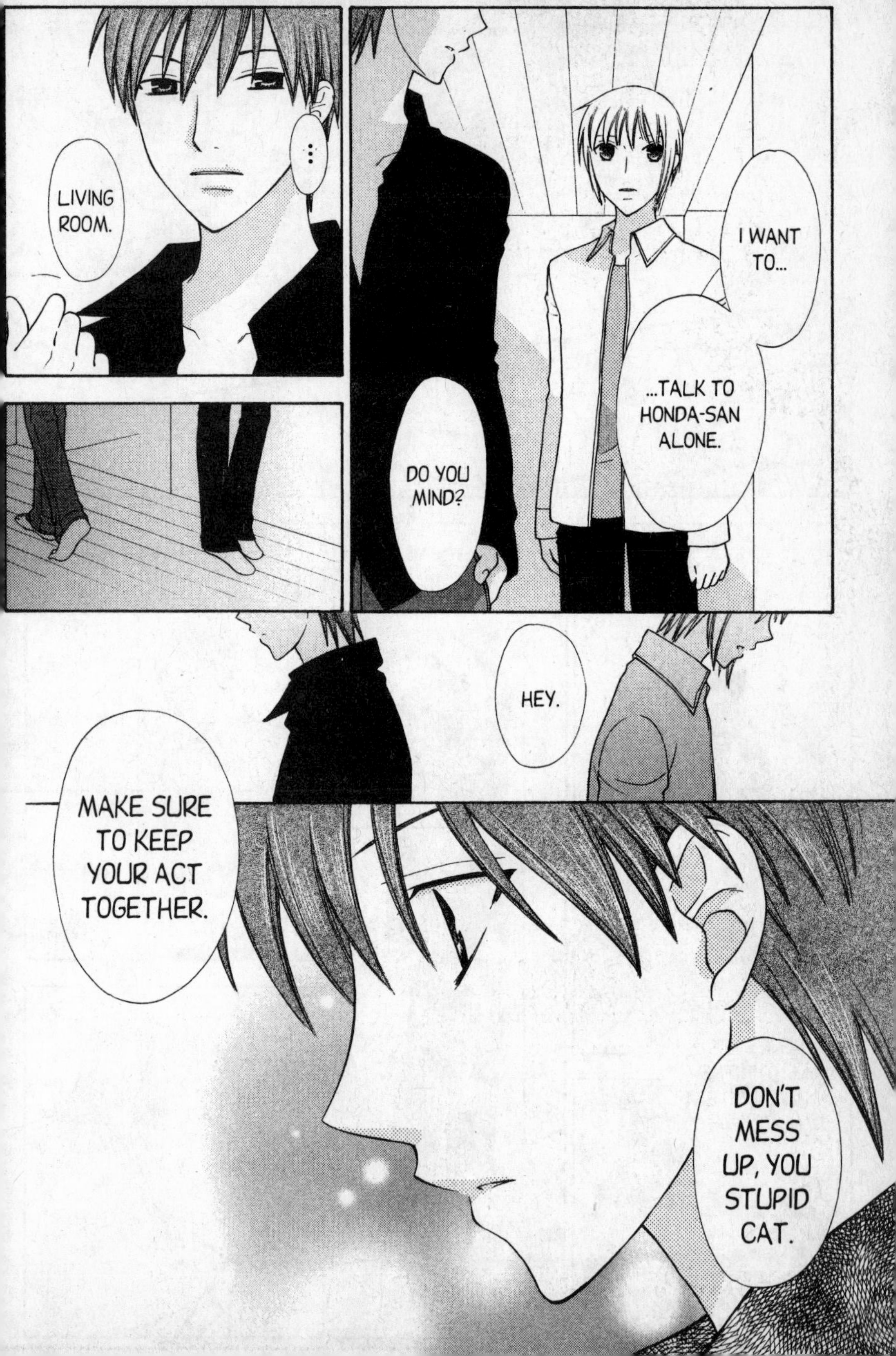
I WANT TO...
...TALK TO HONDA-SAN ALONE.
DO YOU MIND?
LIVING ROOM.
HEY.
MAKE SURE TO KEEP YOUR ACT TOGETHER.
DON'T MESS UP, YOU STUPID CAT.

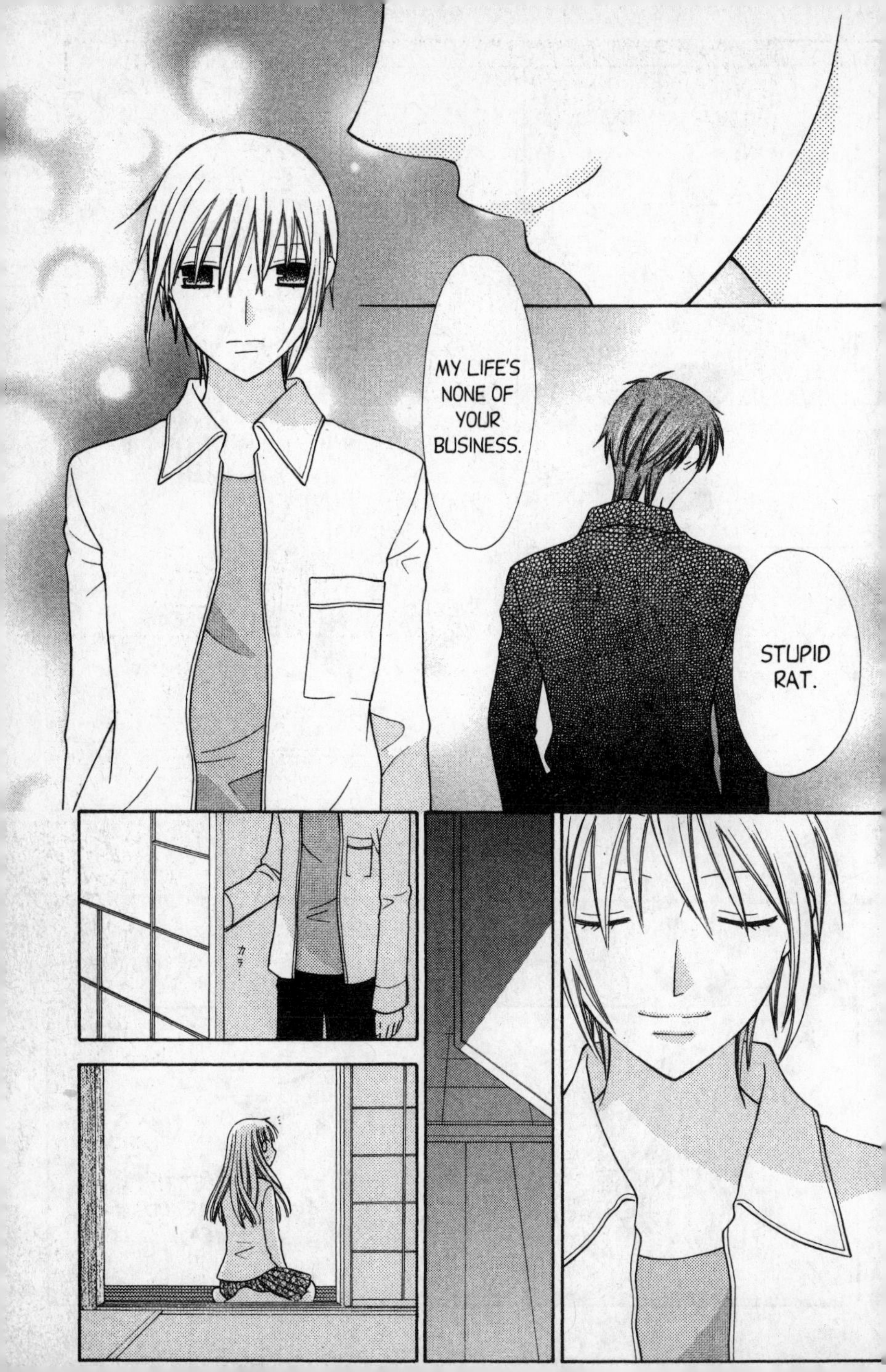
MY LIFE'S NONE OF YOUR BUSINESS.
STUPID RAT.

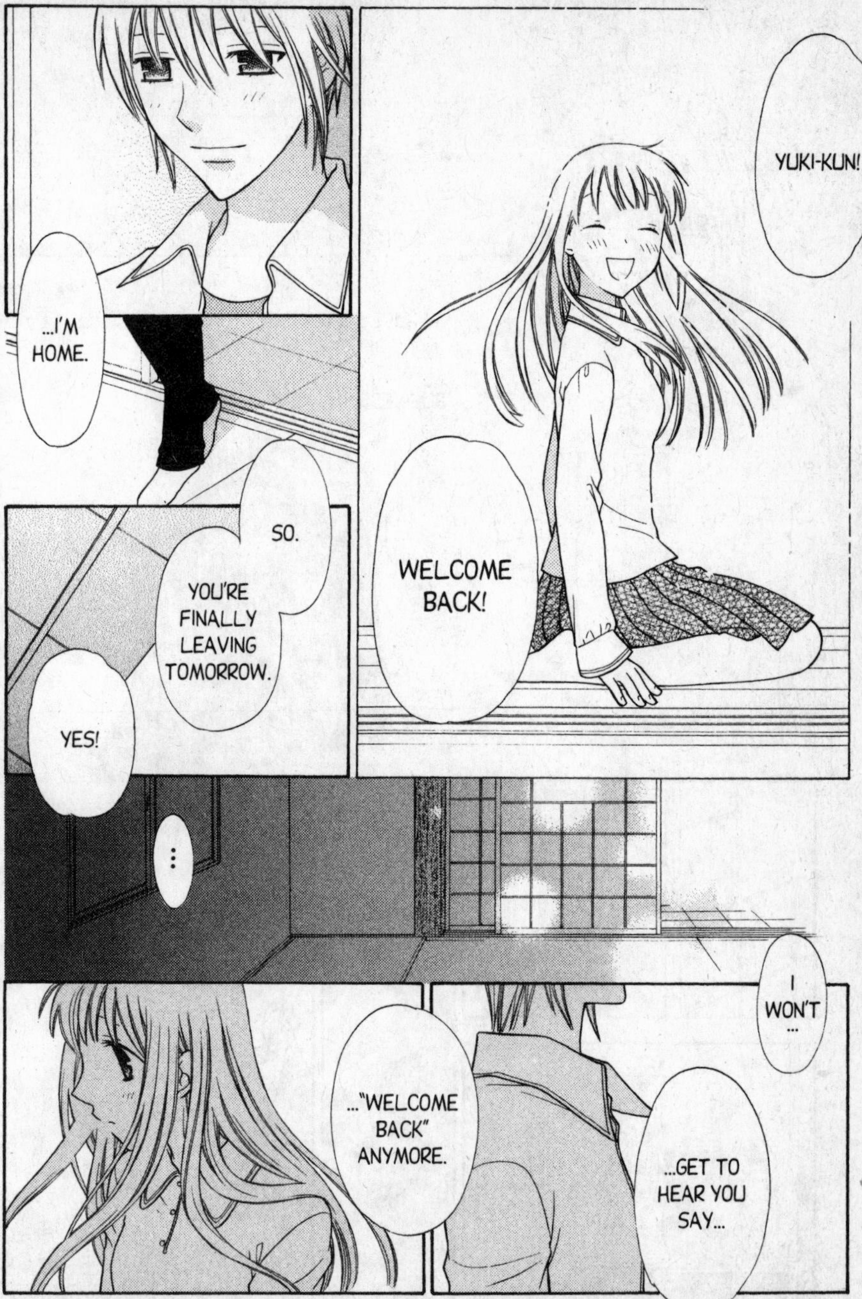
YUKI-KUN!
WELCOME BACK!
...I'M HOME.
SO. YOU'RE FINALLY LEAVING TOMORROW.
YES!
...
I WON'T ...
...GET TO HEAR YOU SAY...
..."WELCOME BACK" ANYMORE.

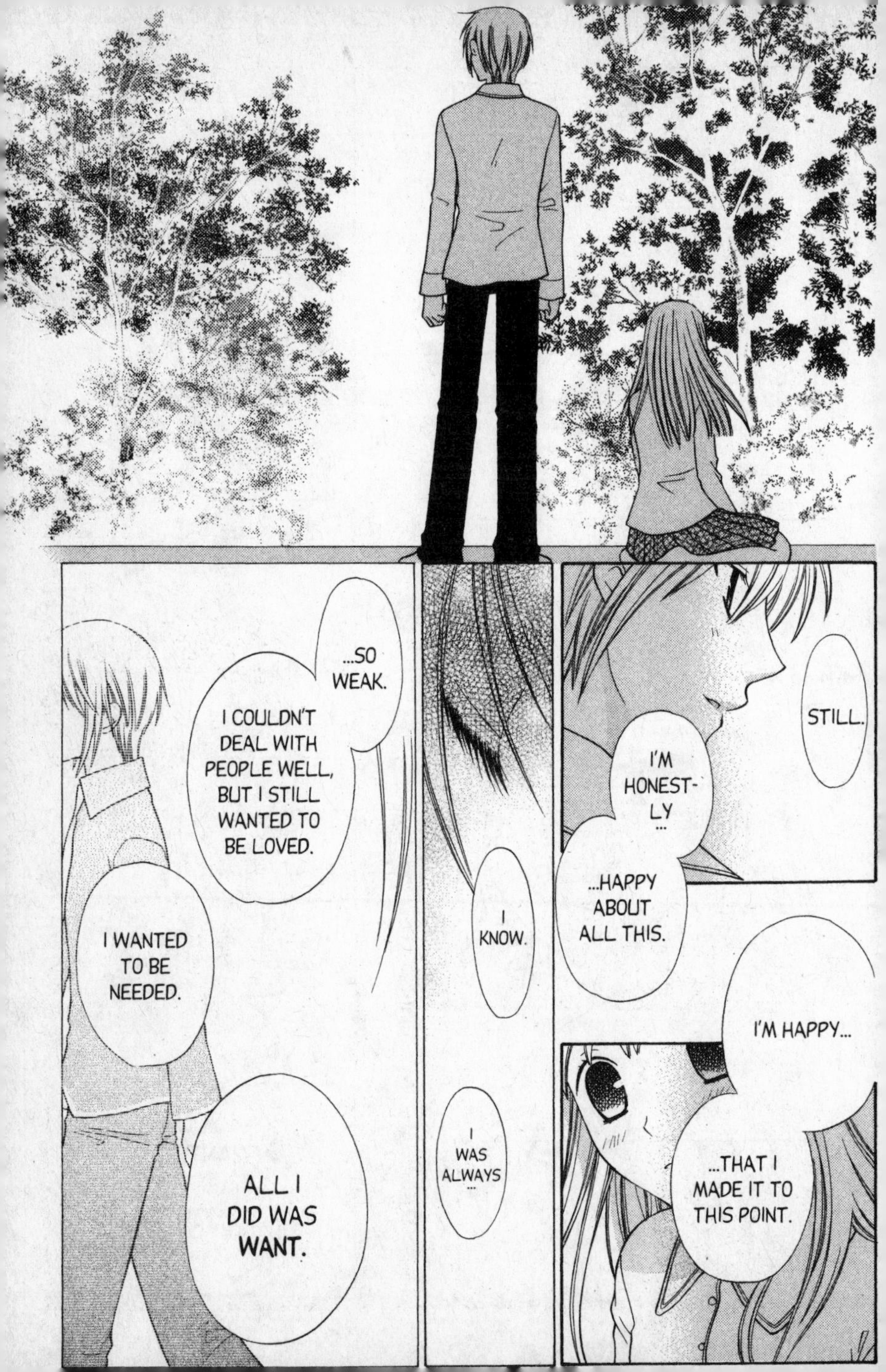
STILL.
I'M HONESTLY...
...HAPPY ABOUT ALL THIS.
I'M HAPPY...
...THAT I MADE IT TO THIS POINT.
I KNOW.
I WAS ALWAYS...
...SO WEAK.
I COULDN'T DEAL WITH PEOPLE WELL, BUT I STILL WANTED TO BE LOVED.
I WANTED TO BE NEEDED.
ALL I DID WAS WANT.

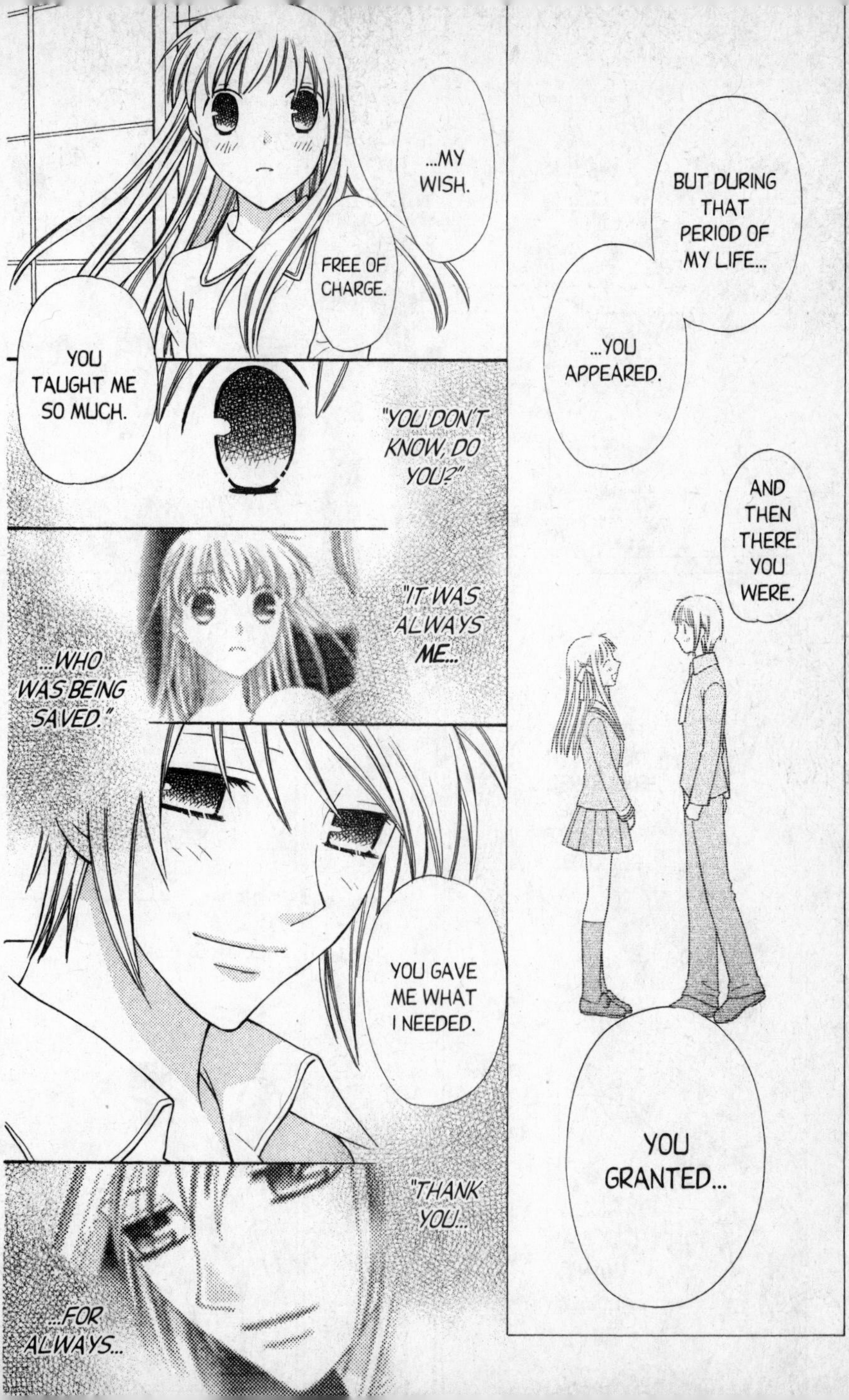
BUT DURING THAT PERIOD OF MY LIFE...
...YOU APPEARED.
AND THEN THERE YOU WERE.
YOU GRANTED...
...MY WISH.
FREE OF CHARGE.
YOU TAUGHT ME SO MUCH.
"YOU DON'T KNOW, DO YOU?"
"IT WAS ALWAYS ME...
...WHO WAS BEING SAVED."
YOU GAVE ME WHAT I NEEDED.
"THANK YOU...
...FOR ALWAYS...

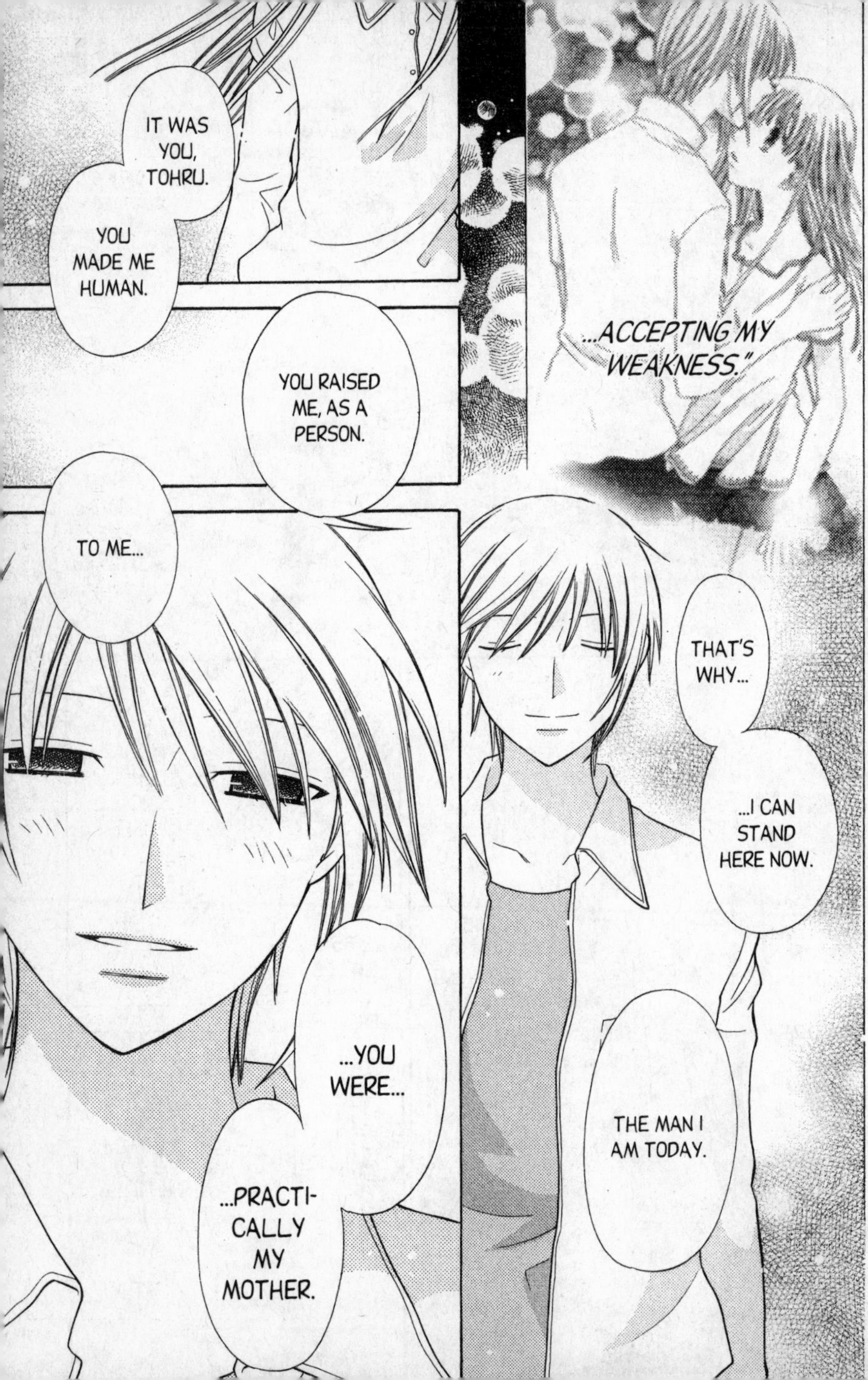
...ACCEPTING MY WEAKNESS."
IT WAS YOU, TOHRU.
YOU MADE ME HUMAN.
YOU RAISED ME, AS A PERSON.
THAT'S WHY...
...I CAN STAND HERE NOW.
THE MAN I AM TODAY.
TO ME...
...YOU WERE...
...PRACTI-CALLY MY MOTHER.

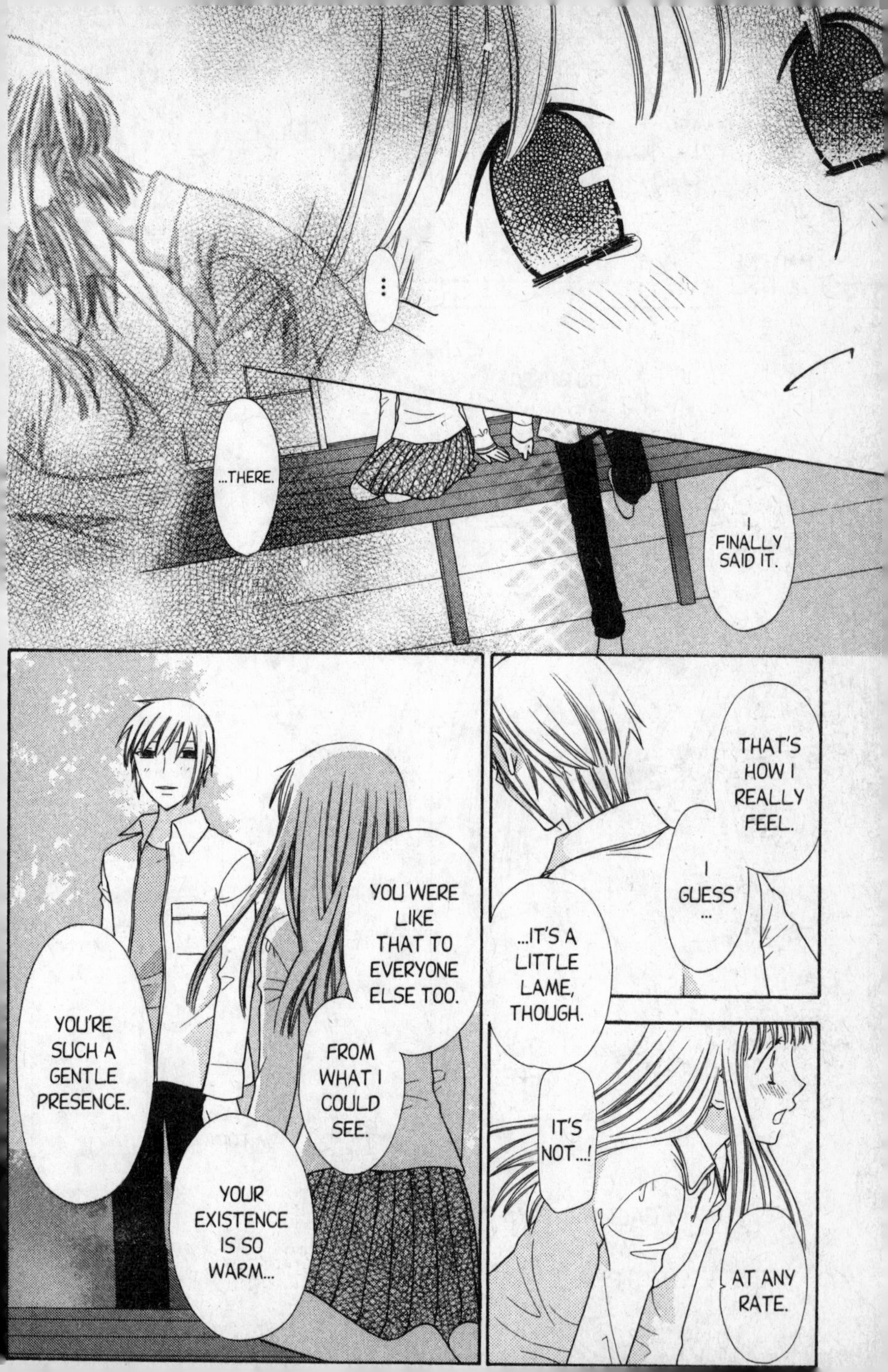
...
...THERE.
I FINALLY SAID IT.
THAT'S HOW I REALLY FEEL.
I GUESS...
...IT'S A LITTLE LAME, THOUGH.
IT'S NOT...!
AT ANY RATE.
YOU WERE LIKE THAT TO EVERYONE ELSE TOO.
FROM WHAT I COULD SEE.
YOU'RE SUCH A GENTLE PRESENCE.
YOUR EXISTENCE IS SO WARM...

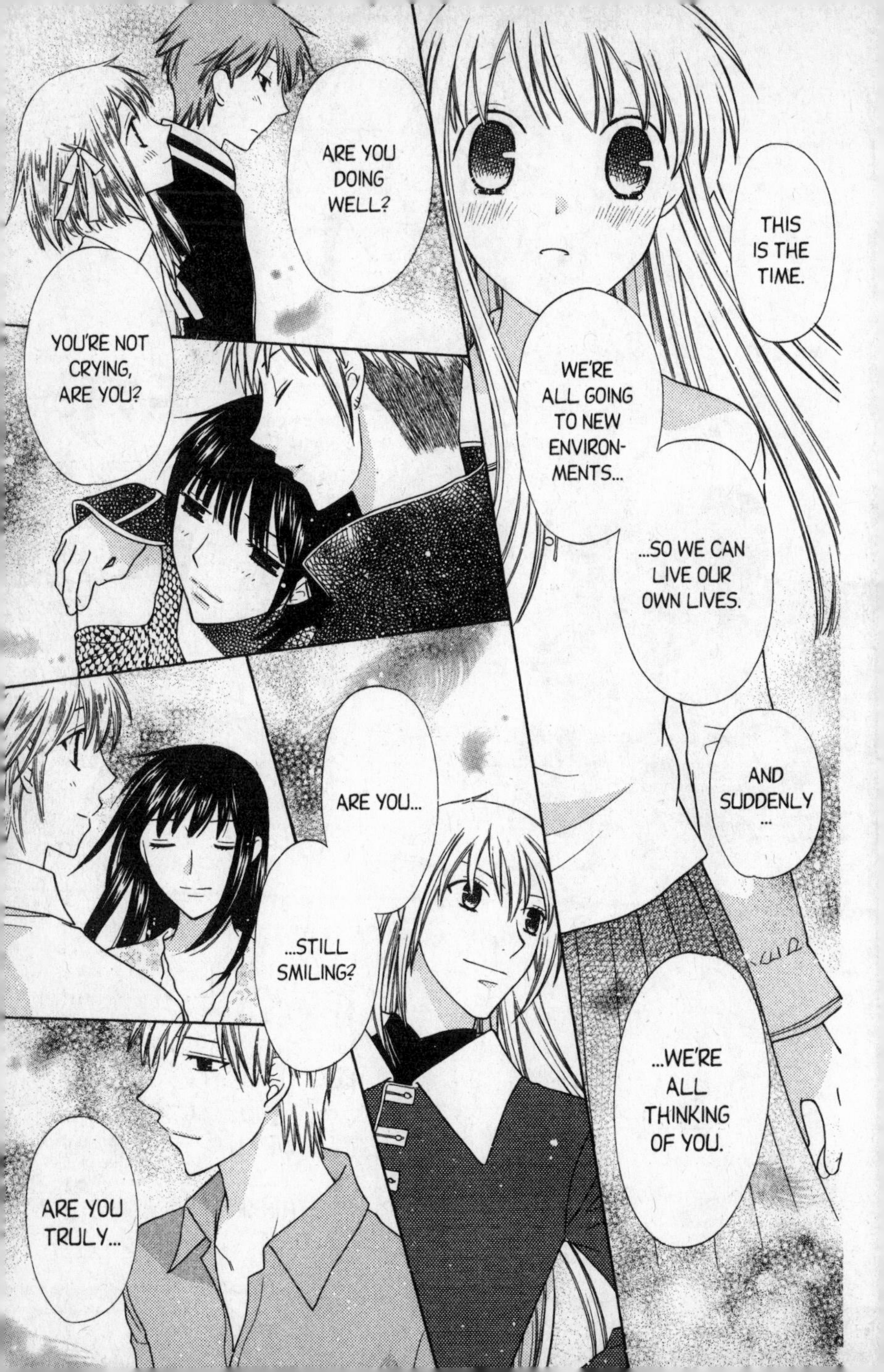
THIS IS THE TIME.
WE'RE ALL GOING TO NEW ENVIRONMENTS...
...SO WE CAN LIVE OUR OWN LIVES.
AND SUDDENLY...
...WE'RE ALL THINKING OF YOU.
ARE YOU DOING WELL?
YOU'RE NOT CRYING, ARE YOU?
ARE YOU...
...STILL SMILING?
ARE YOU TRULY...

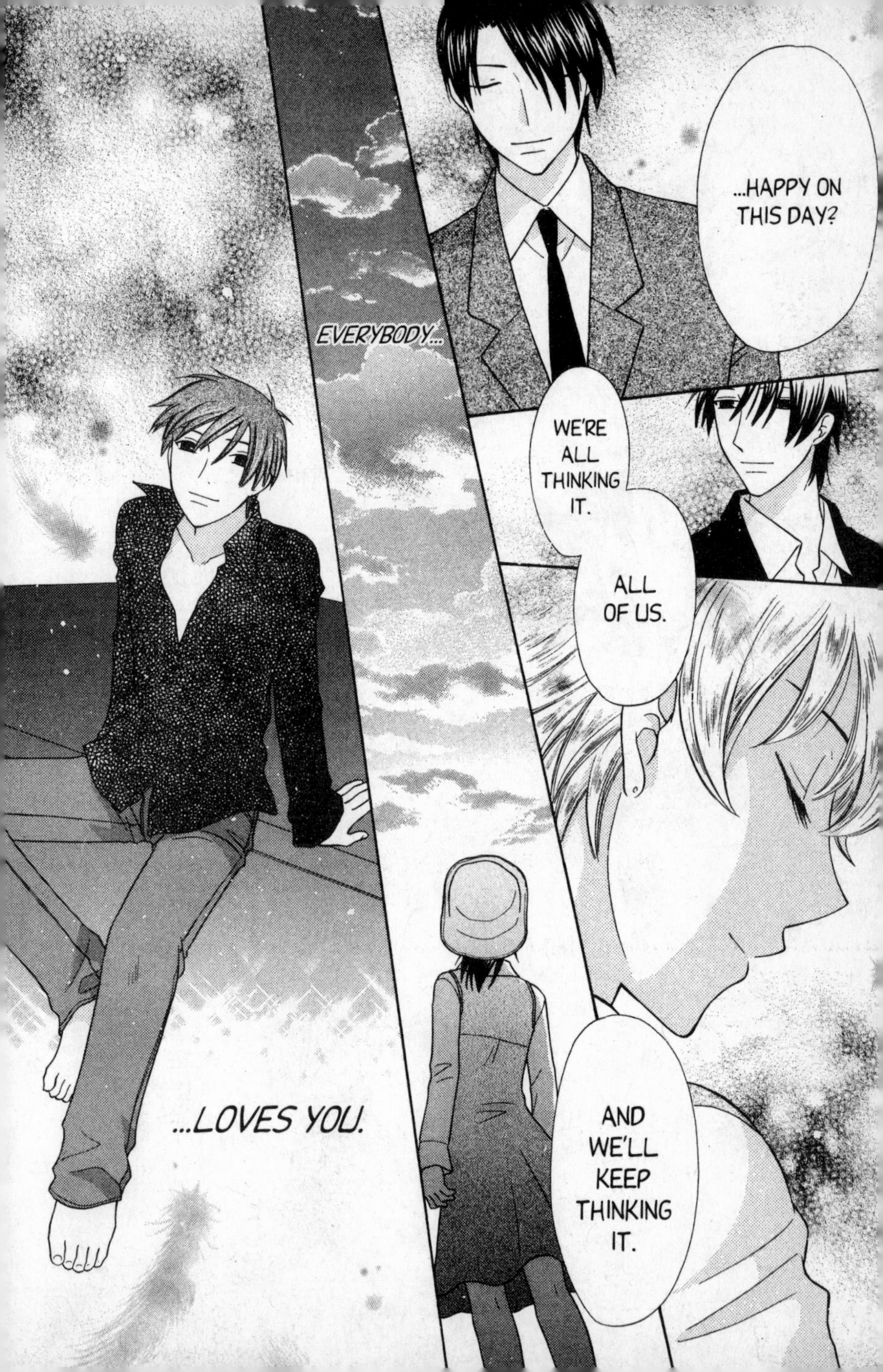
...HAPPY ON THIS DAY?
WE'RE ALL THINKING IT.
ALL OF US.
AND WE'LL KEEP THINKING IT.
EVERYBODY...
...LOVES YOU.

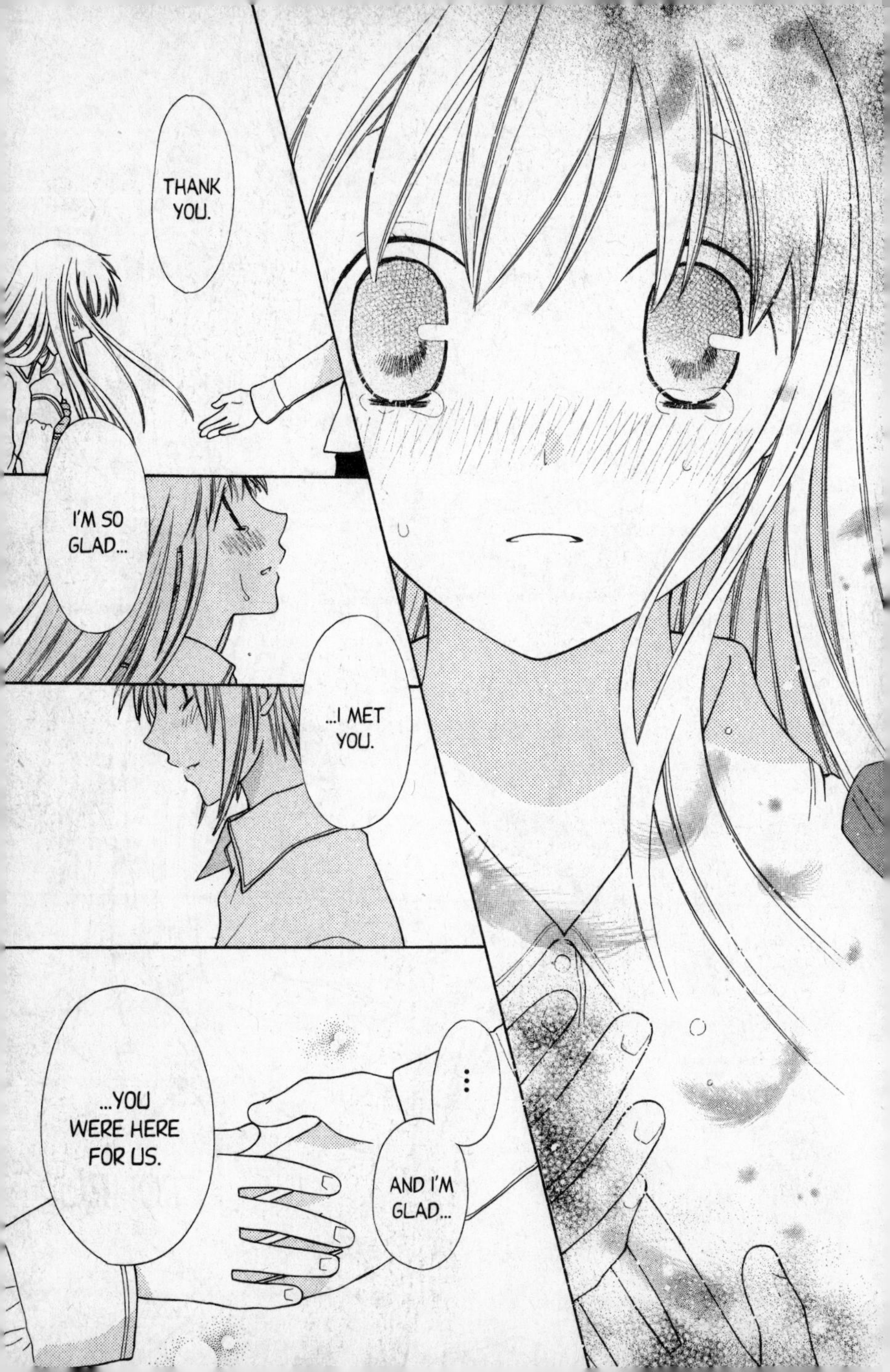

THANK YOU.
I'M SO GLAD...
...I MET YOU.
...
AND I'M GLAD...
...YOU WERE HERE FOR US.

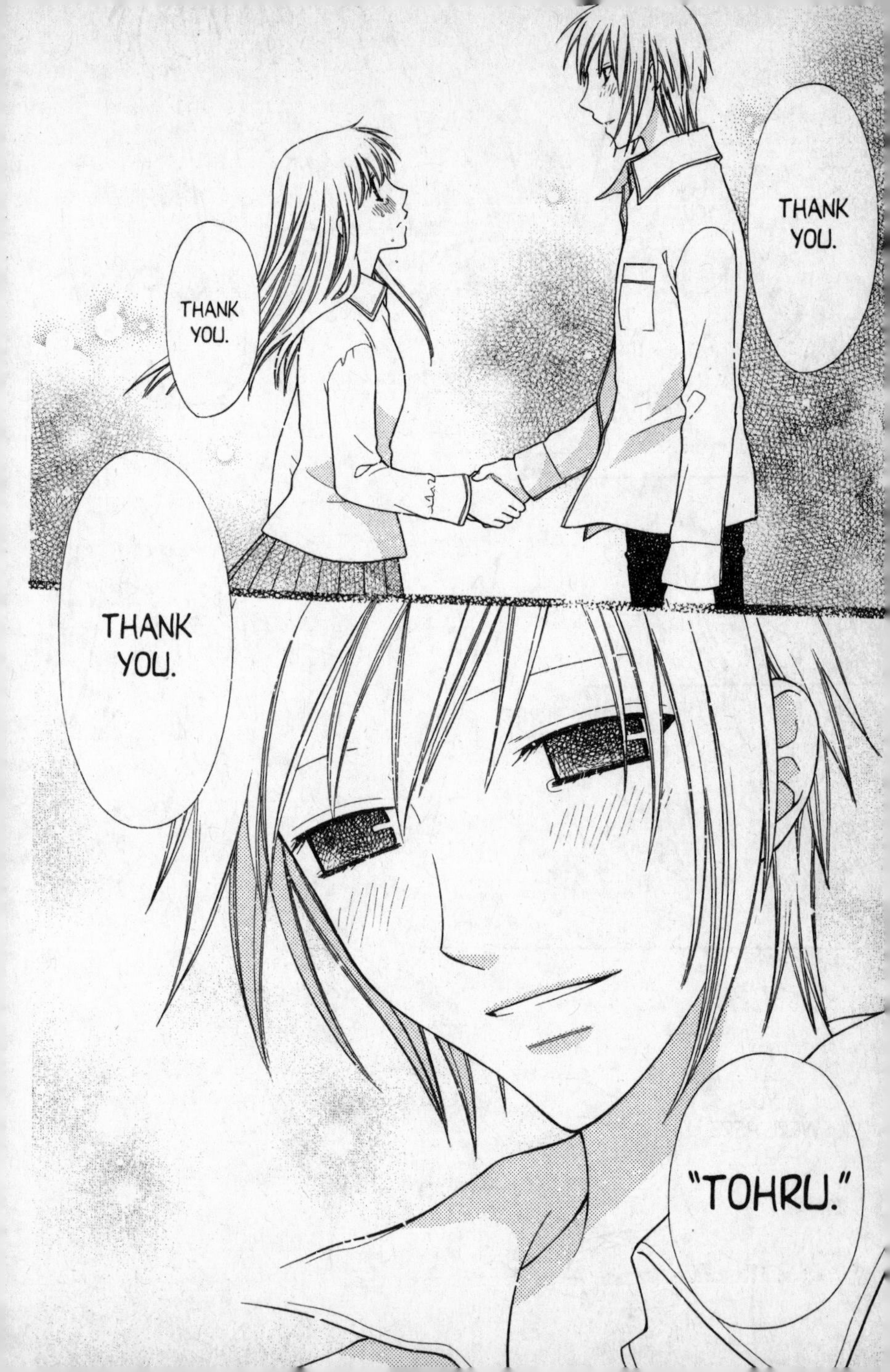
THANK YOU.
THANK YOU.
THANK YOU.
"TOHRU."

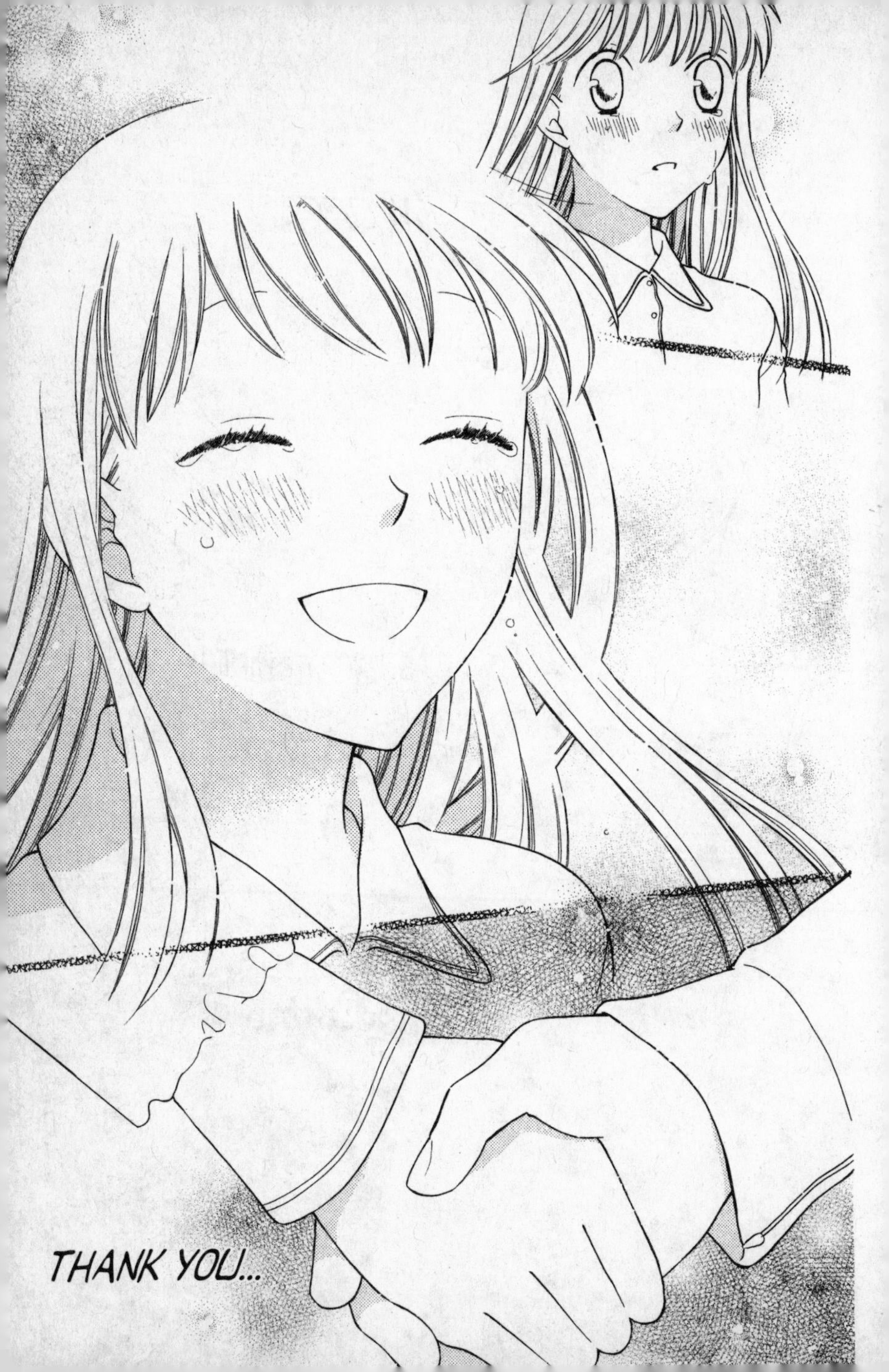
THANK YOU...

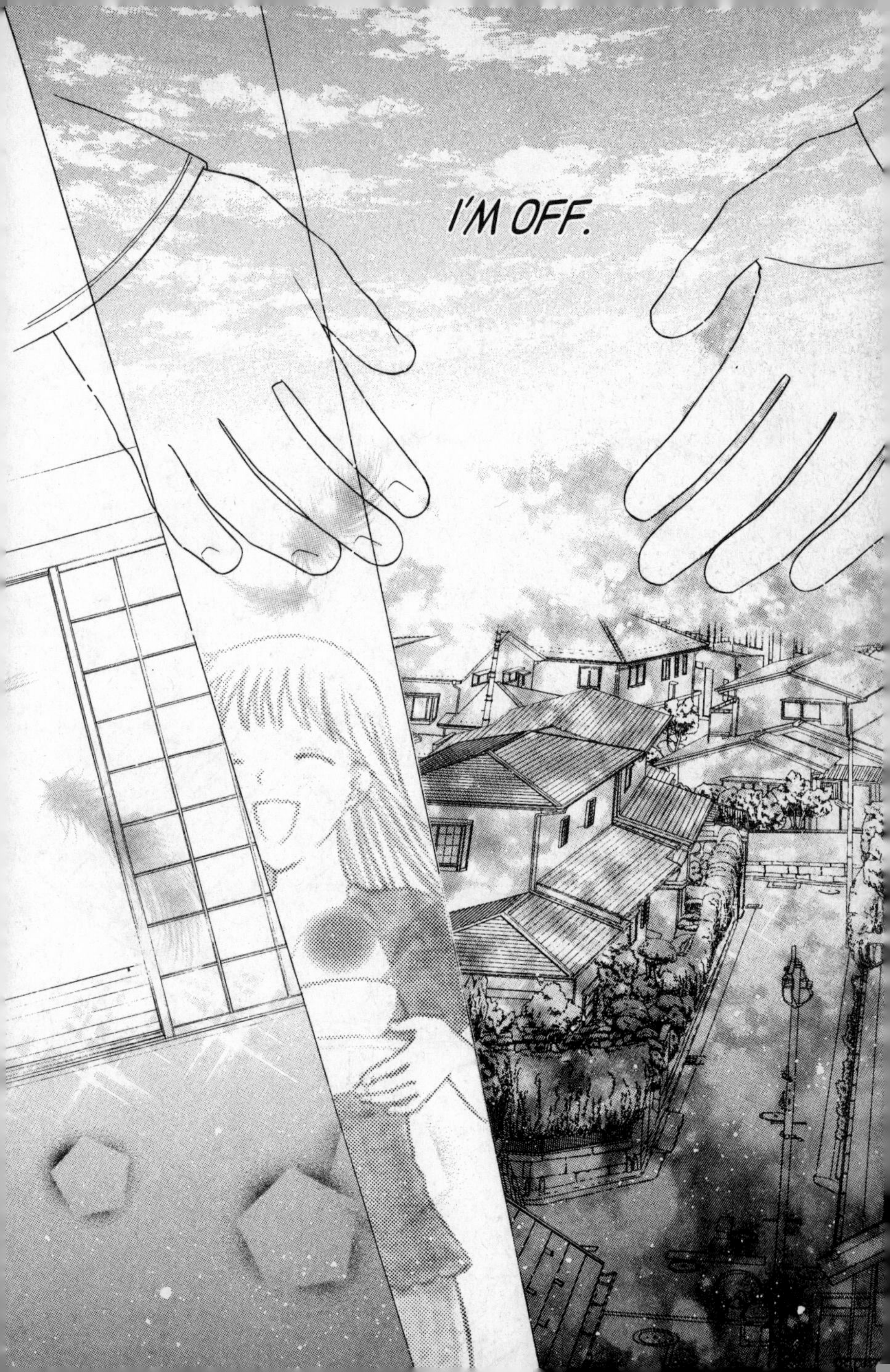
I'M OFF.

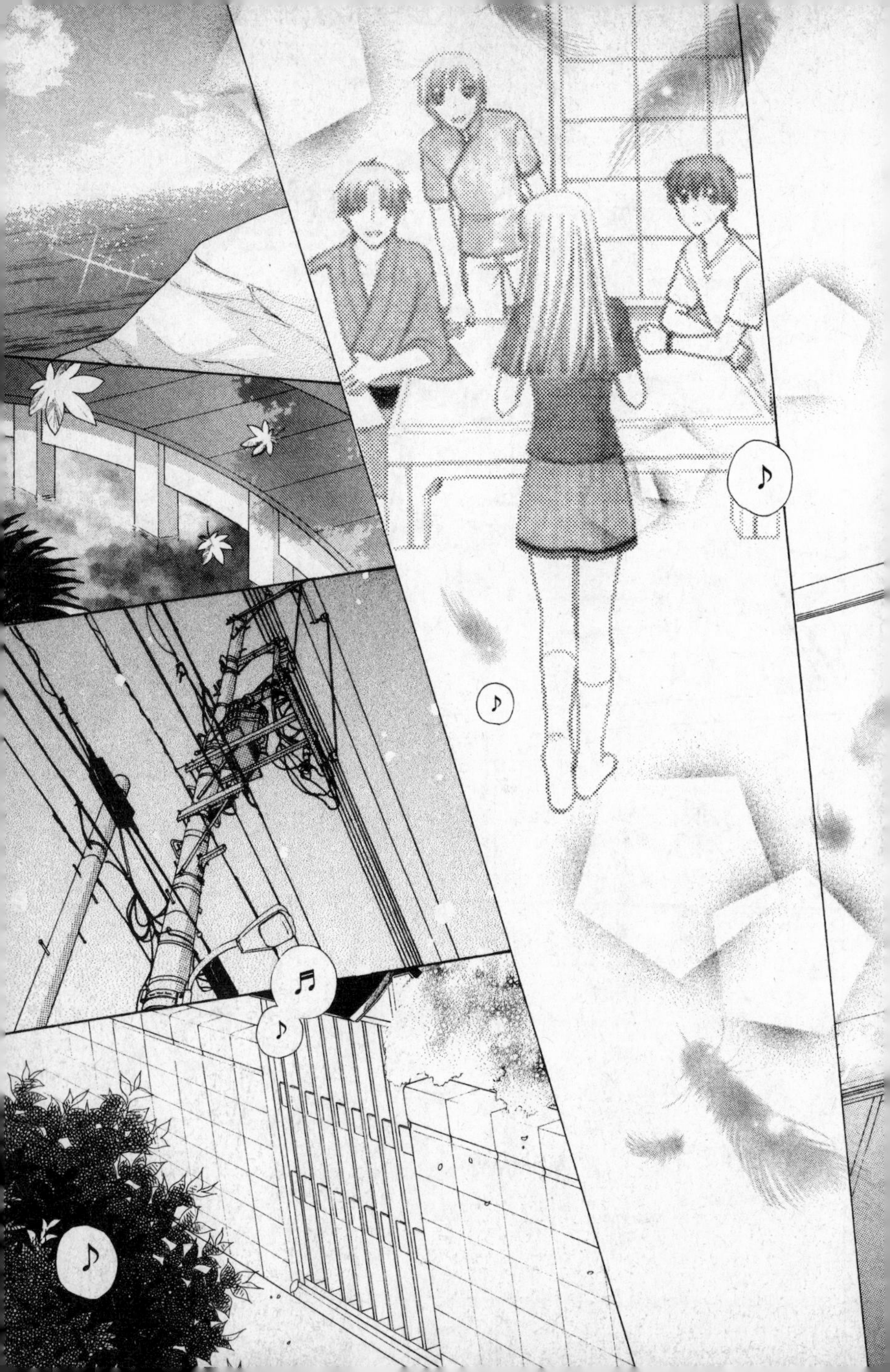
♪
♪
♬
♪
♪

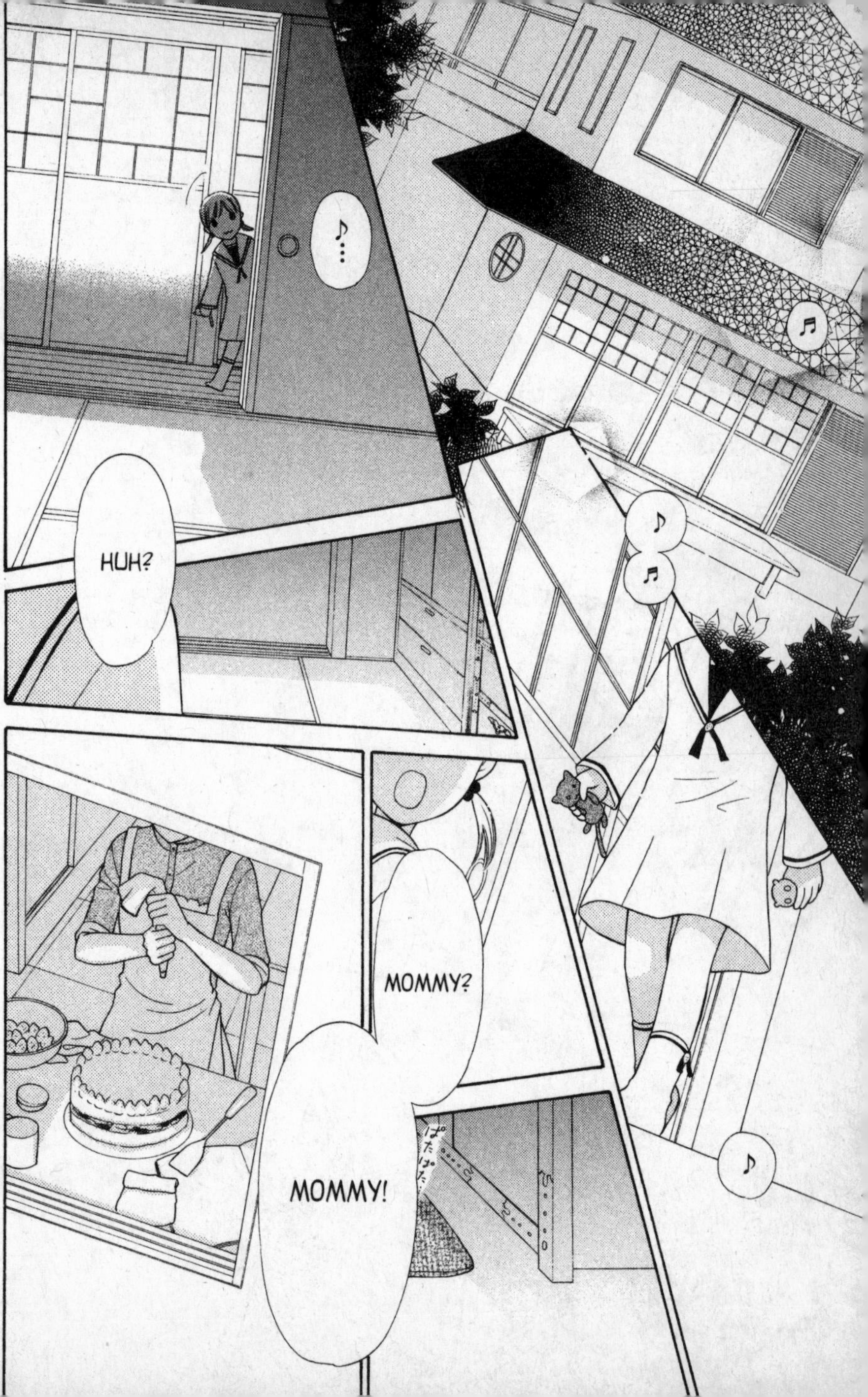

♬
♪
♬
♪
♪...
HUH?
MOMMY?
ぱたぱた
MOMMY!

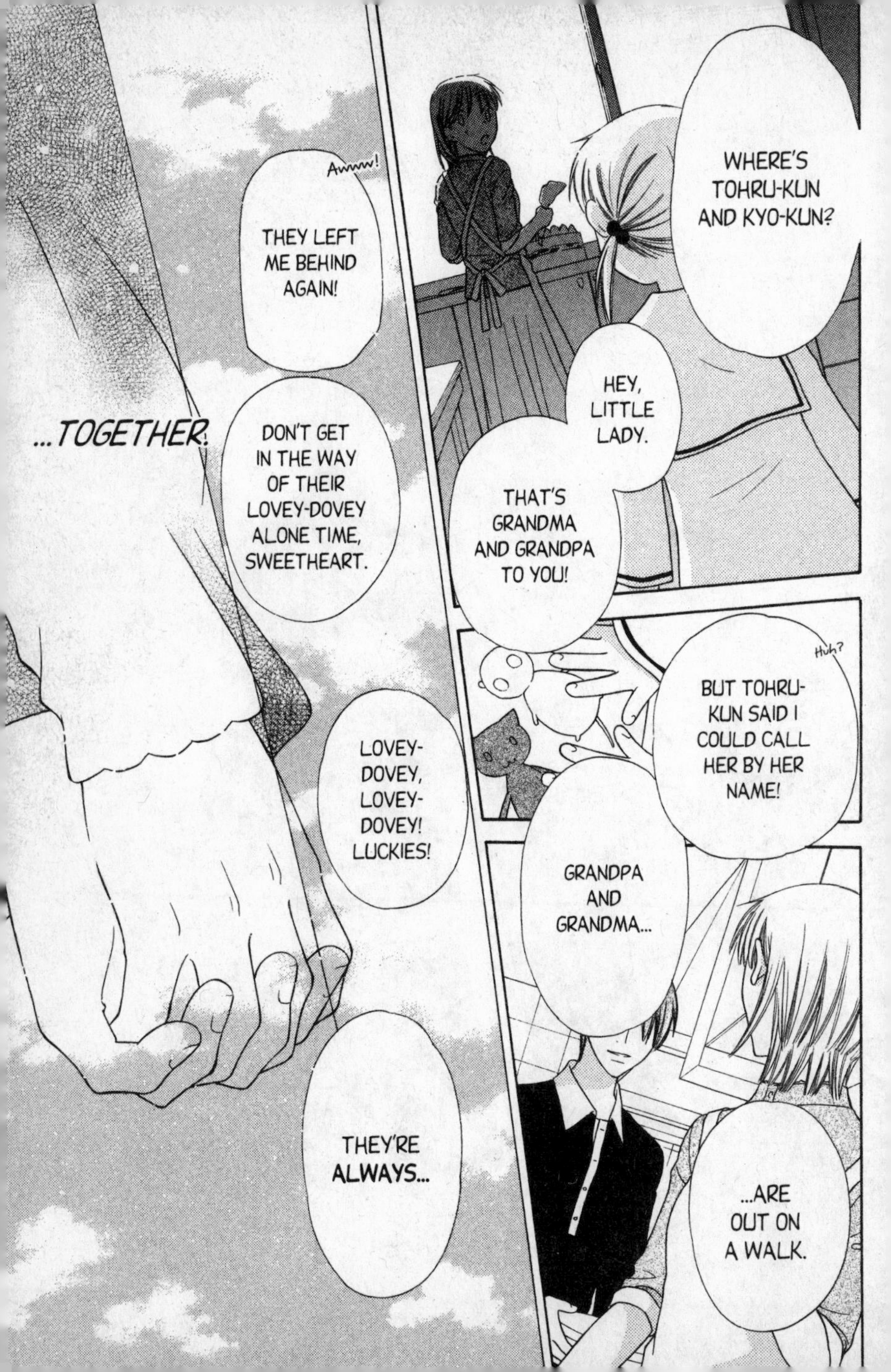
WHERE'S TOHRU-KUN AND KYO-KUN?
Awww!
THEY LEFT ME BEHIND AGAIN!
HEY, LITTLE LADY.
THAT'S GRANDMA AND GRANDPA TO YOU!
Huh?
BUT TOHRU-KUN SAID I COULD CALL HER BY HER NAME!
DON'T GET IN THE WAY OF THEIR LOVEY-DOVEY ALONE TIME, SWEETHEART.
LOVEY-DOVEY, LOVEY-DOVEY! LUCKIES!
GRANDPA AND GRANDMA...
...ARE OUT ON A WALK.
THEY'RE ALWAYS...
...TOGETHER.

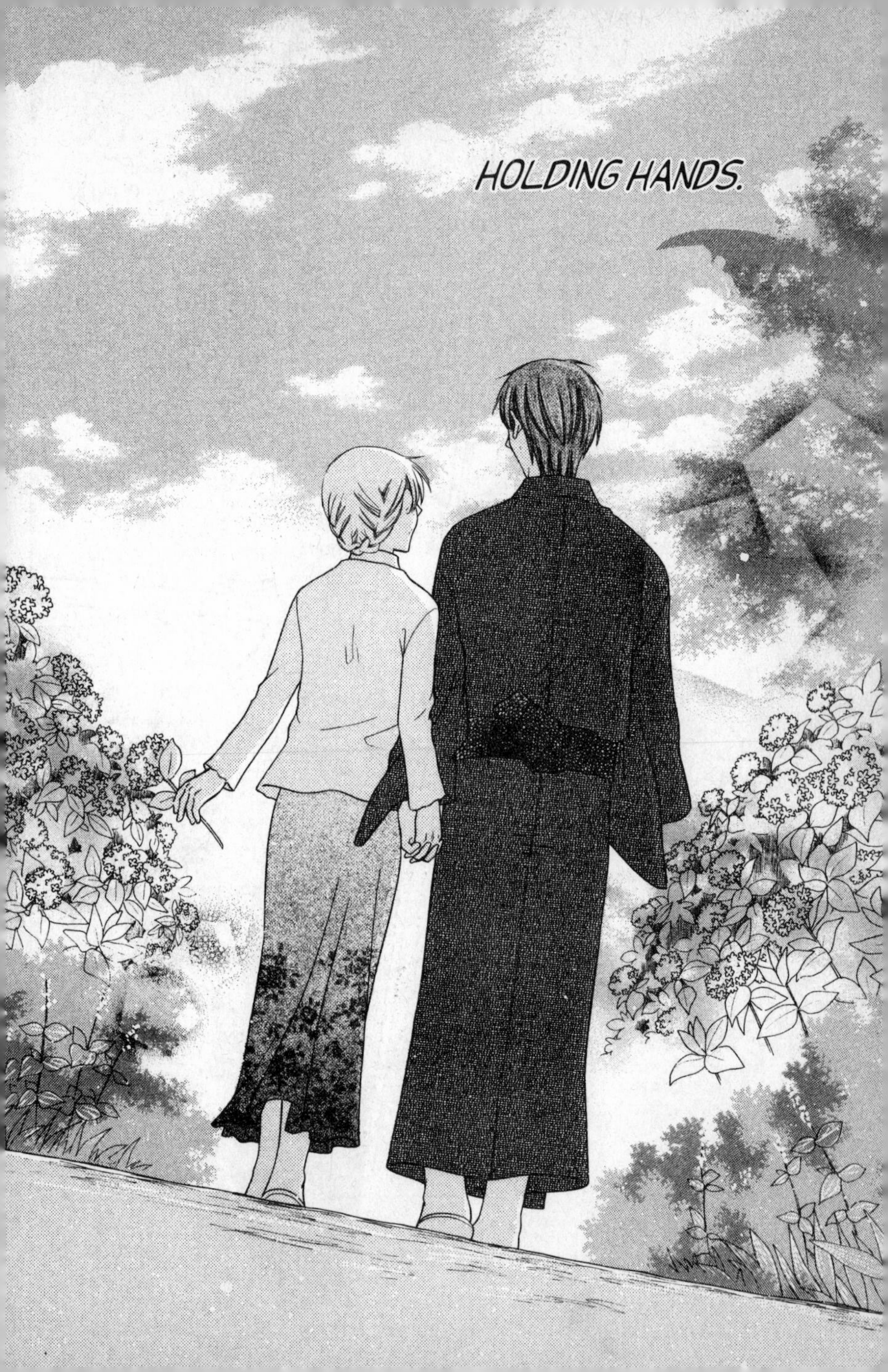
HOLDING HANDS.

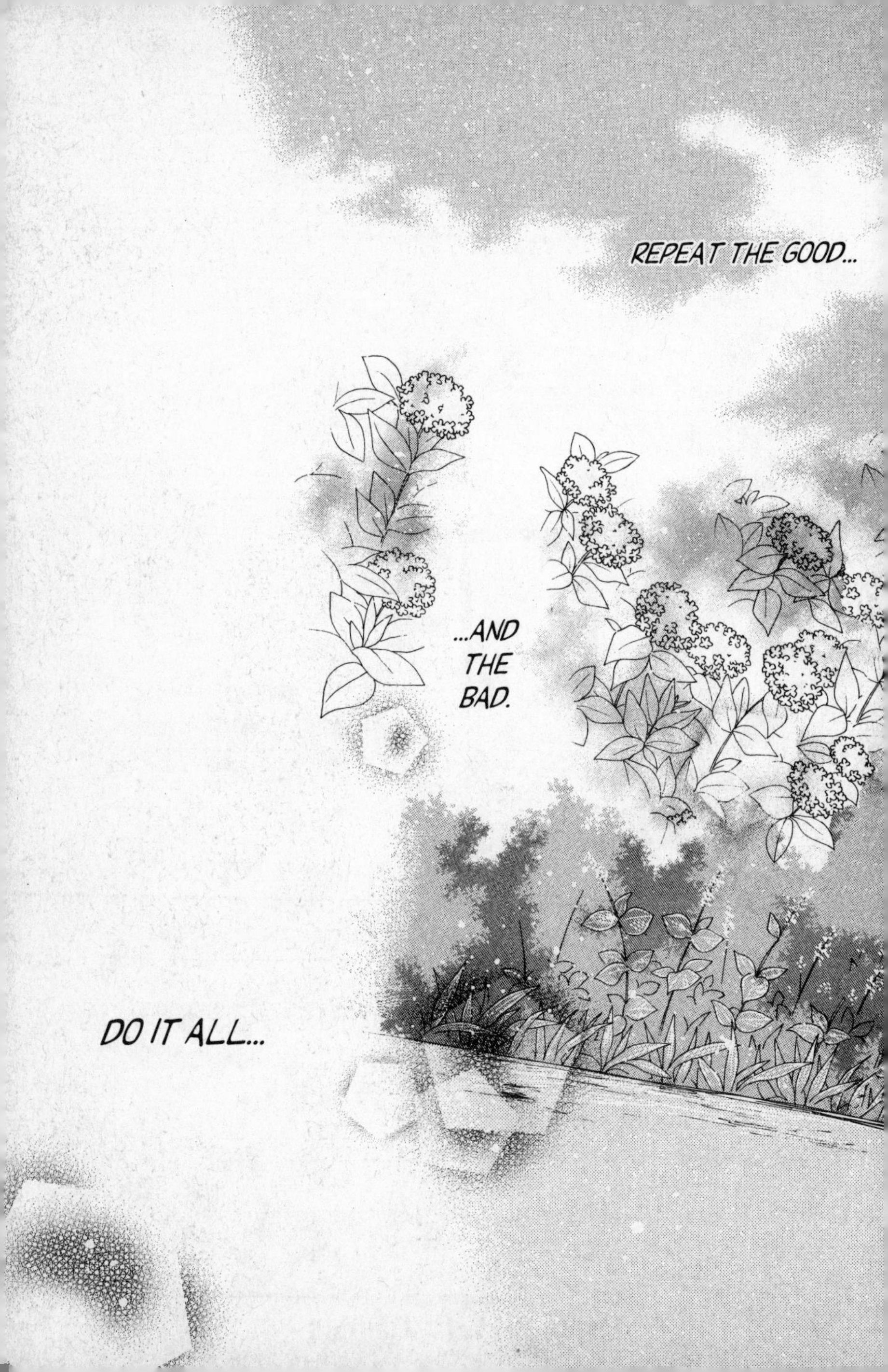
REPEAT THE GOOD...
...AND THE BAD.
DO IT ALL...

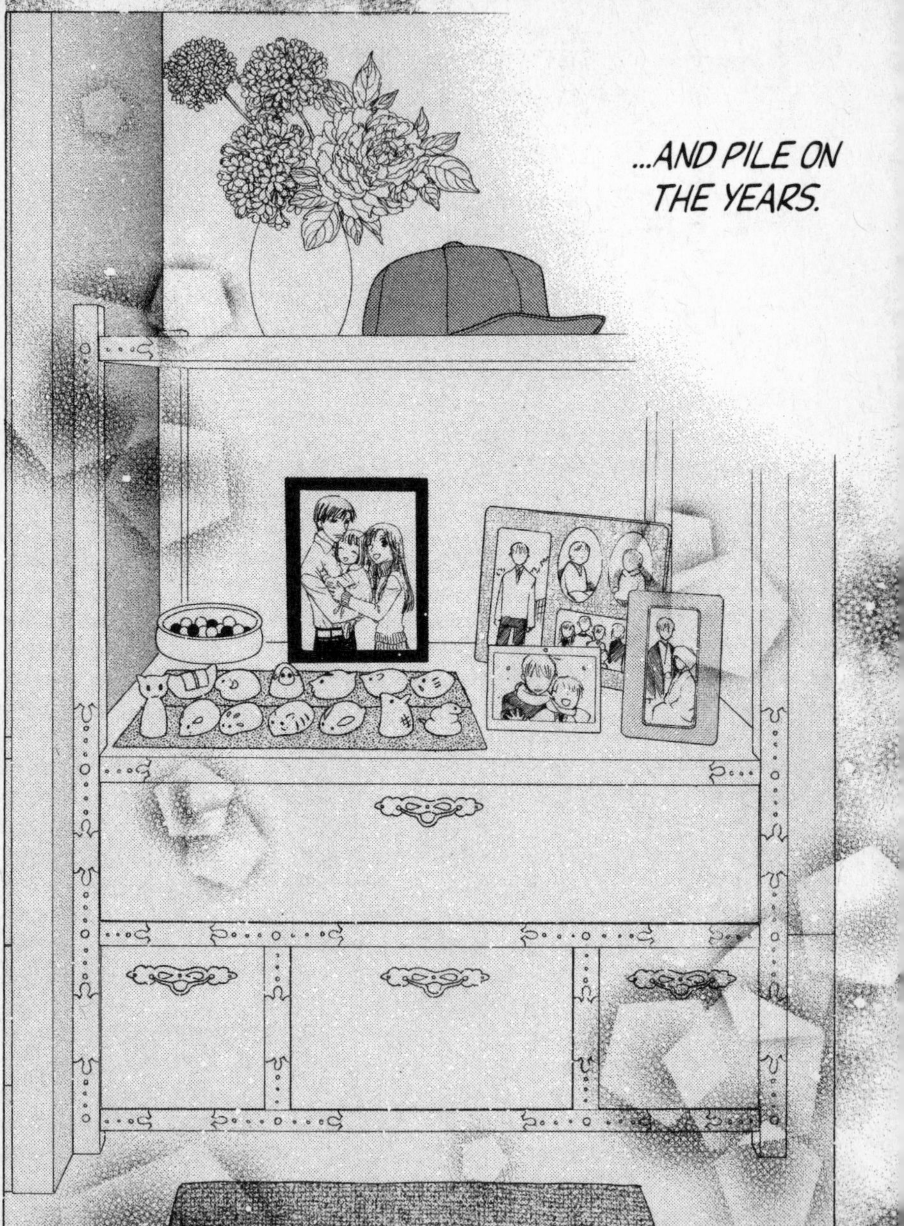
...AND PILE ON THE YEARS.

Fruits Basket / The End

✿ I feel so grateful! ❀

Harada-sama   Araki-sama
Mother-sama   Editor-sama

And everyone who reads and supports this manga.

Everyone and anyone who was involved in Furuba.

Truly, thank you very much...!

This has been Natsuki Takaya.

Fans Basket

You knew it had to come sooner or later, and now it's here! The final printed volume of Fans Basket! We want to express our sincere gratitude to our lovely and hardworking interns - Janice Kwon, Kandice Cho, and Karen Lam! They did a terrific job of picking out some truly inspiring selections of artwork submitted by you, the loyal fans of Fruits Basket. Great job, ladies! And of course, we want to thank all of those who submitted their amazing artwork, not only for this volume, but for all the amazing pieces we've had sent in to us over the years - thank you all!

But just because the series has reached its conclusion doesn't mean you can no longer submit your Fans Basket art! From now on, instead of sending in the original pages to the office, please submit your work to the TOKYOPOP website. This way, we'll be able to keep the Furuba love going on and on! See the last page of this section for details and instructions. And now... enjoy the art of Fans Basket!

Hope
Age 16
Philadelphia, PA

This fan art really captured Isuzu's character! Not only was it drawn very well, but the picture portrayed Isuzu's emotions as well. The detail put into the picture really made this stand out of the piles of fan art. Great job, Hope!

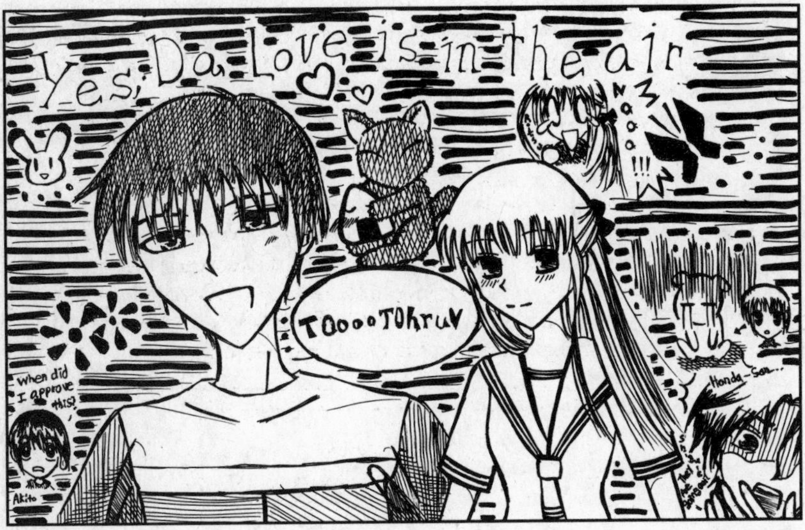
Yes, Da Love is in the air
TOoooTOhru♥
when did I approve this?
Akito
Honda-San...

Hanseul Yoo
Age 14
Leesburg, VA

Aww! Kyo and Tohru look so happy together...I like how Kyo is ignoring all the other people's objections! I also love how Hanseul drew in the other characters' reactions to their relationship... especially Shigure's perplexed look and Ritsu's frantic look.

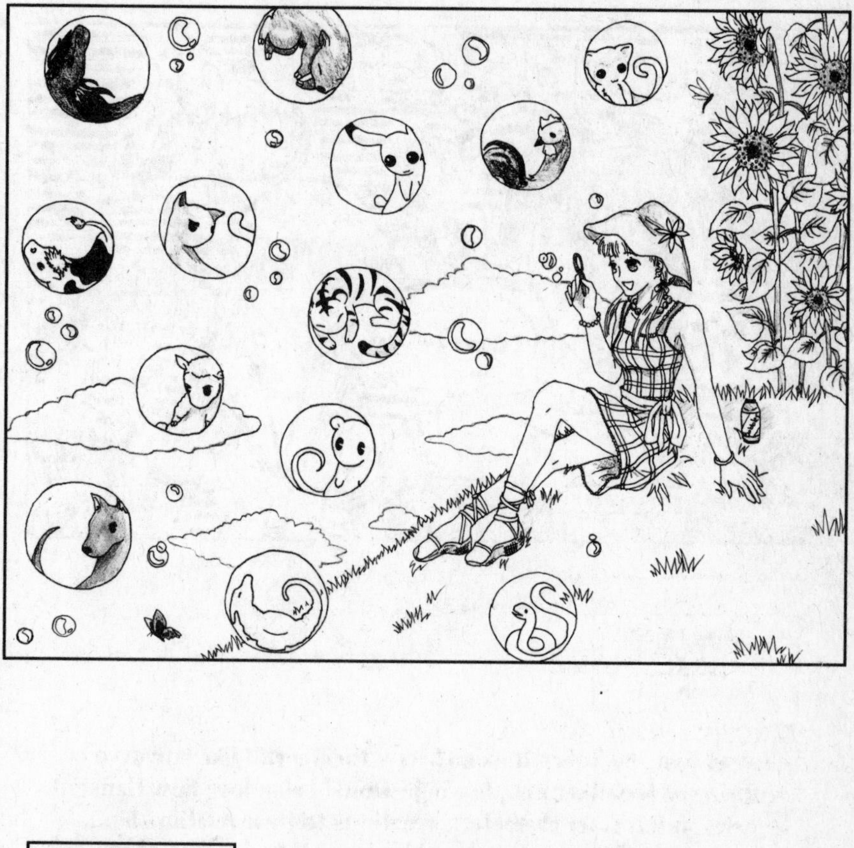

Lacey Hathaway
Age 15
Charles Town, WV

Everyone can see that Lacey put a lot of time and effort into drawing this fan art, cause it looks awesome! So creative, too! I love how Tohru is wearing a cute dress while blowing bubbles filled with each Fruits Basket character.

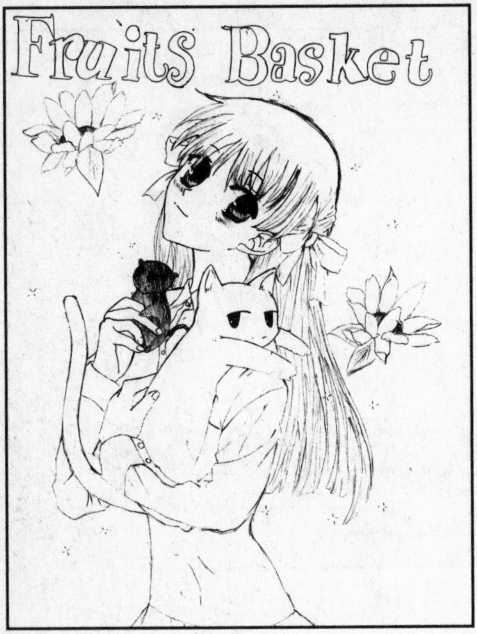
Fruits Basket

Melissa Reña
Age 15
Yakima, WA

Kyo is so adorable in this one! It makes you want to pinch his cheeks through the paper. The expression on his face is hilarious, and you can't help but laugh at his look. Melissa definitely captured all aspects of Fruits Basket in this drawing.

Katie Cunningham
Age 14
Roanoke, VA

Kisa is so adorable here with her absolutely innocent look. Great job on portraying Kisa's shy and gentle personality! The smiling tiger on the side is a nice touch that brings out Kisa's playful side as well.

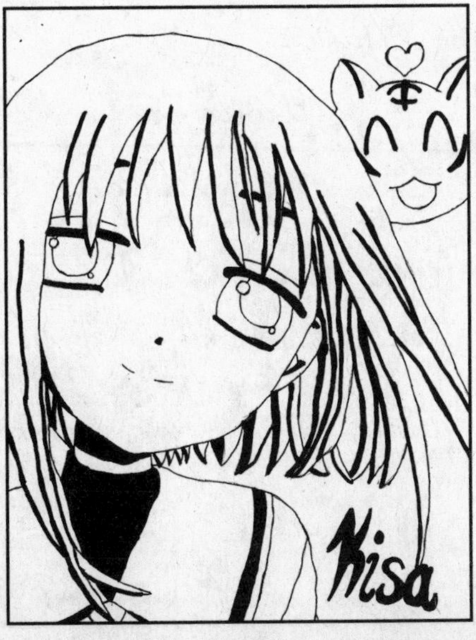
Kisa

Noor M.
Age 12
Kansas

It's hard not to love Kisa when she's this cute with her lopsided tiger hat! Her fuzzy pompoms match her personality perfectly, and the tiger doll next to her foot looks just as clumsy and innocent as its owner! And to the best friend Ami, "Chicken is yummy!" Of course, with no offense to Kureno.

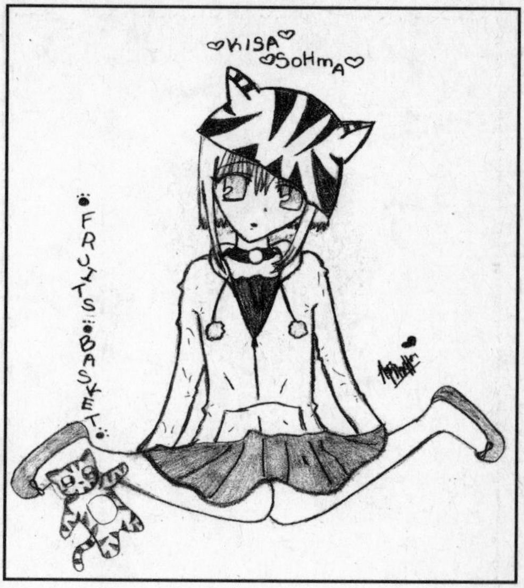
KISA
SOHMA
FRUITS BASKET

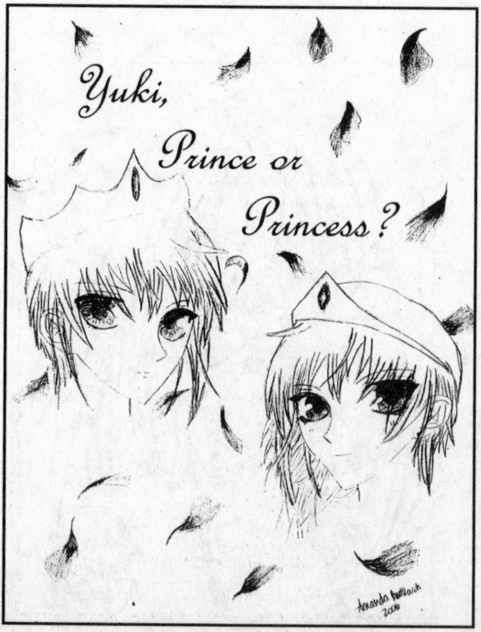
Yuki,
Prince or
Princess?

Amanda Butkovich
Age 14
Molalla, OR

Sometimes Yuki does look like a girl, and I like how Amanda points it out! In Amanda's fan art, you really can't tell which one is the prince and which is the princess. The one on the left is the prince and the one on the right is the princess...right?

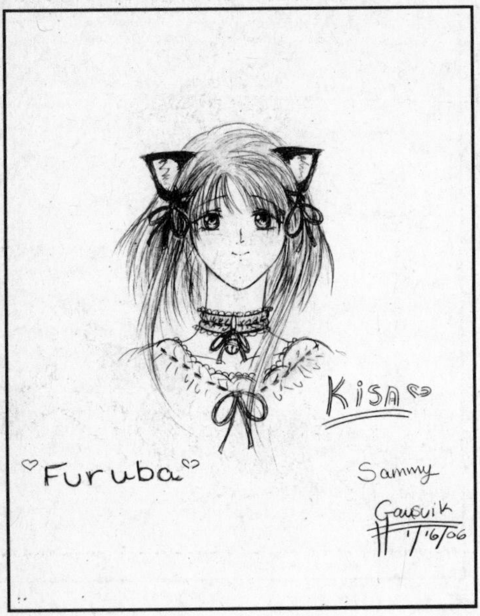
Kisa
Furuba
Sammy
Gausuik
1/16/06

Samantha Gausuik
Age 14
Myrtle Creek, OR

Kisa looks absolutely divine in this drawing. The attention to detail is so careful—the wisps of hair, the gleam in her eyes, the slight flush of her cheeks—and lends this drawing a life-like quality. I love how the innocent look on her face was captured so well!

Lily Li
Age 15
New York, NY

Tohru's hair and eyes bring this drawing to life. I love the way her hair playfully floats in the air and her eyes sparkle with laughter! Lily did an amazing job getting in all the details, especially the feelings between Kyo and Yuki.

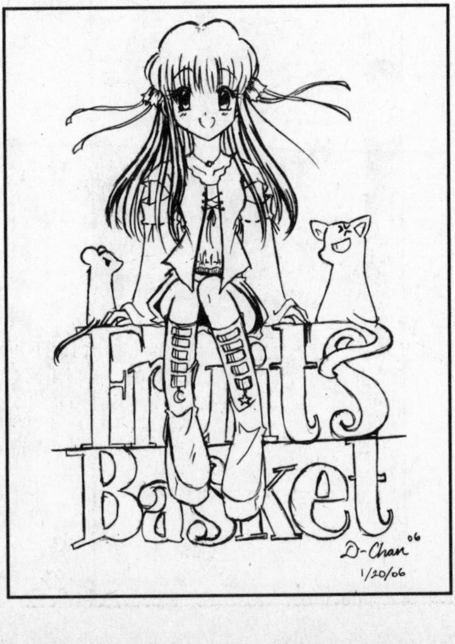
Fruits
Basket
D-Chan '06
1/20/06

Sara Kim Hopkins
Age 11
Berkeley, CA

Kisa doesn't look cold at all out in the snow holding those flowers. She looks like she's waiting for someone—maybe Hiro? For an 11-year-old, Sara did a great job on her fan art! Hope you continue to draw these lovely pictures!

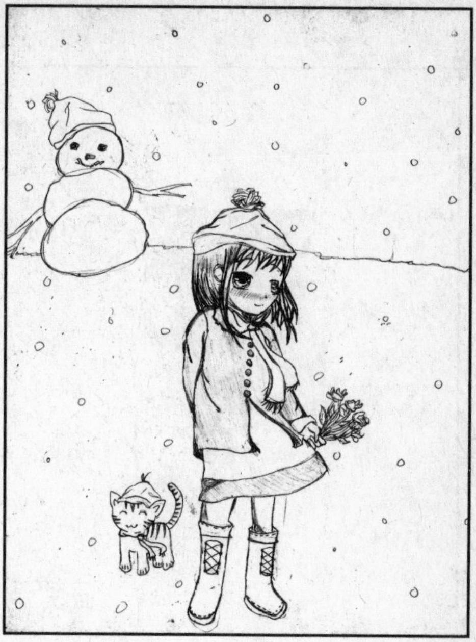

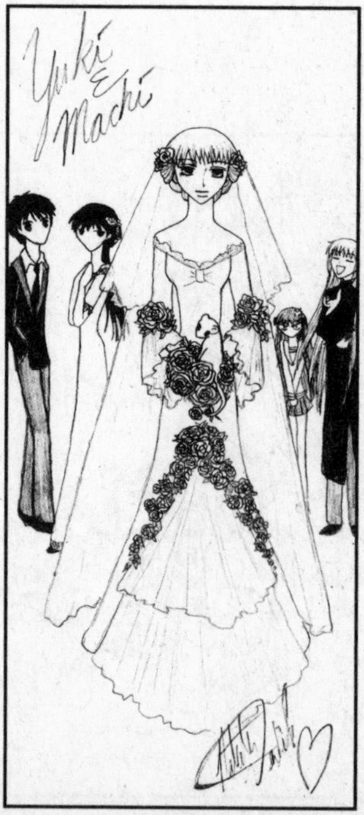
Yuki & Machi

Natalie Vanessa Devick
Age 14
Oronoco MN

I love how Natalie drew Yuki and Machi in a wedding sketch, just because she believes that they need each other. It just shows the imagination and originality of this sketch. Also, the roses and design of the dress are so exquisite. I'm sure it's a dress that every girl dreams of getting married in!

Bianca Tseng
Age 12
Cupertino, CA

I couldn't stop myself from smiling at this sort of dazed Ritsu! She looks so out of it and so funny in her kimono. Too bad you can't see the colored version of this drawing, because it made me so happy just looking at it. I wish I could have drawn this well when I was twelve...

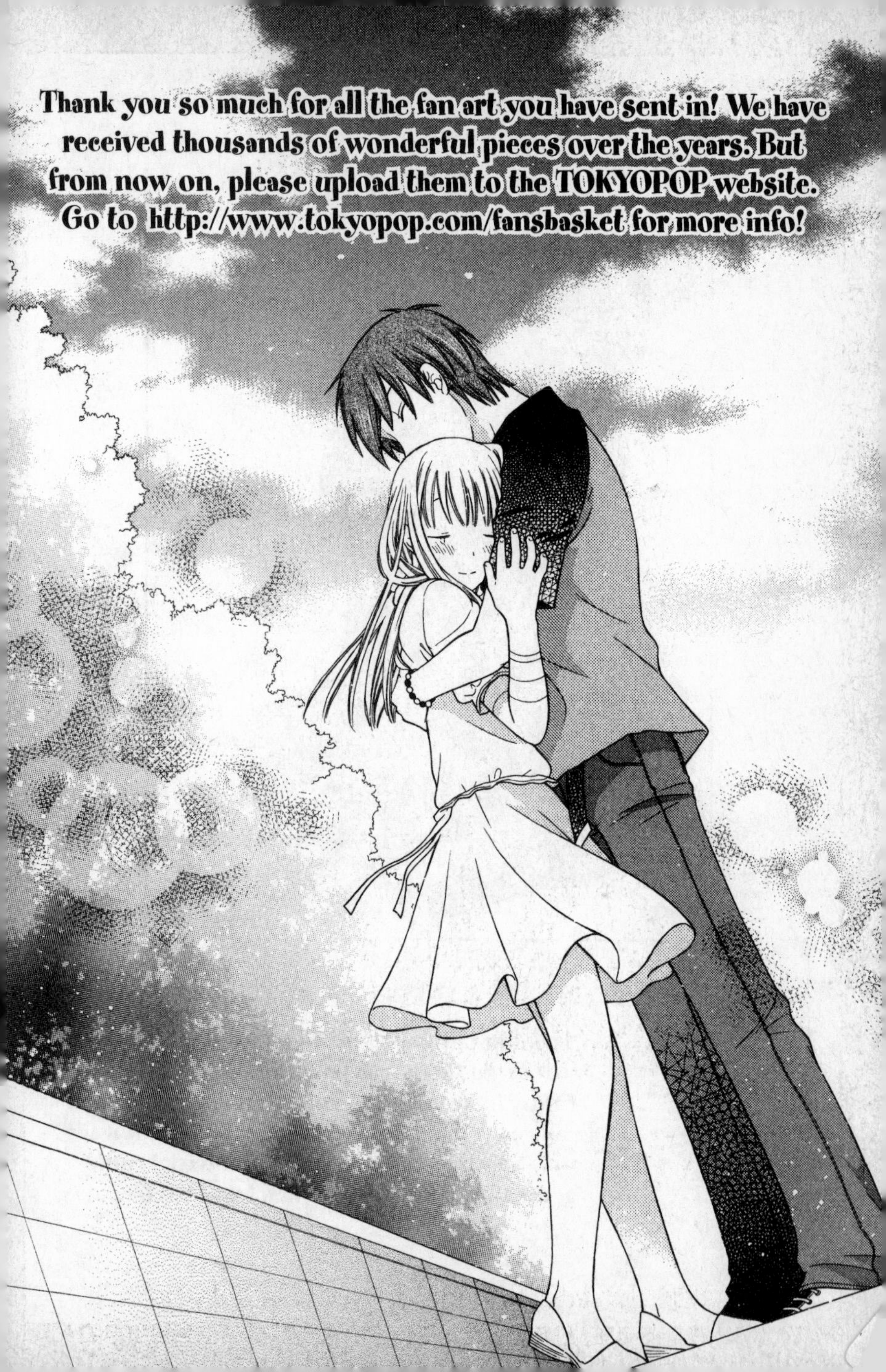
Thank you so much for all the fan art you have sent in! We have received thousands of wonderful pieces over the years. But from now on, please upload them to the TOKYOPOP website. Go to http://www.tokyopop.com/fansbasket for more info!

TOKYOPOP MANGA PREVIEW

TSUBASA

THOSE WITH WINGS

• From the creator of FRUITS BASKET •
TOKYOPOP
TSUBASA
THOSE WITH WINGS™
1
Natsuki Takaya

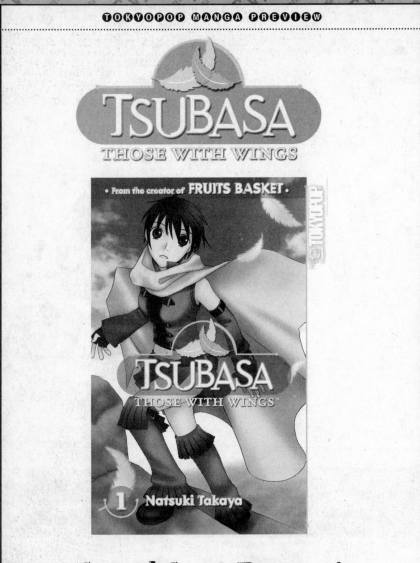

Special Sneak Preview!

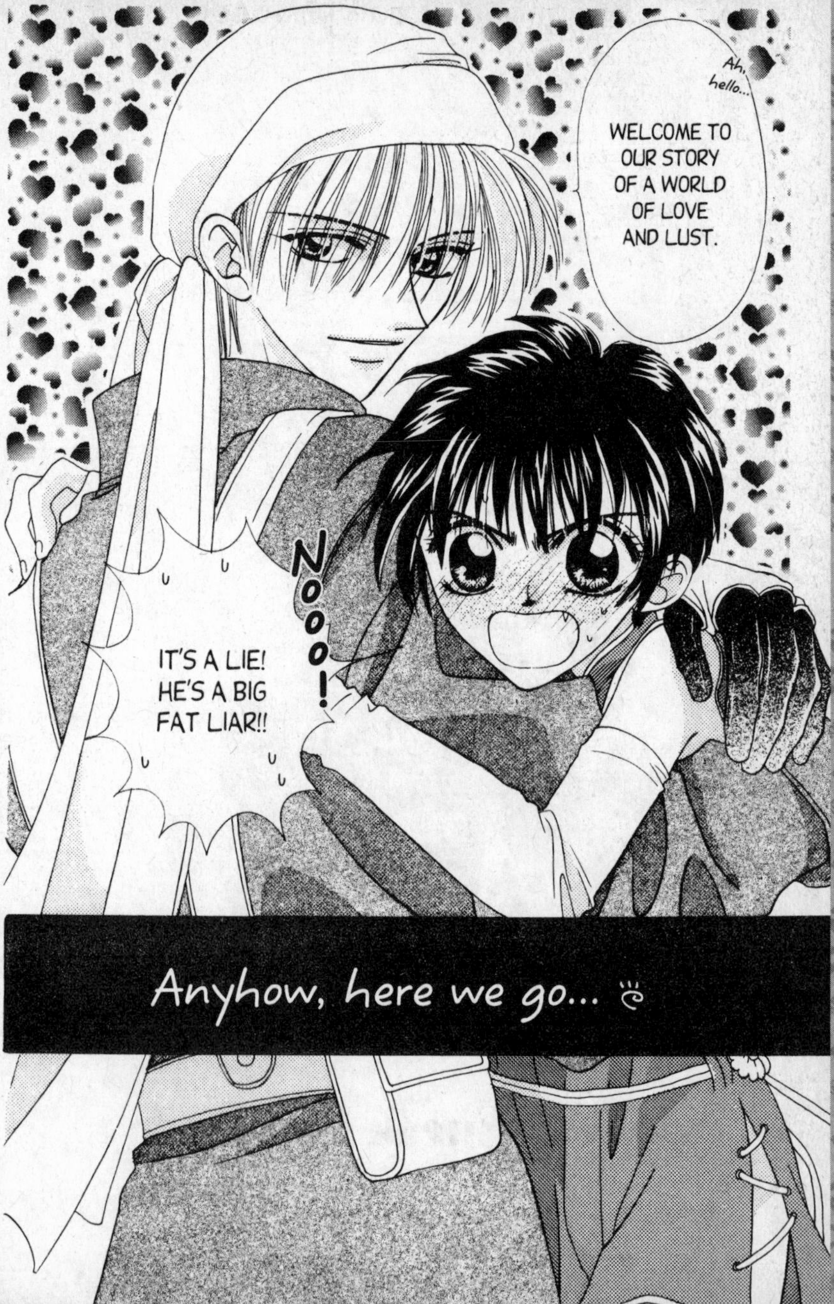
Ah, hello...
WELCOME TO OUR STORY OF A WORLD OF LOVE AND LUST.
NOOOO!
IT'S A LIE! HE'S A BIG FAT LIAR!!
Anyhow, here we go...

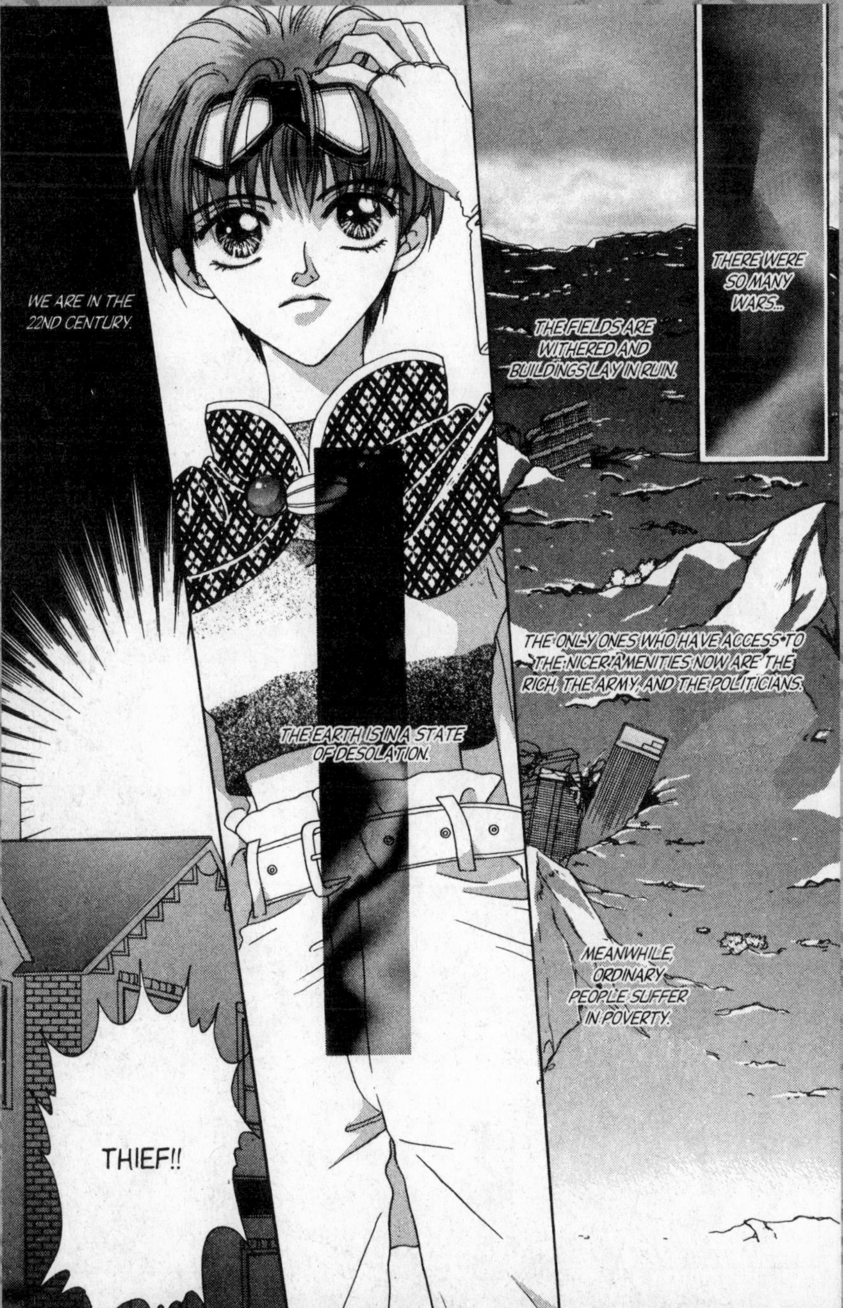
THERE WERE SO MANY WARS...
THE FIELDS ARE WITHERED AND BUILDINGS LAY IN RUIN.
THE ONLY ONES WHO HAVE ACCESS TO THE NICER AMENITIES NOW ARE THE RICH, THE ARMY, AND THE POLITICIANS.
MEANWHILE, ORDINARY PEOPLE SUFFER IN POVERTY.
THE EARTH IS IN A STATE OF DESOLATION.
WE ARE IN THE 22ND CENTURY.
THIEF!!

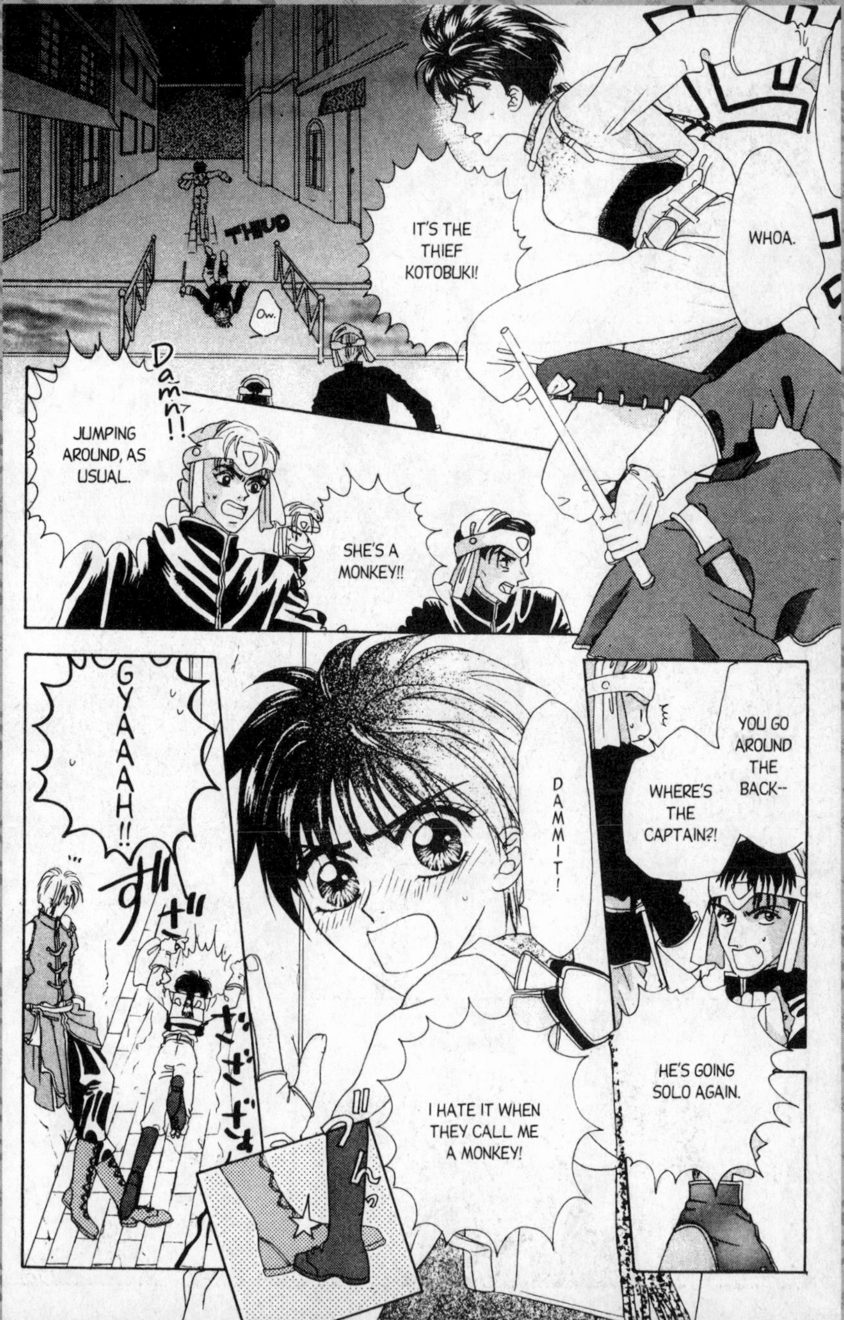
WHOA.
IT'S THE THIEF KOTOBUKI!
THUD
Ow.
Damn!!
JUMPING AROUND, AS USUAL.
SHE'S A MONKEY!!
YOU GO AROUND THE BACK--
WHERE'S THE CAPTAIN?!
HE'S GOING SOLO AGAIN.
DAMMIT!
I HATE IT WHEN THEY CALL ME A MONKEY!
GYAAAAH!!

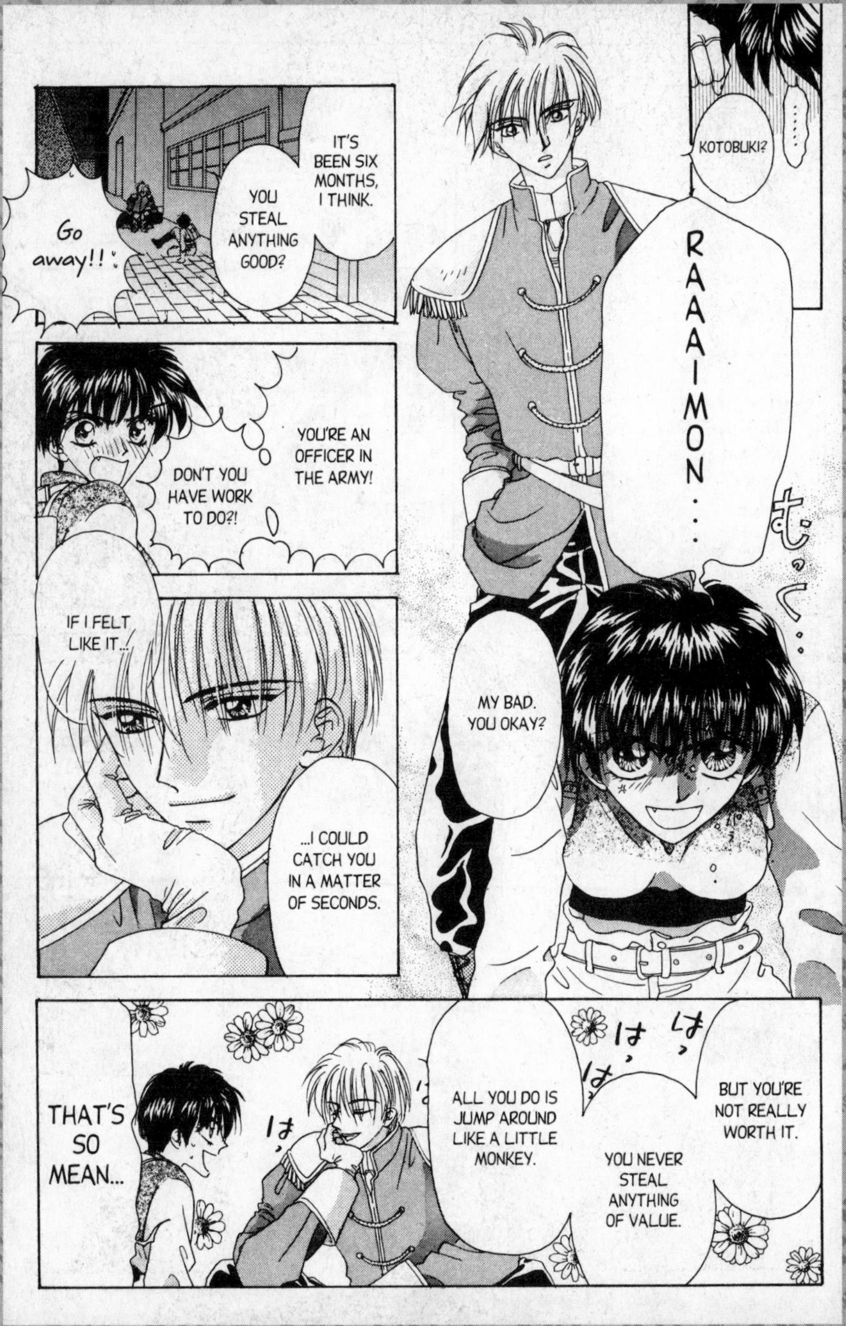
......
KOTOBUKI?
RAAAIMON...
むっく..
MY BAD. YOU OKAY?
IT'S BEEN SIX MONTHS, I THINK.
YOU STEAL ANYTHING GOOD?
Go away!!
YOU'RE AN OFFICER IN THE ARMY!
DON'T YOU HAVE WORK TO DO?!
IF I FELT LIKE IT...
...I COULD CATCH YOU IN A MATTER OF SECONDS.
BUT YOU'RE NOT REALLY WORTH IT.
YOU NEVER STEAL ANYTHING OF VALUE.
はっ は、
ALL YOU DO IS JUMP AROUND LIKE A LITTLE MONKEY.
は、
THAT'S SO MEAN...

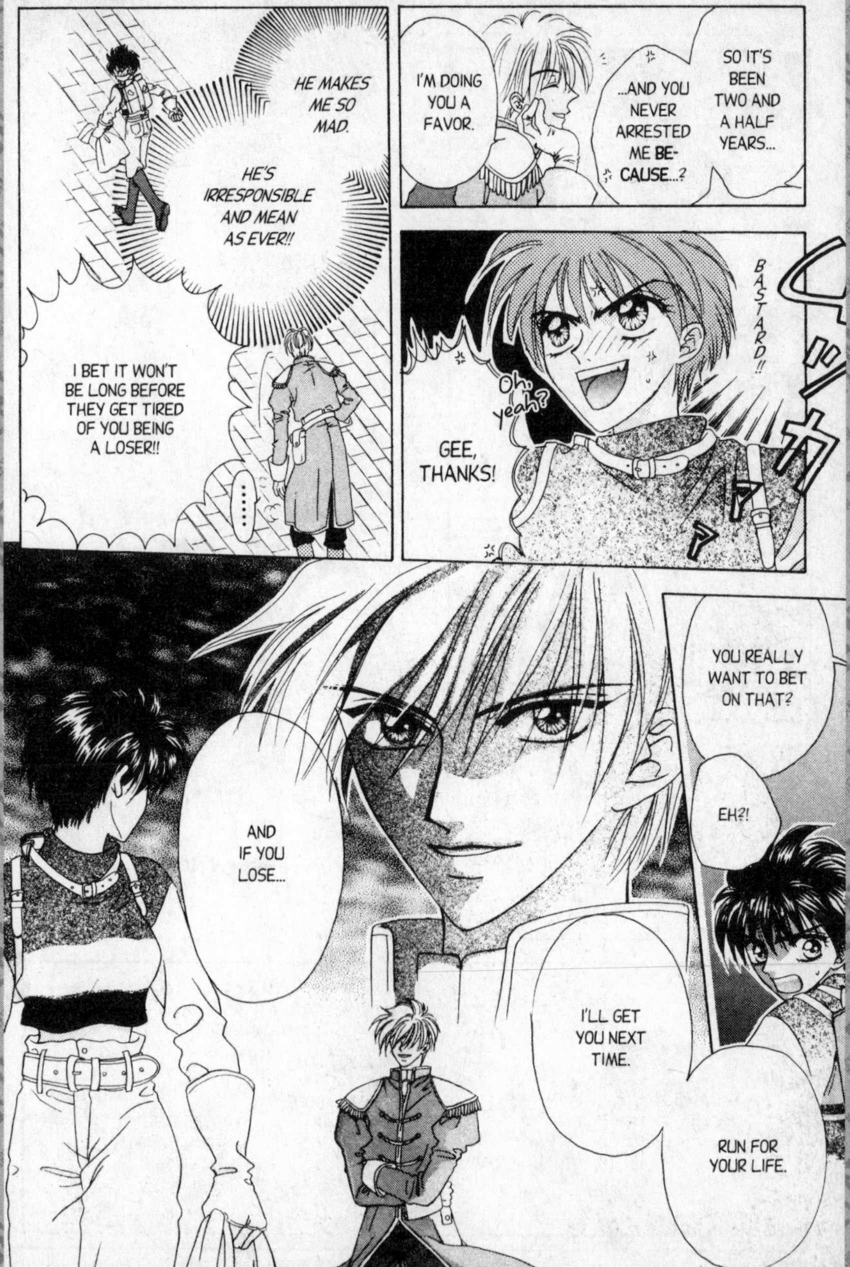
SO IT'S BEEN TWO AND A HALF YEARS...
...AND YOU NEVER ARRESTED ME BE-CAUSE...?
I'M DOING YOU A FAVOR.
BASTARD!!
Oh, yeah?
GEE, THANKS!
HE MAKES ME SO MAD.
HE'S IRRESPONSIBLE AND MEAN AS EVER!!
I BET IT WON'T BE LONG BEFORE THEY GET TIRED OF YOU BEING A LOSER!!
......
YOU REALLY WANT TO BET ON THAT?
EH?!
AND IF YOU LOSE...
I'LL GET YOU NEXT TIME.
RUN FOR YOUR LIFE.

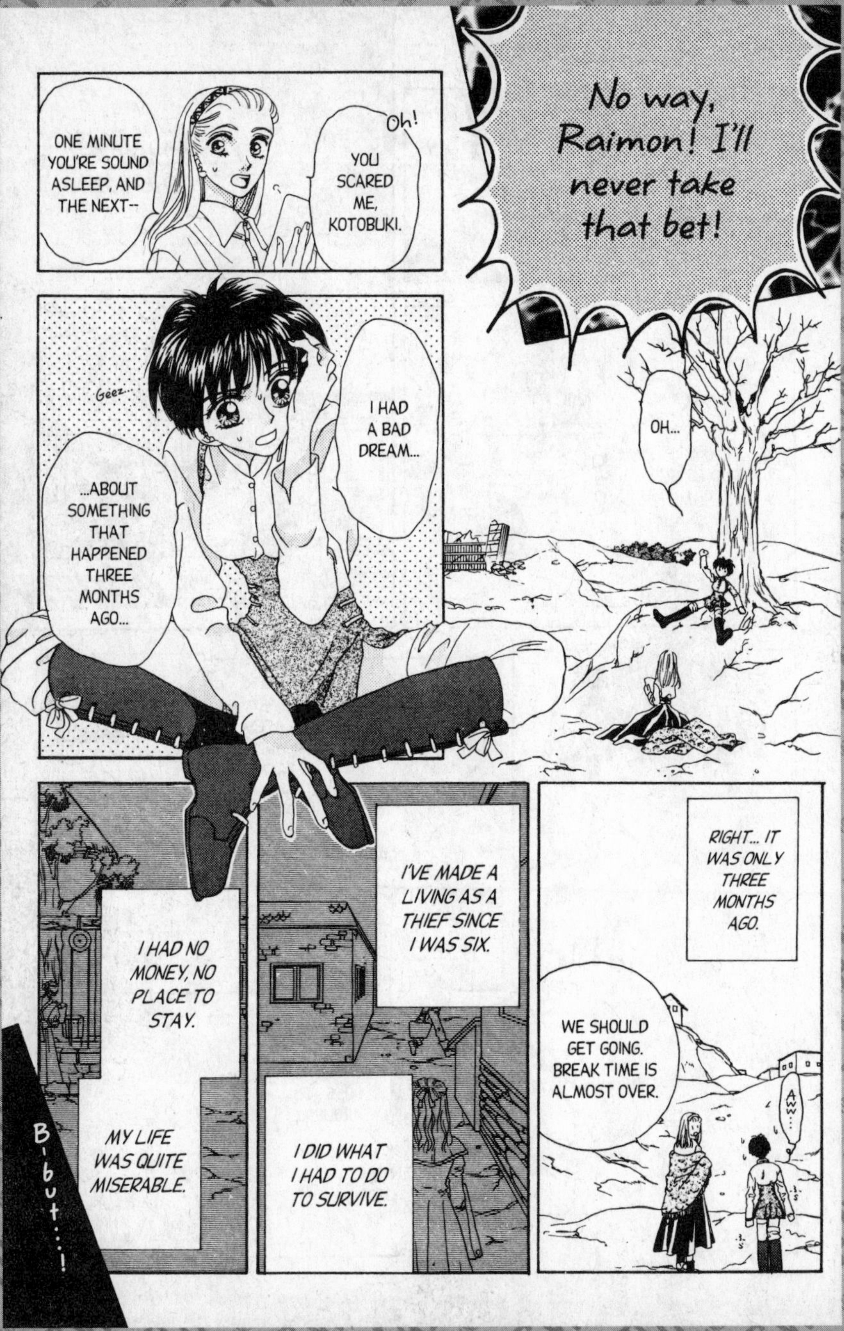
No way, Raimon! I'll never take that bet!
OH...
Oh!
YOU SCARED ME, KOTOBUKI.
ONE MINUTE YOU'RE SOUND ASLEEP, AND THE NEXT--
I HAD A BAD DREAM...
Geez...
...ABOUT SOMETHING THAT HAPPENED THREE MONTHS AGO...
RIGHT... IT WAS ONLY THREE MONTHS AGO.
WE SHOULD GET GOING. BREAK TIME IS ALMOST OVER.
AWW...
I'VE MADE A LIVING AS A THIEF SINCE I WAS SIX.
I DID WHAT I HAD TO DO TO SURVIVE.
I HAD NO MONEY, NO PLACE TO STAY.
MY LIFE WAS QUITE MISERABLE.
B-but...!

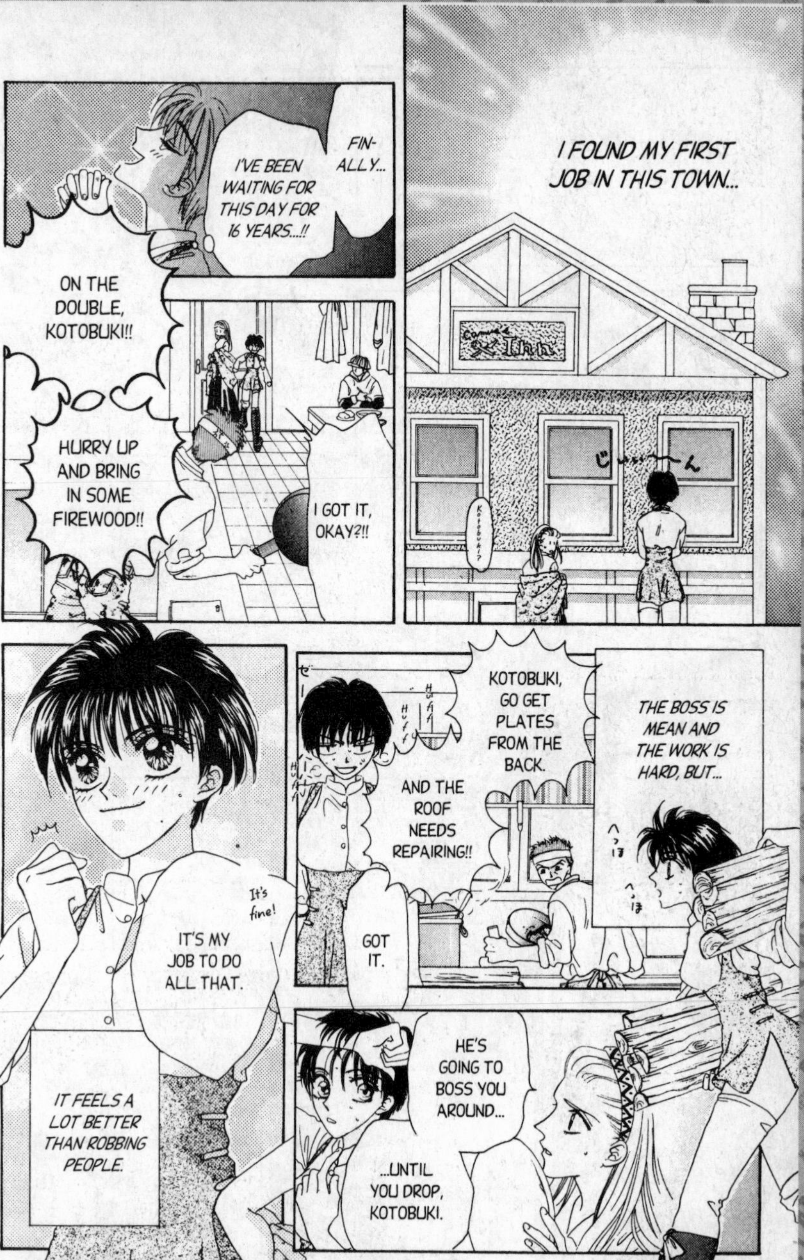
I FOUND MY FIRST JOB IN THIS TOWN...
Kotobuki?
FIN-ALLY...
I'VE BEEN WAITING FOR THIS DAY FOR 16 YEARS...!!
ON THE DOUBLE, KOTOBUKI!!
HURRY UP AND BRING IN SOME FIREWOOD!!
I GOT IT, OKAY?!!
THE BOSS IS MEAN AND THE WORK IS HARD, BUT...
KOTOBUKI, GO GET PLATES FROM THE BACK.
AND THE ROOF NEEDS REPAIRING!!
Huff Huff
GOT IT.
HE'S GOING TO BOSS YOU AROUND...
...UNTIL YOU DROP, KOTOBUKI.
It's fine!
IT'S MY JOB TO DO ALL THAT.
IT FEELS A LOT BETTER THAN ROBBING PEOPLE.

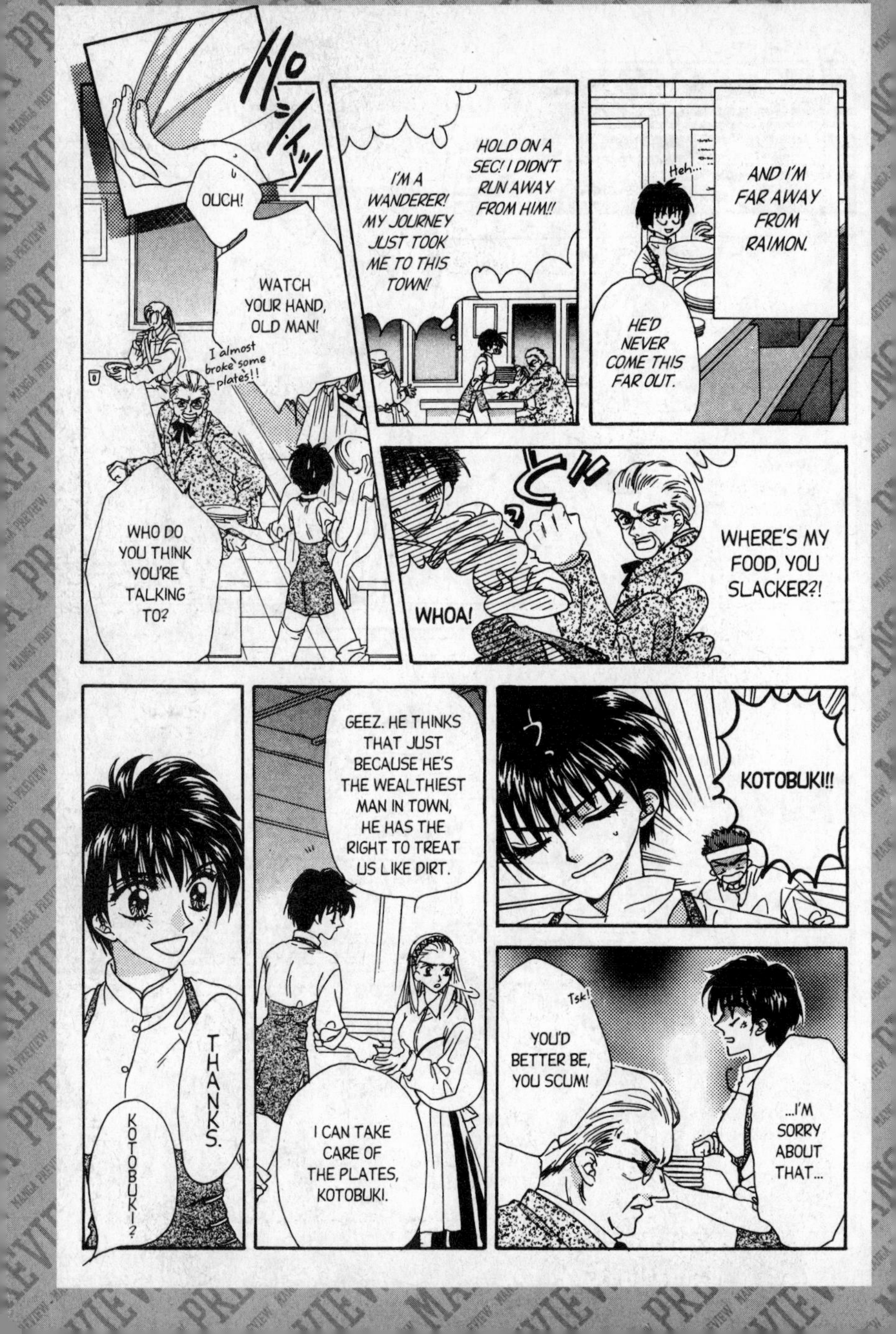
AND I'M FAR AWAY FROM RAIMON.
Heh...
HE'D NEVER COME THIS FAR OUT.
HOLD ON A SEC! I DIDN'T RUN AWAY FROM HIM!!
I'M A WANDERER! MY JOURNEY JUST TOOK ME TO THIS TOWN!
WHERE'S MY FOOD, YOU SLACKER?!
WHOA!
OUCH!
WATCH YOUR HAND, OLD MAN!
I almost broke some plates!!
WHO DO YOU THINK YOU'RE TALKING TO?
KOTOBUKI!!!
...I'M SORRY ABOUT THAT...
Tsk!
YOU'D BETTER BE, YOU SCUM!
GEEZ. HE THINKS THAT JUST BECAUSE HE'S THE WEALTHIEST MAN IN TOWN, HE HAS THE RIGHT TO TREAT US LIKE DIRT.
I CAN TAKE CARE OF THE PLATES, KOTOBUKI.
THANKS.
KOTOBUKI?

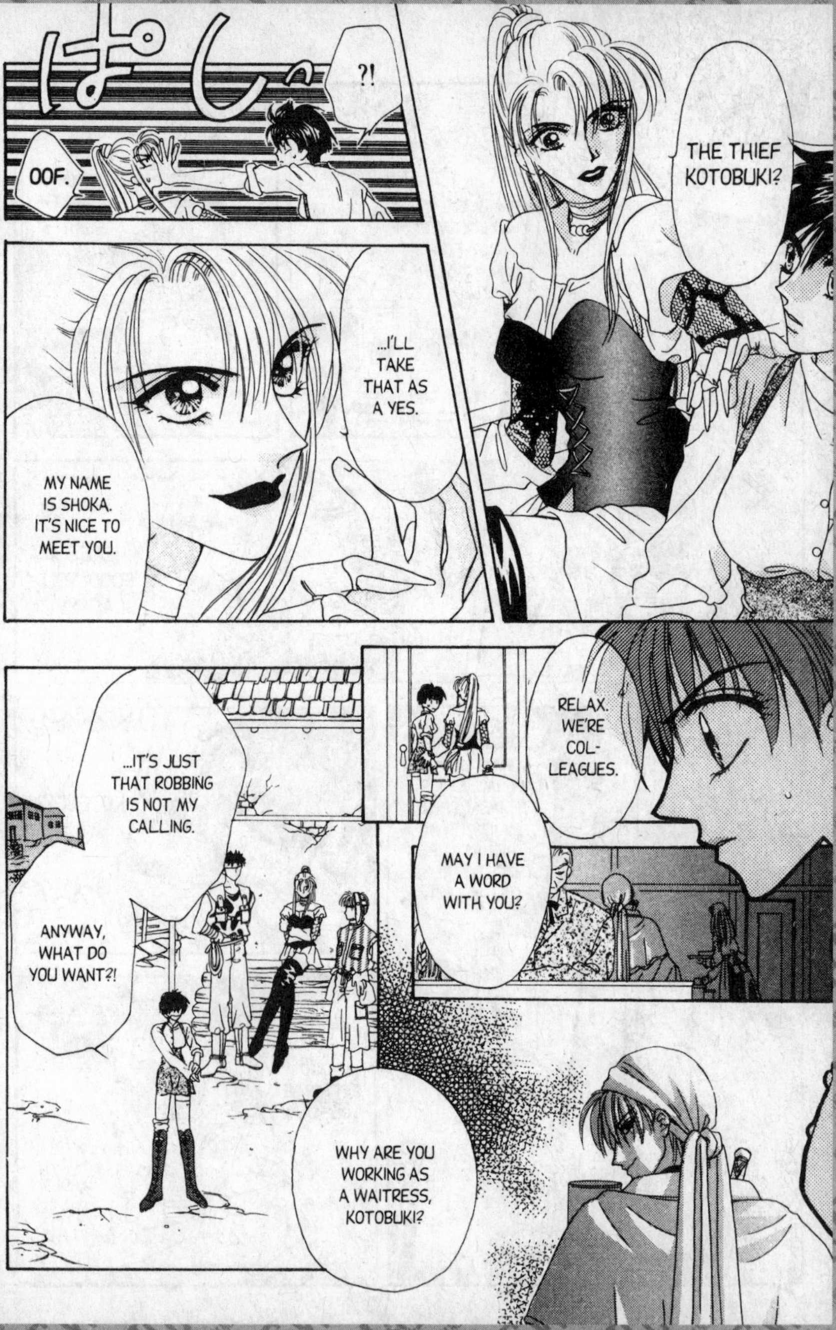
THE THIEF KOTOBUKI?
ぱしっ
?!
OOF.
...I'LL TAKE THAT AS A YES.
MY NAME IS SHOKA. IT'S NICE TO MEET YOU.
RELAX. WE'RE COL-LEAGUES.
MAY I HAVE A WORD WITH YOU?
WHY ARE YOU WORKING AS A WAITRESS, KOTOBUKI?
...IT'S JUST THAT ROBBING IS NOT MY CALLING.
ANYWAY, WHAT DO YOU WANT?!

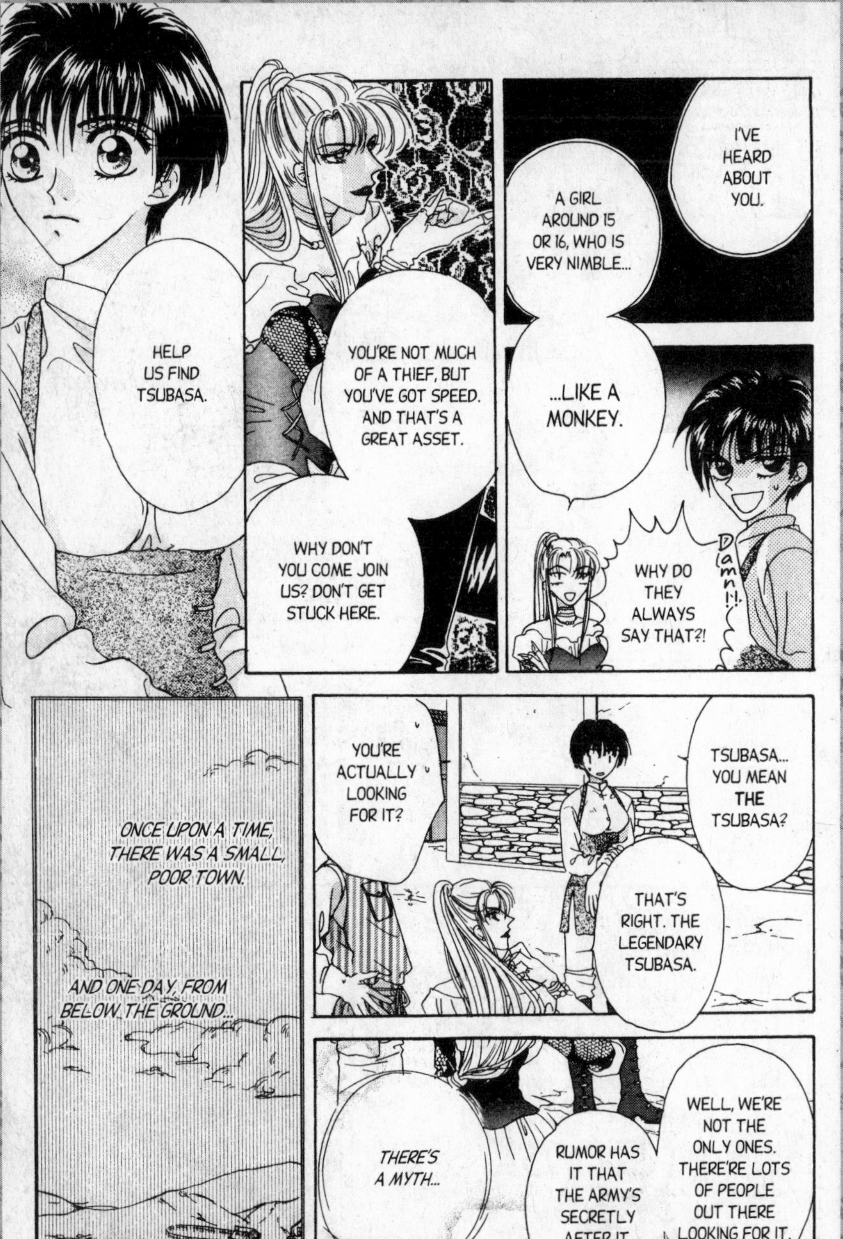
I'VE HEARD ABOUT YOU.
A GIRL AROUND 15 OR 16, WHO IS VERY NIMBLE...
...LIKE A MONKEY.
WHY DO THEY ALWAYS SAY THAT?!
Damn!!
YOU'RE NOT MUCH OF A THIEF, BUT YOU'VE GOT SPEED. AND THAT'S A GREAT ASSET.
WHY DON'T YOU COME JOIN US? DON'T GET STUCK HERE.
HELP US FIND TSUBASA.
TSUBASA... YOU MEAN **THE** TSUBASA?
YOU'RE ACTUALLY LOOKING FOR IT?
THAT'S RIGHT. THE LEGENDARY TSUBASA.
WELL, WE'RE NOT THE ONLY ONES. THERE'RE LOTS OF PEOPLE OUT THERE LOOKING FOR IT.
RUMOR HAS IT THAT THE ARMY'S SECRETLY AFTER IT, TOO.
THERE'S A MYTH...
ONCE UPON A TIME, THERE WAS A SMALL, POOR TOWN.
AND ONE DAY, FROM BELOW THE GROUND...

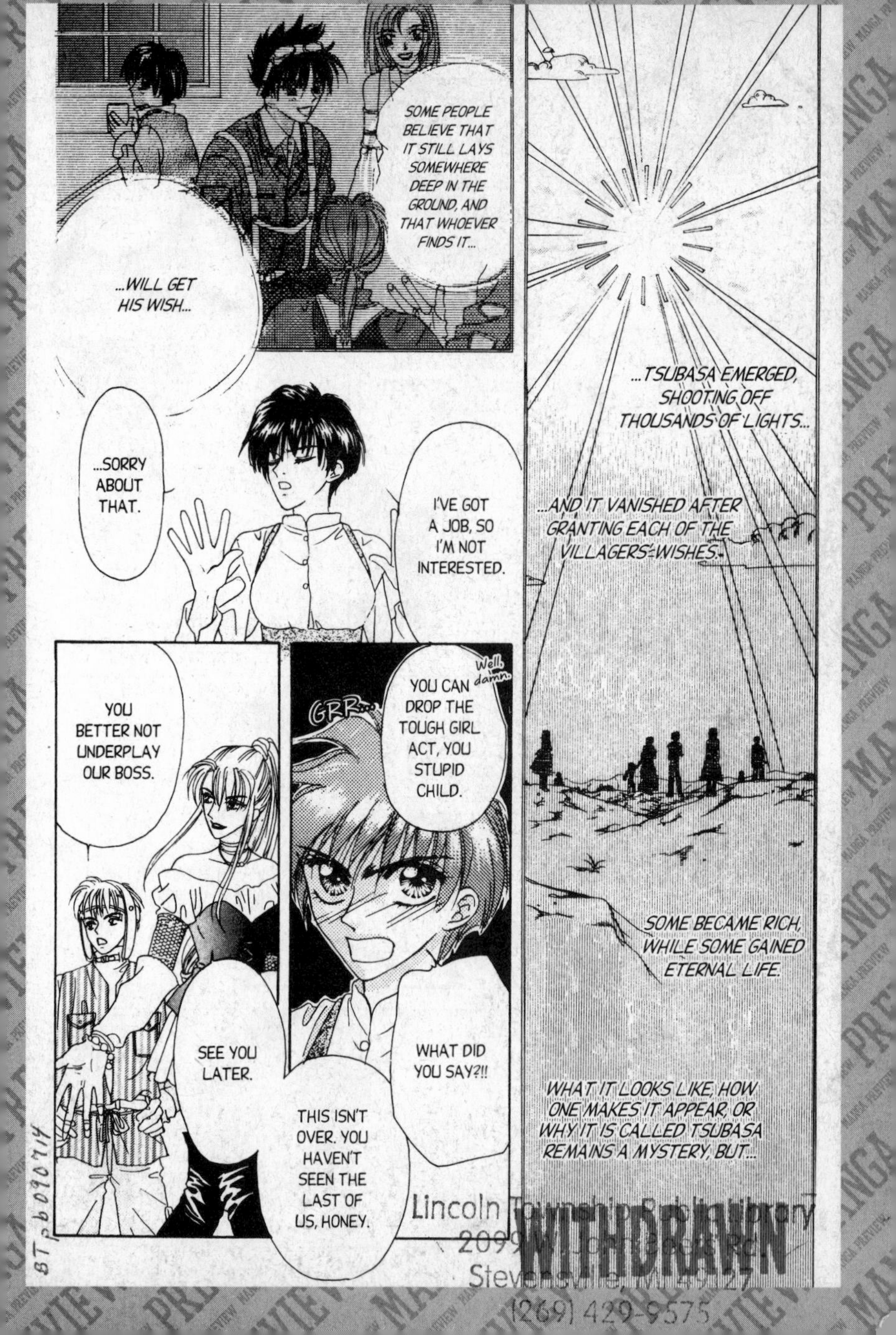
...TSUBASA EMERGED, SHOOTING OFF THOUSANDS OF LIGHTS...
...AND IT VANISHED AFTER GRANTING EACH OF THE VILLAGERS' WISHES.
SOME BECAME RICH, WHILE SOME GAINED ETERNAL LIFE.
WHAT IT LOOKS LIKE, HOW ONE MAKES IT APPEAR, OR WHY IT IS CALLED TSUBASA REMAINS A MYSTERY, BUT...
SOME PEOPLE BELIEVE THAT IT STILL LAYS SOMEWHERE DEEP IN THE GROUND, AND THAT WHOEVER FINDS IT...
...WILL GET HIS WISH...
I'VE GOT A JOB, SO I'M NOT INTERESTED.
...SORRY ABOUT THAT.
GRR...
YOU CAN DROP THE TOUGH GIRL ACT, YOU STUPID CHILD.
Well, damn.
WHAT DID YOU SAY?!!
YOU BETTER NOT UNDERPLAY OUR BOSS.
SEE YOU LATER.
THIS ISN'T OVER. YOU HAVEN'T SEEN THE LAST OF US, HONEY.

STOP!

This is the back of the book.
You wouldn't want to spoil a great ending!

This book is printed "manga-style," in the authentic Japanese right-to-left format. Since none of the artwork has been flipped or altered, readers get to experience the story just as the creator intended. You've been asking for it, so TOKYOPOP® delivered: authentic, hot-off-the-press, and far more fun!

1
2
3
4
5
6
7
8
9
10

DIRECTIONS

If this is your first time reading manga-style, here's a quick guide to help you understand how it works.

It's easy... just start in the top right panel and follow the numbers. Have fun, and look for more 100% authentic manga from TOKYOPOP®!

THE MANGA REVOLUTION • LEADING THE MANGA REVOLUTION • LEADING

漫画革命